M000111396

Technological Innovation in Legacy Sectors

TECHNOLOGICAL INNOVATION IN LEGACY SECTORS

William B. Bonvillian and Charles Weiss

OXFORD
UNIVERSITY PRESS

Oxford University Press is a department of the University of Oxford.
It furthers the University's objective of excellence in research, scholarship,
and education by publishing worldwide. Oxford is a registered trade mark
of Oxford University Press in the UK and in certain other countries

Published in the United States of America by
Oxford University Press
198 Madison Avenue, New York, NY 10016,
United States of America

© Oxford University Press 2015

All rights reserved. No part of this publication may be reproduced,
stored in a retrieval system, or transmitted, in any form or by any means,
without the prior permission in writing of Oxford University Press,
or as expressly permitted by law, by license, or under terms agreed with the
appropriate reproduction rights organization. Inquiries concerning reproduction
outside the scope of the above should be sent to the Rights Department,
Oxford University Press, at the address above.

You must not circulate this work in any other form
and you must impose this same condition on any acquirer

Cataloging-in-Publication data is on file at the Library of Congress

978-0-19-937451-9

9 8 7 6 5 4 3 2 1

Printed in the United States of America on acid-free paper

Contents

viii Contents

Preface

The American economy has long focused on new technological frontiers—on to the new, don't look back to the established. Americans take our technology covered wagons packed with innovations *west* into new frontiers. We don't take our covered wagons *east* back over the mountains to deal with "legacy sectors." In such sectors, technology—like the fossil fuel infrastructure in energy—is entrenched and difficult to displace, and these sectors comprise most of our economy. This failure means that our economy resists badly needed innovation, costing enormous economic benefits, although researchers, inventors, engineers, and entrepreneurs are full of ideas and inventions.

The United States has been at the forefront of almost all the new technologies and industries in the second half of the 20th century. Information technology and biotechnology are only its latest innovation waves. Can we improve our growth rate and our employment and attack other major problems by accelerating innovation in our neglected legacy sectors, energy, healthcare delivery, higher education, industrial agriculture, buildings, manufacturing, and transport, to cite examples we shall address in this book? Can we grow high-productivity, high-wage manufacturing-dependent jobs in the United States? In this, the most innovative society in the world, why are these critically important parts of the economy so resistant to innovation?

Our book uses a new, unifying conceptual framework to address the two major and related problems facing the American innovation system today: "jobless innovation" in high-tech industries and resistance to disruptive innovation in entrenched legacy sectors. Both of these problems arise from the same fundamental cause: a legacy system where incentives for innovators and producers run counter to broader goals of job creation, technical efficiency, security, public health and safety, and environmental sustainability.

The American national innovation system has a dual structure: part suited to rapid innovation, and part stubbornly resistant to disruptive change. The legacy sectors that resist change and erect barriers to disruptive innovation share common features that obstruct the market launch of innovations, over and above the "valley of death" between research and late-stage development and the other "supply-side" obstacles that have been the traditional focus of innovation policy.

Our new, unified analytic framework categorizes the obstacles to market launch faced by innovations in legacy sectors. They must penetrate a well-established and well-defended technological/economic/political/social paradigm that favors existing technology, characterized by (1) "perverse" subsidies and prices, as well as cost structures that create a mismatch between the incentives of producers and broader social goals; (2) established infrastructure and institutional architecture that impose regulatory hurdles or other disadvantages to new entrants; (3) politically powerful vested interests, reinforced by public support, that defend the paradigm and resist innovations that threaten their business models; (4) a financing system for innovation that doesn't support, or doesn't fit the development timeline of, many capital-intensive legacy sector innovations; (5) public habits and expectations attuned to existing technology; (6) a knowledge and human resources structure oriented to legacy needs; (7) aversion to innovation, exemplified by limited research and development and a lack of available alternatives ready for implementation; and (8) market imperfections beyond those faced by other innovations.

The market imperfections that impede innovations in legacy sectors deserve special mention. Some legacy sectors are so decentralized and fragmented that *collective action* is precluded. In others, *network economies* limit entry to new entrant technologies that don't fit those networks. Others require large initial investments, an imperfection known as *lumpiness*. Still others are *nonappropriable*: they require investments that cannot be recouped by the investor, however beneficial they may be to the world.

We apply our framework to a series of legacy sectors: energy, transport, healthcare delivery, higher education, and manufacturing. We explore the legacy sector of manufacturing in special depth, because a significant part of our problem with jobless recovery stems from this industry, which has been in decline in the United States for a decade. Because it employs the majority of the scientists and engineers that constitute the US innovation workforce, and because it occupies a keystone role in an innovation value chain that runs from research, development, and demonstration to production, and in the value network of the service sectors that support it, we can't gain the maximum benefits of innovation without it. Finally, the new generation of advanced manufacturing promises enormous gains in productivity, as well as breakthrough innovations in products and processes. The United States needs to restore its manufacturing sector, with its close ties to innovation, if it is to exploit these advances. To evaluate this, we apply a legacy sector analysis because the problems are joined: manufacturing is a major legacy sector.

Our analysis focuses on the structural obstacles to disruptive innovation in the legacy sectors in the United States because of their importance and because these have received short shrift in the general literature concerned with US competitiveness and innovation. But legacy sectors aren't just an American bad dream; other countries face them as well. We therefore apply our conceptual framework to France, Germany, China, and India. We find that these economies suffer from legacy features that make it hard for entrepreneurs bearing radical innovations with both potential for profit and risk of failure. These legacy features typically lie in the economic, political, cultural, and legal background of innovation—the innovation context—rather than in the institutions and policies directly stimulating research and innovation. On the other hand, these economies have strengths, especially in manufacturing (China and Germany) and infrastructure (France and China), from which the United States could draw valuable lessons.

Legacy sectors go global. American paradigms in many sectors are exported worldwide. Some imported innovations, like cell phones, computers, and modern medicine, can be used directly in poor countries, adding to economic growth and improving quality of life. Others, like high-tech medicine and input-intensive agriculture, may be insufficiently cost-conscious or respectful of environmental sustainability; they may delay the development and spread of needed innovations. India and China constitute new competitive threats, but also represent "innovative developing countries" that have large domestic markets where they are launching innovations—low-cost medical equipment, for example—often better adapted to needs of the poor.

We close our discussion by presenting a policy methodology for launching technological innovation into legacy sectors, and illustrate its use with a case study in manufacturing. If we are to recapture enhanced economic growth, we will need to learn to innovate in legacy sectors to spur innovation-based growth.

We thank Philip E. Auerswald, editor of the journal *Innovations*, and his staff for publishing articles that enabled us to hone our ideas and on which we draw in several chapters of this book, noted in endnotes. We also thank Kevin Finneran, editor-in-chief of *Issues in Science and Technology*, and the managing editors for *Technology Analysis and Strategic Management*, for permission to draw on articles that appeared in their publications, as cited in endnotes. We thank our colleagues and students at Georgetown and the Massachusetts Institute of Technology for their contributions to our thinking as we discussed and taught these concepts. We owe particular thanks to Professor Carl Dahlman, of Georgetown and the OECD, and Professor Suzanne Berger, of MIT, and to the student research assistants who have helped us over the years.

The authors are especially indebted to our families—our wives, Janis and Edie, and our children, Marcus and Raphael, Tamara and Jed—for their support and consideration as we developed the ideas for this book over the past four years.

Technological Innovation in Legacy Sectors

1 The Root Problems

Expanding Innovation and Creating Jobs

The American innovation system is in trouble. Like the innovation system itself, the trouble comes in two parts. One part of the innovation system turns out dramatic discoveries and inventions in information and biotechnology at a breathtaking rate. The trouble is that too few jobs are being created in the United States. The second part has been developing badly needed ideas that address environmental, public health, and policy goals in other, equally important parts of the American economy—energy, manufacturing, transport, agriculture, construction, and health delivery, to cite a few examples. Here the trouble is that these sectors successfully resist the introduction and scale-up of such innovations.

Americans have every reason to glory in the success of US inventors, entrepreneurs and their venture capital backers in creating a steady stream of dramatic innovations. But the extraordinary success of the information technology and biotechnology industries should not blind us to the two critical and neglected problems of job creation and locked-in, disruption-resistant legacy sectors. They are related. The limited examination by technologists and social scientists of the innovation process has focused on the problems faced by radically new products—the collaboration between universities and industry, for example, and the "valley of death" between research and late-stage development. Researchers have shied away from confronting the dual structure of the American innovation system. We tend to explore new technology frontiers, ignoring the legacy sectors where the application and scale-up of new ideas are stymied by entrenched paradigms, sharply limiting our growth rate.

These legacy sectors constitute the majority of the US economy. According to Bureau of Economic Analysis (BEA) data for 2013,[1] the information sector in the United States is 4.6% of its economy. In contrast, legacy sectors that will be examined as specific case studies in subsequent chapters (utilities, construction, building, agriculture, manufacturing, transport, education, and health) constitute 30% of US GDP. Other sectors that could be considered largely legacy (mining, government, much of finance, etc.) constitute another 35%; thus some two-thirds of the economy can be placed in a legacy category without even considering to what extent retail, business services, and other sectors should be categorized as legacy.

These legacy sector and job creation problems require a re-examination of the measures by which the US government has traditionally encouraged innovation in civilian technology. Unsolved, they may threaten support for public expenditure on research, which depends on public belief that research and resulting technological innovation lead to employment and improved quality of life. We set out a summary of basic points below. These will be explored in detail in subsequent chapters.

JOBLESS INNOVATION AND THE ENGINEERING FAULT LINE

At the root of the problem of US job creation lies the fact that national innovation systems, to which policymakers devote most of their attention, are increasingly pillars that support a globalized, international innovation system in which ideas, people, investment, equipment, and services flow relatively freely across borders. This allows relatively easy separation (what economists call "unbundling") of research and new product development, on the one hand, from production and process innovation, on the other. National innovation systems provide the institutional and financial support to basic and precompetitive research and to education in science, technology, engineering, and mathematics, which are direct factors that drive innovation.

So far, so good. The results of the basic research that we and many other countries support are inherently free goods available to anyone that makes the necessary investments in research support and funding to master the emerging field and findings. The United States and the rest of the world have long benefited from the resulting "spillover"—free exchange of scientific information. But the jobs resulting from research funded by American taxpayers now increasingly end up in other countries, most notably China (for manufacturing) and India (for information-intensive services and products). In this way, the growth of the globalization of the innovation system and the rise of China and India threaten to put our system of research support under pressure if the jobs it generates flow predominantly to other countries. The United States is not alone in facing this problem; the EU has announced new rules to make its billions in research-and-development (R & D) investments conditional to follow-on commercialization in Europe.

In brief, the problem arises as follows. Over two-thirds of the US expenditure on research and development takes place, not in the universities and government laboratories of national innovation systems, but in industry—largely in increasingly globalized multinational corporations (MNCs).[2] 500 MNCs control some 70% of world trade; of the 100 largest economies in the world, 52 are MNCs and 48 are nations. In the United States, industry funds 84% of product development but only 5% of basic research; its R & D support is typically for incremental innovation rather than products offering new functionality. Worldwide, over half of R & D is funded by MNCs,[3] again predominantly for development.

MNCs still carry out the bulk of the conception and design of their new products in the United States and other advanced countries, creating areas of high-tech prosperity in Silicon Valley (around information technology), Boston (around biotechnology), and other parts of the United States. However, many such firms have found it increasingly convenient to locate their manufacturing and production activities (we shall use these two terms interchangeably) close to expanding markets in Asia—initially to take advantage of low wage rates and government incentives, but increasingly because of the engineering skills and the ability to rapidly scale up manufacturing processes to be found in China. While critically important to the rising prosperity of the Chinese people and the political stability of their government, this phenomenon of "innovate here, produce there" has contributed heavily to the rapid decline in manufacturing employment in the United States—so much so that we can call it "jobless innovation."

A fault line has thus developed in many industries between research and development, on the one hand, and product design, engineering, and production, on the other. MNCs have vaulted this "engineering fault line" by virtue of their global reach, flexible management, and superior financial resources. Even high-tech start-ups have used their contacts in the venture capital community to identify capable manufacturers in Asian countries, even for their latest products. Both have found it convenient and profitable to "innovate here, produce there." In both cases, only a portion of the gains of innovation—especially the potential gains in employment—are captured in the country in which the innovation takes place. Smaller American firms, on the other hand, lack these advantages. Important parts of the "industrial ecosystem" of training, vendors, technical services, consultants, specialized journals, and university curricula that formerly supported them have thinned out or even migrated abroad, along with their major clients, the production divisions of MNCs and start-ups. For the smaller remaining firms, the fault line between development and engineering can become an insuperable barrier to expansion, denying them the opportunity to generate the employment of which they would otherwise have been capable.[4]

What is more, because of the close links between production and innovation in many industries, the globalization of innovation threatens to erode the long-term competitive advantage of American firms in the development of new processes and eventually of new products. This is particularly true in the case of producers of complex, high-value, capital-intensive goods, such as aerospace and energy technologies, which are characterized by close connections between research, development, and design, on the one hand, and production, on the other. If firms send this production offshore in order to lower costs and to be close to expanding markets overseas, then research, development, and design are likely to follow. In these and other industries, there is thus a danger of losing not only production but also innovation capability—a new pattern of "produce there, innovate there."

In short, the United States is facing two risks: both "innovate here, produce there" and "produce there, innovate there." Taken together, these risks threaten the public support to research and innovation. Since 2009 the United States has been experiencing the slowest job growth in a recovery since the Depression. If the benefits of US innovation increasingly flow abroad, leaving a continuing job crisis at home, what will be the basis of support for investment in federal R & D and innovation?

The debate over slow creation of quality jobs in the United States has taken several directions. Some commentators have argued that the productivity gains from the growing information technology sector are displacing jobs and job categories that will not be replaced, marking a permanent economic shift into declining employment.[5] Of course, this story is an old one. It has recurred every few decades since the Industrial Revolution, creating alarms that the latest productivity gains—such as through mass production and automation—will displace work, although the history to date has always been that productivity gains increase real wealth in the economy and over time net employment gains as new job categories are created to serve the expanded markets and new advances in technology.[6] Others have pointed to the hollowing out of the economy through competition from lower wage, lower cost economies, particularly China, and its effects.[7]

There is another strand in this debate. Economist Thomas Piketty has argued that long-term technology advance is enabling a dramatic new concentration of wealth where gains from capital exceed gain from economic growth for the top echelon of society, with corresponding growing inequality in the remaining parts of the society, to the detriment of overall societal well-being.[8] A society's wealth, of which the level of per capita income is a vital sign, is a critical factor in the ability of the United States and other nations to confront societal challenges, from the cost of healthcare for a rapidly aging population, to new and ongoing infrastructure requirements, to strategies associated with climate change. There is currently a robust debate on "secular stagnation"—the possibility that the global economy, especially in developed nations, has begun a long period of slower growth, with growing inequality as a symptom.

Another way of looking at this inequality issue, however, has been advanced by economists Claudia Goldin, Lawrence Katz, and David Autor.[9] They point out that since the Industrial Revolution, employment has required an ever greater level of technical skill in the workforce. The United States was the first to undertake public mass higher education at scale, through the nationwide creation of higher education institutions under the Land Grant College Act of 1862, which reached ever larger portions of the US population through the GI Bill of 1944 and subsequent federal student financial aid programs. This allowed the United States to stay ahead of that technical advance curve, enabling ever greater numbers in its workforce to master the skills to benefit from the accelerating technologies. However, in the 1970s, the United States allowed its higher education graduation rate to level off, leaving a growing portion of its population without the skills to participate in an increasingly advanced technology economy. The result has been growing inequality: the upper middle class that crosses the higher education threshold dominates the ever-growing skills required by the economy, so commands a premium return and garners higher incomes. The rest of society is left further behind, suffering from a growing income differential and higher joblessness. The Obama administration has recognized this issue and has been moving policies to try to expand the higher education graduation rate. Advances in technology that may assist in this education effort are discussed in chapter 8. But increasing the availability of higher income jobs is also required in a parallel effort to improving the technical skills of the workforce; otherwise the latter is self-defeating.

As suggested in the discussion above, this book takes a slant on these issues different from the current policy debate. The "jobless innovation" problem identified in the discussion above involves another range of causes. Economist Robert Solow demonstrated that the dominant factor in economic growth since the Industrial Revolution is technological and related innovation. However, as noted, the United States has increasingly followed an "innovate here, produce there" model, limiting the gains—and employment—it can achieve from its innovation capability. As set out in chapters 4 and 6, to more fully realize these gains, it needs to rebuild the production stages of its innovation system through new kinds of technology and process innovation. Manufacturing itself has become a legacy sector with resistance to innovation, which is particularly problematic because, as will be discussed, it is also a driver of innovation. The curtailed ability of the manufacturing sector to innovate and therefore to achieve fuller gains from innovation is a root cause of the pattern of "jobless innovation" the United States has fallen into. Important gains arguably could be achieved if this system failure was reversed. But this is not the only approach. There is a second major slant on innovation the book considers: fostering further innovation in legacy sectors to drive further growth, as introduced below.

LOCKED-IN, LEGACY SECTORS

Some of America's greatest needs for innovation lie in complex, established economic sectors[10] that are locked into unsustainable or otherwise undesirable trajectories and resist innovations that would disrupt well-established paradigms and business models. Fossil-fuel-based energy, the electric grid, the health delivery system, highway-intensive transport, and input-intensive agriculture are examples. Since technological and related innovation is the dominant factor in economic growth, these sectors are areas in which innovation can broaden our growth base beyond the frontier-based growth that increasingly lands in a global landscape.

There are two points relevant here to flesh out this logic. First, we need breakthrough, frontier innovations in these legacy sectors. But such sectors have resisted innovation for so long that there are less sophisticated innovations that are also needed. Second, even if we embark on both these kinds of innovations, they may continue to be resisted in the legacy sector because of remaining economic, political and social barriers so still land in a global landscape. For the innovator, this is an acceptable risk; the initiator can often take advantage of a first-mover advantage and realize maximum gains wherever. But it is a problem for the economy that is home to the legacy sector. It is therefore important, from a US perspective, that the technology moves toward implementation, optimally in the United States with first-mover gains, or even if the United States is among the second adaptors and realizes only a secondary gain. Legacy resistance can thwart both.

The obstacles to innovation in these entrenched legacy sectors share a series of common features. As will be explored in detail below, they share one or more of the following characteristics: perverse subsidies and price structures that favor incumbents and ignore externalities like environmental sustainability and public health; an established institutional architecture that imposes regulatory hurdles or other policy disadvantages favoring existing technology; well-established, powerful vested interests, sometimes public and sometimes private, that resist the introduction of technologies; an innovation time horizon that is substantially longer than the five- to six-year time frame of information products on which current capital support systems are focused; public habits and expectations that underpin popular support to policies and government expenditures favorable to existing technology; a knowledge and human resources structure—educational curricula, career paths, and professional standards in medical, legal, and technical fields—oriented to the needs of existing technology; and a dearth of research and development, and hence of innovative alternatives ready for implementation. The dominance of existing technologies is further reinforced by a series of imperfections in the market for technology. These include *network economies, lumpiness, split incentives*, the need for *collective action*, and *governmental, institutional, and regulatory structure*. These obstacles must be addressed if new disruptive innovations are to enter legacy sectors.

There is an interesting contrast here to the concept of systems failure analysis[11] in the field of complex engineering systems. Systems failures generally stem from component failures and defects that prevent the system from achieving its design requirements and prevent the continuous improvements that all systems need to stay healthy. Examples might include hybrid automotive engines that fail to achieve the desired range or fuel economy, or targeting lasers that fail to designate their targets in certain weather conditions. In these cases, a component is typically at fault and can be identified and corrected.

The legacy sector analysis that we undertake here is different. The technology components that make up legacy sectors work well and continue to make incremental improvements so that the system as a whole does not fail to meet its own well-established requirements; the problem is not solved by identifying particular component failures. Instead, the problem is with the whole legacy system, which cannot accommodate breakthrough, disruptive advances that may be needed to achieve new goals but that contradict "root" design features in the legacy system. The problem is not component failure that leads to system failure, but rather a fundamental system-of-systems failure stemming from new requirements.[12] But the legacy system-of-systems needs to be envisaged not simply as a set of engineered technological systems, but much more broadly, encompassing technological as well as related economic, political, and social systems.

DOUBLE TROUBLE

The United States led the major innovation waves of the 20th century—aviation, electronics, communications, nuclear power, space, computing, and the Internet (including its many applications such as social networking)—and reaped the corresponding economic gains, becoming the richest nation in history. The strength of the American innovation system has been in the development of radically new technology that introduces powerful capabilities with new functionalities that never existed, like the computer, genomics, and the Internet. Like pioneers of old, our innovators have driven metaphorical covered wagons westward into uncharted and unoccupied territory beyond the mountains.

Our policymakers have facilitated this cutting-edge innovation by supporting research and education, and by helping to bridge the infamous "valley of death" between research and late-stage development, largely through Defense Department support to emerging technologies.[13] In this they are buoyed by a popular culture that values individualism and freedom of inquiry, welcomes new ideas and new products, upholds merit over ancestry, religion, or national origin, has been open to talent from abroad, and, significantly, accepts the possibility of failure as the flip side of the benefits of change. These cultural values constitute an important dimension of our innovation context and our innovation environment, concepts to which we shall return later in this chapter.

To reiterate, this model now faces double trouble. First, cutting-edge innovation brings profits but creates fewer quality jobs than it could and should—a deficiency that has in recent years constituted our number one economic and political challenge. We therefore must expand our innovation base beyond the narrow band of technology "frontier" sectors to better realize the gains across our innovation system and to innovate more broadly across innovation-resistant sectors. Second, this part of our economy is often locked into undesirable patterns that resist change even when promising innovations are available or within reach. We therefore need to confront the policy challenges that we have so far avoided in these established, legacy sectors. In effect, we need to drive our technology "covered wagons" back east in order to confront the issues we left behind.

This double problem requires a systematic, multipronged conceptual approach that goes well beyond traditional government measures that support research and the early stages of innovation and considers the entire innovative process from ideation through to commercialization at scale. In addition, "change agents" are needed: institutions (and individuals within them) that are in a position to push innovative technology through the barriers presented by legacy sectors at the various stages of the innovation process and to effect any needed institutional and policy changes.

The first problem, jobless innovation, requires measures both to encourage domestic investment in technology and to gain the benefits from the resulting employment. The alternative, "innovate here, produce there," is not a sustainable model. In the United States, the Advanced Manufacturing Partnership collaboration[14] between industries and universities, which proposed measures to restore US production leadership through better integration of productivity-enhancing innovation in manufacturing technology and infrastructure to test out these innovations, coupled with new processes and business models, is a recent example of such a change agent, assuming that its efforts can be sustained and that the government moves to implement its plans. Other change agents whose actions span the innovation process include the Advanced Research Projects Agency for Energy (ARPA-E) in energy technology, whose programs include measures to drive down the costs and move toward commercialization of the advanced technologies it supports. Both these initial change agents require follow-on change agents for further implementation.

In addition, public support needs to be sustained and indeed substantially increased for R & D, the more so since these sectors typically suffer from underinvestment in long-range research and innovation, a problem that has been exacerbated by the cuts that Congress began implementing in 2013. Some engineering-intensive technologies, such as advanced building technologies, carbon capture and sequestration, advanced manufacturing, and enhanced geothermal, also require multiple expensive, well-designed, and carefully monitored demonstrations and test beds, carried out in collaboration with private industry, to prove their reliability, techno-economic feasibility, or environmental sustainability under a variety of geological conditions.

Entrepreneurs may need assistance in introducing new technologies in favorable market niches in entrenched legacy sectors where they can gain valuable practical experience, drive down the manufacturing cost curve, and achieve important economies of scale. Examples from the energy sector have included LED lighting and off-grid power generation for wind and solar energy technology. While the 2011 collapse of Solyndra, the solar photovoltaic company, has led Congress to limit funding for Energy Department loan guarantees, state efforts to meet their energy needs, such as California's, could assist. Here the military has an important role to play in scaling new technologies; examples include developing algal or cellulosic biofuel for aircraft engines, and installing cost-saving renewable energy equipment in stateside military installations.[15]

The second problem, that of locked-in, innovation-resistant legacy sectors, requires systematic analysis of the obstacles confronting the introduction and scale-up of innovation, as well as the gaps in the system of institutional support for innovation. As we explore below, innovation in these legacy sectors requires two approaches: first, lowering the costs, improving the performance, and developing totally new ideas, so that disruptive innovations can compete with established products; and second, confronting the many advantages that favor legacy technologies and drive these sectors in unfavorable directions. The slow growth of the US economy complicates addressing this double problem, since capital investment that embodies innovative technology is naturally drawn to rapidly growing foreign markets, whereas investment in capital plant and equipment in the United States has been at historic lows.

Removing obstacles to innovation in legacy sectors requires more difficult forms of policy intervention that can no longer be ignored by innovation theorists and policymakers, who for these sectors can be important change agents. Altering regulation and regulatory structures to promote the smart grid, establishing focused price signals to discourage carbon dioxide-emitting technologies, implementing environmental regulations to encourage more sustainable agriculture, and changing the fee-for-service tariff structure for health delivery are examples. Here an understanding of launch pathways in legacy sectors—the way technologies move through the development stage and enter the market—and policies designed to facilitate those launch pathways will be a critical step. Fashioning an innovation system where the gaps on both the front end (the phase of the innovation cycle that precedes commercialization, principally research and development) and back end (the phase of the innovation cycle in which a demonstrated technology idea becomes a commercialized product) of that system are filled, will be another. These and other measures are explored below.

THE DYNAMICS OF INNOVATION AND THE INNOVATION ENVIRONMENT

The framework we will erect in subsequent chapters builds on familiar concepts of science policy and innovation theory, but it greatly broadens, extends, and integrates them so as to provide new insights and a new unifying framework. We summarize them here to help the reader see what's coming. In outline, our argument goes as follows.

We begin by asking how innovations that challenge the structure of legacy sectors—that is, "disruptive" innovations—might take place. To answer this question requires an understanding of the dynamics of the innovation process and the kind of change agents required to make each of these models of this dynamic effective. Here we define the *change agent* as the person or organization or institution that makes an innovation happen, either directly or indirectly. A given change may have more than one agent.[16]

We now briefly sketch five basic models, to be elaborated on later, that describe the dynamics that drive innovation in different situations: the innovation pipeline, induced innovation, the extended pipeline, manufacturing-led innovation, and innovation organization. These provide a framework for approaching the twin issues of furthering innovation and job creation.

The "pipeline" model, which dominates US thinking on science and technology, pictures invention and innovation as flowing from investments in research and development at the front end of the innovation system. This is true for major breakthrough inventions. Here the change agents are the researchers, inventors, and entrepreneurs who conceive the initial idea and carry it through to a radically new product.

But most technology responds to market opportunities and incentives, a process described by a second model, that of "induced innovation." This model is important in explaining how the paradigms characteristic of legacy sectors affect the technology in use and the pattern of innovation in a given industry, and how changes in policy can affect the incentives faced by potential innovators and in this way can influence the direction of technological innovation. Here the change agents can include primarily firms, and entrepreneurs and inventors linked to them, but also policymakers in government and standards setters in industry that can affect market signals and regulatory requirements.

In the third model, the "extended pipeline," some US R & D organizations, led by the military, act as change agents to assist in moving nascent technologies beyond R & D through the "back-end" stages of demonstrations, test beds, and initial market creation. Most major innovations depend in some way on this kind of facilitation in order to bridge the "valley of death" between advanced research and an eventual product.

The fourth basic model of the dynamics of innovation, that of "manufacturing-led" innovation, describes innovations in both processes and products that emerge from experience and expertise in manufacturing, typically augmented by R & D closely integrated with the production process. This model underpins our discussion of the impact of globalization on the geography of innovation and hence on the phenomenon of jobless innovation to which we have called attention in the earlier parts of this chapter.

This focus on improving the mechanisms and institutions for innovation over and above those required by the pipeline model gives rise to a fifth basic model of the dynamics of innovation, which we have called the "organizational" model. In this innovation organization model, an integrating mechanism, often involving government, business, and other stakeholders, actively supports the entire innovation process, including production stage innovation captured in the manufacturing-led model. This resembles the extended pipeline model but goes beyond it in that it orchestrates the institutional and policy changes needed to facilitate innovation. While the other models describe existing approaches to innovation, this one represents a new and different approach, namely one of promoting innovation by examining the innovation environment and the institutions and barriers within it, assessing their strengths and potential for improvement, and bringing about measures to build on these strengths and overcome these barriers.

The explanation of this fifth model of innovation requires a brief excursion into the functioning of the national innovation system and of the broader national innovation environment and international innovation system of which the national innovation system forms a part. The national innovation system is defined in the science policy literature as the sum of the institutions and policies that are established for the explicit purpose of encouraging, facilitating, and supporting research, innovation, and the development of technological capacity in a given country.

Beyond this system as it is traditionally defined lie broad features of culture (especially attitudes toward novelty and risk), macroeconomic policy, business climate, legal structure, trade policy, banking, and finance that have a strong influence on the rate and direction of innovation in a given country. These factors have as much to do with the speed and direction of innovation as does the better known and better studied national innovation system. They influence not only the development of individual technologies, but also the general trends in technological innovation, for example toward or away from environmental sustainability or energy conservation. To distinguish these factors from institutions and programs directly concerned with research and innovation, we define them as the national innovation *context* and propose that the sum of the national innovation system and the national innovation context be defined as the national innovation *environment*.

The innovation organization model, then, considers all aspects of the national innovation environment, as well as efforts of the international innovation system to stimulate and mobilize innovations to overcome the barriers to innovation in legacy sectors. This model is important for all legacy sectors and will be especially important in our consideration of the manufacturing sector and the problem of jobless innovation in chapter 4.

GLOBALIZATION, MANUFACTURING, AND INNOVATION

The globalization of the world economy has inexorably led toward the globalization of innovation, so that national innovation systems, which were once relatively independent of one another, have now become pillars underpinning an increasingly international innovation system, dominated by multinational corporations that account for the majority of world total investment in research and development (largely development). While the front end of innovation systems—particularly support for research and technical education—continue to be led by national support systems, the back-end stages that are in the hands of firms are growing international.

The globalization of aspects of innovation and the emergence of an international innovation system, aided by digital production technologies, have made it relatively straightforward for any stage in the back end of the innovation process—from engineering to prototyping and production—to be located anywhere in the world where it makes economic and technical sense. That, in turn, makes the knowledge embedded in the front end more transferrable. Most importantly, the detailed engineering and final production of a good or service—and the employment to which these give rise—are likely to be located together in or near expanding markets, rather than necessarily in the country where the original research and product development were carried out.

This has important consequences for both advanced and developing countries. Historically, advanced countries, and especially the United States, have invested heavily in research and development on the assumption that at least the early versions of a new product would be produced at home, a model we have called "innovate here, produce here." This means that investment in research and development is justified by eventual high-productivity, high-wage employment. The United States achieves in this model the gains from every stage of innovation, from research through production—it can be termed *full-spectrum innovation*.

This model is now threatened by the globalization of innovation, and especially by the rise of China and India as "innovative developing countries" with lower cost technical professionals capable of carrying out especially the last, most labor-intensive stages of innovation. These countries are likely to continue to gain an increasing share of employment from the production of even the latest and most innovative products of the research and development carried out in the United States and other advanced countries, a process already evident in the offshoring of the manufacture of the latest products from Apple. "Innovate here, produce here" is increasingly being replaced by "innovate here, produce there," with serious consequences for the American economy. And another stage may be on the way. The initial production stage can be highly innovative, requiring the original innovation to be rethought and reengineered, closely linking innovation to the production process.[17] If production is moving offshore, much of the capability for manufacturing-led innovation may have to follow it, creating "produce there, innovate there."

TECHNOLOGICAL LOCK-IN IN LEGACY SECTORS

As we have seen in earlier parts of this chapter, many important sectors of the economy are characterized by an entrenched, well-defended technological/economic/political/social paradigm that resists any innovation that might threaten to disrupt the business models of the stakeholders who benefit from it. As long as the technology and the paradigm satisfy users and the larger society, this may be all to the good. Problems arise, however, if that paradigm blocks the entry of more efficacious, advanced technologies. Problems grow if the paradigm begins to create incentives to producers that are not in sync with the needs of the larger society—typically because of environmental, public health, or security "externalities" that do not directly affect the producer or the user of the product and do not figure in their cost structures.

These disruption-resistant, misdirected legacy sectors include some of the most important parts of the American economy. As examples in this book, we examine the fossil-fuel-based energy economy, the national electric grid, the building sector, the input-intensive agricultural industry, air and auto transport, and the manufacturing sector. Parts of the military establishment also display some of the features of a legacy sector, although the military is also capable of achieving astonishing technological leaps by developing means to get around these features. Service sectors such as healthcare delivery and higher education can also operate as legacy sectors. At the international level, the resistant paradigms of legacy sectors in advanced countries often result in the importation of inappropriate technologies by developing countries, a phenomenon that may be mitigated by imports from "innovative developing countries" whose markets more nearly resemble their own.

The process of defining the barriers to transformative technology in these legacy sectors illustrates the need for policies to overcome the obstacles to bringing innovation into these sectors. We believe, as will be reviewed later in detail, that these require improving the front end of the innovation system, designing launch paths for advancing new technologies, tying incentives to these paths to encourage their launch, analyzing the gaps in the sector's innovation system, and making systemic efforts to fill those gaps. The policy approach we hammer out also requires an overall strategic approach, and the complexity and difficulty of change in a legacy sector demands change agents prepared to push innovative advances relentlessly through barriers at each innovation stage.

Returning to our covered wagon metaphor, it is critically important to remove the obstacles to the movement of innovation in both eastward and westward directions. The nation's economic prowess, including its capability for job creation, arguably rides on the outcome. An understanding of how to innovate in legacy sectors will be a key task in this effort.

Other nations face legacy features, as well, as we will explore in chapter 9, where we apply the framework we have developed for the United States to the innovation environments in Russia, Scandinavia, China, India, France, and Germany, and draw lessons from this brief "world tour" for the United States. What is more, legacy sectors from the developed world tend to define the innovation space for developing and emerging economies, and in this way to narrow the possibilities and economic promise of innovation worldwide. Efforts to tackle legacy sectors in advanced countries thus promise worldwide benefits.

This chapter, then, has defined the questions that subsequent chapters attempt to answer. To return to the two core issues, while one part of the US innovation system is just that, highly innovative, in areas like information technology and biotechnology, it is creating too few jobs to optimize the benefits of that innovation. Important roots of this problem lie in the production system and the ability of firms to "innovate here, produce there." By distributing the gains of its innovation capability, the United States fails to realize the full spectrum of gains possible from its innovation system. Ultimately, this may threaten the strength of the innovation system itself.

A way out of this dilemma—the second core issue—could be to expand the reach of innovation not only to the new sectors it periodically creates, like information technology, but to the established legacy sectors of the economy that constitute much of the economy. However, in sectors like energy, transport, construction, healthcare delivery, and education, there is systemic resistance to innovation. These sectors successfully evade the introduction and scale-up of innovation unless they perpetuate the existing legacy system. If technological innovation is a dominant cause of growth, this resistance acts as a profound drag on overall economic strength as well as on needed societal advances. These are the twin innovation problems we must confront.

2 The Legacy Sector Challenge

In the most innovative society in the world, why are certain parts of the economy—like the health delivery system and the electrical distribution grid—stubbornly resistant to innovation?[1] Why is it hard to launch sustainable innovations in energy, health delivery systems, manufacturing, buildings, and agriculture at a scale sufficient for substantial impact? In short, why does the United States have what amounts to a dual economy: breathtakingly rapid innovation, capable of disrupting long-established practice and structures in the information, pharmaceutical, industrial agriculture, and military and aerospace industries—at the same time that other, equally important parts of its economy successfully resist disruptive innovations that would address broad environmental, security, and public health goals?

These questions highlight an important gap in the American literature on innovation, which is focused largely on the problems facing radical innovations that introduce new functionality but does not address the interlocking obstacles encountered in the disparate, disruption-resistant "legacy sectors" cited in the preceding paragraph. These legacy sectors share common features that, taken together, define a technological/economic/political/social paradigm that enables them to resist fundamental change.[2] The resulting market forces lead to the evolution of dominant designs for products that embody or are consistent with that paradigm, leading to technology "*lock-in*"[3] that further reinforces the resistance to technological alternatives.[4]

These paradigms have implications beyond America's borders. First, they set limits on the ability of other countries to develop and launch desirable innovations in these sectors, since their efforts to penetrate some of their biggest potential markets for these products will be blocked by deeply entrenched obstacles. Second, most developing countries lack the technological and innovative capacity to strike out in fundamentally new directions, so that they largely accept the direction of innovation charted by technologically advanced countries and adapt the resulting innovations to their needs. This process occasionally produces remarkable results, as in the case of mobile finance in Africa and the application of biotechnology to problems of tropical medicine and agriculture. It has, however, delayed essential innovations in sustainable agriculture, energy conservation, and other areas of great importance to developing countries.

WHY LEGACY SECTORS?

Americans pride themselves on the scientific and technological prowess that has given rise to a steady stream of innovations in information and communication technology, along with medicine, agriculture, military, aerospace, and many other fields. For more than a quarter-century, innovation policy in the United States has focused on the problems encountered by innovations—in these and many other areas—especially on "the valley of death," the gap in implementing innovation that occurs as technologies bring new functions to create new markets and as innovators move from research to late-stage development. In contrast, almost no research has focused on a different but critical problem in innovation: introducing new technologies into established economic sectors where innovation is needed and potentially transformational and where the record of success is much more meager. This is the problem we confront here.

Complex, established legacy sectors—such as those cited above—present acute needs for system-wide technological innovation. Typically, the United States launches new technologies, and the new functionality they offer, into new territory, creating new economic activities. There was nothing quite like computing, telecommunications, aviation, electricity, or railroads before their advent, and no entrenched incumbent to resist them. It is harder to launch innovations into established sectors occupied by incumbent firms and their aging technologies because they resist any change that threatens their business models. Therefore, the United States tends to incubate the new rather than fix the old, leaving established sectors isolated from innovation, so that they tend to stagnate. That's why Thomas Edison would be comfortable with the electric grid, why the United States has been working on electronic medical records for twenty years, why energy losses from its buildings are major contributors to global warming, and part of why a cab ride from Kennedy Airport to Manhattan over potholed highways is something of a Third World experience. The resistance to innovation in US established sectors becomes a drag on its long-term viability and economic growth.

The technological systems in these established legacy sectors are the result of stable and well-defended technological, economic, political, and social paradigms that have developed over decades of history. This multifaceted legacy sector paradigm—and the technology lock-in that it ensures—provides the overall structure into which any innovation must be introduced, even though its original purpose, however justified it may have been at the time it evolved, may have long been overtaken by events and become broadly counterproductive. While established sectors will allow "sustaining" advances to existing technologies that slot into and are consistent with the paradigm, they resist breakthroughs that make fundamental structural, "disruptive" changes.

US inability to introduce innovation into such legacy sectors ties an anchor to its economy. Emerging nations climbing toward developed world status tend to have growth rates two to three times that of the United States, in part because they are starting afresh and bringing the latest innovations into all sectors. The US growth rate is based largely on innovating at the frontiers of technology, so it leads new innovation waves[5] that generally recur every four or five decades. If we worked not only on innovation at the frontier but also on innovation in established sectors, both our growth rate and our quality of life could be significantly enhanced.

US growth might look different if it could find ways to cut the Gordian knots that tie up the ability of its people to innovate in legacy sectors and bring innovation into the territories they occupy, rather than confining themselves to cutting-edge advances in new breakthrough technologies. This might mean bringing innovation into its inefficient and expensive healthcare delivery system along with new biotech-derived drugs. It could mean bringing computer simulations and online, game-based learning into K-12 education, new materials and information technology into our transportation or construction infrastructure, or e-government into the widespread delivery of government services. The list of possibilities is long.

Perhaps the United States could even take its innovation covered wagons back east and bring innovation into our complex, deeply entrenched, heavily subsidized energy sector. Our energy sector paradigm supports legacy technologies based on fossil fuels, a structure that is now backed by the power of huge corporations, buttressed by strong and deeply felt public expectations of cheap energy, that mobilize opposition to any proposals for fundamental change.[6] The result is a complex set of interlocking obstacles to the development and market launch of technologies based on alternatives to fossil fuels.

Analogous paradigms exist in transport, food, health delivery, building, the electric grid, and many other sectors—based, respectively, on the strong public support for personal as opposed to mass transportation, on the political power of industrial agriculture, and on the inability of our fragmented systems of healthcare, of building, and of the regulation of electric utilities to promote innovation and efficiency. These paradigms guide not only investments in existing technology, but also the direction of investments in research, development, and demonstration of new technologies.

"DRIVING COVERED WAGONS EAST"

We use the image of "driving covered wagons east"[7] as a metaphor with which to capture the difficulties of introducing innovations in the broad set of legacy sectors mentioned in the previous paragraph: the fossil fuel economy, the health delivery system, the long-distance electricity grid, the building sector, air transport, and industrial agriculture. In all of these sectors, the social benefits of a technological revolution justify public intervention[8] to speed technical change beyond what might be expected from the ordinary activity of free markets, just as they would in energy. In all of them,[9] the chief obstacles to innovation lie in the problems of *market launch*. This means that policymakers need to go beyond support to research and development—the traditional focus of American science and technology policy—and examine the entire innovation process.[10] The obstacles to market launch in these systems are known to specialists in all these areas but have not received the attention they deserve from general innovation theorists.

Our logic, in brief, runs as follows. All innovations face obstacles as a result of a variety of market imperfections. (They can benefit from market imperfections like patent monopolies, too, but that is another story.) Innovations that seek to disrupt legacy sectors face numerous additional obstacles because they must break into a long-established and well-defended economic, political, social, and cultural paradigm that encourages compatible innovations—the sectoral version of the technological lock-in made familiar to students of innovation by the QWERTY keyboard, a parable recounted in chapter 3.[11]

This phenomenon of the techno-economic paradigm is well known to students of the waves of technological innovation that have swept over the world every 50 years or so, only to be succeeded as a new wave came to predominate. The cluster of iron, steam, coal, and textiles, for example, set the tone for industry in the first half of the 19th century, only to be supplanted by the railroads, steamships, and telegraph in the second half. Economic historians who study these so-called Kondratiev cycles acknowledge the obstacles that each new cluster must overcome before a new cycle can supplant the old, but their main interest is in the process by which each new wave replaces its predecessor by dint of its technological superiority and the superior returns it offers to investors.[12]

Our emphasis, however, is different. In the legacy sectors that we explore, the obstacles to innovation are so well defended and of such long standing that it is unlikely that they will be overcome simply by virtue of the superiority of a new Kondratiev cluster. Besides, the need for innovation in these sectors often arises, not so much from the needs of users and consumers as expressed in market forces, but from "externalities" like security, reliability, safety, and environmental sustainability. For this reason, while technological advance is essential, it is unlikely to be sufficient to disrupt existing paradigms in the absence of policies that align the incentives of producers with these larger goals.

MARKET IMPERFECTIONS AFFECTING "NORMAL" INNOVATIONS

We now continue to develop our unifying conceptual framework so as to illuminate the common features of these apparently disparate sectors in order to facilitate the discussion of policies that can stimulate innovation in these critical and apparently disparate economic sectors. We first use the concept of market imperfection to distinguish between the obstacles faced by all innovations, on the one hand, and the special hurdles faced by innovations seeking to disrupt a legacy sector, on the other.

The market for technology is inherently imperfect. Some of these market imperfections reward private investments; others impose obstacles to innovation. We therefore begin by exploring the market imperfections that affect the development and launch of *any* innovation, some for better and some for worse.

We first need to recall the properties of a free market as they are defined by economists. The free market is a theoretical concept; in reality, there are very few if any truly free markets. But we shall find that it is a useful starting point for analysis. In principle, a free market for a product has a very large number of buyers and sellers, all of whom act individually, all of whom are equally well informed about the properties of what is being bought and sold, and none of whom incur "transaction costs" in obtaining this information or in completing the purchase and sale. There are no environmental or other externalities that require individuals not involved in the transaction to absorb related costs or that allow them to gain benefits. If the product is the end result of a "value chain" of successive processes, each of these can be "unbundled" from the others and treated as a separate transaction, each of which has all of the properties of the free market. Even the technology itself can be separated from the company that manages it. Most importantly for our analysis, the seller receives the full value of his or her investment in the product being sold and need not share it with anyone else—a characteristic known as *full appropriability.*

In a perfectly free market, the price of an object is set by supply and demand, just as it is in any market. What sets a perfect market apart—and the reason it is the subject of such admiration and research—is that this market price is equal to the value of the product, not only to the buyer and seller, but also to the whole world. This is true not only of the product itself, but also of its "inputs," that is, the things that went into its production. In other words, if it was profitable to the investor to combine the inputs to create the final product, his or her investment also added value to the entire world—all of which the investor gets to keep. In such a world, then, market prices give perfect signals to investors as to where to put their money—not only for their own good, but for the good of the world as a whole. If a prospective investment fails to attract capital, it wasn't a good investment to begin with. In more technical terms, in a perfectly free market, capital markets—the market for investments, "Wall Street"—are the best arbiters of the allocation of capital.

This theoretical picture plainly does not apply to technology. On the contrary, as we have pointed out earlier, the market for technological innovation is inherently imperfect, and it is to these market "imperfections" that we now turn. Many of these market imperfections work to the strong advantage of the innovator. Even before an innovation is ready for market, for example, the underlying science or generic technology is likely to have benefited from *public support*—a market imperfection—to research, development, prototyping, or demonstration. Once a product or process is fully developed, the innovator gains "economic rents"— that is, extra profits—through his, her or its *monopoly* on technology, guaranteed by our system of intellectual property and further reinforced by the fact that the owner of a technology knows more about it than does a prospective buyer—an advantage known to economists as *asymmetric information*. Once their new product has been established in the market, innovators benefit from *barriers to entry* by competitors. The innovator further benefits from various *first-mover advantages*, for example, the fact that consumers are more likely to identify the new product with the innovator, even after competitors have appeared on the market.[13]

Other market imperfections, on the other hand, work to the innovator's *disadvantage*. These constitute the first theoretical justification for specific policy interventions intended to stimulate research and innovation. (We shall explore other, more expansive justifications in chapter 11.) Of these imperfections, probably the most important is the fact that the innovator does not keep all of the benefits of his or her invention, a market imperfection known to economists as *nonappropriability*. First of all, the innovator must share the value-added of innovation with a variety of stakeholders—most obviously with the user, given the rule of thumb that an innovation must be at least twice as cost-effective as whatever it replaces. Beyond this, technology may "leak" away from its originator by such means as the departure of key personnel or successful patent infringement, or it may even be stolen outright. This appropriability, or "knowledge spillover," is the basic policy justification for public support to research and development, since it implies that aggregate private investment in innovation will be less than optimum for society, even ignoring environmental and other externalities.[14]

We have already mentioned the well-known "valley of death" between applied research and the late-stage development of commercial products; from this point of view, it is an imperfection in the capital markets in the sense that potentially profitable opportunities fail to attract investors.[15] A less obvious market imperfection affecting all innovations is the frequently difficult link between technology and management; for example, a company with excellent technology may suffer from poor management, and vice versa. This is an imperfection because in an ideal free market, technology and management could be "unbundled" from each other, like design and manufacturing in the semiconductor and other IT sectors.[16] The most famous case of this pattern is the failure of the Xerox Corporation to capitalize on the seminal inventions of its own Palo Alto Research Center (Xerox PARC), including the desktop computer, the graphic interface, the mouse, and the Ethernet.[17]

To be sure, the status of first mover involves costs as well as benefits. The innovator must achieve sufficient *economies of scale* to be able to introduce the new product into the market at a cost low enough to be competitive with any existing products. The innovator must absorb the cost of educating consumers, developing distribution channels and repair and maintenance capabilities, driving product costs down the price curve, developing incremental improvements and second-generation products, and identifying and seeing to the production and marketing of complementary products.[18]

We now define a "normal" innovation as one that is subject to these particular market imperfections, but not to the many others that characterize legacy sectors. The term "normal" does not suggest that such innovations face an easy path; on the contrary, they typically face an uphill struggle. The obstacles they face, and the policy measures needed to help them overcome these obstacles, have been the near-exclusive focus of the general literature on innovation theory. Analysis of these "normal" innovations has led to the definition such important and well-studied categories as "induced" innovation,[19] "discontinuous" or "transformative" innovations,[20] "enabling" or "generative" innovations,[21] and many kinds of "disruptive" innovations.[22] Such innovations may be "radical" (new functionality), "secondary" (major improvement of established functionality), or "incremental."[23] We shall use many of these categories in the discussion that follows.

These obstacles justify the interventions that characterize the national innovation system—standard recommendations that are valid for virtually all innovations. The organization of the innovation process, both at the institutional level and at the face-to-face personal level,[24] likewise presents a profound challenge. In particular, the link between technology and management constitutes much of the theoretical justification for establishing the Defense Advanced Research Projects Agency (DARPA)[25] and its counterparts in intelligence (In-Q-Tel[26] and IARPA[27]), biodefense (BARDA),[28] homeland security (HSARPA),[29] and energy (ARPA-E),[30] which provide various forms of support extending into the applied development area to firms with technologies deemed critical to defense, intelligence, health, and energy capability, respectively.

OBSTACLES TO INNOVATION IN LEGACY SECTORS

We now review in more detail the concept of the legacy sector by explaining the additional obstacles to innovation, over and above those faced by "normal" innovations, that create and sustain a technological/economic/political/social paradigm that favors existing technology and supports a legacy sector.[31]

As we explained earlier, innovations in a legacy sector that are consistent with and fit into the prevailing paradigm face only the same obstacles as any other innovation. Innovations that threaten an established paradigm, on the other hand, face many additional hurdles on their way uphill. They must contend with policies, institutions, subsidies, prices, price structures, standards, regulations, incentives, infrastructure, political support, expert communities, technological institutions, innovation systems, career paths, and university curricula and market imperfections that protect the "legacy" technology, all backed by the competitors that benefit from the established paradigm. To return to our "covered wagons" metaphor, these are the conditions that led our technology pioneers to head westward in the first place.

We define the typical legacy sector as displaying eight paradigmatic features:

1. A tilted (nonlevel) playing field caused by *"perverse" subsidies and cost or price structures* that are favorable to existing technologies,[32] and that create a mismatch between the incentives of producers and innovators and the goals of the larger society, typically by ignoring externalities such as environment, public health, and security.

2. An *established institutional architecture* that imposes regulatory hurdles or other policy disadvantages favoring existing technology or discouraging new entrants, accompanied by public support to infrastructure adapted to the requirements of existing technology.

3. *Well-established and politically powerful vested interests*, reinforced by public support, that defend their sectoral paradigm and resist the introduction of technologies that threaten their business models.

4. A *financing system geared to incumbents* and reluctant to extend risk capital to disruptive, new-entrant technologies.

5. *Public habits and expectations attuned to existing technology*, price structures, and dominant products, that underpin popular support to the policies and public expenditures favorable to existing technology.

6. An *established knowledge and human resources structure* that includes educational curricula, career paths, and professional standards in fields that are adapted to the needs of existing technology.

7. *Limited investment in research and development* and a consequent dearth of alternative technologies that are ready for implementation at scale.

8. A set of *market imperfections* specific to one or more innovations within the sector, over and above those facing "normal model" innovations. These may include network economies, lumpiness, split incentives, requirements for collective action, and transaction costs.[33] We explore these in detail in chapter 5.

We define in the next chapter, drawing on these points, the paradigms that characterize these legacy sectors. These paradigms do not inhibit all innovations. On the contrary, innovations that reinforce them constitute the basis of much of the United States' comparative advantage in pharmaceuticals and in fossil fuel, agricultural, military, and aerospace technology. The structures supporting these paradigms have grown up over the years precisely because they fulfill their functions well, at least for a substantial proportion of their stakeholders. Indeed, in many cases there would be no issue at all if it were not for some overwhelming nonmarket collective benefit, such as the environment, public health and safety, or (in the case of energy) geopolitics and national security.

But for innovations that do not slot readily into a given legacy paradigm, for example those in sustainable agriculture, this structure presents multiple obstacles that inhibit investment at every stage, from research to market introduction. The prominence and obvious importance of the critical societal problems raised by this paradigm may attract the attention of creative individuals and companies, resulting in a substantial supply of promising ideas at various stages of development and small-scale implementation—just far enough along to give rise to excited stories in the media and to create major frustration on the part of the innovator, but far short of readiness for the large-scale deployment that would be needed to make a significant dent in the overall problem.

To further complicate matters, policymakers seeking to promote innovation face the problem of defining and obtaining agreement on a clear and measurable standard or metric by which to gauge whether the externalities have been overcome and the social goals have been met, for example for evidence-based medicine or sustainable energy. The same interests that benefit from the existing paradigm are likely to oppose efforts to define and implement such standards.

In the next chapter, we explore the characteristics of a legacy sector paradigm in greater detail.

3 Paradigms as Obstacles to Innovation in Legacy Sectors

To understand legacy sectors we need to tackle several fundamentals. First, we need a working theory of the dynamics of the innovation process in order to understand how it plays out in legacy sectors; in particular, we need to understand the five models for the dynamics of innovation, particularly "innovation organization," a new concept that we define in this book. We must also understand some basics about how legacy sectors are organized. As we suggested in the previous chapter, they are characterized by a "paradigm"—but what does this mean, and how does it relate to more familiar concepts of technology lock-in and dominant design?

FIVE MODELS OF THE DYNAMICS OF INNOVATION

In order to contemplate bringing our scientific and technological capabilities to established legacy sectors of the economy, we need a working theory of the dynamics of innovation for these sectors. The design of this theory depends on a clear concept of how technological innovation takes place in the sectors in response to both technological advance and market forces, and how this process can be influenced by public policy and institutional forces. We identify five models of this process,[1] each of which is the product of a particular period of technological history and each of which requires a different kind of change agent. Each was briefly cited in chapter 1, and also is elaborated on in more detail in subsequent chapters on policy, but for coherence the ideas need to be anticipated here.

The first of these models is the so-called pipeline or linear model, identified with Vannevar Bush,[2] in which basic research operating at the frontiers of knowledge leads to applied research, which in turn leads to invention, to prototyping, to development, and finally to innovation, by which we mean widespread commercialization or deployment. Here the researcher is the prime agent of change, along with the company or entrepreneur that translates his or her idea into a practical product. While subsequent literature showed that this process isn't really linear—technology influences science as well as the other way around[3]—"pipeline" is still the term generally associated with this approach.

This model was inspired by the World War II–era success of atomic energy, radar, and other technologies derived from advances in fundamental scientific knowledge;[4] it regained prominence in the 1990s from the examples of the information revolution supported by DARPA and the National Science Foundation (NSF),[5] the biotechnology and genomics revolutions derived from research supported by the National Institutes of Health (NIH), and the promise of a similar revolution in nanotechnology. In these examples, the government played a prominent role in shepherding these technologies through the initial stages of the innovation process.

The pipeline model is a "technology push" or "technology supply" model, with the government supporting initial research but only to a limited extent helping to push the resulting advances toward the marketplace. In strict logic, it implies that government should support basic and perhaps the early stages of applied research, but should leave development and the later stages of innovation to private industry. In practice, this "front end" support is often augmented by a variety of "bridging" methods intended to overcome the "valley of death" between applied research and late-stage development for a marketable product, including support to "translational" medical research (research intended to carry through the results of basic research toward a usable product), support or encouragement to venture capital, the work of technology transfer offices at universities and government laboratories, support to regional clusters of innovative industries, etc. In the United States, such support is limited and often tends to be politically controversial.

The second of these models is based on the "induced innovation" concept explored in detail by Vernon Ruttan,[6] in which technology and technological innovation respond to the economic environment. This concept holds that the technology in use in any economic sector—and given enough time, the direction of development and research—is shaped by the structure of the market and responds to market changes, for example by responding to price signals by minimizing the use of expensive inputs and maximizing the use of inexpensive ones. By extension, this model would predict that technology and technological innovation would also respond to the policy environment, for example by improving worker and product safety and decreasing pollution as policies in these areas are tightened. In response to such changes in markets or policies, firms would quickly adopt relatively straightforward innovations that were ready for implementation and would also invest in longer term research and development to support and improve them.

The induced model involves "market pull": the market inspires and pulls technological innovations from firms toward implementation in the market. Innovation of this kind is typically led by firms; in meeting market opportunities, they generally pursue incremental advances that are more foreseeable than the radical technology advances that come from the pipeline model. The model can also apply to innovations induced by the change in market incentives that results from a change in public policy, from a new standard developed by the private sector, or even from a prize to or a guaranteed purchase from the developers of a particular product (a vaccine for a particular disease, for example).

The third model, the "extended pipeline," is also a technology-push model— but in contrast to the simple pipeline model, it involves governmental action at all stages of innovation, not simply the early ones. This model was pioneered by the US Department of Defense (DOD), which not only funded the early stages of research but often sponsored all the follow-on stages: the development, the prototype, the product design, the demonstration, the test bed, all the way to the creation of the initial market. While interventions based on this model can support incremental advances, its most powerful role is in nurturing radical technology. Important parts of the information technology revolution—the Internet for example—were developed in this way. Before this, as Vernon Ruttan has elaborated, the DOD used this model to spur innovation in aviation, electronics, space, nuclear power and computing.[7] Other R & D agencies are starting to emulate this more connected system.[8] Given its powerful contribution to 20th-century technology advance and its importance in counterbalancing the common supposition that the latter stages of innovation will take care of themselves once research has been completed, the extended pipeline deserves special notice as a full-fledged model unto itself.

The fourth basic model of the dynamics of innovation, that of "manufacturing-led" innovation, describes innovations in both production processes and technologies that emerge from experience and expertise in manufacturing, typically augmented by R & D closely integrated with the production process. Production, particularly the initial production stage, can be highly innovative; this is where product design is completed and a new technology advance is reworked and re-thought to become a product that can be made at scale and can fit into a market need. It involves extensive and creative engineering and often requires that the original innovation and the scientific and technological learning behind it be completely reworked. Japan's economic success in the creation of the quality manufacturing system in the 1970s and 1980s is emblematic of the importance of this stage. This model also underpins our discussion of the impact of globalization on the geography of innovation and hence on the phenomenon of jobless innovation to which we have called attention in chapter 1.

The fifth model, which we call "innovation organization," encompasses the first four models and reaches beyond them to take into account the broad structure into which the innovation is to be introduced. We need this fifth element in our framework if innovation theory is to encompass not only ideas but the means to implement them despite the barriers that they are likely to encounter. This innovation organization model is based on the idea that innovation, especially in legacy sectors, requires not only a supply of technology and a market demand for that technology, but also institutions that are anchored in both the public and the private sectors—and organizational means for connecting them—that can facilitate and guide the evolution of new technologies that may not fit prevailing paradigms.[9] There must be concrete institutions for innovation to facilitate the evolution of new technologies in response to forces of technology push and market pull.

Innovation in these sectors also requires a mechanism that orchestrates these institutions in such a way as to facilitate the formation and launch of new technology, beginning with an assessment of the likely impact of the innovation environment and then using the full panoply of mechanisms and agents that are needed to surmount the obstacles it poses, which as we have seen are especially serious in legacy sectors. Researchers and entrepreneurs are of course central to any innovation, but in the innovation organization model these orchestrating mechanisms are also critical change agents.

In applying the innovation organization model, then, we must also take into account the dynamics of the innovation process, including the kind of change agents required for a given disruptive innovation. Here we define the *change agent* as the person or organization or institution that makes an innovation happen, either directly or indirectly. A given change may have more than one agent.[10] The *instrument* of change—the way in which the change agent makes the change happen—may be an idea, an invention, an entrepreneurial effort, the championing of an idea or a change within a business, an organization or a government bureaucracy, or (in the case of an induced innovation) a policy or standard. The change agent's work can be enabled and abetted by a policy or economic shift or crisis, or by sectoral or global competition.

Our new concept of the innovation organization model for the dynamic of innovation thus goes well beyond the pipeline, induced, extended pipeline, and manufacturing-led models, which underlie the dominant approaches to the organization of innovation in the United States. As we have seen, these models are limited in their reach, especially when they address the need for innovation in legacy sectors. In short, we would suggest that introducing innovation into legacy sectors requires a much more far-reaching approach than the methods that are now in use in the United States.

All of these models fit into a historical context. The pipeline model was inspired by the dramatic advances seen in World War II deriving from basic science, such as nuclear energy from particle physics, in the 1940s–1950s. The induced innovation model responded to the realization that nations that were superior in basic research, such as the Great Britain of the 1950s, were not necessarily leading innovators, and that a majority of new products used modifications of existing technologies to meet new market needs—incremental advances—rather than emerging from basic research. The pipeline and extended pipeline models best fit breakthrough or radical innovation, while the induced model best fits secondary or incremental innovation. The manufacturing-led innovation model recognizes that innovation does not occur only at the front end—the R & D phase—but can depend on highly creative "back-end" production technologies and processes.

Japan's "Toyota" system of quality manufacturing, which scaled up in the 1970s and 1980s to lead the auto sector, illustrates the importance of this model.[11] Economies like Taiwan, Korea, and now China are following its example. None of these models addresses the underlying yet largely unexplored organizational issues that are particularly critical for innovation in legacy sectors. We shall later argue that the innovation organization model is required for confronting the problem of legacy sectors developed here.

The dominant literature on technological innovation in recent years has remained focused on the strengths and weaknesses of the pipeline model, because of the importance of the innovation waves in information technology and biotechnology, for which this model provides a good description. The innovation literature has not confronted the problems involved in legacy sectors, which have been relatively unaffected by these waves. Neither the pipeline literature nor the literature on other innovation models pays sufficient attention to how the overall economic and policy environment affects technological innovation in complex networks of both related and unrelated technologies. The extended pipeline is a term we have coined here; the literature on this category is still very limited. The induced technology model often pays too little attention to the governmental role.[12] The literature on this model has rested primarily on market pull and the role of firms in filling technology needs based on changing market signals, ignoring governmental policy interventions. The manufacturing-led model, because of its focus on the back end of innovation, misses the front end; Japan, Taiwan, and Korea, for example, are now scrambling to build stronger front-end innovation to complement their success with back-end production.

Most importantly, the two pipeline, the induced, and the manufacturing-led models have been viewed as separate and distinct paths; to date none has focused much on the possibility of combining these approaches into what we have called the innovation organization model. If we are to adequately describe the institutional framework required for innovation in the complex range of technologies to be introduced into legacy sectors, we need to use the innovation organization model to combine and integrate the other four models and consider the need for change agents—institutional and individual actors that are prepared to push innovations through the sectoral barriers that exist at each stage of innovation. We can then move toward a better grasp of the task before us: innovation in complex established legacy sectors. This will lead us to draw a new series of policy prescriptions quite different from the existing policy literature, focused as it is on the "valley of death" and other approaches that have been articulated to date for nonlegacy sectors.

PIPELINE AND EXTENDED PIPELINE MODELS IN US INNOVATION

In order to show the need for the innovation organization model of innovation, we now explore the pipeline and extended pipeline models as they work in practice in the United States. A weakness in the American innovation system is that most of government support for innovation is based on the pipeline model for technology push, and is therefore organized around the early stages of the innovation system, especially research and development. It emphasizes support for basic research in universities or government laboratories in order to nurture discoveries on the disciplinary frontiers of scientific knowledge. The original assumption embedded in Vannevar Bush's postwar model for science organization was that industry will pick up on the resulting discoveries and commercialize them. This linear or pipeline model, as noted, stresses technology supply-push, in which new technologies evolve and push themselves into the marketplace, rather than the market or demand pull around which Ruttan's induced innovation model is organized. The technologies spawned by the application of this pipeline model became so central to US economic growth[13] that it became accepted as the standard innovation model underlying most American science policy legislation and the institutions it supports.

As this pipeline model was examined over the last two decades, the policy focus, explored most prominently by Lewis Branscomb and Philip Auerswald, turned to the major obstacle to innovation of this kind, namely the "valley of death," the gap in support and financing between basic research and later stage development, or in other formulations, between proof of concept and a commercial product.[14] This obstacle is in significant part the result of the institutional gap between performers of basic research (typically in universities or publicly funded research institutes), on the one hand, and the private firms that carry out commercially oriented development, on the other—an institutional disconnect that was designed into our national innovation system as it evolved in the post–World War II era.

This gap results in a deficiency, articulated by the late Donald Stokes, of research in "Pasteur's quadrant": basic research inspired not by curiosity but by the hope of practical application.[15] Even private venture capitalists accustomed to taking speculative bets on new technology avoid financing the early stages of revolutionary technological advance, deferring investment until a technology is no more than a few years away from production.[16] The result is a valley of death for many, many technologies. The extended pipeline model was introduced by the defense innovation system to help bridge these gaps.

Innovations that could transform legacy sectors are not likely to come from the operation of Ruttan's induced innovation model. Nor are they likely, at least at the early stages, to come from established firms undertaking what firms do best, the development stage for incremental and engineering advances for existing technologies. These firms usually are part of their legacy sectors and are less likely to pursue high-risk technological advances that will break their own business models, since their incentives derive from the existing paradigm. Indeed, they may be inclined to suppress such disruptive technologies if they have the power to do so.

Instead, the advances that will transform legacy sectors will more likely come from the application of the pipeline model, and particularly its variant, the extended pipeline model, and the technology-push approach they embody. The pipeline model works well for "breakthrough" or "radical" innovations because these are typically based on government-funded research support. Breakthrough innovations often create a "new functionality"—that is, a capability that has not previously existed and hence has no real competition and can command a premium price as it enters the market. There was nothing, for example, quite like desktop computing before the Apple IIe, the Mac, and the PC. As a result, the Apple II with 48K RAM sold for $2,638 when introduced in 1977; the Mac portable sold for $6,500 when introduced in 1989—sky-high prices in the context of today's radically more capable computers.[17] As long as pipeline innovation systems are pushing out technologies that create significant new functionality, those systems don't have to worry too much about the opening price; firms can drive this opening price down the production cost curve over time as production efficiencies and incremental advances are incorporated into the product.

However, the first generation of technologies that parachutes into legacy sectors typically does not offer significant new functionality; in the jargon, these are "secondary" innovations. To cite energy examples, for example, consumers will still plug their appliances into wall sockets whether the electricity is derived from wind farms or coal-fired power plants; driving a car with a hybrid engine is still very much like driving a car with an internal combustion engine.

The new technological innovations seeking to enter legacy sectors must therefore be price competitive from the moment of market launch. This means that the pipeline innovation system portrayed above, which produces the bulk of the breakthrough technological advances in the United States, is not well suited to innovation in legacy sectors. In addition, it is organized around the front end of the innovation system, and pays little attention to the back end—the stages of demonstration, test bed, and initial market creation. This creates serious additional implementation issues for this model.

Happily, the picture is somewhat more complicated than this portrayal. The United States doesn't have one pipeline innovation system; it has two. There is, as noted above, the Vannevar Bush universe of government support predominantly for basic research that still dominates US civilian R & D agencies such as the National Science Foundation, the Office of Science in the Department of Energy, and the National Institutes of Health. This is a disconnected model that severs the research system from the industry-led development and implementation systems.

But there is also a parallel universe, the well-funded system of defense research and development that funds all of the stages of the innovation process, from research to initial market creation[18]—the extended pipeline model. As a result, the success of many major innovations with wide economic ramifications has typically depended on a strong injection of public money, often (as Ruttan has illustrated) from the military, enabling them to bridge the valley of death.[19] This military innovation system has been the foundation for most of the innovation waves of the second half of the twentieth century: aviation, electronics, nuclear power, space, computing, and the Internet.

While the connections are far from perfect in this military pipeline system,[20] it is much more connected than its civilian pipeline counterpart. Could this connected military system play a significant role in bringing disruptive innovations into legacy sectors? It depends. The military will fund innovation only in its mission territory, where it has a direct and substantial stake. For example, it could support and fund some energy technologies[21] that fit directly into its mission needs. It has had an interest in reducing its dependence on petroleum-based fuels for its aircraft and ships, for example, and so has supported an effort to develop biofuel alternatives. However, it has little interest in carbon capture and sequestration, a technology that would affect public utilities. Nor can it be expected to take on the transformation of industrial-scale agriculture. Will it fund new healthcare delivery systems? Conceivably—the military's "Tricare" health system for the military, military families, and retirees is a major one, and the DOD has a stake in upgrading its efficiency and cutting its costs.

This brings us to a problem we will discuss later in much more detail. Using the traditional linear pipeline model, we have been labeling R & D and prototyping to promote technology creation as *front-end support*, and the demonstration, test bed, and initial market creation, and the economic incentives and regulatory requirements or mandates to encourage technology implementation and deployment as *back-end support*. Technologies entering legacy sectors generally must be price competitive at the moment they launch into the marketplace, and therefore require attention on both front and back ends of innovation. The pipeline, technology-push approach to innovation is key to shifts in legacy sectors. Some technologies will come to legacy sectors from research, via the pipeline or extended pipeline. Others will require changes in incentives to enable entry. Some innovations in legacy sectors will result from market mechanisms via the induced model, initially filling niche markets. But the bulk of breakthrough innovative technologies will come from the application of the two pipeline models because the induced model favors incremental advances.

Therefore, the fact that, except for the military, we have a largely disconnected federal innovation system that does not operate beyond the front end is a significant challenge at the very outset of the process of bringing innovation into legacy sectors. A particular need will be creating connections between innovation organizations operating on the front and back ends, and then finding change agents: institutional and individual actors in the innovation system prepared to bridge these organizations and force change. These structural problems will require attention as we design possible approaches to spurring innovation advance in legacy sectors.

THE ORIGINS OF THE PARADIGM CONCEPT

In the previous section, we argued that problem of introducing innovations into legacy sectors is particularly complex because of the nature of the paradigm that such an innovation must confront. This leads naturally to the critical question, what do we mean by paradigm?

The modern concept of a paradigm, which we have used to describe the properties of an entrenched legacy sector, originated in the study of the "structure of scientific revolutions" by the distinguished historian of science Thomas Kuhn,[22] who brought the word *paradigm* into common usage and gave it a new meaning: "the world view underlying the theories and methodology of a particular scientific subject."[23] Scientific revolutions, Kuhn found, like the change in chemical theory from the phlogiston model to the concept of oxidation, or in physical theory from Newton's laws to the laws of quantum mechanics and relativity, resulted from a scientific advance that was "sufficiently unprecedented to attract an enduring group of adherents away from competing modes of scientific activity." It constituted "universally recognized scientific achievements that, for a time, provide model problems and solutions for a community of researchers."[24] Such a revolution resolved anomalies in its predecessors that had become so prevalent as to create an intellectual crisis. For each individual scientist, the shift from established to successor paradigm was akin to a religious conversion.

Once accomplished, each of these scientific revolutions provided a framework for what Kuhn called "normal science," by which he meant research that did not challenge the fundamental tenets of the new paradigm, but that rather explored the many problems that remained to be resolved within it. To be sure, there remained champions of the earlier paradigm, who fought back with new experiments and new arguments, but these arguments were refuted and their advocates became converted or were increasingly marginalized or ignored as time passed, and eventually died off.

Christopher Freeman, Carlota Perez, and other students of technology used the concept of a paradigm by analogy to denote the social, economic, infrastructural, legal, and cultural structure that grew up around a cluster of technologies that defined a 50-year period that marked the duration of an innovation wave,[25] in accordance with a model developed by the Russian economist Nikolai Kondratiev. In Perez's words, each Kondratiev wave developed a paradigm that constituted a "best practice model, made up of a set of all-pervasive generic technological and organizational principles, [leading to] a common-sense basis for organizing any activity and structuring any institution [that] becomes imbedded in social practice, law and other elements of the institutional framework, facilitating compatible innovation and hindering incompatible ones."[26]

Each Kondratiev wave was in this way supported by a wholesale change in technology, infrastructure, laws, and institutions, as well as the structure of careers and of educational curricula and institutions. This is a deterministic perspective, according to which shifts in technology drive significant societal reorganizations.[27] In Perez's perspective, the first such Kondratiev wave, the Industrial Revolution, was succeeded in turn by the age of steam and railways, the age of steel, electricity, and heavy engineering, the age of oil, the automobile, and mass production, and the present age of information and telecommunications.[28] The fossil fuel economy, for example, brought about extensive infrastructure for the extraction, refining, transportation, and distribution of coal, oil, and (later) natural gas, as well as infrastructure designed for the users of fossil fuels, such as universal electricity, roads, and airports.[29] Robert Atkinson, evaluating the US economy, charts the innovation waves somewhat differently, but his underlying findings are comparable.[30]

In Perez's, Freeman's, and Atkinson's pictures, each new paradigm was able to succeed its predecessor by dint of the superior technical capacity of its associated technologies via their support from capital markets. Investors sensed that the pent-up demand for superior new technology would make possible much greater returns than could be achieved by investments in legacy technologies that were nearing the exhaustion of their technical possibilities. These competitive market forces enforce what Schumpeter called "creative destruction;" in his words, the "industrial 'mutation' that revolutionizes the economic structure from within, incessantly creating a new one."[31]

In Perez's formulation, the obstacles faced by the new paradigm are more social and institutional than technological or economic, precisely because of the efficiency of the capital markets. During the first phase of a new cycle—what Perez calls the "irruption period"—the technological revolution may encounter "powerful resistance" from dominant predecessors and may be held back by "routine, ideology and vested interests, leading to a mismatch between economy, society and the regulatory system."[32] "The socio-institutional framework," she observes, "has much greater inertia than the techno-economic sphere, which is spurred by competitive pressures,"[33] because of the difficulty of "overcoming the inertia of vested interests, long-held prejudices and dogmas, cultural views, practical routines and ingrained habits, especially when they had been previously successful."[34] In this discussion, Perez thus takes these competitive market pressures for granted and does not pose the question of what might overcome a paradigm in their absence.

In our discussion, we build on the work of Perez and the thinkers whose work she extended. On the other hand, Freeman, Perez, and Atkinson were studying the innovations that have happened and we are studying innovations that don't happen. We therefore explore the characteristics of the paradigms that enable legacy sectors to resist disruptive innovations in more detail. This question of what can overcome a paradigm will become critical when we turn again in later chapters to the established legacy sectors that are the focus of this book.

SECTORAL PARADIGMS AND DOMINANT PRODUCT DESIGNS

The paradigms that characterize successive Kondratiev waves provide a socio-economic structure for technological innovation analogous to the intellectual structures that Kuhn's scientific paradigms provided for the conduct of scientific research. As Perez explains, innovations that are consistent with the prevailing paradigm and that take advantage of its superior capabilities (what we, following Christensen, term "sustaining" innovations) can flourish to the extent that they provide advantages sufficient to overcome the competition from existing products, while those inconsistent with the prevailing paradigm tend to languish.[35] The result is a form of technological lock-in, defined as occurring when users "continue to employ an existing technology even though potentially more productive technologies can be found."[36]

The paradigm that characterizes a legacy sector is intermediate in scope between the larger paradigm that is the hallmark of Kondratiev waves as described by Perez, Freeman, and Atkinson, and the analogous pattern that takes place at the product level through the evolution of what James Utterback calls "dominant designs."[37] When a new product is first introduced, a number of alternative designs compete for dominance. In the early days of the automobile, for example, it was not clear whether the internal combustion engine would win out over the Stanley Steamer. In due time, the market shakes out, leaving a few dominant companies and a particular product design that has come to shape user habits and expectations—in this case, the internal combustion engine and the shape and function of the modern automobile.

At this point, the focus of technical change shifts to innovations that are compatible with that design—namely in manufacturing process, the value chain, the value network, and the design of product components.[38] Market entry becomes more difficult, as potential competitors must achieve economies of scale and possible network economies comparable to those already enjoyed by the dominant product, not to mention the market development, switching, and training costs involved in capturing customers from the dominant brand and the costs of building a new value network of vendors and distributors.

This pattern of innovation persists until the dominant design is replaced by another one that is sufficiently superior technically that it can overcome these obstacles, as for example an electronic as opposed to a mechanical calculator—a "discontinuous," that is, major, secondary innovation. Such innovations often emerge from a company in a different industry that is not wedded to a specific set of technical capabilities and hence is not bound to any historical "technological trajectory." As in the case of the succession of paradigms representing successive Kondratiev waves, the success of each new dominant design derives from the forces of market competition and the operation of capital markets. Such innovations are often disruptive, in the sense that they upset an established market structure, typically by starting in a niche market and gradually improving their performance and expanding their market until they can successfully challenge market leaders, a pattern again driven by market forces.[39]

The paradigm concept in essence is thus an extension of and follow-on to the concept of dominant design. But we must distinguish among the dominant design of products, the larger paradigm that is the hallmark of a Kondratiev wave as described by Perez, Freeman, and Atkinson, and what we can describe as a legacy sector paradigm. The first concerns a product, the second, a technology cluster, and the last, an entire economic sector.

TECHNOLOGICAL LOCK-IN IN ENTRENCHED LEGACY SECTORS

The switching costs, network economies, and other obstacles to innovation suggested in the previous chapter can be sufficient to block even a superior technology from replacing a dominant predecessor, which resists change even though the problem it was designed to solve has long been overtaken by events. The exemplar of this pattern of technological lock-in is the QWERTY keyboard on which this manuscript is being typed (or if you insist, inputted). As has been recounted by the well-known economist of technology Brian Arthur,[40] this keyboard was designed in the early days of typewriters as a means of *slowing down* typists, lest the keys of the typewriter (remember them?) get entangled with each other and jam up.

The jamming problem disappeared with improved typewriters (and much later, word processors and computers), and a new keyboard layout with improved ergonomics and faster potential speeds was soon developed.[41] This "Dvorak" keyboard made possible faster typing speeds but never caught on. It was never worth typists' time and effort to relearn to type. As time went on, more and more typists were trained on QWERTY keyboards, more and more typewriters were manufactured to equip them, and the Dvorak keyboard has continued to languish to this day. This is an example of the phenomenon of "path dependence" or technology lock-in.

Disruptive innovations in the legacy sectors that are the focus of this book face many of the same obstacles as disruptive innovations in other sectors, with the difference that the legacy paradigm can effectively stand in their way. In addition, the driving force for innovation in legacy sectors is not always market-driven but can consist of externalities, typically environmental (such as the need to limit carbon dioxide emissions) or geopolitical security (such as the need to defend the Straits of Hormuz, through which 35% of the world's oil carried by sea must pass), that are not immediately costly to the consumer or user. No matter how badly they are needed on environmental or geopolitical grounds, innovations in such sectors therefore can lack the forces of market competitiveness that enable successive Kondratiev paradigms and dominant designs to overcome all obstacles and overwhelm their predecessors, since they must face incumbent technologies in these sectors that benefit from prices and price structures that do not reflect the costs of the externalities that they inflict on the larger society.

In established legacy sectors like energy, then, candidate replacement technologies face a chicken-and-egg situation, especially if driven by externalities like environment. They often tend to offer capabilities that are at best the same as the incumbents and offer little or no direct advantage to the user (wind- and coal-generated electricity, for example, will both power your lights). Alternative technologies need time to develop and drive down their costs before a new dominant product emerges that is capable of competing at scale with a well-established incumbent, if for no other reason than applied research that might lead to a radical innovation is likely to have been underfunded due to the lack of foreseeable market demand—precisely because of the entrenched character of the dominant paradigm. In contrast, incumbent sectors are likely to use at least part of their revenue streams to increase their efficiency and expand their capacity—witness the revolution in oil and gas exploration due to implementation of microseismic imagery and fracking. This is a different kind of technology lock-in. While QWERTY locked in through network economies derived from user familiarity, utilization, and convenience, in a legacy sector, the lock-in is driven by the dominating paradigm.

In entrenched legacy sectors, therefore, paradigm succession cannot be ensured even if it is needed on social grounds. As will be elaborated on in chapter 11 on policy interventions, both policy change and support to research and development are needed if technological innovations are to emerge to support the new value structure. Ideally, the policies that encourage innovation should not favor one technology over another—in the jargon, they should be as technology neutral as possible—as long as the technologies to be supported satisfy the criteria dictated by the new value structure. However, even with explicit neutrality policies, change agents are still a vital input to innovation. This requirement gives these change agents an additional duty: maintaining a system where the best technologies can win over time, avoiding lock-in of inferior technologies.

The desirability of a technology-neutral policy leads to a still further problem. If policy is to encourage the development of technology that supports a certain set of values, those values need to be clearly defined and embodied in a new, dominant standard. But these values themselves may well be in the process of evolution. Should, for example, the standards for "organic" or "sustainable" agriculture forbid the use of genetically modified food crops or beef growth hormones? Disagreements of this kind may complicate the development of a technology-neutral policy, especially since the various possible alternative technologies are likely to lobby for policies favoring their particular approach, regardless of whether its superior potential has become clear. This pattern is already apparent in renewable energy, where separate lobbying groups for each alternative energy technology argue for legislation specifically supporting their industry, as well as in the disagreement over the relative merits of hybrid versus all-electric cars.[42]

OBSTACLES TO CREATIVE DESTRUCTION IN LEGACY SECTORS

Creative destruction in entrenched legacy sectors therefore faces almost insuperable obstacles in the absence of specific interventions to overcome them. In some cases, a disruptive technology—say, off-grid wind energy or photovoltaics—may be able to expand from a niche market. Alternatively, a key player may act as change agent by changing the incentives that have distorted the market, as when the health insurance industry changes the fee structure for health providers so as to encourage preventive medicine rather than medical procedures, or a single payer (such as the Veterans Administration or the Defense Department) insists on a single, unified system of digitized health records.

The final, and in most cases the most difficult, option is that new policies can be instituted that favor disruptive change, like a carbon tax or cap-and-trade system to minimize carbon dioxide emissions. As is evident from the current controversy over climate change, such policies are likely to face strong opposition from the stakeholders in the legacy sector. The fossil-fuel-based economy is in many ways the case in point for the staying power of legacy technologies, and indeed has grown in importance over three full Kondratiev waves.[43]

There are thus clear parallels between the concepts of technological lock-in, dominant design, and the technological/economic/political/social paradigms that affect legacy sectors. In each of the first two cases, an entrenched technology, product, or technological cluster is superseded if and only if its candidate successor is sufficiently technically superior to overcome the paradigm that precedes it. The fact that potential successors to entrenched legacy sectors in many cases have only nonmarket externalities to recommend them adds an additional, almost insuperable layer of difficulties in the way of disruptive innovation. To overcome these difficulties will require explicit attention to policy issues that stand in the way of innovation, in addition to support to the research, development, and innovation process itself.

In sum, the structural obstacles that block disruptive innovation in legacy sectors derive from a technological/economic/political/social and indeed institutional paradigm, a concept that has its origin in the research on scientific revolutions and on the Kondratiev cycles that describe the historic succession of technological clusters. This paradigm creates a sector-wide technological lock-in that is analogous to, but much broader and more pervasive than, the "dominant design" of a product.

To introduce disruptive technologies into legacy sectors requires both policy and institutional measures to help overcome these structural obstacles, and a change agent to push new technologies from research through to implementation at scale. In this process, all five models of innovation need to be brought to bear: the pipeline, to develop radical new ideas; induced innovations, to respond to new and more appropriate incentives once these come to pass; the extended pipeline, to link researcher to implementer; manufacturing-led to capture the innovations that can occur in the back end of the system; and innovation organization, which encompasses the others and provides the organizing principles for examining the structure of an innovation system and orchestrating the development and deployment of needed technology. The problems of legacy paradigms are thus deeper than can be addressed with the earlier simple models of innovation. Rather, they require a more integrated conceptual framework and a deeper policy response.

4 Production Matters

In the first chapter we described the "double trouble" the US economy now faces. First, legacy sectors operate as a drag on technological and related innovation, the major driver of economic growth. This problem is compounded by the second: jobless innovation, of which weaknesses in the production sector are a leading cause. (We here treat production and manufacturing as synonymous.) These two problems are profoundly linked because manufacturing is itself a legacy sector, characterized by numerous barriers to innovation. The knotty problem of innovation in legacy sectors, then, must be seen against the backdrop of the overall US economy, particularly in production and the challenges it now faces.

There are two fundamental parts to our innovation system, as we briefly introduced in chapter 1. First, there are new, innovation-oriented *frontier sectors*, such as information technology and biotech, that tend to arise every few decades out of transformative technological advances.[1] Typically, they are built around core, enabling technological advances—for example, semiconductors played this role in the IT innovation wave.[2] This core technological advance is joined by a mass of compatible applications that grow the innovation wave, enabling broader productivity savings in the economy; over time, the new sector becomes significant to the economy, producing productivity gains and contributing to growth. The second part of our innovation system, as discussed in chapters 2 and 3, consists of legacy sectors that are technologically mature, locked into a technological/economic/political/social paradigm, and resistant to innovations that are not consistent with their underlying paradigm. While legacy sectors accept some innovations—typically, incremental or secondary as opposed to radical innovations—they tend to do so only if it is consistent with their existing legacy paradigm.

Frontier sectors have been a critical source of new growth in the United States, consistent with the lesson of growth economics that technological and related innovation is the dominant contributor to economic growth.[3] Legacy sectors, by contrast, create barriers to technological advance and in this way limit the potential for growth. There is, therefore, a deep contradiction between the economy's need for growth and its legacy sectors—which are, after all, the dominant economic sectors from the perspective of this study, frontier innovation sectors by definition being still at the frontier.

However, in the frontier sectors and elsewhere, the United States has now stumbled into a new problem: job creation. Having created an increasingly international, dispersed innovation and production system, the United States is less able to realize the full economic gains of innovation through all the stages of the innovation and production process—it is losing the advantages of *full-spectrum innovation*. To state the problem another way, the United States has unbundled and globalized the innovation value chain, and in this way it has *disrupted its domestic element* and lost much of the potential gain from innovation in its economy.[4] The result is that the new innovation sectors will deliver less than their potential share to job creation. When this is coupled to the fact that innovation-resistant legacy sectors won't deliver their full potential for innovation-driven growth and jobs either, we end up with an inability to deliver the full range of innovation and corresponding job gains in both frontier and legacy sectors.

How did we reach this point? How extensive is this problem? Historically, US innovation policy has focused on the R & D stage, particularly on the gap known as the "valley of death" between research and later stage development. This problem of a disrupted domestic value chain is different from that of the valley of death. It occurs at a later stage, along the *engineering fault line* between research and development and engineering, production, and implementation.

This chapter examines in detail this problem of the disrupted value chain of innovation. First, it explains why goods, not just services, remain important in our economy. Against that backdrop, it looks at the status of the past implicit assumption of growth economics, that we would gain employment from the first stages of the production of innovative products that we invented—that is, that we would both *innovate here and produce here*. In contrast, we find that this is being increasingly replaced by a new pattern of "innovate here, produce there" and may be replaced in turn by "produce there, innovate there." We explore these trends through a review of data on the strength of the US production system, the area along the engineering fault line where significant job losses have been occurring, and on the strength of the R & D elements in the US innovation system on the other side of the engineering fault line. Both these sets of data illustrate the problem of the disrupted domestic innovation value chain and the erosion of job creation to which it leads.

We then ask the key question: How did we reach this state? This leads to a review of the new "geopolitics" of production. We close this chapter with a discussion of the emerging fusion of production and services, a phenomenon that increases the stakes involved in a disruption of the innovation value chain still further. Chapter 6 will explain why we consider our manufacturing sector itself to be a legacy sector and why the disruption of the domestic innovation value chain is having a major effect on innovation in the United States.

THE "INNOVATE HERE, PRODUCE HERE" ASSUMPTION

The story of the US economy between 1840 and 1940 was one of the creation of the world's first true system of mass production. By 1840, initially through long-term R & D to meet War Department requirements for musket production, the US developed a system for interchangeable machine-made parts[5] that turned north-eastern towns into factory towns. This capability became known as the "American System" of production. Tied to the first continent-sized economy, it made mass production possible.[6]

Since the onset of World War II, the US economy has shifted. It has been organized around the objective of leading the world in technological advance. Spurred by the wartime innovations that were built at scale in that war, extended by the creation of federally funded research universities,[7] and then supported by the defense innovation system refined to meet Cold War demands,[8] the United States placed its economy at the innovation frontier, bringing on a sequence of waves of worldwide growth through the 1990s. In this way, the United States developed what economists call a comparative advantage in innovation, and as a result, it led all but one of the significant world innovation waves[9] of the 20th century: aviation, electronics and communications, space, computing, the Internet,[10] and biotech. The operating assumption was that the United States would both innovate and translate the resulting innovations into both products and supporting services.

By innovating here and producing here, then, the United States would realize the full range of economic gains from all the stages of innovation, from research and development, to demonstration and test beds, to production and initial market creation, to production at scale, and to the follow-on life cycle of the product. It worked. The United States became the richest economy the world had ever seen. The United States for the past half-century has been playing out the theory of economic growth that holds that the predominant factor in economic growth is technological and related innovation—and demonstrating that it works.

But in recent years, with the advent of a global economy, this "innovate here, produce here" model no longer holds as strongly as it used to. In some industrial sectors, firms can now unbundle the innovation value chain by severing R & D and design from production. Codable, IT-based specifications for goods that are tied to software-controlled production equipment have made possible this "distributed" manufacturing by enabling precision parts and components to snap together with the exact fit of Legos, no matter where they are produced.[11] While manufacturing once had to be vertically integrated in order to ensure that exact component fit, firms using the distributed model increasingly can *innovate here, produce there*. It appears that this distributed model works well for many IT products, and for many commodity products as well. Apple is the standard-bearer for this model, continuing to lead in dramatic IT innovations, retaining most of the value-added and profit in the United States, but "offshoring" virtually all its production to Asia.[12]

Nonetheless, there are many sectors where the distributed model doesn't work and that still require a close connection between research, design, and production. Capital goods, aerospace products, energy equipment, and complex pharmaceuticals are examples of this phenomenon. In these sectors, production and R & D / design are the complementary yin and yang of innovation, in that production infrastructure often provides constant feedback to R & D / design infrastructure and vice versa. In these industries, incremental innovation in products is most efficient when tied to a close understanding of, and linkage to, manufacturing processes, a phenomenon that is part of what we have called "manufacturing-led innovation." This means that R & D, design, and production are tightly linked, so that R & D and design—and with them the capacity for discontinuous secondary and eventually for radical innovation—are likely to follow production offshore. This phenomenon of "produce there, innovate there" may thus be even more disruptive than "innovate here, produce there."

These twin developments bring the economic foundations of America's innovation-based economic success into question. What good is a world-leading innovation system if much of the gain flows elsewhere? We now examine the economic and production data to see to what extent these phenomena are actually taking place.

"PRODUCE THERE, INNOVATE THERE": THE INNOVATION DATA

If there is a serious potential for *produce there, innovate there*, what is the picture on the innovation side? We begin by examining the data on overall national investment in R & D. The United States has been maintaining the same national innovation intensity (R & D relative to GDP) as it developed in the 1960s, while other competitive economies have steadily increased theirs.[13] A group of leading Asian nations has now collectively passed the United States in total R & D investment, as well.[14] Economist Gregory Tassey suggests that "input/output" theory in economics applies: if you freeze a major input to growth, which the United States has increasingly been doing through stagnant innovation intensity, then your growth rate will be limited.[15]

The ratio of federal R & D investment to GDP has been in decline for decades, falling from nearly 2% of GDP in 1965 to 0.7% of GDP in 2010; this has been offset by a rise in R & D in industry to nearly 2% of GDP in that same period.[16] However, the latter is now leveling off. One reason is that the two sides undertake different tasks: The federal government funds predominantly research, while industry funds development. But much of the strength of the development system depends on the strength of the research system. They are on a two-way street—each influences the other, so that reducing the former affects the latter. Strength in research provides the basis for radical or breakthrough ideas; strength in development makes it possible to translate these ideas into innovations. Both are required.

Another reason for this stabilization of innovation intensity is that US industrial firms have significantly shifted their R & D investment strategies during the last decade and a half to reflect an increasingly global perspective. Their offshore R & D investment has increased at three times the rate of their domestic R & D spending. Tassey further argues that US production firms have shifted the composition of their R & D portfolios toward shorter term development objectives[17] to meet the demands of an increasingly competitive international marketplace. Thus the institutional barriers between R & D and later stage development—the so-called valley of death—are actually widening in the United States as firms focus more on shorter term incremental advances and pull back from investment in radical or breakthrough innovation, leaving the latter to universities and government laboratories.

Nonetheless, the United States retains the world's strongest innovation system, although it faces growing competition in this area. American innovation strategy logically should seek leverage from this comparative advantage in innovation. The problem lies in the fact that US R & D has had only a very limited focus on advanced technologies and processes needed for leadership in production as opposed to product conception and design;[18] this is in sharp contrast to the approach to manufacturing R & D taken by Germany, Japan, Korea, Taiwan, and China. While the major US-based multinational manufacturing firms fund most of the nation's development of production technology and so have the capacity to keep up on this innovation front, the majority of US production takes place in 300,000 small and midsize firms that lack this capacity. The base of small and midsize manufacturers represents 86% of our manufacturing establishment and employs more than half of our manufacturing workforce.[19]

As we shall see, these firms are largely outside our innovation system. This support structure—what we shall in a later chapter call their "innovation ecosystem"—has been eroded by the globalization of the innovation ecosystem and value chain, a phenomenon with major implications for innovation and competitiveness in the United States. As we shall later argue, manufacturing is a legacy sector deserving of policy attention based on the innovation organization model.

PRODUCTION OF GOODS, NOT JUST SERVICES

Are these shifts toward *innovate here, produce there* and *produce there, innovate there*, and the corresponding disruption in value chains, reflected in production data? As we have noted, production lies on the far side of the engineering fault line and is the sector where job loss is likely to concentrate—and in fact, the data on US production and trade deficits in goods do indicate declining US production capability:

Employment: Over the past 50 years, the share of manufacturing in US GDP has shrunk from 27% to below 12%. For most of this period (1965–2000), manufacturing employment generally remained constant at 17 million; between 2000 and 2010, it fell precipitously by 31.4%, to below 12 million.[20] All manufacturing sectors saw job losses between 2000 and 2010, but lower value-added sectors readily subject to globalization, such as textiles and furniture, were affected most adversely, losing almost 70% and 50% of their jobs, respectively.[21]

Investment: Fixed capital investment in manufacturing (plant, equipment, and IT) grew from 2000 to 2010 at its lowest rate as a percentage of GDP (below 1.5% annually) since this data began to be compiled at the end of World War II.[22] If this number is adjusted for cost changes, actual fixed capital investment in manufacturing declined from 2000 to 2010 (down 1.8%)—the first decade this has occurred since data collection began in the 1950s. In contrast, manufacturing actual fixed capital investment grew at an average of 5.5% annually in the 1990s.[23] Investment declined from 2000 to 2010 in 15 of 19 industrial sectors measured by the Bureau of Economic Analysis (BEA).[24] This has important implications for process innovation, which is frequently introduced through capital investments in new equipment embodying new technology.

Output: While the United States had been assuming from published government statistics that US manufacturing net output as a share of world output has been stable, passed only recently by China,[25] it may have been misleading itself. An Information Technology and Innovation Foundation (ITIF) report[26] and other economic evaluations[27] suggest that the official US output data have been significantly overstated. These data indicate that net output in 16 of 19 manufacturing sectors actually declined from 2000 to 2010, in many cases significantly, but also show that these declines were offset by increases in two sectors, namely computing and energy.[28] Analysts now say that the overall decline was real and only partially offset.

The ITIF and these other economists make three arguments in support of this conclusion.[29] First, the number of foreign components in US-manufactured products has risen sharply, and these have not been adequately accounted for in the official data, overstating US output. Second, government data included an inflationary output factor for increased computer quality and performance that caused the output of the computing sector to be significantly overstated from 2000 to 2010, failing to take into account the facts that employment in the computer sector declined by 43%, that a significant amount of computer production moved offshore, and that nominal US industry shipments in this sector barely grew. Third, the supposedly offsetting output in the energy sector was also significantly overstated. Adjusting for these factors, ITIF found that the net value of US manufacturing actually fell by 11% from 2000 to 2010.

Productivity: Conclusions about strong productivity growth in manufacturing must be scaled back as well, since output is the numerator in calculations of productivity—although to be sure, productivity in manufacturing still significantly exceeds that in the service sector. ITIF finds that manufacturing productivity grew by 32% between 2000 and 2010, not by the BEA's much higher estimate of 71%.[30] Thus adjusted, against 19 other leading manufacturing nations, the United States was 10th in productivity growth and 17th in net output growth.

Many thought the United States was losing manufacturing jobs because of increased manufacturing productivity. This argument has suffered two criticisms from opposite angles. First of all, productivity gains have historically led to net job growth, a pattern recently confirmed by a Brookings study.[31] Second, the study by ITIF finds that productivity gains accounted for only about a third of the 5.8 million loss in manufacturing jobs during the past decade.[32] Either way, we have to look elsewhere for reasons why manufacturing lost nearly one-third of its workforce in a decade.

Trade deficits: The highly competitive world economy rewards nations and regions that succeed in producing complex, high-value-added goods. While world trade in services is growing, world trade in goods is close to five times the trade in services.[33] Complex, high-value goods (including capital goods, industrial supplies, transport goods, and medicines) make up over 80% of US exports and a significant majority of its imports. These goods are engineering-intensive and often contain numerous components (which may be customized), require a wide breadth of knowledge and skills in their creation and production, embody a range of technologies and technical novelty, and require groups of firms in their production. World trade increasingly is dominated by such high-value goods, and will remain so indefinitely. Yet the United States was running a $500 billion trade deficit in manufactured goods in prerecession 2007, and is returning to that level.[34] As of 2011, that total included a $100 billion deficit in advanced technology products.[35]

Will services offset the US production decline? After all, since services are now 80% of the US economy, can't it just continue this growth trend? The problem is that the modest and gradual growth in the US trade surplus in services ($160 billion in prerecession 2007) is dwarfed by the size and continuation of its deficit in goods; the former will not offset the latter any time in the foreseeable future.

To summarize, US manufacturing employment is down, manufacturing capital investment is down, manufacturing output is down, manufacturing productivity is lower than previously estimated, and the trade deficit in goods is up. Overall, the argument appears strong: the US manufacturing sector is hollowing out. This appears to be a substantial causative factor in the overall erosion of jobs and consequently of the American middle class, and is symptomatic of a disrupted domestic innovation value chain, as discussed below.[36]

Does this matter? We would argue that it does. Production remains a major element in the US economy: it contributes $1.7 trillion to the $15 trillion economy and employs 12 million[37] of a total employed workforce of some 140 million. Manufacturing workers are paid substantially more than service sector workers, 20% higher than nonmanufacturing.[38] Since, as suggested earlier, 60% or more of historic US economic growth comes from technological and related innovation,[39] we need also to recall that manufacturing dominates the innovation system. Manufacturing firms employ 63% of our scientists and engineers, and this sector performs some 70% of industrial R & D.[40] Thus our production strength and the strength of our innovation system are directly linked, illustrating the significance of the problems of *innovate here, produce there* and *produce there, innovate there* that affect both frontier and legacy sectors.

Production pulls more than its weight in the economy; its importance should not be measured only by its present contribution to GNP and employment. We have already called attention to the pervasive ties between the production and innovation systems and to the data that show its importance to the trade balance. The production sector is also the largest multiplier in the economy, both in jobs and in GNP; each manufacturing job is estimated to create between 2.5 and 2.9 jobs in other sectors, as explained in the ensuing paragraphs. High-tech production sectors have higher multipliers than this; estimates range from a jobs multiplier of 5.2 for a digitized modern factory, to one of 16 for the electronic computing sector.[41] Gains from production processes can be scalable, unlike those from services, a point to which we shall return shortly. For this reason, manufacturing operates as an output multiplier—every dollar in final sales of manufactured products results in $1.40 in additional output in other sectors.[42] No other economic sector approaches this level.

This multiplier tells us that we need to see the employment created by production as significantly more than the 12 million production workers that constitute some 10% of the US workforce. Measuring employment only at the moment of production provides only a partial understanding of the role of this critical sector. We now need to explain this concept of the multiplier.

Production is best viewed as a system. At the center of this system is the production moment. Tied to the production moment is a considerably larger employment base, which includes those working in resources, those employed by a wide range of suppliers and component makers, and the innovation workforce, the 63% of scientists and engineers employed, as noted above, in the production sector. This is the input side of the system. Flowing out of the production moment on the output side of this system is another larger host of jobs: those working in the distribution system, retail, and sales, and on the life cycle of the product. The employment within this production system is significantly higher than that at the production moment itself, as the multiplier data attest.

Arranged throughout this system are lengthy and complex value chains and value networks of firms involved in the production of the goods—from resources to suppliers and components to innovation, through production, to distribution, retail, and life cycle—a great array of skills and firms. Many of these would be counted as services in economic statistics, but are actually tied to production. If we remove the production element, the value chains of connected companies face significant disruption. While the output end of the system (sales, marketing, repairs, and maintenance, for example) may be partially restored if a foreign good is substituted for a domestic good—a Hyundai for a Chevy, say—the input side of the system (as well as design, engineering, and manufacturing), with its firms and their employees, generally doesn't get restored.

When these complex value chains and value networks are disrupted, it is very difficult to put them back together. That's why, historically, once the United States has lost an economic sector, it has been so hard to resurrect—it won't come back. The United States doesn't collect data on our industrial sector to reflect these phenomena; the closest data are the job multiplier data cited above, which don't tell the full story. Understanding manufacturing employment as a system that contains complex value chains within it provides part of the explanation for the economy's current predicament over job loss, job creation, and declining median income.

Production, after all, is the central way an economy as a whole can accelerate growth. This is because services tend to be more face to face and therefore to scale more gradually, but production can scale more rapidly and make possible geometric economic increases. In other words, while production of semiconductors or cell phones can scale up very rapidly, and can act as a growth accelerator, services such as accounting or restaurants scale up much more slowly. So production is a critical enabler of increasing returns[43] in an economy; selling high-value goods is still the largest societal wealth creator.[44] Because of its potential for rapid scaling, production requires specific policy attention. Because they scale more slowly, it is not enough to settle for services alone.[45]

THE GEOPOLITICS OF INDUSTRIAL PRODUCTION

Production leadership, after Alexander Hamilton put the financial building blocks in place to transform the United States into the world's largest commercial economy, has historically been central to US geopolitical strategy. Barry Lynn argues that the United States has gone through three evolutionary phases. From the time of Hamilton until 1945, the United States pursued national industrial self-dependence as key to its security.[46] Hamilton saw that in a world of dominant and colonizing European powers, the United States would retain its independence on the world stage only if it magnified its commercial power, with industrialization as a critical component.

The United States pursued Hamilton's basic strategy through World War II; US industrial might and corresponding economic strength as the world's largest economy were critical to its military superiority and ability to sustain its allies, and therefore to its subsequent victory in that war. This strategy lasted until the beginning of the Cold War. From 1945 until the end of the Cold War in 1991, faced with a struggle with a Marxist economic model, the United States built a series of postwar agreements that entwined the United States, Europe, and Japan in a system of mutual economic dependence around America-centric consumer markets and production. The geopolitical concept in this period was that US national security would be enhanced through the economic embrace of our Cold War allies—a system of mutual economic interdependence designed to build the economic strength to fend off Marxist geopolitical competitors.

The third period began in 2001 with the entry of China into the WTO under President Clinton's leadership. The geopolitical concept was to bind the world, not just our allies, into an interdependent economic system tied together by open trading, financial integration, and joint manufacturing.[47] The aim was to integrate China into the world economy so as to ensure peace in a way comparable to Jean Monnet's design for a postwar common market to ensure future European peace. Clinton's perspective, in effect, embraced a laissez-faire perspective toward production. Integrated industrial sectors would assure an integrated world economy, and the earlier Hamilton concept of industrial production ensuring national security was set aside.

China, meanwhile, pursued a different approach, perceiving that production- and innovation-based growth would be key to its ascendency and using neomercantilist policies[48] to accomplish its objectives. It has sought to build a rim of Asian economies increasingly dependent on China's economy for their exports and production facilities, running a huge trade surplus in manufactured goods with the United States to generate the capital to finance internal growth and offset trade deficits with its Asian rim dependent economies. Economist Carl Dahlman has portrayed this strategy as a hollowing out of the economies of developed-economy competitors to finance its own geopolitical rise.[49]

Samuelson in 2004 asked how the United States could be an economic loser with a low-cost, low-wage competitor like China, in apparent violation of Ricardo's accepted economic theory of comparative advantage that trade benefits everyone by encouraging specialization.[50] Samuelson pointed out that if China makes productivity-enhancing gains in its production, coupled with a continuing low-wage advantage, US wages could drop after a time to the point where China's advantage in production costs is offset. In other words, nations like the United States that base their comparative advantage on innovative capacity face the problem that such an advantage can be captured by others as they build their own innovation systems. The United States would still benefit from lower prices for goods, but there are now "new net harmful U.S. terms of trade"—that is, US workers would have to work at lower wages for longer hours or US firms to sell more output in order to buy the same Chinese goods. Samuelson cites many historical examples of this phenomenon, from the shift of the US textile sector from the Northeast to the Southeast in the early 20th century, to the way Midwestern agriculture surpassed eastern agriculture in the United States in the second half of the 19th century.

Economists David Autor, David Dorn, and Gordon Hanson have validated Samuelson's concerns.[51] Studying labor markets in regions of the United States where Chinese-produced goods have captured markets, they found widespread patterns of rising unemployment and reduced wages, not only in the affected manufacturing sectors but also in a wide range of dependent and related job sectors in both services and production. They found that the gains from increased trade were almost equally offset by what they term "deadweight losses" to the economy, particularly through the rise in transfer payments for unemployment, health, and disability insurance and food stamps required to cope with declines in employment and real wages, which are compensatory, not immediately economically productive investments. As economics Nobelist A. Michael Spence has noted, "Globalization hurts some subgroups within some countries, including the advanced economies. . . . The result is growing disparities in income and employment across the US economy, with highly educated workers enjoying more opportunities and workers with less education facing declining employment prospects and stagnant incomes."[52] Just as manufacturing employment was a key to enabling less-educated workers to enter the middle class after World War II, the loss of manufacturing jobs is correspondingly a key element in the decline of the American middle class in the past few decades.

The United States faced an intense competitive challenge in the 1970s and 1980s with Japan and Germany. That was a simpler and more straightforward competition with comparable high-technology, high-wage economies, as opposed to the much more complex competition it faces with emerging nations like China and India. At the time, the Japanese were recognized as being "number one" in industrial management and in quality manufacturing and a major threat to US competitiveness, especially in automobiles and consumer electronics.[53] This concern ended when the United States achieved dominance in IT-related industry and Japan went into prolonged recession, in large part because of problems in its financial sector unrelated to technology.

Table 4.1 illustrates some of the differences in competitive patterns the United States faces, comparing the US competition with Japan versus the competition with China.

Table 4.1 Competitiveness Then and Now

Japan as a competitor to the United States, 1970–1990	China as a competitor to the United States today
High-cost, high-wage, export-oriented, advanced technology economy—comparable to that of the United States	Low-cost, low-wage, export-oriented economy with a huge population, pursuing increasingly advanced technology
Postwar industrial expansion began based on low-cost labor but quickly absorbed the available labor supply, leading to high wages as productivity increased.	Technological advance is taking place in parallel with expansion of low-wage manufacturing, since there is still an ample supply of underemployed labor to keep wages relatively low compared to developed economies.
Little or no direct foreign investment or MNC research in Japan	Huge potential market and generous incentives in targeted industries encourage foreign investment, but with required local procurement and pressure for technology transfer and local R & D.
"Flying geese" model[69] of economic interdependence encourages Japanese investment in Southeast Asia to take advantage of low-cost labor.	Development of Southeast Asian suppliers as Chinese wages rise with increased productivity; dependence of other Asian economies on Chinese markets
US had entrepreneurial advantage; Japan had industrial policy advantage.	Entrepreneurial culture and pursuing industrial policy

(continued)

Table 4.1 *continued*

Japan as a competitor to the United States, 1970–1990	China as a competitor to the United States today
US breakthrough innovation capability enabled its leadership of IT and biotech waves, which Japan missed. Japan has strong R & D, but it is still industry-oriented and aimed at incremental innovation; it is working to strengthen breakthrough innovation capability.	Rapidly increasing government support to industry-oriented research; weak on research aimed at breakthrough innovation
Rule of law	Limited rule of law
Substantial early IP theft, but now part of international IP system	Extensive semiofficial IP theft
Subsidized currency to sustain exports and economic growth. United States tolerated for geopolitical reasons. Japanese government buys US debt and assets, many of which declined in value. Japanese firms established manufacturing plants in United States, in order to limit US opposition and forestall trade barriers.	Follows Japan's model: subsidizes currency to sustain exports and economic growth. United States tolerates so as to maintain access to Chinese market and to obtain financing for its trade deficit. China is the largest holder of US debt and uses its foreign currency reserves to acquire US assets.
Legacy agriculture and service sector, plus financial crises, problematic macroeconomic policy, and slow population growth led to a prolonged recession.	Authorities are aware of the Japanese experience but face political problems in shifting their economy to address domestic needs.
National security ally for 60 years	Potential national security peer competitor

To summarize the table, in competing with China, the United States faces a huge, low-wage, low-cost, increasingly advanced technology economy that lacks shared systems for the rule of law, IP, and national security, presses foreign investors to transfer advanced technology in exchange for access to its major market, and is only slowly moving away from a long-standing policy based on currency subsidy and acquisition of foreign debt, which creates competitive pressures that have some similarity to those that the United States faced in the 1970s and 1980s but are much more complicated. At the same time, largely from inattention or lack of understanding of its own past successful model, the United States has departed from a geopolitical strategy of economic and security advantage built around leadership in both the development and the production of innovative products.[54]

ERODING ADVANCED IT SECTORS

While many economists in the past have argued that the United States should cede lower-end industrial sectors and offset these losses with success in high-end, high-value-added goods emerging from its frontier sector innovation system,[55] the picture in this advanced technology sector is now unsettling and has brought this standard thesis into doubt. Gary Pisano and Willy Shih[56] have examined the advanced IT sector and found, for example, that the most recent edition of the Kindle could not be made in the United States. The flex circuit connector, controller, lithium polymer battery, wireless card, and injected molded case are all produced in China, and the electrophoretic display is made in Taiwan. Every brand of US notebook computer (except Apple) and every mobile/handheld are now not only manufactured but also *designed* in Asia. In these sectors, design capability is the key to the next generation of innovation. Reviewing advanced technology sectors innovated in the United States and in danger of shifting abroad, Pisano and Shih conclude that major erosion has already occurred in technological leadership for advanced materials, computing and communications, renewable energy technologies and storage, semiconductors, and displays. They suggest that the next generation of technological leadership in these areas is facing an imminent shift, including production, design, and by implication, the capacity for manufacturing process and secondary product innovation, along with their production and innovation value chains and attendant employment.

This loss of technological leadership is the reason why the United States has run a trade deficit in advanced technology goods every year since 2002, and that that deficit has now reached the $100 billion annual level.[57] Continuing to contend the United States will make up for economic declines in lower margin sectors by assuming it will always capture high-end industry through its leadership in radical innovation amounts to a game of "Let's pretend," given the pattern of decline in US production dominance of advanced technology sectors.[58] The problems of the United States are deeper than it has acknowledged them to be.

The offshoring of innovative capacity is likely not to end with manufacturing, design, and process and secondary product innovation. China, Taiwan, and many of their Southeast Asian neighbors are making substantial investments in R & D, with the explicit objective of moving up the innovation value chain to radical and breakthrough innovation. They are also investing in advanced manufacturing, which they see as essential to preserving their comparative advantage in production. (We shall return to this subject in the last section of this chapter.) They are still weak in both of these areas, but their determination to master them should not be underestimated.

There is an analogy here to the phenomenon of disruptive technology in product design. Clayton Christensen found that, faced with disruptive innovation, established firms in many industries cede low-margin production and work in order to retain leadership through incremental ("sustaining") advances in high-margin production. But these firms end up ceding the high end as well, because as the disruptive advances that allow capture of the low end mature and improve, their lower costs allow expanded customer bases, enabling the low-end disruptor to capture the high end.[59]

This argument may prove relevant to overall US innovation strategy. The United States may be facing disruptive innovations in manufacturing technology that it has not recognized. China has now passed the United States in manufacturing output, and is not simply exploiting its low-cost production advantage but is innovating in the rapid scale-up of production, initially in low-end products like inexpensive motorcycles but now also in high-tech IT products, through advances in production processes that are integrated across groups of firms, in this way making possible gains in production tempo and volume, with corresponding cost savings.[60] While China faces its own legacy sector challenges, as we discuss in chapter 9, its innovations in production technology and its efforts to move up the innovation value chain should not be underestimated. It intends to follow a "manufacturing-led" model up the innovation value chain, at the same time that the United States has allowed its historic production leadership to slip, endangering its innovative capacity in important areas of technology.

IMPLICATIONS ALONG THE "ENGINEERING FAULT LINE"

To summarize, production as the final stage of the implementation of innovation matters in a number of ways throughout our economy. Successful nations still capture wealth from around the world predominantly by trade in complex, high-value goods, not from trade in services. The shift by US multinational production firms to distributed manufacturing—the industry's term for "innovate here, produce there"—not only shifts gains and employment from the implementation of innovation abroad, but because of the interrelationship among R & D, design, and production in many sectors, risks shifting leadership in innovation as well. This could lead to an even more problematic pattern of offshoring of both innovation and production—what we have called "produce there, innovate there."

This failure to understand the geopolitical importance of manufacturing jeopardizes future American leadership in both production and innovation in a number of advanced technology sectors, and may over time cost the US economy a crucial economic multiplier. The United States can hardly expect to lead in manufacturing-led innovations if there are too few US-based manufacturing firms left to devise them and put them into practice.

Today, this production challenge lies along the *engineering fault line* between development and engineering in the innovation system. The United States does the R & D, but engineering and production and the jobs that go with them too often go abroad. A bigger problem lies ahead. The loss of comparative advantage in manufacturing may lead to the loss of the leadership in innovation on which the United States has based its national comparative advantage for the past 70 years. The decline of production in the United States thus threatens American long-term competitiveness even in frontier sectors.

AN INNOVATION-INTENSIVE RESPONSE

Given the critical need to reconnect innovation and production across the engineering fault line in both frontier and legacy sectors, what is the basic direction the United States could pursue?

The United States has systematically turned to technological innovation to work its way through past economic dilemmas; there is every reason to believe that this is how it must approach this one. Given that its leading competitors have a significant advantage in production costs and wages, it must compete by leading in technological and process innovations that support major productivity and efficiency gains, so as not to be forced to compete by driving down wages and standard of living. Restoring the innovation-oriented value chain and value network must be a critical strategy for both legacy and frontier sectors.

The emphasis here on an innovation-intensive approach is a critical complement to the macroeconomic strategies centered on trade, tax, currency valuation, and regulatory policies that are the near-exclusive focus of most industrial trade associations. The slow pace of the recovery from the Great Recession that continues to affect the US economy suggests that it is at least in part due to structural features rooted in shifts in particular parts of the economy.[61] A macroeconomic stimulus will have only a limited effect on these structural characteristics.

The data discussed above on the extent of the decline in production in the United States suggest that there are structural issues in the US economy's recession, rooted not only in the housing and financial sectors but also in the production sector. Structural problems are the most likely explanation for the significant decline in manufacturing employment, capital investment, and output, and lower than assumed increases in productivity. These developments are not explainable as a business cycle response or indeed as an effect of financial panic. If there are structural problems in the production sector, a macroeconomic response alone is not going to work in the longer term.

Instead, a deeper structural focus on this sector is required and an innovation-oriented response must also be considered, since advances in technology and technology-related processes are the best source of the gains in efficiency and productivity that are needed to alter sectoral performance.[62] This approach must stretch across the engineering fault line between the development and the later stages of engineering and implementation, not simply the traditional "valley of death" gap between research and late-stage development. As discussed in chapter 6, US manufacturing has many of the characteristics of a legacy sector, a fact that complicates the introduction of innovation. Structural changes in its system of innovation organization will be required, and change agents will be needed to effectuate these changes. Chapter 13 focuses on these issues in detail.

THE FUSION OF PRODUCTION AND SERVICES

The 21st-century firm increasingly fuses services, production, supply chain management, and innovation. Many of these fused capabilities are knowledge "intangibles," not fixed assets, and will require learning to tie advanced production, including new technologies, equipment, and processes, with IT-informed service delivery. This fusion is another reason why production and its tie to innovation are important: the fused model suggests that stand-alone services or stand-alone production will not be the dominant successful model of the future. Instead, in many sectors, an approach that fuses services and production will be required. Thus a lack of leadership in production could jeopardize leadership in services as well, since the fused model requires both.

US firms have played a leadership role in the modern fused model of production and services and are well positioned to take advantage of it, if they retain manufacturing capability. IBM was probably the first large firm to create this model and to put it into practice. When CEO Lew Gerstner arrived at IBM to pull it out of a financial crisis, the prevailing approach was to carve up firms into smaller focused units and sell them off—to go "asset light."[63] Gerstner decided to do the opposite, electing to build a unified firm with greater breadth, keeping historically strong R & D with a range of IT hardware offerings and tying both to a new services effort, offering customers not only technology but what IBM called "solutions" to IT challenges. The result was one of the great business turnaround stories in the late 20th century; IBM's fused model subsequently was emulated throughout the IT sector.

To be sure, the fused production/services model doesn't have to be vertically integrated in a single firm; it can be horizontal, with linkages among firms with a range of services and production capabilities, leveraging specialized capabilities from particular partner companies. The model is not only about business organization; there is an increasing number of merged products with both hardware and services features. Apple's iPod was emblematic of this approach, combining a capable MP3 player with a new highly efficient, low-cost system for delivering music and now other applications. The fused services/production approach has significant advantages for business models for advanced production because it enables services and production to be deeply tied to each other, with corresponding interdependent strength and increased potential economic gains. We can see this in firms like Google, Amazon, and Microsoft, which are tying hardware to their software so as to enhance the ability of both to scale. The fused model will be relevant to both legacy and frontier sectors and will require new approaches for bridging the engineering fault line and correspondingly restoring the innovation value chain.

The fused model offers a new approach to the question of scalability. As we have seen, a produced good is tradable and can scale. Services are often face to face and generally slower to scale. However, if a service is tied to a tradable good, it can scale in parallel with the tradable good. This means that the dynamic part of a services economy may be increasingly tied to high-value, complex tradable goods. Firms in many sectors will increasingly offer high-value goods tied to services to provide customers with "solutions." This means that the tradable goods can scale, which in turn enables the accompanying service to become tradable and scalable as well.[64]

For this reason, the success of services-dominant economies like the United States will increasingly be linked to their success in manufacturing. Services already represent half of the value of US manufactured exports.[65] In this important evolving area of advanced manufacturing, production and design will in most cases be closely linked in fused model products, as well, so that there is a danger of losing the benefits of employment and later innovation from this area as well. Overall, production is an important enabler of "increasing returns" in an economy,[66] which means that it must be considered a foundational societal wealth creator.[67] The fusion of production and services adds to the importance of production as a link to the service sector.

THE DISRUPTED DOMESTIC INNOVATION VALUE CHAIN

To review, both the frontier and legacy sectors of the US economy are facing structural challenges at a time when its growth depends on innovation. Legacy sectors make up a large part of our economy but resist innovation and so fail to maximize their potential for economic growth and job creation. The dominant source of new growth in the United States has been frontier sectors that evolve periodically through innovation waves. However, in these sectors, the United States has been creating an increasingly international, dispersed, "unbundled" production system, and so is less able to realize the full economic gains of innovation through all the stages of the innovation and production process. The result is that the frontier innovation sectors are delivering less than their potential share of job growth.

The globalized innovation value chain has *disrupted the* domestic *innovation value chain* on which American small- and medium-sized manufacturers depend and has reduced the potential gain from innovation in both areas of our economy, the frontier and legacy sectors. Historically, US innovation policy has focused on the R & D stage, particularly the gap known as the "valley of death" between research and later stage development. This problem of a globalized and disrupted innovation value chain is different. It occurs at a later stage, along the *engineering fault line* between the research and development stages and the engineering, production, and implementation stages.

Against that backdrop, the implicit assumption of growth economics, that we would both "innovate here and produce here," becomes open to question. With the arrival of IT-enabled distributed manufacturing, we have instead evolved a pattern of "innovate here, produce there," in which we are able to disperse the production stage abroad in IT and similar sectors. However, in other sectors less amenable to dispersal, where R & D and design remain closely tied to production, we face an even more problematic tendency: "produce there, innovate there." In this situation, a shift to global production may be leading to a shift in innovation capability as well. The data on US production capability, as far as it goes, appears to substantiate these dual concerns about "innovate here, produce there" and "produce there, innovate there." Data on the stagnation in the support for US R & D intensify these concerns, suggesting that the US may over time lose its predominance in breakthrough innovation as well. This will particularly affect production firms with high-value complex goods that are innovation-dependent. A review of the production sector as a system suggests that the job losses in that sector will have ramifications for job losses in connected sectors as well. We are now at the root of the job erosion problem arising from the disrupted innovation value chains in both frontier and legacy sectors.

A review of the geopolitics of innovation suggests both a decline in the US political focus on its production capacity and a simultaneous and related rise in the capacity of its economic competitors. Restoring this capacity will require a policy emphasis on innovation. But innovation must be looked at as a whole, across not only the "valley of death" between research and late-stage development, the traditional innovation policy focus, but across the engineering fault line that reaches to the engineering, production, and implementation stages. Initial production is a highly creative stage, requiring critical engineering and design advances as a raw innovation is transformed to a product that will fit a market. Often the original innovation is completely reworked. We have therefore identified one of the five innovation models in chapter 3 as "manufacturing-led"; production is a stage in the innovation process and can be an important driver because of this creative role.

Yet the United States has tended to view the early R & D stages as *the* innovation system; production has been assumed to be an automatic follow-on, on autopilot. This inability to see innovation as stretching from research through production is a major systemic problem.[68] The need to stretch the view of innovation will be both complicated and enhanced by a new development—the increasingly fused nature of the production and services sectors. This will affect both legacy and frontier sectors; new innovation business models will need to reflect this growing combination.

In sum, production is a legacy sector, as will be explored further in chapter 6, below. It is also a crosscutting sector that is critical to other parts of the economy, both to other legacy sectors and to frontier sectors. Production, particularly initial production and when fused to IT-based services, constitutes an important part of the back end of the innovation system. This is an important example of a connection between a legacy sector and the innovation system and of a two-way interchange between legacy and frontier sectors.

5 What's Blocking Innovation in Legacy Sectors?

In this chapter, we explore in detail the properties common to the technological/economic/political/social paradigms that underlie each of a series of legacy sectors in the United States.[1] These paradigms inhibit the development, the market launch, and the implementation at scale of technologies that do not fit neatly into them, such as those for renewable energy, energy conservation, sustainable agriculture, and the "smart" grid for the distribution of electric power in the United States.

The idea of a paradigm parallels the concept of technology lock-in as it is used by other innovation researchers, specifically business-oriented researchers exploring disruptive technology,[2] and science, technology, and society (STS) researchers exploring the properties of socio-technical systems.[3] Some of the most important characteristics inhibiting innovation in legacy sectors are imperfections in the market for technology.

In the three chapters that follow this one, we explore these paradigms and market imperfections as they affect a series of domestic legacy sectors. We show in chapter 9 how the idea of legacy sectors can be extended to entire economies and illuminate the obstacles to innovation in a number of foreign countries. We extend the discussion to international markets in chapter 10, showcasing the agricultural and fossil energy sectors, in order to show how asymmetries in technological and innovation capacity can result in the export of these paradigms to developing countries and hinder the development and flow of technologies that could make important contributions to global social, environmental, and security problems. We close by articulating strategies that might be employed on overcoming the obstacles to market launch in legacy sectors.

PARADIGMS INHIBITING INNOVATION IN LEGACY SECTORS

We begin this journey by defining the common features of legacy sector paradigms. Here we build on our previous work and also on the literature of sociotechnical systems,[4] with the difference that we drill more deeply into the role of economics, policy, and regulations, and into the politics that underlie them. As we have previously mentioned, these characteristics are known to specialists in each of the legacy sectors that we shall explore. Our contribution is to define them and point out the commonalities. These common features are the following:[5]

1. *"Perverse" subsidies and prices* that *neglect externalities* like environmental sustainability and create *cost structures* favorable to existing technologies that create a mismatch between the incentives of producers and innovators and the goals of the larger society.[6] These include the numerous subsidies to fossil fuels[7] and the regulated electric power tariffs that discourage investment in the electricity distribution network. The concept here also encompasses cost structures that tend to offset or impair innovations and to ignore positive externalities accruing to others. Examples include the procedure-oriented fee structure used by doctors and hospitals, and the power-sales-oriented profit structure of electric utility companies. As discussed below, the cost structure of the military services, with their long-term procurement contracting, tends to lock in budgeting for existing technology platforms and crowd out funding for newer technology advances, affecting security.

2. A *government or other institutional architecture* that favors existing technology or discourages new entrants, accompanied by government support to infrastructure adapted to the requirements of existing technology. Here we distinguish the institutional or regulatory structure from the substantive content of the regulations themselves, which we discuss below. Examples include the balkanized or overlapping regulatory structures that affect the installation of large-scale solar and wind power installations, all of which require multiple approvals from separate jurisdictions for the installation of high-voltage power lines to connect them to the main electric power distribution grid. Other examples include the federal highway construction trust fund that has historically promoted highways over mass transit investment, and the government-financed system of research and development that has revolutionized natural gas extraction by fracking and other "nonconventional" methods.[8] By this we do not mean that government intervention inevitably impedes innovation. On the contrary, government institutional arrangements can also act as a change agent to promote new entry, as illustrated, for example, by DARPA's strong history of promoting technological advance.[9]

3. *Well-established and politically powerful vested interests*, both in private industry and in government, that resist the introduction of technologies that threaten their business models. In private industry, these include oil, coal, and natural gas companies in energy, health insurance companies, hospitals and medical associations in health delivery, and large telecommunications firms in the

wireless phone sector, and the broadcast and cable television industry. Legacy sectors can take the form of oligopolies, where a small number of firms dominate an industry or market, with each firm able to affect the overall market. Such firms tend to be price setters and may be able to retain abnormal levels of profits and create barriers to entry to potential competitors. In government, the vested interests in legacy sectors include state regulatory agencies in the utility industry, the multiple state and local jurisdictions that control the siting of energy facilities and installations, like wind and solar energy farms and their associated long-distance power lines, and the local control over building codes, which creates an approval structure that sharply limits the ability to adopt innovations to improve the efficiency of energy use in buildings.

4. *Financing support geared to incumbents* and reluctant to extend risk capital to finance disruptive new entrant technologies. In the United States, this typically takes the form of financing support attuned to the time horizon and relative simplicity of information technology (IT) and biotechnology and relatively unsuited to more complex industries. IT and biotech are typically financed by "angel" investors and venture capital (VC) companies, a brilliant new launch system for disruptive innovations originally built to accompany the emergence of the IT sector in the 1980s and 1990s.[10] VCs invest in a firm with innovations that are generally no more than two to three years from commercialization and can be produced at scale three or four years later, at which time venture investors can recoup their money when the firm goes public. Software-based firms can be on an even shorter time frame because their capital requirements are minimal and the scale-up can occur in the cloud. While venture firms may continue interim funding in particular non-IT, capital-intensive firms they have invested in for a longer period—10 years or more—if they are still promising, they will not finance the production scale-up stage. Typically they push these firms abroad for this step, to contract manufacturers or sovereign wealth funds, and they will not support other firms in the sector once they find that the time frame for returns is longer than the IT sector yardstick.[11] In contrast, the time frame for firms attempting to innovate in legacy sectors, such as energy, may be a decade or more. The capital required for the complex technologies involved may be much higher, and the market less familiar, than they are for IT and biotech.

5. *Public habits and expectations* attuned to existing price structures, dominant products, and technology, that underpin popular support to the policies and public expenditures favorable to existing technology. These include public expectations of cheap and convenient energy, widespread satisfaction with existing health delivery options (for those who receive adequate care and do not have to pay for it directly), tolerance of existing single-passenger highway auto transport despite mounting delays and energy effects, and public reluctance to pay higher prices or rents for energy-efficient buildings.

6. An *established knowledge and human resources structure*: educational curricula, career paths, and professional standards in medical, legal, and technical fields that are oriented to the needs of existing technology. For example, nanoscale

fabrication is widely understood to be a breakthrough area, yet the legal, regulatory, and health sectors are not ready for it because of a series of unresolved safety questions; nanotechnologies largely remain at the lab bench because we lack engineers with the training to introduce them into efficient manufacturing processes.

7. *Aversion to innovation*, as indicated by very limited investment in R & D on breakthrough innovations that could improve efficiency and outcomes, both for lack of interest and because the other obstacles make them unlikely to be implemented. This, for example, is a characteristic of the higher education and healthcare delivery sectors discussed in chapter 7, and of the fossil fuel energy sector, which spends, as detailed in chapter 6, less than 1% of its annual revenues on R & D.

8. *Market imperfections* that reinforce the position of existing technologies. These include network economies, lumpiness (minimum required size) of investments, split incentives ("nonappropriability"), and requirements for collective action. These will be explored in more detail later in this chapter.

These features of the paradigms underlying legacy sectors often occur in combinations that reinforce each other. For example, the private broadcast information industry has been particularly prone to resistance to disruption at different stages of its evolution, often by means of market imperfections reinforced by government institutions and regulations for which the industry itself had lobbied. In radio and television, for example, the dominant industry repeatedly developed a potentially disruptive successor technology but used weapons of intellectual property protection and other methods we have already discussed to suppress it, sometimes for decades, because it threatened its business model. In two significant examples, television was delayed because it was thought to have the potential to destroy radio, and FM broadcasting was delayed because it required less power than AM and would have made possible many small stations that could have challenged the dominant handful of big networks. A similar dynamic may be occurring today in broadband.[12]

In some legacy sectors, such as energy and developing country agriculture, innovation is further inhibited by a general underinvestment in research and development, and in some cases, as in public transport and electric power distribution, by underinvestment in or undercapitalization of the sector as a whole. As we shall see in chapter 10, the paradigms we have described also impose obstacles for the development of technologies for developing countries that must depend on advanced countries for technologies that can be applied or adapted to their own particular needs.

PARADIGM-COMPATIBLE INNOVATIONS

Despite the very real obstacles that they face, innovations that reinforce existing paradigms—or are at least compatible with them—are often successful and indeed constitute the basis for much of the United States' comparative advantage in biopharmaceuticals, fossil fuel, and agricultural, military, and aerospace technology. Even in legacy sectors, technologies like light-emitting diodes (LEDs) and off-grid wind and solar energy have been successfully launched into niche markets from which they can expand and perhaps challenge established competitors.

These paradigm-compatible innovations can slot into a market niche that falls within the existing paradigm, and can be profitable reasonably soon after market launch, ideally even despite the subsidies to competing legacy technologies. Building up in a niche, they can, over time, go through engineering improvements and move down the production cost curve to build momentum for broader entry into the sector. Here, private market mechanisms are more important than interventions through public policy.

If these innovations become sufficiently superior to the technologies they replace to overcome the subsidies to their competitors, their market adoption can follow the "normal model" described earlier. LEDs provide a good example of this category. This technology began in specialty niche lighting sectors, and went through cost-cutting and incremental engineering improvements to build up its market base to a point where the technology may emerge as the dominant lighting technology.[13] In other words, over time LEDs, while displacing existing incandescent lighting, constitute a technology that is still compatible within the existing lighting/electric utility paradigm.

LEDs exemplify the situation in which a new technology is likely to be competitive only in special situations at the beginning, but may have the potential to improve and expand into existing markets and become a disruptive innovation in the sense originally defined by Christensen.[14] However, such innovations typically face a series of marketing and design challenges when they attempt to move from early-adopter niche markets into broader use markets,[15] including engineering incremental improvements for the technology, selecting the right target markets, developing a concept of the "whole product," positioning the product in the market, formulating a marketing strategy, finding distribution channels, and pricing for emerging markets.

This "self-expanding process" has to attract the market segments characteristic of the successive stages of the classic technology adoption lifecycle:[16] innovators, early adopters, early majority users, late majority users, and laggards. This process could in principle be accelerated by public policy intervention, including subsidies, regulatory requirements, guaranteed purchases, or other interventions intended to encourage scale-up or to provide incentives or regulatory requirements for adoption by users in cases in which this is justified by some environmental or other social benefit. Examples of technologies that merit such intervention might include renewable energy and most new drugs and medical devices.

PARADIGM-INCOMPATIBLE INNOVATIONS AND DISRUPTION-RESISTANT LEGACY TECHNOLOGY

As they are erected and evolve, legacy sectors erect paradigms that create a set of protective barriers that entrench the innovations that created them and protect them from disruption. As we have seen, these paradigms are not simply castles of technological incompatibility, but include economic, political, legal, and social barriers as well. Each reinforces the others; a legacy sector is not guarded by a single defense but by a group of paradigm walls and moats. It is these interlocking paradigm defenses—a system-of-systems as noted above—that make innovating in legacy sectors so difficult.

Paradigm-compatible technologies, as we have noted, tend to be either incremental or secondary advances that enhance the strength of the legacy sector, or in some cases, potentially disruptive technologies that can nevertheless be launched in modest market niches, although eventual scaling may be difficult. Paradigm-incompatible technologies are by definition disruptive, challenging the business and organizational models that dominate the particular legacy sector. Thus, unless they can locate a market niche in which to begin, they must assault the legacy citadel.

At least in their first generation, these paradigm-incompatible technologies are often secondary innovations or innovations to components of larger systems. For example, the advanced lithium battery that will underpin electric vehicles is a component of a complex automotive platform, and electronic medical records still serve physicians and hospitals. This means that these technologies cannot be launched at scale unless they are cost-competitive from very beginning, a fact that adds a major complication.

As we have discussed, our pipeline-oriented innovation system is organized around the launching of technologies that offer new functionality; these do better landing in new markets—open fields where they can be built up without immediate cost competition from existing technologies. Our system is simply not organized to help new entrant technologies drive down the cost curve to compete in complex, well-established sectors. This is a deep problem of innovation organization that policymakers in the United States have yet to understand and confront. Indeed, it constitutes a profound challenge to the institutional paradigm that underlies our support to the development of science and the outset of a technology, a theme to which we shall return in chapter 11.

EXPLANATION OF THE IMPERFECTIONS IN TECHNOLOGY MARKETS THAT AFFECT LEGACY SECTORS

Our list of the typical characteristics of the paradigms that underlie legacy sectors included a brief summary of the market imperfections that form key elements of these paradigms.[17] A dramatic demonstration of the existence of such market imperfections is the fact that for some interventions, for example in the building industry, the sum of the financial benefits to the various stakeholders that would result from widespread implementation would actually exceed their aggregate financial costs.[18] In other words, implementing these technologies would not only achieve social benefits, but would actually save money overall. In the jargon of economics and finance, these interventions would have positive aggregate financial net present value. (As we shall see, the problem lies in "nonappropriability"—the fact that the people who pay the costs don't reap the benefits.) More frequently, however, paradigm-threatening innovations in these sectors are driven by nonmarket considerations: externalities (costs that users do not pay directly) involving the environment, public health, security, or other collective benefits that may be critically important to the country or the world but inevitably cost extra money.

We now return to these imperfections and explore them in more detail. The first imperfection is that of *network economies* that apply to industries organized around national or large-scale regional networks. As a way to visualize these networked sectors, picture the vast system of telephone lines or of wireless cyber connections—or the advantages enjoyed by widely spoken languages or widely used computer programs. Examples include the network dominance of Microsoft's operating system in personal computers or the existing grid system in long-distance transmission of electricity. Here a major obstacle is often the absence of agreed standards that facilitate interoperability within the network. Innovations in the air traffic control system, many elements of the smart grid, and many applications of information and communications technology to the delivery of health services fit into this category. These innovations require the adoption of standards, regulatory incentives, or other policies to facilitate the establishment of such networks and to ensure the interoperability of components and subnetworks.

If the required innovations are purely technical, they may be introduced by agreement among stakeholders, as long as these are consistent with their competing business strategies. Or they could be imposed by a dominant firm (such as Microsoft in desktop computer operating systems), or directed by a single health payer (such as the US Veterans Administration, the Defense Department, or Medicare regarding electronic medical records). The absence of such standards in these networks in effect squanders the advantages conferred by the huge American mass market, a fact that long slowed the adoption of cell phones in the United States. Their rapid deployment in Europe can be ascribed to the rapid adoption of a uniform Europe-wide standard. If the required standards cannot be set by agreement or by a dominant player or product design, federal government intervention may be necessary, especially if different regulations in different states have the effect of imposing divergent standards.

A second market imperfection that may impose barriers to innovation is known as *lumpiness*. This term is applied here to innovations that require a substantial minimum investment in order to be introduced at full scale against entrenched competition. It might be visualized as a boa constrictor trying to swallow an elephant. These technologies often involve large-scale, engineering-intensive installations that must first be the subject of full-sized, expensive, and risky demonstrations in order to prove techno-economic feasibility, safety, and environmental sustainability. Examples are the technologies for enhanced ("hot rocks") geothermal systems or fourth-generation nuclear power plants. The need for public intervention to promote the introduction of these "elephant" technologies is especially acute if they are likely to involve extra costs even when fully developed in order to compensate for environmental or other externalities. As an extra complication, the implementation of these technologies may also give rise to issues of ownership rights and legal liability, in addition to those of economics and technology.

In the energy field, this set of conditions applies directly to carbon capture and sequestration (CCS) technology; such major engineering systems, even when fully developed, will add major new facilities and costs to coal-fired generation plants. This technology will require billion-dollar investments in demonstration projects that are likely to be funded privately only if investors are reasonably sure that such technology will eventually be required of them in one way or another. Public-private partnerships and international collaborations are needed here in order to share demonstration costs, to offer financing support, and also to ensure that performance, safety, and environmental data are collected in a manner consistent with the needs of eventual private investors.

CCS presents a case study worth elaborating on because it illustrates the complexity and difficulty of interventions to overcome market imperfections. It has been difficult for the Department of Energy, despite years of effort and $3.4 billion in CCS funding available under 2009 stimulus legislation, to get significant demonstrations at scale underway because it has been hard for politicians or private investors to invest large sums in expensive full-scale CCS demonstrations as long as there are few prospects for a carbon tax or other incentives to carbon conservation in the reasonably near term. To date there are no commercial ventures in the United States that capture, transport, and store CO_2 from power plants on a large scale solely for the purpose of sequestration. A series of demonstration efforts are underway, although others have been canceled, that are focused more on demonstration for separate CCS stages, for example for capture and for industrial recovery.[19] The DOE has awarded $270 million to date, for example, for a major precombustion gasification technology project in Mississippi designed to capture 65% of CO_2 emissions from the plant and to become operational in 2015. However, total costs of the full project appear to be rising toward $5 billion.[20] Most seriously, DOE's FutureGen project was scaled down in 2010 from a new plant to a retrofit of an existing power plant and was finally suspended in 2015 for lack of timely industry co-sponsorship support.[21] Yet projects on this or even larger scale will be required to fully demonstrate the technology, if it is ever to have a major effect on carbon dioxide emissions from the electric power industry or other major point sources of CO_2 emissions. Even the recent efforts of the Obama administration to classify CO_2 as a pollutant, if they survive expected court and congressional challenges, are more likely to stimulate a switch to natural gas than interest in CCS technology.

Given that coal is cheap and abundant in the United States, China, India, and other countries, it is important to find out whether CCS technology is going to be techno-economically feasible and environmentally acceptable at a scale consistent with the size of the global energy industry. Assuming that the world at some point is forced to deal with the issue of climate change, the future of the coal industry— and indeed of the energy industry as a whole—will be very different depending on the answer to this question. And it will take some time to arrive at this answer even after serious effort is undertaken to do so.

A third kind of market imperfection that may impose barriers to innovation is the need to effect *economies of scale*. This barrier especially affects technologies that cannot be launched from market niches. In these cases, special intervention may be needed to bring down unit costs, to improve performance, or to organize the market for complementary products and infrastructure. To visualize these economies of scale, one need only imagine the vast array of resources, suppliers, components, and production facilities—the "value network," in Christensen's terminology—needed to produce a million cars. The cost and complexity of assembling this vast production system at sufficient scale to be competitive is what makes entry into such sectors as auto or aircraft production so difficult.

This market imperfection is especially important in the manufacture of hardware or of electronic components of information systems; for example, a single semiconductor chip fabrication plant (known as a fab) is a massive production facility requiring a multi-billion-dollar investment. Here public intervention—for example, low-cost financing of capital equipment—may be justified if there is an urgent social need to expand production beyond that required to meet the needs of assured future markets. The federal government did this to produce aircraft during World War II, as did the Japanese government during the 1970s in many areas of manufacturing. A well-tested policy measure to encourage expansion of production facilities is guaranteed public purchase. For example, the government can issue a public tender for a quantity of solar water heaters or photovoltaic panels to be installed on military housing, to be awarded to bidders meeting specified conditions. The same technique could be used to incentivize the development and manufacture of vaccines, which face a different set of market imperfections.

A fourth kind of market imperfection that may impose barriers to innovation is that of *nonappropriability*. This refers to innovations (or other economic decisions) whose benefits accrue to someone other than the investor or to others who are separated from the transaction; it can also be called the problem of *split incentives*.[22] Doctors, for example, may be reluctant to invest in information systems for medical records that benefit patients but whose costs cannot be passed on to them. Builders and landlords may be unwilling to invest in energy conservation that will benefit purchasers and tenants, respectively, but who may be unwilling to pay extra for them. In such cases, it is important to devise ways of overcoming these imperfections, for example by a mechanism that finances extra initial costs at favorable rates. Even so, the practical difficulties of implementing such systems may require some form of subsidy or regulation, for example through revisions in building codes or other standards.

This is especially true in situations where the nonappropriability was created by government institutions or by regulation. For example, in the case of the electric grid, state-regulated electricity rates may prevent utilities from recovering the cost of investments that could result in a more reliable and efficient national supply of electricity. In this case, it is a set of government agencies rather than a private industry that constitutes the disruption-resistant vested interest. Alternatively, these innovations may simply be imposed by fiat by a central paying or management authority, such as electronic medical records by the US Veterans Administration or the Kaiser-Permanente healthcare system, or by the national health services of the United Kingdom and the Scandinavian countries.

A fifth kind of market imperfection is *requirements for collective action.* These typically involve fragmented industries with many units, none of them large enough to invest in innovation. Picture the housing construction industry, for example. It is highly decentralized, with thousands of small firms. Few of them have even a regional, much less a national presence, and only a tiny number have the capital depth to support research and development for the sector. This sector is risk-averse and therefore innovation-averse, and is therefore unwilling to implement new advances until their costs and efficiencies are fully and convincingly proven—a sort of catch-22. Innovations in such industries can come from suppliers, who, however, face a significant threshold for proving costs and quality for this highly decentralized sector.

Other similarly fragmented industries have organized themselves for collaborative, precompetitive research, sometimes with government help. Picture another example, the farming sector, where millions of farms cannot implement or finance innovation without the systematic support of the Agriculture Department's research and development efforts, without its dissemination efforts through county extension agents who bring these innovations to individual farmers, or without its massive financing programs.[23] Another example is Sematech, a public-private partnership—initiated by leaders of the industry—that helped to pull together the semiconductor industry and its diverse equipment suppliers and bring productivity gains and cost efficiencies to equipment-manufacturing processes.[24] In the energy sector, the Electric Power Research Institute supports sector-wide research and development. Such cross-sectoral efforts can suffer from underinvestment due to the free rider problem, in which members of the industry benefit from collective research without contributing to it.

The need for collective action is also a factor in the commercial airline industry, which is also undercapitalized and which has benefited from innovation historically funded by the military budget, a pattern that has been undermined by the reduction in the procurement budget for military aircraft—partly due to precision strike and stealth, which have greatly reduced the number of sorties needed to destroy a target, and by the divergence between civilian and military performance requirements.

Many of the market imperfections in the previous discussion arise from a sixth barrier category: *governmental or regulatory* impediments to innovation. Here we refer to the substance of these regulations rather than the institutional structures that create them. Regulation can protect incumbents from more innovative new entrants, as exemplified by the history of commercial aviation,[25] trucking,[26] and telecommunications[27] before these sectors were deregulated. Alternatively, regulation can operate to encourage the entry of new technology, as with the acid rain provisions of the Clean Air Act Amendments of 1990[28] that encouraged new entry of SO_2 scrubber technology through a cap-and-trade system. In other words, regulation can either encourage or discourage innovation, depending on how it is structured and designed.

This problem is not restricted to regulatory agencies but may also extend, for example, to the particular institutional structure of agencies and programs, including in research. The organizational structure of the National Institutes of Health, for example, is decentralized around some 27 institutes and centers so as to fulfill the political demands of historical disease groups, a structure that limits crosscutting research initiatives that could accelerate medical innovation. In other cases, government interventions have misdirected the development of technology, for example when interest-group politics dictated huge subsidies for corn-based ethanol although it is at best a suboptimal biofuel technology and a competitor for land used to grow food crops. In another example, the political demand for manned space exploration has curtailed less expensive and more scientifically rewarding robotic exploration.

The lack of agreed standards by which to assess alternative technologies can also impede disruptive innovations in legacy sectors, especially when these depend on environmental or other nonmarket considerations that are driven by government policy (as for example, carbon charges) or by consumer willingness to pay extra (as for example, organic produce or sustainably grown timber). These drivers require agreed external criteria that embody these desired values and can be the basis for an agreed replacement standard against which candidate alternatives can be judged. These criteria and standards tend to be works in progress (examples include standards for evidence-based medicine, "smart" grid standards, and information technology standards for health services delivery) and are frequently contested (for example, low-carbon versus renewable energy technologies, or the many different standards for sustainable agriculture and forestry). This lack of agreed standards adds to the usual problems that face all innovations, disruptive or not, and makes it difficult to achieve the necessary economies of scale and network economies for market launch at scale.

SUMMARY OF THE MARKET IMPERFECTIONS AFFECTING LEGACY SECTORS

For clarity and emphasis, we briefly summarize the set of market imperfections that can infect legacy sectors. These imperfections can affect legacy sectors singly or in groups. This is a working list; market imperfections differ from sector to sector; not all legacy sectors display all these imperfections and there may be many more such imperfections that we have not considered, so we should not assume these categories form a complete list.

1. *Network economies.* Some sectors organize around network economies to achieve large-scale efficiencies, such as the grid or common IT operating systems. These can act as barriers to the introduction of innovations, such as those based on information technology for the healthcare delivery system.
2. *Lumpiness.* A minimum investment size and scale, known to economists as *lumpiness,* limits the entry of new technologies into some sectors—for example, in the pharmaceutical industry, whose business model depends on highly profitable "blockbuster" drugs, and in the development of engineering-intensive

technologies like carbon capture and sequestration and enhanced ("hot rocks") geothermal in the energy sector. Only technology "elephants" can enter the sector.

3. *Economies of scale.* There are sectors that require a vast array of resources, suppliers, components, and production facilities, and distribution, sales, and service systems, for entry. For example, the cost and complexity of assembling the huge production system and value network constitutes a significant barrier to outside innovators in such sectors as auto or aircraft production.

4. *Nonappropriability or split incentives.* This imperfection occurs when the benefits of innovation go to someone other than the inventor or investor; the innovation gain is *nonappropriable.* This hinders, for example, innovation in the application of information technology both to the "smart" electric power distribution grid, in which the cost of investments in increased reliability cannot be passed on to consumers, and in the delivery of health services, in which the cost of investments in increased efficiency cannot be passed on to patients and insurance companies. This imperfection also applies to energy conservation technologies for buildings, where owners and landlords are reluctant to make efficiency investments whose benefits they cannot recapture.

5. *Collective action.* Sectors that are composed of numerous undercapitalized firms typically lack the ability to collaborate and cooperate on common problems. The need for *collective action* is, for example, an important obstacle to innovation in the highly decentralized and small-scale building industry. The need for collective action has also been an important factor in the government's interventionist role in agricultural innovation.

6. *Government, regulatory, or institutional structure.* Innovation can also be severely impacted by the *pattern of government regulation,* which is often influenced by the *structure of regulatory institutions.* Regulation and standards structure, in particular, can be forces that limit innovation entry or support it.

In the next chapters, we review the obstacles to innovation in a number of representative legacy sectors, using the conceptual framework set forth in the last few chapters.

6 Six US Legacy Sectors

Energy, the Grid, Buildings, Air and Auto Transport, and Manufacturing

We now summarize the obstacles to innovation in a series of legacy economic sectors, using the conceptual framework set forth in the previous chapters. We provide snapshots of these sectors, briefly noting the technology challenges and the barriers to meeting them. For each sector, we briefly set forth the general structure of its technological/economic/political/social paradigm, the market imperfections that affect the sector, the new considerations that create the need for disruptive technology, the desirable characteristics of such a revolution, and the difficulties involved in achieving them.

We then characterize some of the most prominent possibilities for technological improvement in the sector, and note the obstacles to launching them in the marketplace, using some of the relevant concepts set forth in the preceding chapters: the subsidies and price structures creating a tilted playing field, the market imperfections and other obstacles for innovation resulting from the existing legacy paradigm, and the existing policies, standards, regulations, and economic and political factors that affect the speed and direction of technological change and innovation. We also note some of the policy interventions that could lead to a technological shift in the sector, and the change agents that would be needed.

ENERGY

Energy is the poster child for a legacy sector. The major problem facing innovations in the energy sector[1] is a deeply entrenched, nonlevel playing field, backed by powerful companies and public support, in which legacy fossil-fuel technologies have benefited from a variety of incentives and tax advantages that historically have been much richer than those for carbon-efficient technologies.[2]

Fossil fuels are convenient and cheap if externalities like environment and war are excluded. The fossil fuel economy is huge, mature, heavily subsidized, and pervasive; it is deft at fending off competition, deeply entrenched in the economy and the political system, and sustained by the public expectation of cheap energy. Except in limited circumstances, a new energy technology must compete at scale with existing technology from the moment that it is launched into the established energy market, a difficult prospect for new technologies. As a result, any innovation in energy technology faces a playing field that is far from level.

Legacy fossil fuel technologies deliver cost-effective, reliable, and convenient energy to users. As a result, the driving force for change comes from the serious environmental and geopolitical externalities of fossil fuels, rather than from market demand. The resulting watchwords have been sustainability and energy security—objectives that overlap although they do not always coincide. Meanwhile, warnings about climate change effects grow, with the energy sector as the leading culprit.[3]

For two decades, the United States and much of the rest of the world have operated on the assumption that putting a price on carbon would be the strategy for addressing climate change. Nations would price carbon emissions, cap their production levels, ratchet down the cap over time, allow carbon dioxide emitters to pay for their emissions at an ever increasing price, and use this market mechanism to price carbon dioxide emissions into a gradual multidecade decline. As a result of this market forcing, innovative new technologies would be induced into energy markets to substitute for fossil fuels.

The United States based this approach on the successful use of a cap-and-trade mechanism against acid rain through the Clean Air Act Amendments of 1990. At the Kyoto Framework Convention in 1997, the United States persuaded participating nations that the cap-and-trade approach with which it had successfully experimented would work against carbon dioxide emissions. The subsequent Kyoto Protocol eventually obtained enough initial signatures to go into effect, and Europe subsequently enacted a cap-and-trade program. However, the biggest carbon emitters, the United States and China, did not ratify the agreement. Concerned US policymakers assumed after Kyoto that cap-and-trade over time would still be adopted there and would be the US mechanism to tackle the climate challenge. This would bring the United States into Kyoto compliance and encourage China to join. At the outset of the Obama administration, the House in 2009 passed cap-and-trade legislation,[4] and the Senate subsequently came within a handful of the votes needed to break a filibuster.[5] But in one of the periodic tectonic shifts in congressional politics, cap-and-trade became anathema to conservatives, so that the legislation was pulled and now appears to be indefinitely postponed.

It is time to cite a parable. The movie *Armageddon* was about a different form of planetary impact. An asteroid the size of Texas is 18 days away from smashing into planet earth. NASA develops a plan to land an expert drilling team, implant a nuclear weapon, detonate it, and split the asteroid in half, deflecting the two halves so they bypass the earth. Perceiving this plan as, to say the least, risky, actor Bruce

Willis, playing the leader of the drilling team, approaches a senior NASA official in a spacecraft hanger and the following dialogue ensues:

> BRUCE WILLIS: What's your contingency plan?
> NASA: Contingency plan?
> BRUCE WILLIS: Your backup plan, you gotta have some kind of backup plan, right?
> NASA: No, we don't have a backup plan.
> BRUCE WILLIS: And this is the best that you, that the government, the US government, could come up with? I mean, you're NASA for crying out loud, and you put a man on the moon, you're geniuses! You're telling me you don't have a backup plan . . . [You're] the world's hope, that's what you're telling me?
> NASA: Yeah.

The United States has not managed to assemble over the past 20 years a backup plan, apart from carbon pricing, for the impending climate change, either. As we shall see, a technology strategy is both a backup plan and a necessary complement to cap and trade or other means of carbon dioxide pricing.

Carbon Dioxide Pricing and Technology Policy

The carbon dioxide charge approach (often abbreviated as "carbon pricing") was in significant part the product of the neoclassical economic thinking that has dominated US economic policymaking since the 1950s. It has emphasized allocation efficiency through pricing and markets but has exhibited only a limited focus on innovation and innovation systems.[6] As a result, this approach employed a pricing system approach to climate that missed many of the subtleties of innovation policy. While the 1990 acid rain legislation, which was the stalking horse for climate cap-and-trade policy, worked well, the SO_2 scrubber technology required for that approach was already at hand when the legislation was passed, so implementation by industry worked smoothly.

In contrast, the history of climate change legislation shows the limitations of the use of policy-driven price changes as a tool with which to induce technological change. At the time of the legislative debates on climate change (2007–2010), few of the technologies required to meet cap-and-trade requirements were either technologically mature or economically viable at the scale that would have been necessary to enable them to be implemented in the nationwide energy economy. Nor was there a program of sufficient size that offered realistic prospects of developing and demonstrating such technology. This created very significant risk for the many major industries that would have had to adopt the technologies, from transport to utilities, over and above the strong resistance from the coal and oil fossil fuel industries that were directly affected. While some firms, particularly those making larger platforms in which clean technologies were housed (for example, automakers prepared to develop battery-powered engines), might have tolerated such transformative technologies if they were competitively priced, others, whose business models were directly threatened, would not have done so.

Because the carbon pricing strategy dominated the policy debate, accompanied by what we can now see was a somewhat naive assumption that needed technologies would evolve without an accompanying technology strategy, in retrospect it appears that the pricing strategy inevitably faced even more opposition than it had to. While some companies would never have come around and had already developed sophisticated opposition tactics,[7] others that might, in some less directly affected industries, had no clear or manageable pathway to compliance. In addition, the political challenges to a carbon tax—that is, a direct charge on carbon dioxide emissions—discouraged research on low-carbon solutions.

This history provides an example of how the obstacles posed by legacy sectors might discourage others that would otherwise have acted as change agents. While price certainly can induce technology shifts, its disruptive impact can be mitigated by an accompanying technology strategy that precedes and accompanies it. That technology strategy—a backup plan—was largely missing from the climate policy battles.

Where do we now stand on energy R & D and technology development? We clearly failed to maintain a focus on energy technology development following the oil price crisis of 1978–79. Although study after study has called for major new investments in energy R & D,[8] it is still not at robust levels that could drive a technology strategy in either the public or private sectors. Federal R & D in new energy technology in real (inflation-corrected) dollars as of 2007 was only about half its 1980 level—the high-water mark for energy R & D.[9] Private-sector R & D had similarly fallen; studies indicate the energy industry invests less than 1% of annual revenues in R & D for new energy technology, far below the US industry average, and far, far below the 15%–20% levels in industries (semiconductors, biotechnology, pharmaceuticals) that are innovating new technologies.[10] While venture capital funding for clean energy technology grew significantly, reaching $4 billion by 2008, it declined to $3.3 billion in 2012.[11] In any event, this funding is for commercialization and is not a substitute for R & D.

The low level of private-sector R & D suggested a larger initial role for public-sector R & D. The Obama administration understood this and through its economic stimulus legislation made a major investment in FY2010 funding in energy technologies. The Department of Energy (DOE) funded some $5 billion in energy R & D and $34 billion in technology implementation above historic "baseline" appropriation levels. However, that was a short-term spurt and those levels have fallen back in FY2011–14 funding.[12] The additional funding was welcome, but it has created the risk of building up the energy technology enterprise and then letting this expanded capability wither for lack of follow-up funding, thereby "pushing it off a funding cliff."[13]

Meanwhile, the US energy supply situation has become more complex. While the United States has long been dominated by the politics of a perceived scarcity in fossil fuels, that underlying assumption has now shifted, and it faces a politics of surplus. Fracking technologies for shale gas extraction, initially developed by the DOE,[14] have created a natural gas boom, and oil production is up as well. DOE research, although small compared to the magnitude of the energy sector, here produced a revolutionary but paradigm-consistent innovation-in the classification presented earlier, a "discontinuous secondary innovation." The United States is significantly expanding natural gas production, which is underpricing coal and rapidly expanding in electric power and industrial uses.[15] In 2012, the United States became a net petroleum product exporter for the first time since 1949.[16]

While a carbon pricing system is likely still necessary to meet the challenges of climate change, a technology strategy is both a necessary backup plan *and* a necessary complement to a pricing system. We do not now have such an adequately funded strategy. The needed levels of R & D and technology implementation worldwide still do not exist.[17] This appears to be a direct result of the legacy features of the energy sector, which must be addressed if an energy technology strategy is to emerge. It is to these legacy features that we now turn.

Legacy Features of the Energy Sector

Although investment in energy research and development has been modest, considering the enormous size of the energy economy, it has still been enough to give rise to a wide range of promising alternative energy technologies. These face the gamut of categories of impediments to innovation that we defined earlier: from impediments to *early stage innovation*, as characterized by hydrogen fuel cells and fusion, to potentially *disruptive secondary innovations*, like off-grid wind and solar, that are already established in special niches but still face impediments, to *paradigm-compatible innovations*, like fracking.

The litany of other legacy sector characteristics also fit fossil-fuel-based energy like a glove: (1) it is subject to *"perverse" prices* that do not reflect the externalities associated with carbon dioxide emissions and thus underprices fossil fuels and creates a mismatch with the broader social goal of carbon dioxide reduction; (2) it benefits from an *established infrastructure and institutional architecture* oriented around fossil fuels that disadvantages alternative energy technology new entrants; (3) it has a *financing system* where venture capital, after an initial phase of support, is declining[18] because it doesn't operate on the longer term timetable required for new entrant energy technologies, effectively protecting incumbents from innovation; (4) it is backed by politically and economically *powerful vested interests* that defend the existing energy paradigm, resist innovations that threaten their business models, and have battled attempts to pass climate change legislation to a standstill; (5) it has been *averse to innovation*, as a system where industry conducted very *limited R & D* and resists disruptive, paradigm-inconsistent technologies; (5) it is *sustained by public habits and expectations* attuned to cheap energy from energy resources and technologies; and (6) it rests on an *established knowledge and human resources structure* oriented to the existing industry's own needs and resistant to change.

Energy is also characterized by a series of market imperfections. These include an inability to muster *collective action* in particular energy sectors.

Energy itself encompasses disparate elements: transport is very different from electric power generation and transmission, requiring different strategies and technologies. The electric grid gives rise to important issues of collective action. It is very difficult, as discussed below, to organize collective efforts on behalf of electric utilities because their national governance system is highly decentralized and balkanized, with regulatory control scattered among at least a hundred institutions, each jealously guarding its function. The energy sector also includes "elephant" technologies like solar and wind farms, carbon capture and sequestration, enhanced geothermal, and next-generation nuclear, secondary innovations that must be launched at large scale and thus suffer from innovation impediments due to *lumpiness*.

Impediments to innovation due to the need for *economies of scale* create inherent costs and risks and require special intervention, as, e.g., in hardware manufacture for electric vehicles, which require major initial investment levels and so risk overexpansion of manufacturing and marketing capacity beyond anticipated market needs. Technologies that face impediments to innovation due to *nonappropriability* offer positive aggregate net value but suffer from market imperfections that make it difficult to translate this into a practical incentive structure, a situation that applies to many technologies for conservation and efficient energy use. The energy sector is also laced with *governmental and other institutional* impediments, notably the lack of mechanisms to translate research advances from federal laboratories and university research into scaled technologies.

Each of these barriers and impediments to innovation requires a strategic policy response. Are there change agents that will press for change? The Obama administration and its secretaries of energy have been doing so, with such resources for technology development as they can muster from a reluctant Congress. ARPA-E was designed to be a DARPA-like change agent. Residual Environmental Protection Agency (EPA) regulatory authority can be a force. For example, EPA and National Highway Traffic Safety Administration (NHTSA) regulations for Corporate Average Fuel Economy (CAFE) are now set to rise to 54.5 miles per gallon by 2025 for cars and light trucks.[19] This will press ongoing industry experimentation with electric engines, hybrid engines, more efficient internal combustion engines, and vehicle lightweighting. As another example, EPA proposed in 2013 and reproposed in 2014 regulations on CO_2 emissions on fossil fuel plants that, if implemented, would compel new coal-fired power plants to adopt carbon capture and sequestration technologies by 2020.[20] Some states are continuing to press for alternative energy. And clean energy firms are starting to develop market share as their technologies move beyond niche markets, often aided by states that have adopted renewable portfolio standards requiring a percentage of state's electricity generation to be from clean energy sources. The question remains whether these efforts, coupled with efforts in particular states and increasingly in cities, will be politically sustainable over time and at a scale that would constitute a backup plan. In the meantime, innovators in other countries are hard at work. Other regions, led by China and Europe, are supporting clean energy technology implementation, offering alternatives to US development.

The high-voltage, long-distance, interstate electric power grid in the United States has been the subject of criticism because of limits on its reliability, its inability to accommodate renewable power sources, its vulnerability to hacking, and its inability to adapt to advances in information technology (IT).[21] The recent emphasis on environmental issues has created pressures for increased efficiency, as well as measures to facilitate the incorporation of intermittent, renewable sources of energy, and has stimulated discussion of possible means to overcome the many obstacles created by a fragmented regulatory system.

Electricity charges in the United States, to summarize briefly, are largely regulated by 50 state commissions. These generally ensure utility revenues as a fixed percentage of investment, making regulators reluctant to permit new investments, since they are likely to result in rate increases that consumers will resist. Different parts of the long-distance electric power grid in the United States are owned by different electric utilities, depending on geography, with the result that no single entity feels responsibility for the reliable and cost-effective operation of the whole grid, and no state commission is eager to approve utility investments with that purpose. In any case, the benefits from such an investment would redound to the consumer in the form of increased reliability and lower rates, and to the environment in the form of reduced carbon dioxide emissions and other forms of pollution, rather than to the utilities in the form of increased profits—a classic example of *environmental externalities* and *nonappropriability* due to *split incentives.*

The result is a grid that has relatively poor reliability, unnecessarily high costs, below-standard efficiency, and consequently a high environmental footprint, specifically high carbon dioxide emissions and their consequent contribution to global warming. Underlying these problems is a long-standing under-investment in the long-distance grid and in research and development on ways to improve it.

Thus, any effort to restructure the electric grid system runs headlong into a highly balkanized structure, with different jurisdictions controlled by different institutions at different levels of government. The number of utility actors involved is startling. "America's electric power industry is highly fragmented, divided among more than 3,100 separate entities, under a variety of forms of investor and public ownership."[22] Apart from the pricing of generation, transmission, and distribution noted above, "Diverse state regulatory policies predominate regarding electric industry structure, generation adequacy, energy resource mix, transmission siting and cost recovery and retail electricity prices."[23]

The process of generating and distributing electricity has three stages—generation, transmission, and distribution, as we describe in more detail in the ensuing paragraphs. The pricing and regulation of these stages is not integrated, so that electricity market transactions are divided, as discussed below, based on location and on the type of distribution system. The Federal Energy Regulatory Commission (FERC) has sole jurisdiction over pricing rates in wholesale high-voltage transmission, but cannot set prices for the local systems that distribute lower voltage power to end users. FERC has very limited authority over the construction of utility lines; pricing of generation and transmission over local distribution systems is set by state regulators under varying state laws. To add to the complexity, the 1990s saw partial and piecemeal deregulation. Some states deregulated, some did so partially, and others didn't deregulate at all. The generation market therefore contains both deregulated and regulated elements operating under a regulated wholesale high-voltage system under FERC. The result is a classic example of *governmental and other institutional* impediments that affect a broad range of promising innovations.[24]

Reliability oversight of the grid as a whole is the responsibility of the FERC, which delegates some responsibilities to the North America Electric Reliability Corporation or NERC. The latter divides North America into eight regulatory regions, which do not match up with the three major grid "interconnection" regions. Since relatively few high-voltage transmission lines connect any one region to the others, consumers in one region are largely limited to energy generated in that region.

Large-scale renewable energy sources—wind and solar farms and geothermal fields—have to be built in areas separated from existing transmission facilities, requiring major new build-out. However, the regulatory structure is so divided and generally reluctant to embrace major and costly infrastructure investments that developers face almost insuperable obstacles in obtaining the multiple regulatory approvals needed, both for the build-out itself and for absorbing the extra costs that they entail into the rate structure. What is more, the business model for most utilities is based on the sale of power, a system that does not reward conservation, efficiency, or reduced fossil fuel use. In other words, the system does not *align producer incentives with social goals.* Many state regulators require that a portion of their energy be generated from renewable sources ("renewable portfolio standards") but some do not. Since renewables are still more costly than coal or gas, accommodating renewables within the existing balkanized structure of the grid is problematic.

The next level of grid innovation is even more complex. The "smart grid"— which can integrate IT into the electricity grid—promises information flows that could yield both increased reliability of supply and major efficiency savings.[25] The cost of electricity varies widely over the course of a day or an hour, so a technology that allows users to see these varying costs and adjust their consumption to reduce them could help level out usage and therefore costs, avoiding peaks in consumption and spikes in prices. These technologies could also automatically program in these efficiencies based on preset user demand choices and preferences. At present, however, electricity users are largely blind to these cost-saving opportunities. Nor are utilities equipped to handle the flows of "big data" that such technologies would require.

A smart grid also offers individual households the ability to move from being simple users to becoming storage and generation sites, and selling power into the grid. Such a two-way system would offer dramatic new flexibility, making electricity markets and therefore consumption significantly more efficient. However, achieving this advance involves overcoming the highly fragmented and decentralized system described above, with its many participants, each with differing interests and many constraints.

The two-way features of the smart grid can also play a critical role in enabling the small-scale installation of renewable resources (wind, solar, geothermal, tidal, hydropower) and the widespread use of electric or hybrid vehicles. The current grid system, which long predates interest in renewables, is limited in its ability to incorporate them, despite the need to reduce the amount of electricity derived from burning coal, currently the source of half the electricity the country uses. Many renewable technologies could be introduced at the household or local scale, but these sources are outside the grid and can serve only the particular household or local, not broader needs; a smart grid could be a significant inducement to introducing smaller scale renewables.

A smart grid system would also support the broader introduction of electric and hybrid vehicles. These vehicles can be recharged at times that take advantage of optimal pricing, with corresponding gains in efficiency. Once recharged, the storage systems for these vehicles could sell power back into the grid at times when generation is more expensive, offsetting charging costs. The grid is also fragile, facing threats of blackouts; to avoid these, utilities must always have significant excess capacity. Smart grid technology includes automated information systems that "could mean a self-healing, self-optimizing power-delivery system that anticipates and quickly responds to disturbances."[26]

Implementation of a new grid will require overcoming obstacles posed by several of the market imperfections that are characteristic of legacy sectors. First, innovation in the grid is hindered by the need for *network economies* that can be achieved only through national or large-scale regional networks. These will require the adoption of *standards*, and of *regulatory policies and incentives* to ensure the interoperability of components and subnetworks, and to facilitate the establishment of new innovative networks within the established grid network.

Second, innovation within the grid is impeded by the problem of *nonappropriability*, in which the benefits of innovation accrue to someone other than the investor. While utility investors would have to accommodate and implement smart grid features that could benefit consumers, for example, the power-sale business model that underlies price regulation in most states treats such investments as non-recoverable costs. These and other obstacles derive from *governmental and other institutional* impediments that are largely regulatory, the product of historical developments in an earlier technological era, and embedded in entities unwilling to surrender jurisdiction or power—in this case regulatory authorities rather than the operators of older technologies. The highly balkanized regulatory structure, divided between state and federal agencies and imposing varying business models on operating utilities, creates *collective action* impediments to the introduction of innovation. In other words, the numerous regulators, locked into varying legal and regulatory systems that are hard to alter, cannot readily band together to develop and pursue common concerns, and the regulated correspondingly face a similar problem. This, in turn, creates a collective action problem for innovators: they have difficulty in finding markets at the scale needed to justify their technologies and investments. Finally, electric distribution utilities lack the pressure to innovate that would accrue if, because of their public monopolies, they had not in the past been substantially free of the problem of acquiring or retaining customers.

The IT technologies and software that would form the foundation of the smart grid are largely available, although cybersecurity, transmission efficiency, and other particular R & D challenges still remain to be resolved. Technology implementation is the central problem, requiring, initially, setting of common standards, and establishment of test beds and demonstrations. The Commerce Department's National Institute for Standards and Technology (NIST) has worked on smart grid standards with industry,[27] and the 2009 economic stimulus legislation[28] provided $4.5 billion for initial efforts at technology implementation. The Department of Energy's initial Quadrennial Energy Review has focused its planning on energy transmission, storage, and distribution because this infrastructure is inherently inflexible and has a major effect on energy supply and end-use decisions.[29] However, the scale of work required to extend the reach of transmission and to incorporate smart features will require a much larger scale of investment in this sector, which already has some $800 billion in established capital plant and infrastructure.

There are some transformative technologies in the wings. The DOE's Energy Efficiency and Renewable Energy (EERE) office has launched a new advanced manufacturing institute to pursue wide band gap semiconductor technology that could be transformative of power electronics, including in power transmission efficiency.[30] While these advances could ensure dramatic new energy efficiencies and savings, there is a technology development cost to get there.

In sum, establishing an interstate grid that is both smart and more efficient will require federal leadership, public and private financing, common standard setting, and a major effort at regulatory harmonization between state and federal agencies to overcome these structural barriers. Are there change agents available? Leadership at the federal level from FERC and the Department of Energy will be key. Reform-minded state agencies, such as California, can experiment and provide models for best practices.[31]

BUILDINGS

Some 40% of US carbon dioxide emissions come from buildings,[32] making building technology one of the most important areas for stimulating technological innovation. Saving carbon dioxide emissions and mitigating global warming is a nonmarket objective; even so, energy is a cost to the occupants of a building and saving it should be a market incentive. A study by McKinsey & Company found that investing in energy-efficient buildings, combined with certain other nontransportation efficiency steps, could reduce energy consumption in the United States by 23% by 2020.[33] This would amount to annual savings totaling $130 billion to $1.2 trillion, with reductions in greenhouse gas emissions of 1.1 gigatons annually, or a complete "stabilization wedge" in the Pacala-Socolow construct.[34]

These gains could be achieved largely by using existing efficiency approaches and technologies for an investment of about $50 billion per year over a period of 10 years. The McKinsey research found that a comprehensive strategy, executed at scale, could reduce the annual consumption of nontransportation end-use energy from 36.9 quadrillion BTUs in 2008 to 30.8 quadrillion BTUs in 2020, saving 9.1 quadrillion BTUs relative to a business-as-usual baseline.[35]

There are extensive efficiency options currently available, and new modeling simulation tools to help deploy them optimally are also in development. New efficiency technologies, including new advances in building appliances, heating and cooling system efficiency and in the electric motors that power many of these are also within range.[36]

There are significant barriers to achieving these gains. Energy efficiency typically requires a significant up-front investment in exchange for savings over the lifetime of the deployed technologies and measures. But the benefits from grid improvements are strewn across some one hundred million locations and billions of devices used at residential, commercial, and industrial sites; this dispersal of benefits, plus the *transaction costs* involved in choosing and implementing the necessary technology, means that efficiency is rarely a leading priority for anyone.[37] *Nonappropriability* is also a significant problem in this sector: in many cases, the financial benefits go to someone other than the investor. Why should a builder undertake efficiencies that benefit the purchaser, or a landlord undertake those that benefit tenants, when they cannot pass along the extra costs? These environmental benefits go largely to the public at large, making them a valuable but nonmarket incentive.

Other structural barriers abound. The manufacture of efficiency hardware and the technical services involved in supporting them for many innovations are subject to *economies of scale* and therefore may require special intervention to bring down unit costs and service cost to improve performance. Because efficiency is, in effect, optional to most consumers and owners because of the comparative low cost of inefficiency and the higher initial cost of many efficiency technologies, many of these new technologies have to enter at low cost and hence at large scale to make entry feasible. These economies of scale may require policy interventions; DOE's building efficiency hub noted below is an example of the role of a proof of concept and technology testing program to lower entry costs.[38] In addition, the construction sector is highly decentralized, consisting of huge numbers of small, geographically dispersed and undercapitalized firms that are not well set up for *collective action* and hence undertake very little research and development, or indeed experimentation of any kind. As a result, the cost, reliability, and efficiency savings from building efficiency technologies must be proven at major scale before these firms will take the risk of implementing them.

In addition, the sector is rife with *governmental and other institutional* impediments to innovation. While building codes could in principle provide a regulatory mechanism to encourage efficiency improvements, these codes are a regional responsibility, with thousands of jurisdictions involved. Few jurisdictions have an incentive to take on a national energy goal, since they would have to impose significant new requirements and costs on their construction firm constituents. Besides, the social goal of energy efficiency is very hard to measure; only the federal government could likely assemble the expertise and investment required to develop the accurate *efficiency metrics and standards* that are needed.

Recognizing these deep problems, the Department of Energy formed an R & D Hub around energy efficient buildings in 2010 as a collaboration between university and industry.[39] The Hub is undertaking applied R & D and serving as a test bed for new building efficiency technologies, so as to get around some of the problems of market failure in this sector. Change agents are also needed; Department of Energy agencies can support the needed R & D on standards and technology development, but state and regional government will need to apply regulatory forcing mechanisms and to create incentives for utilities to foster conservation and not just consumption. Again, states like California can foster best practices.

AIR TRANSPORT

The area of transport is huge, encompassing a significant portion of the economy with very different industries and business sectors. To discuss it we must narrow the questions we are pursuing. We therefore have elected to cover two problems linked to possible new advances in technology in two parts of this massive sector. In the field of air transport, we discuss possible entry of biofuels, and in the area of surface transport, we discuss the possible entry of intelligent vehicles and driverless cars. Each presents significant legacy sector challenges.

The technological/economic/political/social paradigm of air transport presents a somewhat different picture from the legacy sectors discussed above. In this case, the end of the era of new aircraft designs being spun off from military to civilian use has left a legacy of undercapitalized, low-margin airlines, which as a group are not organized for *collective action* in technology introduction. This limits the ability of manufacturers to undertake major research and development efforts for new advances on their own behalf. Here the early history of the aviation industry provides instructive background.

American aviation evolved as a close collaboration between military and civilian aircraft firms. For example, in the 1920s and 1930s, the navy's aviation leadership carefully planned and organized its procurement spending so as to nurture and build a strong network of aircraft and engine makers and in this way to ensure the military of a strong industrial base of aircraft suppliers.[40] In the post–Cold War period, however, military and civilian aircraft markets increasingly diverged. The military required highly maneuverable supersonic aircraft with advanced avionics and fire control systems; civilian markets required stable, long-range reliable aircraft of limited maneuverability. Military jet engines were designed more for maximum thrust, and civilian engines more for low fuel consumption. The focus of military aircraft on stealth technology found no counterpart in civilian markets. The development of stealth, cruise missiles and precision-strike technologies, first exhibited during the Gulf War, allowed the military to reduce the number of strike aircraft it required significantly, reducing federal focus on the development of new aircraft and further limiting the ability of aircraft makers to transfer innovation from the military to the civilian sector.

Even in military transport, the military's need for short-distance landing capability (C-17) created a divergence from civilian airliner prototypes that could use longer runways. The one type of military aircraft that could be used both for civilian and military purposes was the military tanker, which can double as a civilian transport plane. This seemed readily transferable between the two sectors, but contracts over the past decade for military tankers became bogged down in a long-term procurement battle.[41] To be sure, some underlying technologies are transferable between sectors; composites; "fly by wire" (electronic as opposed to hydraulic controls), GPS navigation, and various engine advances have been shared. Overall, however, the close convergence and mutual support between the military and civilian sectors, which historically was highly productive, has declined significantly.

The aircraft manufacturing industry has consolidated as well. Boeing is the only remaining US maker of civil aircraft, and there are only two US jet engine makers. Globally, Europe has one civil aircraft maker and one engine maker, and those in Russia face financial challenges. There are successful and growing makers of smaller civil transport aircraft in Canada and Brazil, component makers in Asia, and a potentially emerging aircraft sector in China. With the US military's cancellation of the procurement of the F-22 as a new generation of interceptor to replace the F-15, only one aircraft is now under development for the military: the F-35 Joint Strike Fighter. This aircraft has been long delayed, requiring a two-decade design and development process, and rapidly rising per-unit costs have sharply curtailed the number of planes likely to be purchased by the military.[42] Aside from unmanned aerial vehicles (UAVs), a classic disruptive innovation, no new fixed-wing aircraft are under design in the United States for either civilian or military needs, probably for the first time in a century. Boeing faced a major struggle in completing development and scaling up production for its newest civilian airliner, the 787, and the military has faced similar problems with the F-35; the drawing boards are now largely empty.

While incremental advances are being achieved in composite materials and improved avionics, overall larger scale innovation is on the decline in air transport. The cause is largely the market imperfection of *lumpiness*: the requirement for large-scale, engineering-intensive investments to develop advanced new aircraft prototypes, which are no longer financed by the military at traditional rates. While supersonic airliners could cut travel time on long-distance routes, for example, these time savings cannot be priced high enough to offset the major additional development costs and higher operating costs. A possible priority for such a larger scale undertaking would be R & D leading to the design and manufacture of an aircraft with much wider body and much larger carrying capacity that could transport significantly more people or cargo without much more (or reduced) fuel load. This would be of interest both for military and civilian applications. It would require significant research on airframe design, materials, aerodynamics research, and engine efficiency. But this is only at the idea stage.

Breakthrough innovation is now being sought in one area in aviation: developing a nonpetroleum fuel source, essentially a secondary innovation in the energy sector. This is an area where the older model of defense technology leadership benefiting the civilian aircraft sector could again come to bear. As the military faces both strategic and tactical problems because of its dependence on petroleum, it is working to develop biofuels for operational energy as an alternative source. Although petroleum resources in North America are expanding, oil is a commodity in a global market that faces growing demand and therefore remains subject to price spikes and supply vulnerabilities.

The military is reviewing applications for its tactical weapon systems, particularly aircraft, but also for combat ships and vehicles and supporting equipment. The navy has been a leader in this effort; navy secretary Ray Mabus has worked toward operating a carrier task force, including its aircraft and support ships, on biofuels, and over time extending this technology to the rest of the fleet.[43] Using Defense Production Act powers, the DOD has teamed with the DOE and the Department of Agriculture in creating pilot plants to test processing technologies for a series of nonfood biofuels ("farm to fleet").[44] Although the program has faced resistance over costs from conservatives in Congress, support from farm interests has tended to offset this, and the navy has continued to move ahead.[45] Debate has sharpened, however, with the recent advent of a US net export position in petroleum products.[46]

Fuel constitutes some 40% of the costs of the civilian airline industry; volatile oil prices have brought the industry to the brink of collapse several times in recent decades. Like the military, the industry is interested in an alternative fuel. However, the civilian airline sector is undercapitalized and is not equipped to undertake a research-and-development effort. Because of the vast number of existing aircraft and the low rate of fleet turnover, any alternative fuel that is developed must operate in existing engines—it must be a "drop in" fuel. Engine makers are interested and prepared to cooperate, but are awaiting military research, development, and procurement.

While the civilian sector will cooperate and is interested in the results, continued defense leadership as the change agent will be mandatory if progress is to be made. The Department of Defense could apply its traditional systems approach to this effort, as it has in many other sectors. It could undertake the research, the development, the prototyping, the demonstrations, and the test bed analysis, and then create an initial market for a new technology, using patient capital outside of market pressures. As we have pointed out in chapter 3, this "extended pipeline," system-wide approach to innovation enabled the DOD to lead American technological advance in the second half of the 20th century in such areas as space, nuclear power, computing, and the Internet.

What are the technical issues facing the DOD if it were to undertake such an approach in biofuels? The established Fischer-Tropsch methods of processing coal, biomass, or a combination for biofuels have limited advantages for reducing greenhouse gas emissions.[47] Interest has therefore shifted to research and development in hydro-treated renewable jet fuels.[48] Among these, algae may over time prove the most promising biofuel candidate, because they have high oil content and do not require the diversion of croplands for production. However, the research and development in this area will require considerable time and additional investment; it will need to drive down production costs to be competitive with oil. A Rand study[49] found that the prospects are uncertain for the commercial production of alternative fuels at a level adequate to meet military goals by 2020. Efforts by the military to test and certify alternative fuels are ahead of actual commercial development and new infrastructure for such fuels. The Rand authors also argued, although some in the military argue otherwise, that DOD goals for alternative fuel use in tactical weapons systems should be based on potential national benefits because the department itself can likely continue to access petroleum fuels despite any supply threat; it can obtain priority access even if it has to pay a premium price.

Air transport faces impediments to innovation due to the requirement for *economies of scale*, and therefore may require special intervention to bring down unit costs, improve performance, or organize the market for complementary products and fuel supply infrastructure. This, combined with the impediment of *lumpiness* in the form of the requirement for massive engineering-intensive investments, makes innovation increasingly difficult.

In sum, innovation in air transport has traditionally evolved through military support of the sector. But the introduction of new military aircraft has dramatically slowed and the introduction of new aircraft for civilian transport has slowed in parallel. The shift from petroleum to biofuels may be the most significant area of pending innovation for air transport. As suggested above, these benefits could be significant: mitigating the economic effects on civilian and military air transport of their exclusive dependence on petroleum-based fuels. This would strengthen the air transport system and aid in reducing CO_2 emissions.

However, only the military is equipped to make the large-scale, systemic investment required. Even for the military, the new technologies for accessing gas and oil supplies have removed much of the pressure for developing alternative fuels. The civil transport sector is ready to cooperate, but it remains to be seen whether the military will muster the scale of effort and longer term focus required of a change agent. This constitutes an innovation impediment due to *nonappropriability*; neither the private nor the governmental aviation sectors may be able to fully realize the societal or economic benefits.

DRIVERLESS CARS AND INTELLIGENT TRANSPORTATION SYSTEMS

Imagine traveling along an interstate at 60 mph and seeing the driver in car in front of you take his hands of the steering wheel, climb into the back seat and watch a movie. We are starting to approach the technological capabilities to enable driverless cars (or automated vehicles), a key potential component in "Intelligent Transportation Systems" (ITS).[50] But there isn't one single legacy sector here to transform; rather there is a whole collection of them, a fact that complicates the problem and makes this technology an interesting variant of the legacy sector problem. Will the affected legacy *sectors*—automotive, insurance, regulatory, and legal—be willing to be enablers of this promising innovation?

Automated vehicle ITS come about because of the inherent inefficiency of the automobile. Cars evolved by simply replacing the horse with internal combustion engines to create horseless carriages. These have proved to be inherently highly inefficient. Why did we have to come up with a 3,000-pound vehicle to transport a 170-pound person? A huge amount of wasted energy is required to move this excessive mass. While a car moving at say, 2 mph may in principle have to stay only a few inches behind the next car, the headway required between cars grows as speeds increase because braking distances multiply with the square of the speed and because human reflexes take time to click in to brake and slow the vehicle. These requirements make the space required to move a person in a car at 60 mph resemble the length of a small train; yet all this space typically moves only one person because most driving is solo. Altering headway distances through ITS could significantly improve fuel efficiency. ITS could also program system software to make fuel efficiency an engine priority, and linking vehicles together into chains sharing engine power could also increase efficiency.

Mass transportation radically reduces the inherent inefficiencies of the auto. But the other surface transportation options—train, light rail, subway, or bus travel, which improve the efficiency in weight, energy, and space per person, are largely limited to prescribed routes and schedules. In the end, while societally advantageous, they are not as personally convenient as a car in which a driver can select his or her own destination, route, and timing. Given the convenience factor, most people will not be willing to surrender their cars, and governments are unlikely politically to require them to do so.[51] So cars will not disappear any time soon. But could cars be made more like mass transit without their drivers having to give up their personal convenience?

Driving is often repetitive and boring, and increasing amounts of time in ever-growing metropolitan areas worldwide are spent in congested, stop-and-go traffic, interrupted by the occasional accident. Traffic conditions in places like Cairo or Shanghai resemble living nightmares of both danger and congestion. In Moscow, traffic jams can last for a day or more. In an increasing number of urban areas, driving resembles the definition of military combat: countless hours of congestion boredom followed by seconds of terror. If you live in an area of especially heavy traffic congestion, you multiply the moments of terror. Could all the time spent in congestion be more productively used? Could safety be improved?

A major motivation for automating vehicles is that removing human error could avoid nearly all of the 371,104 traffic deaths over the previous decade in the United States.[52] Driverless cars are based on the assumption that computers can compute and link to automatic, drive-by-wire car braking and operating systems far faster than human braking reflexes. Computer-operated driverless cars could also significantly reduce the congestion inefficiency of cars by cutting headways; in theory, cars could travel at 60 mph only inches apart. To accommodate that fundamental feature of American civilization, the song of the open road and the unwritten "constitutional right" to road freedom, drivers presumably could revert to hands-on control whenever they chose.

Where does driverless car technology stand? The US military is very interested in driverless vehicles because the majority of the 8,148 deaths in the conflicts in Iraq and Afghanistan have been in vehicles, often in supply convoys hit by small, cheap hidden mines. DARPA's 2007 "Urban Challenge"[53] came out of this problem; DARPA invited teams, nearly all from university computer science departments, to compete to develop driverless vehicles and operate them in a performance contest in the Nevada landscape designed to replicate urban driving conditions. While DARPA distributed GPS (Global Positioning System) points of the driverless route in advance of the contest, one team developed both GPS location identification technology linked to responsive automatic car operating technology ("drive-by-wire"), and tied it to a Light Detection and Ranging (LIDAR) pulsed laser to develop three-dimensional data about objects. It also developed other technologies that enabled its vehicle to "read" the road, traffic, and obstacles as well as travel between GPS points.[54]

Although DARPA conducted no follow-on research program, this contest nonetheless nurtured groups around the country interested in the problem. The technology now emerging will likely combine GPS, LIDAR, and Ground Penetrating Radar (GPR).[55] The reasons are as follows. Driverless vehicles must grasp their location well enough to remain within a travel lane. The existing sensor system for this level of identifying vehicle location ("localization") consists of, to use the unavoidable technical terms, GPS/INS (Inertial Navigation System) units, which in turn can be tied to LIDAR 3D scan matching (laser-based remote sensing technology for measuring distances),[56] with prior image registration linked to the scan matching.

However, even high-performance GPS/INS units today must operate in relatively clear skies and even then may not be able to determine locations well enough to keep a vehicle in its lane. Performance further declines when GPS reception is limited by trees or buildings, or when the vehicle is moving in tunnels or underpasses or under bridges. Performance significantly improves in reasonably good weather when GPS/INS is linked to 3D LIDAR, which maps the road surface and distances, enabling the driver not only to locate but also to "see," a feature known as "feature mapping." However, there are still problems when the road surface is obscured by obstacles like other vehicles or people, or by heavy rain, snow, ice, dust, fog, or smoke, in which case image registration deteriorates.

LIDAR can be augmented by GPR to read below-surface conditions like snow-covered roads; route options can be premapped and then can be "read" as the vehicle travels with a unit mounted under it. This gets around the image registration problems. Already used in civil engineering, geophysical evaluation, and forensics, GPR can assist significantly in solving the localization problem. Even this technology has gaps. It has problems with bridges and metal road surfaces that are reflective, and with soil absorbency that can affect radar signals. So redundant systems will be required for optimal performance under a range of driving conditions.

The cost of these systems, moreover, presents a significant barrier to implementation. GPS/INS can cost over $60,000, depending on the capability of the unit. LIDAR adds approximately $75,000 to that cost, and GPR can cost $50,000.[57] Clearly, these systems are not ready for adoption for average family travel until they go through a major effort to move down the cost curve.

But do all vehicles have to be autonomous? There could also be communication and collaboration between vehicles, where highly equipped vehicles can lead others, or road networks equipped with sensor and communication systems that can link to vehicles to enable them to move together in "platoons." These vehicle-to-vehicle and embedded communications could also help to get around the problem that fleet turnover in the auto industry is quite slow—approximately 15 years—so that autos can only gradually be equipped with driverless technology. However, these intervehicle tracking systems could raise significant privacy issues. Information on exactly where vehicles have traveled at what times will be transmitted and recorded. Autonomous vehicle technology is more attractive from a privacy standpoint but faces a more gradual introduction rate.

Despite its promise, driverless car technology faces a significant legacy sector *collective action* problem. The auto industry will likely view driverless cars as "paradigm compatible" and a number of major auto companies are interested and experimenting with these technologies, including General Motors, Volvo, Volkswagen, Daimler-Benz, and Toyota, as are auto OEM (original equipment manufacturer) suppliers such as Delphi and Continental. Outside the auto sector, Google has undertaken vehicle experiments, and a series of start-ups are interested and developing IT-based applications. There were some 100 experimental driverless vehicles traveling US roads as of 2013. But these firms are by no means the only players. A wide range of federal, state, and local governments that regulate transportation, auto safety and insurance must actively participate and collaborate if this technology is to be introduced successfully, as must the insurance industry and the legal and liability system.

The situation cries out for an effective *change agent* to orchestrate the many actors. Could this collective action problem be mitigated through the Department of Defense? The DOD is very interested in R & D in this area, and the technologies developed to date—GPS and radar—have developed from the defense innovation system. While military stealth technology has to date had only military applications, "inverse stealth technology" could increase the radar signature of vehicles so as to make vehicles much more visible on each other's radar systems and in this way improve the reliability and safety of driverless systems. The DOD interest could over time assist both incremental advances in technology and in driving the needed technologies down the cost curve, a critical task. Despite the defense interest, it will be extremely difficult to get this multitude of sectors to align to accommodate this complex and potentially extremely dangerous technology to the point where it is fully tested and reliable. In this case, the legacy sector problem isn't from the technology user industry, but rather from the wide range of other sectors that must enter into the innovation process.

Aside from the market imperfection problem of *collective action*, there are a series of other legacy sector elements that affect the prospects for driverless cars. *Established infrastructure and governmental institutional architecture* is completely oriented to existing live-driver systems and will have to be completely rethought and revised to allow driverless cars; this imposes major regulatory hurdles on sector entrants. While three states (California, Nevada, and Florida) as of 2013 have allowed driverless vehicles on their roads, to create a market, even a niche market, many more states will have to adopt this position, as well as to adjust a long list of other regulatory provisions.[58]

Politically powerful vested interests, reinforced by public support are present as well. In particular, the legal system will resist the introduction of a new system after over a century of evolving an intricate tort law system to cover autos and trucks. Legal costs, including those of litigation, can make the introduction of a new technology prohibitively expensive, and lawyers are likely to use their ability to sue to resist innovations that disrupt lucrative tort business models, as they did in the 1970s when they blocked no-fault auto insurance reforms. This having been said, there are real legal issues that need to be resolved. If a driverless car misbehaves and does damage—or worse, kills or injures someone—whom does the injured party sue? The owner of the car that did the damage? Its manufacturer? The company that made the sensors or the software? The resulting litigation will take years to sort out in the courts and create corresponding uncertainty, with the possibility of different answers in different jurisdictions

The capital costs connected with the introduction of driverless cars will be significant but the *financing system for innovations* is organized around an IT sector timeline that does not fit capital-intensive legacy sector innovations. While the major auto companies can leverage off of advances in military technology and likely can raise capital, investment in public infrastructure will be needed as well for nonautonomous vehicle approaches (such as sensor systems embedded into roadways) at major additional expense to the state and local governments that manage road infrastructure. New entrants from the IT or other industries may be needed to drive the technology applications that are outside the scope of auto industry expertise. They will be deterred if the timeline for this sector to reach scale and for production to drive down initial high technology costs for vehicle systems is well beyond the venture capital timetable, although niche interim technologies and niche sectors could fit, for example, in off-road applications.

Public habits and expectations are attuned to the existing technology; the public will be willing to accept interim advances but it may be some time before they are prepared to accept the unfamiliarity and the risks of truly driverless technology. There is also *an established knowledge and human resources structure* oriented to the needs of the existing system; the new sector will need a talent base to implement and maintain advances; it will face delays as educational curricula, career paths, and professional standards in new technical fields become oriented to the needs of new technology.

There are other *market imperfections* beyond collective action requirements present as well. *Network economies* could be an issue; if there is to be continuous communication between vehicles, a vast system of potentially expensive and highly reliable wireless cyber connections will be required; gaps and interruptions in wireless communication cannot be tolerated and will have to be resolved. Here, a major obstacle will be the absence of agreed standards that facilitate interoperability within an ITS network. *Lumpiness* could be an issue because vehicle ITS will require substantial minimum investments in order to be introduced at scale. While there isn't a set of direct competitors, ITS still must be the subject of full-sized, expensive, and risky demonstrations to prove techno-economic feasibility and, particularly, safety. Finally, there are significant barriers to driverless ITS because of the need to effect *economies of scale*; special interventions—including some by government—may be needed to bring down unit costs, improve performance, and to organize the market for complementary products and infrastructure. A significant array of technology suppliers, component makers, and production facilities will be need to needed to introduce driverless technologies into a substantial part of the auto and truck fleet. The cost, the complexity and the required economies of scale involved in assembling this vast production system or "value network" will be significant.

In summary, there are substantial barriers to ITS implementation due to a series of established technological/economic/political/social paradigms in a large group of affected economic sectors. The auto sector may view ITS as a "paradigm-compatible" innovation that can improve the utility of its product line by making it less prone to congestion and potentially safer, and the insurance sector may view it as potentially improving auto safety and so reducing the industry's risk. However, other sectors may be harder to bring along—particularly the dense and decentralized legal and regulatory sectors across an array of political jurisdictions, which have only limited incentives to collaborate.[59] This "legacy network" makes accommodating driverless vehicles complex from a policy perspective.

How could this new technology evolve? Incremental advances can already be seen in components that are required for driverless vehicles and that also aid live drivers. These include automatic braking systems, GPS navigation systems in cars, video cameras to assist backing up, and automatic parking features. Live-driver cars could use radar, linked to automatic braking, that identifies objects and other vehicles. Mercedes Benz vehicles are already introducing computer, radar, and sensor technologies that both warn of potential collisions and automatically adopt collision avoidance braking, that preclude lane changes when another vehicle is in a "blind spot" and automatically position the vehicle in a lane and block unintentional swerves out of that lane. Daimler Benz is thus using its high-cost vehicles to introduce these technologies, in effect "selling safety," and using this system to drive these technologies down the cost curve for more widespread application. If these technologies can be shown to reduce collisions, insurance firms may offer discounts to customers adopting them, and governments may move toward regulatory requirements for those with most life-saving potential, as they did for seat belts and airbags. Automobiles are already starting to embed as much software code as fighter aircraft and these new technologies will accelerate the trend. After-market introduction is possible for a number of these technologies; they don't all have to be embedded when the car is produced. Because auto companies historically are not IT-oriented, a growing number of IT and sensor start-ups are entering this new sector as suppliers and acquisitions. The staid and stable auto sector overall is starting to look more interesting with new forms of auto usage and sharing, apart from traditional ownership, emerging in cities (Uber and Zipcars, for example), and even new start-ups (like Tesla). The IT-sensor start-up firms are a new wave of secondary technology entrants contributing new incremental IT-based safety features.

If we build up enough such features and capabilities, could there be a day when people other than professional test drivers take their hands off the wheel? More likely, there could be niche users, with highly equipped vehicles introduced into specialized sectors already prepared to invest in expensive vehicles, including mining, surveying, agriculture, military combat, and off-road trucking. Low-speed shuttles on defined routes are another possible niche market.[60] In parallel, incremental advances in automatic safety technologies for driver vehicles will also contribute. Once progress in such niche markets is in hand and costs reduced, the technologies can scale into broader applications. However, even these incremental advances that are compatible with existing vehicle paradigms and niche markets will still face a "legacy network" before the first drivers on public highways can take their hands off the wheel.

MANUFACTURING

Manufacturing is both an important part of the innovation process and a critical enabler of innovation. It also constitutes a legacy sector that suffers from systemic problems that pose obstacles to the introduction of innovation. This point needs emphasis: if manufacturing is both a critical stage of the innovation process *and* embedded with a legacy sector's resistance to innovation, this is a major innovation system problem for the United States and worthy of major policy attention. American manufacturing is hollowing out, and also may be at the heart of a series of problems in the strength of the US economy, as we have explained in detail in chapter 4. Absent transformative innovative inputs in process technologies that improve production efficiency and productivity, the future of this sector in the United States is in jeopardy, which in turn affects its innovation system. What are some of the problems the US manufacturing sector is facing?

The disconnect between innovation and production: the United States generally has failed to understand that manufacturing constitutes an important part of the innovation process.[61] This is a fragmented, disconnected view; innovation demands to be looked at as a system, from research through production. Initial production is a highly sophisticated stage, requiring complex engineering, often extensive reworking of the initial R & D, and complex feedback loops between research, development, and both design and production engineering. In contrast, Germany has a culture of engineering and Japan of artisanship and quality that embrace histories of innovation in production and success in manufacturing. Both nations have higher wage and higher cost manufacturing sectors than the United States. Yet both have run major trade surpluses in manufactured goods, whereas the United States has run large deficits.[62]

Despite the deep American strength in manufacturing in the 19th and the first half of the 20th centuries, US innovation since World War II and the Cold War has become front-end loaded, largely focused on early-stage R & D. In industries in which an innovation system must also encompass the back end—the prototype, demonstration, test bed, and initial production phases—the United States has a gap.[63] China, which has passed the United States in manufacturing net output, is focused on the back end of innovation, particularly on production, as it works to build its front-end R & D system. Although many have assumed that China has achieved its leadership in production through lower wages and costs, recent work suggests that it is able to rapidly scale up production volume through advanced processes that are integrated across regional firms and tied to system efficiencies and cost saving.[64] Given the connections we explored earlier between manufacturing and innovation, the US failure to treat production as a critical and integral element of the innovation system rather than an afterthought risks erosion of its comparative advantage in innovation.

The thinned-out ecosystem: As a major MIT report has argued, the US ecosystem for manufacturing has been eroding.[65] For three decades, the United States has been thinning out its manufacturing sector. Formerly, it had firms and supply chains that were much more vertically linked, supporting a kind of "commons" where larger firms tended to support their small and mid-sized suppliers in the development of best practices in processes and technologies, as well as in workforce training. A major cause of this change has been a model of financial services focused on short-term returns and risk avoidance that has led firms to emphasize "core competency" and "asset-light" approaches to business strategy.[66] Increasingly, the 2013 MIT report found, small and mid-sized firms are "home alone," lacking the support systems that used to enable them to scale up efficient production more speedily.

The production scale-up problem: There is a gap in the financing system for manufacturing. The many industrial sectors in the United States have three kinds of firms in common. The first are major multinational corporations (MNCs), a category that the United States still dominates. These firms are affected by a financial model that drives them toward core competency and the correspondingly thinned-out ecosystem discussed earlier. They are global, must be active in all global markets, and can seek production efficiencies by producing in lower cost nations, especially those with expanding markets.

The second and third categories of US manufacturing firms are more vulnerable. The second category encompasses the 300,000 small and midsize enterprises (SMEs)—"Main Street" firms—that perform the majority of US manufacturing. Although they are typically undercapitalized and must be risk averse in order to survive, these firms can be quite innovative. While they typically do not perform science-based R & D, the MIT report, evaluating high-performing firms from a sample of over 3,000 production firms that doubled their revenues in a difficult financial period from 2000 to 2010, found that these firms, for example, can be quite good at repurposing existing technologies into new markets or at reengineering existing product lines.[67] The problem lies in the fact that they have difficulty in obtaining financing to scale up their innovations. The MIT report found that they must finance these primarily out of ongoing revenues because "local banking," the system by which the local bank historically understood its local industrial customers, has been largely displaced by national and indeed international banking models that are disconnected from local customers. This means that the capacity of Main Street firms to scale-up the production of their innovations is declining, slowing the introduction of these innovations, in contrast to the rapid scale-up that China has achieved.

The third category of firms comprises the start-up and entrepreneurial firms that manufacture products based on their own new technologies. The MIT report studied a group of highly innovative such firms and found that these also have a problem in scaling up production.[68] While their innovations can command venture capital funding, their venture firms lack the financing capacity to stand up significant production. As explained in chapter 5, venture firms are typically on a timetable that is well suited to the IT firms that have historically led the sector, in which the technology becomes a product after five to seven years. The MIT study suggests that many venture firms do not abandon their start-up firms after more than five to seven years, but rather put them into what could be termed "income maintenance." This means that when such firms ask the venture firm for financing for scale-up to actual production, they are usually told that no, the venture firm lacks the depth to finance the capital requirements required for investment in local production, and they are often referred to contract manufacturers in Asia.

This has important implications. The initial stage of production involves significant engineering and innovation. The US firm's innovation team often spends significant time abroad with the contract manufacturer; much of the innovation is transferred in that process, and the capability for follow-on incremental advances shifts overseas. So while the start-up may have its technology produced and enter into markets, important aspects of its "know-how" move offshore; this means that when production capability shifts, significant aspects of innovation capability shift with it. These advanced technology start-up firms represent the next generation of US technology firms; this gap in scale-up financing means that important in-depth features may be transferred abroad, and may become the basis for future major innovations in both processes and products.

Workforce talent: The MIT study found that three-quarters of US manufacturing firms were able to fill vacancies in less than a month; one-quarter took longer.[69] While this shows there is no overall shortage of manufacturing workers—after all, the United States lost over 30% of its manufacturing workforce in the past decade—the fact that one-quarter of these firms faced hiring delays is interesting, as they tend to include the firms involved in more innovative technologies and advanced manufacturing processes. This means that a gap in workforce skills may be emerging in high-end production. If the United States needs to shift to advanced manufacturing to compete, more attention to skills training in these areas is required. In addition, there is a significant demographic problem ahead; the manufacturing workforce is aging and will need replacing and training.

Contrast with Germany: Most Americans believe that it is foreordained that they must lose manufacturing jobs to low-cost, low-wage competitors in Asia because the United States is a high-cost, high-wage producer. But Germany is also high-cost and high-wage. Wages in Germany are some 60% higher than the United States, and yet it runs a major surplus in manufactured goods, including a significant surplus with China. The MIT study found that Germany has moved in the opposite direction from the developments in the United States that are described above.[70] It emphasizes advanced engineering in its production system, seeing it as critical to innovation. It is deepening its manufacturing ecosystem. Its small and large firms use strong collaboration networks, sharing R & D in a joint industry-government-university support system focused around its system of Fraunhofer Institutes. It retains strong regional and local banking, with close ties between its producers and financing institutions, so that production scale-up is not a major issue. It retains a strong workforce training system based around apprenticeships; it may have the strongest skilled workforce system in the world. While some German practices, such as the Fraunhofer system, could fit into US practice, the multiyear apprenticeship system, anchored in a workforce that is 80% unionized with union training requirements, doesn't readily fit US approaches to training. But overall industrial strength in Germany, despite its high costs, demonstrates that a highly developed nation can stay industrialized. In short, it's not a mission impossible.

Innovation in production: Historically, nations that have succeeded to manufacturing leadership have created new production technology paradigms, and have combined these with new process and business models to support them.[71] These are technological paradigms because they constitute a combination of technological advance with supporting policies, incentives, and institutional linkages, as suggested in chapter 3, along with implementing process and business models. This was the means that Britain used to achieve leadership of the Industrial Revolution built around steam engine and textile machinery,[72] for America's manufacturing leadership starting in the second half of the 19th century through interchangeable, machine-made parts and mass production capability serving the first continental-sized market and mass middle class,[73] and for Japan's consumer electronics and auto leadership, which was achieved in the 1970s and 1980s through its paradigm of high-quality production.[74]

The United States could compete with low-cost, low-wage, increasingly innovative emerging nations by slashing its wage base and lowering its standard of living, but this is not an appealing course. The alternative is to improve its manufacturing productivity and efficiency to be cost competitive. There appear to be new manufacturing paradigms at hand that could play roles in transforming production.[75]

But to get to these production innovations, the United States must find ways across a series of barriers created by the legacy sector features in its manufacturing system. Many of the problems discussed above—the disconnect between innovation and production, the thinned-out manufacturing ecosystem, the production scale-up problem, the workforce talent issue, and the need for new innovation in production—derive from legacy sector characteristics. This needs fleshing out: how do these manufacturing issues translate, then, into the characteristics of a legacy sector that we have previously identified?

US Manufacturing as a Legacy Sector

The barriers faced by American manufacturing, set forth in the previous section, exemplify the characteristics of established technological/economic/political/ social paradigms that define legacy sectors, as we have explored in the previous chapter.

First, US manufacturing is subject to a *"perverse" price structure* in that the currencies of its chief competing countries, specifically China, Japan, and Germany, are undervalued relative to the dollar, giving their exports an advantage over US products. This statement requires some historical background. The dollar was in a strong position relative to other currencies as a result of the dominant position of the US economy as the world emerged from World War II. It regained its strength through its leadership of the information technology innovation wave in the 1990s. While a strong dollar demonstrated economic strength, it also tended to penalize production sectors by raising prices in foreign currencies and in this way limiting their exports. The problem is exacerbated because some nations, earlier Japan and now China, have devalued their currencies against the dollar to capture production advantage.

The current problem, therefore, lies in the fact that China has intervened in different ways to lower the value of its currency so as to enable its goods to gain entry into US markets.[76] At the same time, China is the leading purchaser of US debt, which has grown significantly in the past decade and a half exacerbated by the fact that the United States imports much more than it exports. The two countries are now locked in curious embrace. China needs to continue to buy US debt in order to keep its exchange rate low, its products competitive, its growth rates high, and its political system stable. Because the Chinese are, in effect, America's bankers, the United States has been in a weak position to complain about China's intervention in currency markets. (China has announced its intention to move away from this position, and is gradually doing so.) Japan had long engaged in similar practices; the United States acquiesced in its doing so because of the country's geopolitical and strategic importance as an ally.

Germany, the largest European economy, gains its advantage through a different mechanism, namely through its participation in the euro zone, which includes the much weaker economies of southern Europe. If Germany still retained its own currency, it would have a much higher value. Its membership in the euro effectively lowers the prices of Germany's manufactured goods, giving them an artificial advantage over US products.

These currency problems with China, Japan, and Germany, the major US competitors in manufactured exports, are politically hard to alter. As will be further discussed in chapter 9, China also keeps energy prices low and makes low-cost capital available to favored industries. While in other sectors in the US economy discussed in this chapter, the system of perverse prices typically centers on the ability of legacy technologies to underprice and block new entrant technologies and to ignore the effects of externalities like environmental damage for which others must pay, the world manufacturing sector works the opposite way for the United States, effectively raising its prices against key competitors in produced goods, forcing the United States toward either sectoral decline or efficiency gains to offset its exchange rate disadvantages.

US manufacturing is also characterized by an *established institutional architecture* that discriminates against new entrants, the second typical characteristic of a legacy sector. Here the key obstacles to innovation lie in the structure of the financial services that serve the different kinds of industry. As described above, SMEs, the Main Street firms that often act as suppliers and component makers, and the start-up and entrepreneurial firms that typically develop new technologies, face significant difficulty in obtaining financing for the scale-up of production.[77] Multinational corporations have been disinvesting in plant and equipment[78] and thinning out the system of support for manufacturing in the United States, in part to produce near their main expanding markets and in part because the financial system is driving them to maximize short-term returns by focusing on their "core competency," producing abroad with contract manufacturers and spinning off "noncore assets." This "asset light" structure is intended to reduce risk and to maximize short-term returns on a reduced capital base.[79] This strategy in turn profoundly affects their supplier and component makers, the small and medium-sized "Main Street" firms that must now survive in a thinned-out ecosystem with less of a "commons" of support.[80] These firms in turn are further affected by the shift to more national and international banking and away from the traditional local banks that understood and were loyal to their producer customers and were active in the regional economy.

The end result of this process is an *innovation time horizon* for manufacturing that is substantially longer than the financial system is prepared to support, another typical characteristic of a legacy sector. Start-ups trying to bring innovative technologies to market often find themselves in a multiyear process of product design and unable to obtain venture capital support for scaling up to production.[81] Venture firms lack the capital depth to finance the costly stage of initial production and frequently point their start-ups toward contract manufacturers abroad,[82] severing the stages of innovation and production from each other. In sum, the architecture of established financial institutions curtails or slows the introduction of innovations in multinationals, Main Street firms, and start-ups.

Manufacturing also contains *powerful vested interests*. Major firms tend to dominate their sectors—for example, the big auto companies—and therefore still tend to dictate to their networks of suppliers, including veto power over the level of innovation they will accept. Many multinationals, under pressure to engage in distributed manufacturing following a short-term, asset-light financial model, have tended to abandon their US supply chains and distribute production abroad.

Therefore they have not been in a position to promote innovation-based production efficiencies at home, tending to defend the existing distributed production paradigm and to resist the introduction of innovations in production, such as the new advanced manufacturing production methods, that threaten their business models. So the multinationals don't have to innovate in production because they can achieve cost gains and stay competitive by producing abroad in nations with low wages and low production costs, using low-cost contract producers or locating their own production abroad. Thus, many have tended to be *averse to innovation*, to *underinvest in R & D*, and to be locked into existing systems of production, and so have relieved themselves from having to pursue expensive and higher risk innovations that could lead to productivity gains and efficiencies in the United States.

Inattention to manufacturing innovation as an economic priority has been *sustained by public habits and expectations*. As we have explained earlier, manufacturing itself is not well understood as an aspect of innovation. The American public tends to believe that the United States is fated to lose manufacturing because it can't compete with low-wage nations like China. They aren't alone; the economics profession in particular has largely missed the economic importance of manufacturing. Christina Romer, for example, spoke for most neoclassical economists in a widely distributed column written shortly after her departure as chair of the President's Council of Economic Advisors, arguing against making manufacturing an economic priority.[83] Although Adam Smith accorded added value to manufacturing over other sectors,[84] Romer's piece reminded many of the problems neoclassical economics has had in differentiating between the value of producing "potato chips versus computer chips"[85]—that is, the economic value of producing a low-value commodity good versus a high-value, complex good that enhances productivity. In contrast, we argue that production is a critical way that an economy can scale its growth.[86] In addition, the growing fused production-services model, tying goods to services so both become tradable and scalable, is increasingly important to both sectors. Yet few in the public or in the policy community, as illustrated by the problems cited above with neoclassical economists, grasp the implications of these distinctions.

Manufacturing also contains a *knowledge and human resources structure* that hinders innovation in production processes. At all levels from workforce to engineering, the US training system has suffered from the thinning out of the industrial ecosystem. With the sharp decline of manufacturing jobs, unions have pursued unionization of service sectors and placed less emphasis on their traditional industrial job base, decreasing the organizational and political pressures for strong programs of worker training. Public schools have largely abandoned vocational education. Engineering education lacks a significant focus on production.[87] Not surprisingly, a recent survey of undergraduate students found that only 50% of engineering students and 20% of math and science students found manufacturing an attractive career option.[88] As a result, the manufacturing employment demographic is aging. It will be harder to introduce new technologies and processes into production unless the declining talent base can be reinvigorated, trained, and educated so as to be ready for new, advanced manufacturing paradigms.

Finally, there is only *limited R & D* being undertaken in manufacturing technologies and related processes, both at the federal level and in industry. While there are technologies evolving, as discussed in chapter 13, that could be transformative and create a new kind of advanced manufacturing, there is little organized focus to date to bring them into the manufacturing sector. Further breakthroughs are required, and those emerging are not yet ready for implementation.

Market Imperfections That Affect Manufacturing

US manufacturing is also characterized by a number of market imperfections characteristic of legacy sectors. In the absence of government intervention, manufacturing faces a critical inability to muster *collective action*. With the manufacturing ecosystem increasingly thinning out and with what Pisano and Shih call "the industrial commons"[89] in decline, as discussed above, the Main Street firms that constitute the majority of US manufacturing increasingly find themselves, in Suzanne Berger's term, "home alone."[90] Collaboration with each other and with major producers becomes increasingly difficult. As we have seen, major manufacturers that are able to move offshore to lower wage and cost economies have limited interest in pursuing productivity gains through innovation in onshore production even though this may be important to Main Street firms.[91] Start-up producers, for their part, are increasingly driven offshore as well because their venture backers cannot finance production scale-up. These deep disconnects between manufacturing sectors complicate the organization of collective efforts around production innovation.

Innovation in US manufacturing faces obstacles derived from additional market imperfections. The first of these is *lumpiness*. New advanced manufacturing technologies require significant investment in equipment, in addition to investments in process innovations to implement the new production technology in a factory, business model development to show its efficiency, and cost reductions to justify the investment. Multinationals can avoid these investments simply by continuing lower tech operations in low-wage countries abroad. For their part, as we have seen, start-up manufacturers and Main Street firms often face a problem of production scale-up financing that is too large for them to handle.

There is a *split incentives* problem here as well. Why should a multinational support the adoption of production innovations or the maintenance of domestic technical services that are of marginal or no net benefit to itself, even though these innovations may be of significant benefit to its onshore supplier and component makers—the Main Street firms—and hence of major overall benefit to the US economy? In other words, the benefits for production innovations may be split—they may accrue primarily to small and midsize firms to enable them to compete with manufacturers abroad, not to the multinationals that have the resources to sponsor their development but that are already partially based abroad. Why should they, in effect, cross-subsidize the smaller firms for the greater benefit of the local economy?

Underlying these problems of lumpiness and split incentives may be issues of *economies of scale*. A dramatic transformation of production systems through new technologies and related processes may require a vast array of resources, suppliers, components, and production capabilities, and distribution, for entry. Nanofabrication, a potential advanced manufacturing paradigm, for example, requires mastery of considerable cost and complexity—with required *economies of scale*—if it is to create a new production system and "value network" around this new paradigm.

In summary, if the US manufacturing sector is to compete through innovation advances in complex, high-value goods—the major driver of wealth in an intensely globalized economy—it faces many of the barriers from existing technological/economic/political/social paradigms and from a set of market imperfections as well. Chapter 13 sets out a series of policy prescriptions for advanced manufacturing to meet these challenges.

7 Applying the Legacy Framework to Service Sectors

Higher Education and Healthcare Delivery

We now turn our focus to the application of our framework to two major service sectors. The US R & D system is organized to focus on goods-related technologies with little attention on service sectors. Partly as a result, the services economy generally experiences significantly lower rates of productivity gains than the production sector. However, if a technological advance can transform the service sector by providing an alternative means of service delivery, the resulting disruption can shake the affected sector to its foundations. Travel agents, for example, were largely displaced by Internet-delivered air travel reservations systems.

The scalability of this kind of technological innovation—that is, the fact that it can rapidly expand its numbers and use—enables it to disrupt a legacy service sector. The critical change takes place when the service—for example an installation, repair, or upgrade—stops being a personal service, delivered person-to-person, one by one, and becomes tied to a tradable good that can be mass produced. When this happens, the service becomes more tradable and scalable and hence more subject to the introduction of disruptive innovation.[1] As discussed in chapter 4, there is an increasing movement toward fusing services and products; if more innovation can be introduced into legacy service sectors, there is an opportunity to improve overall efficiency and growth.

HIGHER EDUCATION

We now examine higher education as a case study of a legacy service sector, considering whether it will be transformed by pending technological developments.

For two thousand years, the talking head—the lecture—has been the dominant learning model in higher education. This is the case in the humanities and social sciences as well as the natural sciences. Occasional advances in technology have supplemented this model. Movable type in the 16th century was the most important of these, allowing widely accessible published materials to supplement the lecture. However, higher education is now facing the introduction of online course delivery at increasing scale.[2] The entry of this new technology has potential for bringing tradable good and service features to higher education, which, depending on how the technology is implemented, could have positive or negative consequences. This carries particular significance because of the importance of higher education to modern society.

Societal Role of Higher Education

Higher education since the industrial revolution has become increasingly tied to societal economic well-being. Harvard economists Claudia Goldin and Lawrence Katz have portrayed the societal advantages and necessity of continually raising the college graduation rate, as briefly noted in chapter 1. Their book, *The Race between Education and Technology*,[3] argues that the continuing advances in industry since the Industrial Revolution require an ever-increasing level of technological skill in the workforce. In effect, there are two curves: an ever-growing curve of the technological advance implemented by industry, and a corresponding curve of the technological skill base in the workforce needed to support this technological advance. In a successful, technologically advanced economy, the societal skill base curve must stay parallel to and ahead of the technology implementation curve.

From this point of view, the rise of American technological and industrial leadership to ascendancy in the closing decades of the 19th century was significantly furthered when the United States became the first nation to develop mass higher education through the passage and implementation of the Morrill Land Grant College Act in 1862. This law created a nationwide system of public higher institutions of education. It was supplemented by the GI Bill following World War II, which in turn moved a growing portion of the middle class through higher education. Together, these two pieces of legislation may have constituted the most important social legislation ever passed in the United States. Mass higher education was a critical step in ensuring that the skill base of the US workforce stayed ahead of the technology implementation curve. Expenditures on higher education amount to 2.6% of US GDP, still the highest percentage in the world.[4]

For a hundred years, the United States kept the education curve ahead of the technology implementation curve, but starting in the late 1970s, it allowed the higher education graduation rate to stagnate. Goldin and Katz argue that this development is a major cause of the growing income disparity in the United States. While the US upper middle class kept ahead of the technological skill curve, increasing its graduation rate, the lower middle and lower classes did not. While not all experts agree,[5] they argue that this created a gap in the skill base, allowing the upper middle class a wage premium and leaving the other classes behind, with an income gap growing in recent decades between the two. Goldin and Katz as well as economist David Autor track these income disparities against the college graduation rate and find a close correlation.[6] Their work suggests the societal importance of higher education; the question here is whether innovation-based solutions might make possible improved graduation rates without debasing the quality of higher education.

Higher Education Cost Structure

The need for a healthy and more economically mobile society is not the only driver of innovation in higher education. Higher education faces what some are calling a perfect storm: (1) rising costs that are met by raising posted tuition rates at a rate well above inflation, a trend that does not appear sustainable in the long term; (2) systematic cuts in state support for public higher education in nearly all states; (3) a student base that faces changing population demographics; and (4) competition from private, for-profit institutions with low-cost faculties and campuses using federal student aid to fund their operations. All four translate into major financial threats to the existing system; because these cost questions are central to whether higher education must innovate, they deserve examination.

Concerning the first point, ever-increasing published prices for tuition and fees—that is, the "sticker price" posted by colleges and universities—have significantly exceeded the national inflation rate.[7] These are the numbers decried by politicians and the media.[8] Colleges respond that when "net tuition"—the sticker price minus student aid—is examined, the picture is not as grim,[9] and public higher education remains less expensive than private or for-profit. Although education can be valued for its own sake, the return to college graduates in additional lifetime earning power compared to those with high school education makes college a very sound investment.[10] The extent of student loans exacerbates the cost problem, although the size of average student loans has not grown greatly in recent years.[11]

Even so, deep cost problems remain. A year in college does take an increasing share of annual incomes, and college nontuition costs are rising as well. With widening income disparity, some families may be affected more than others; while Pell grants and financial aid may create a safety net for most college students from low-income families, students from income levels just above this range may face more problems. The rate of tuition "sticker price" increases, which primarily affect the middle and upper middle class, may not be indefinitely sustainable; when these are coupled with the effects of rising tuition and other costs of education on other parts of the population, schools may find that they are pricing themselves out of markets they need to retain.

The problem of increasing tuition and other costs is particularly acute at the institutions that provide some three-quarters of college education, the public four-year institutions. These schools are facing a steep decline in state support, which is the driving force behind the increases in tuition at public universities. A decade ago, state governments paid about two-thirds of the cost of education at those schools; tuition paid by students and families paid the remainder. Now, states pay only one-third of these costs. Increases in tuition at these public universities closely track the declines in state support. The largest single annual decline in state appropriations to public colleges in a half-century, 7.6%, occurred in 2011–2012. Seventeen states have experienced more than 20% reductions in state support in the past five years; an additional 15 states experienced declines of more than 10%.[12] The third problem is demographics: the number of college-age students (ages 20–24) in the US population will grow more slowly, from 22 million in 2010 to 28 million in 2050, with increased percentages from minorities as the US populations diversifies.[13] To keep its student base up, colleges will need to increasingly embrace students outside the traditional college age bracket.

Higher Education and Baumol's Cost Disease

The data on the "sticker price" of college significantly exceeding inflation rates suggests an analogy to "Baumol's Cost Disease." This concept explains how certain service sectors experience ongoing rises in wages[14] without corresponding productivity gains. While classical economic theory held that wages are tied to productivity gains, William Baumol and William Bowen in studying the performing arts sector in the 1960s[15] identified a different phenomenon: the size of the orchestra it takes to perform a Beethoven symphony today has not significantly changed since 1800. Musicians' wages have risen even though there have been no productivity gains.

Employers in such sectors must compete with wages for talented musicians, so wages escalate; higher education, a profession in which credentials, publications, and research enable capable faculty to seek a premium, has operated in a similar way. Employers in such service sectors have several options: they can increase prices, decrease quality, decrease quantity, or use "volunteers." While decreasing quality is a problematic option for higher education given the competition between institutions and it can't decrease quantity because that would mean fewer students and reduced tuition income, it has systematically increased prices through raising tuition and fees, and employed increasing numbers of "volunteers"—in this case, systematically underpaid "adjunct" part-time faculty.

Higher Education and the Legacy Sector Framework

Higher education fits most of the legacy sector characteristics:

1. It is subject to a cost structure and hence a *price structure* that, due to Baumol's cost disease problem discussed above, has continued to increase its published tuition and fees at a rate higher than any other significant economic sector including healthcare, and created a mismatch with the broader social goal of a highly educated public. (Its demand structure could be characterized as "perverse" in a different sense, namely that the system tends to equate higher tuition with education quality, as with perfume or champagne).
2. It constitutes an *established infrastructure and institutional architecture* based on a "prestige" factor that disadvantages new entrants.

3. It contains *powerful vested interests*—particularly faculties and the academic departments they control—that defend the paradigm, are reluctant to adapt education reforms, and resist innovations that threaten their business models.

4. It has been *averse to innovation*, as a system that conducted almost no R & D on educational reforms that could improve learning—innovation is even harder to adapt if there are no innovations.

5. It is *sustained by public habits and expectations* attuned to existing education approaches.

6. It contains an *established knowledge and human resources structure*—particularly universities, faculties, and departments oriented to their own needs and disciplines and resistant to change.

Higher education is also characterized by the market imperfection of an inability to muster *collective action*. It is very difficult to organize collective efforts around reform of learning because the system is highly decentralized, scattered among thousands of institutions. Even university systems that join public colleges and universities together in a particular state remain quite decentralized, and not all fifty states have organized such systems. The decentralized nature of higher-education institutions means that reforms adopted in one or even some are hard to spread to the others at scale. As is typical of legacy sectors *averse to innovation*, there has been almost no R & D on education reforms, as noted, that could improve learning and hence a dearth of innovations ready for adoption. Nor has there been until recently an obvious potential change agent with the interest and influence to effect reform.

Finally, reform in higher education has been hindered by genuine controversy over the purpose of higher education, which translates into earnest ongoing discussion over how the efficiency and effectiveness of any proposed reform should be judged, even over and above the resistance described above. Are universities to convey marketable skills and information, to educate an informed and conscientious citizenry, to develop in its graduates lifelong intellectual and cultural interests on which they can construct more rewarding lives, or all of the above or something else? In our framework, this controversy hinders innovation in a manner somewhat analogous to the proliferation of standards that besets such potentially disruptive innovations as sustainable agriculture or forestry.

Entry of Online Education Reform

Higher education, largely immune to technological innovation since the invention of the printing press, began to shift in 2012 as online, Internet-based education technology began to scale up in long-established institutions.[16] While online courses have been offered at modest levels at colleges for over a decade and a half, the diffusion of technological advances—particularly broadband access and the prevalence of personal and handheld computing—have changed this landscape.

A key component of this emerging higher educational world is the "massive online open course"—popularly called MOOCs, a term just a few years old.

Early MOOC providers were for-profit firms that saw opportunities to capture higher-education markets. At the University of Phoenix, a leader in online education, total enrollment by 2012 was approximately 308,000. At Kaplan University, another major online provider, enrollment was 78,000. Universities began to respond to this market threat. As of 2014, at Coursera, an initial university MOOC platform originating from computer science faculty at Stanford, over 90 universities from 21 countries now offer at least one course. Coursera adopted a for-profit model and obtained venture funding. In 2013, Udacity, another for-profit MOOC provider developed by Stanford faculty, announced a master's degree in computer science program in conjunction with Georgia Tech and AT&T.

Concerned about the implications of grafting a for-profit approach onto non-profit institutions, the Massachusetts Institute of Technology, later joined by Harvard University, launched edX as a nonprofit educational venture, with $60 million in experimental funding from the two schools. The edX alliance as of 2015 had 54 university members, including ten leading universities in Asia. Each school is creating courses for its own use and the use of others. The edX consortium has posted the courses to universally available websites, making them available without charge, although charges are imposed for students seeking a validated certificate of course completion.

The first edX course, from MIT, was on computer and electronic circuit design, taken directly from MIT's introductory circuit design course. It initially drew some 154,000 participants worldwide. Other MOOC providers saw comparable initial numbers. No one had seen such numbers attending a single course. They continued to rise. Operating since 2012, edX counted its millionth student halfway through 2013. Most of these viewers, however, proved to be "shoppers," testing the buzz and content.[17]

Even so, some 7,000 people eventually completed the edX course for a certificate. Even this number is startling—60% more than MIT's total undergraduate enrollment. Online students completing courses tended to be self-assembling—assisting each other, organizing online and in-person discussion groups. EdX has become the theater, staging the show, with the participating universities developing the course content around evolving edX design standards. EdX is developing and offering the platform and assessment software, serving as the common technical support mechanism.

However, the MOOC business model is by no means clear. Developing quality online courses, assuming they are not mere videos of lectures, is much more expensive and demanding than developing a physical classroom course. Schools are starting to see that alongside their established university they may have to form a "Pixar" branch for the development of online courses. MIT, Harvard, and Stanford can afford for a time the costs of offering these courses for free and making them universally available, but this is not true for most other universities. Most schools offering MOOCs will need to charge more for completion certificates to cover development and presentation costs. These business model issues will be reviewed in detail below.

For a time, many politicians in the United States seemed to feel that MOOCs represented a kind of "new magic"—online higher education for free. Although it was never explicitly stated this way, conservative politicians seemed to be hoping that for-profit online higher education could finally rid the republic of those pesky, left-wing universities. Progressive politicians, on the other hand, seemed to be hoping that MOOCs will end what they view as outrageous university tuition rates, driving tuition through the floor and making higher education more accessible than ever before. This initial overoptimism has been superseded by a backlash, led by faculty groups threatened by potential job loss who have attacked the online model.[18] They realized the pressure to cede education to online courses is growing as states cut funding for higher education to pay for the growth of Medicaid expenditures and prisons. Since some 72% of US higher education is provided by state-funded systems, this is powerful pressure.

Given the pressures of declining state support, unsustainable posted tuition levels, and student population demographic shifts, what will happen to the campus and to residential higher education?[19] Although MOOCs will affect all types of higher education—from community colleges to private colleges to the several tiers of regional state universities to for-profit education providers—we focus here on the first tier, of research universities, public and private, and particularly on education in science, technology, engineering, and mathematics (the STEM fields).

The research university has evolved over the past 150 years or so into the most important home for scientific advance; it is the base system for global knowledge. The research university is a comparatively new creation in the United States, modeled in the late 19th century on the German university and coming into its own through the massive federal investments in research and development during World War II and the subsequent Cold War. The brilliance of this model lay in its combination of research and education, which allowed learning to become hands-on. Research and learning became mutually reinforcing, and learning became continuous. This learning-by-doing model, though remarkably effective, has also contributed to the high cost of undergraduate science education, as students need increasingly expensive laboratories.

The entry of the laboratory into science education was a creation of mid-19th-century reformers such as William Barton Rogers, who helped shift natural science away from the lecture model and its accompanying recitation and memorization.[20] This critical education reform was followed by the introduction of the seminar in the first part of the 20th century. Education philanthropist Edward Harkness, a Standard Oil heir who felt that middle-range students (such as himself) were left out of a system that focused only on students at the top and bottom of classes, funded Phillips Exeter Academy faculty to study Oxford University and Cambridge University as models for education ideas. Finding that the one-on-one tutorial systems at those schools was prohibitively expensive, the Phillips Exeter faculty created the seminar of 12 or so students around an oval "Harkness Table" in the 1930s to bring all participating students into the common discourse. The model spread to the Ivy

League and widely to US universities for upper-level courses. However, the bulk of STEM education is still in lecture-based classes.

MOOCs potentially could reform the lecture model. They may represent a particularly interesting new tool for education in STEM fields because the problem-solving approach to education in these fields may fit more readily into online courses than the emphasis on discourse in humanities or social science courses. Online features can make possible dynamic visualization of data and the ability to interact with that data, allowing better identification of data patterns. It provides new ways for mapping the content and core ideas of a field, with new options for visual representation of both information and concepts. And online can offer tools for real-time assessment of content acquisition and of knowledge transfer and application, together with the ability to improve reinforcement of content.

But online education has serious limitations. Even as online education advances, vital education components will remain face to face for at least a significant time to come. Developing expertise through oral expression and presentations remains especially critical to the learning process. Online education simply cannot handle these discourse aspects of learning very well. Conventional education methods can also more effectively promote written analysis, a key aspect of learning. Machine evaluation of written papers is improving, and edX, for example, has a team working on this technology. But while software can capture key words and rubrics supplied by faculty—what might be called established concepts—it will not be good at recognizing out-of-the-box new ideas or evaluating fresh approaches. For a very long time to come, writing will require human assessment except for the most straightforward assignments.

Conventional education will also remain vital in research, where online capabilities can be limiting. Performing research is central to learning-by-doing in science—indeed, it is what scientists do. Although computer simulations and modeling can capture elements of how to perform research, in many fields the student ultimately needs to be at a lab bench or in the field, interacting with a research team in an apprenticeship and in project-based learning. Online features can enhance research. For example, data visualization and display and computer simulations can be critical tools. MIT has an "iLab" for high school science students where they can run real experiments online from any location on real MIT equipment. But there is no getting around the reality that research in many fields requires critical face-to-face dynamics and interactions with the natural world that will be hard to replace. So relying on online learning alone, perhaps in the name of saving money, could damage learning quality; essential aspects of learning—discourse, writing, and research—still require face-to-face interaction.

Blended Learning

In the end, then, MOOCs may change many things, but they shouldn't be allowed to kill everything. Indeed, for the foreseeable future, as a Department of Education study found in 2010,[21] the most effective education will combine online and face-to-face approaches into "blended learning" that captures the best of both worlds.

In this scenario, online education will continue to evolve. In some ways, it will become better at doing some of the jobs that are the hallmarks of conventional education. For example, with growing broadband capability, it will be possible to make online discussion groups easier to assemble and more dynamic. Videos will increasingly be able to use high-definition capability for improved realism. Machine evaluation of writing will get better. Even now, for shorter papers—where software can increasingly evaluate key word use, rubrics, and core concepts—MIT's machine grading software matches the score of a human grader as accurately as a second human grader 85% of the time. And as we have discussed earlier, research can be complemented by online simulation and modeling, and can offer online access to laboratory equipment and the ability to run experiments online.

There is a larger point, as well. "Face to face" conventionally has implied physical proximity, but there are significant learning areas where, as technology continues to improve, face to face is transforming into "person to person," where virtual personal connections are online. Personalized education need no longer be entirely face-to-face education if online education can integrate personalized tutorial systems into large-scale courses. So even as online and face-to-face approaches manage a certain détente, online is likely to become over time a more and more disruptive force—another example of how new firms embracing new technologies can disrupt and eventually displace legacy firms.

Clayton Christensen[22] argues that in the days when nonprofit higher education was a service-only sector, it was protected. Its service model had long since absorbed books as its one technology base, already a mature sector after five centuries of development. It had been successful in evading any significant new technology component, facing only modest incursions from a private-sector online education system that had been slowly evolving. When a point was reached where online entry could scale—via significant broadband access and smartphone entry—the way was open for a new technology component to enter higher education. It was the arrival of this new technology that created the possibility of disruptive displacement for the existing higher-education system.

Christensen proposes an analogy: online is analogous to the steamship. Early steam engines were very inefficient, requiring great volumes of wood and then coal. They could not power a ship across an ocean, but they found a niche market, starting out on rivers. It is difficult to sail upriver with contrary current and winds and often narrow channels, and rowing anything sizable upstream requires impossible levels of manpower. But steam engines, although initially inefficient, had a compelling advantage. They could move steadily upriver into current and wind, and replenish at frequent riverside wood or coaling points. As engines became more fuel efficient, it became possible to venture across part of an ocean. The answer was hybrid technology: ships that carried masts for sails as well as steam engines, using both means to cross an ocean. Eventually, through development over most of the 19th century, the engines became efficient enough, sidewheels were replaced by more efficient screw propellers, and iron and later steel ships could carry more fuel. Ships became steam-only—true steamships—discarding the hybrid model.

Will this be the higher-education story? Will "blended learning"—the hybrid model—eventually fade and be displaced by an online steamship? Will universities go the way of sailing ships? For the foreseeable future, we would argue, online education will continue to depend on conventional education, especially in universities.

The fundamental problem is that if universities were to disappear, the institutional source for course content would collapse over time. Universities are also research engines as well as teaching and learning centers; at least in science, that research side has a separate funding system that could be maintained, apart from education tuition (although in current practice, tuition revenues provide subsidies to research because universities do not fully recover their indirect costs from the federal government).

In a knowledge economy, there is no substitute for universities, which are literally innovation systems that are critical for societal growth. With industrial research ever more focused on incremental advances in later development stages, the breakthrough stage increasingly is a university role using federal science research funds. University research, by providing a foundation for learning by doing, is also central to science education for both undergraduate and graduate students.

The fact that universities are needed does not ensure their survival. Although there is no real replacement for many functions of the research university, it is possible that the university in its present form will survive only if it significantly reforms its face-to-face learning model. Its age-old primary delivery tool, the lecture, is no longer the optimal model from a learning science perspective.[23] A head-to-head competition between a live "talking head" in a classroom and an online presentation with assessment and interactive features built in is not a winning long-term proposition for the classroom lecture.

So the online education revolution is here. Universities can take an ostrich approach and allow continuing and systematic market incursions from for-profit online operators. Or they can figure out how to integrate the new online tools for learning and reform their face-to-face course offerings in parallel. Given the increasing pressures on tuition revenues, the reality is that universities cannot ignore the new, disruptive technology of online education. On the other hand, they have an opportunity to adapt to a blended model, taking the best attributes of online and face-to-face learning, to form over time a more nearly optimal learning environment.

This model will require a division of tasks that reflects the strengths of each environment. As Sanjay Sarma and Isaac Chuang, directors of MITx (MIT's online course development entity), have stated, "This new [online] tool might streamline first-order learning and free us up to enrich second-order learning."[24] They propose that online can absorb much of the information and content-conveyance tasks—first-order learning—and the face-to-face classroom can focus on the understanding and conceptual depth of second-order learning. The online element in the blended model can integrate the lecture model, but space it into shorter, more absorbable segments, reinforcing each segment with the interactive features at which online excels, such as visual data displays, animations, and problem simulations.

Application of computer gaming to courses is particularly promising.[25] Online will take advantage of emerging software for continuous assessment that will test student understanding frequently and will reinforce concepts and practices that were not adequately understood. Online also may prove a good tool for lifelong learning. Once a student develops discourse, writing and research skills, online may enable lifelong updating of content and information. Course and sequences of course completion certificates offered online may fit well with the skills updating increasingly sought by employers.[26]

Meanwhile, the face-to-face classroom can benefit from the significant advances in learning science in recent years.[27] It can become a space for more seminar-like discussion sessions, where students can learn to express and organize expertise, engage in participatory laboratory work and demonstrations, and frame overall problems that they then will mine the online resources to help resolve. Apprenticeship learning-by-doing and learning progression approaches, using teachers as mentors, also become possibilities. Basic short papers to test the students' information acquisition can move online; conceptual papers to demonstrate creative thinking and problem solving could receive more attention from faculty members freed from lecturing. Problems initially could be framed in the classroom, followed by supporting online material, so the classroom is "flipped" in the most productive direction.

The science of learning will advance through analyses of massive data from students learning online and will inform both the virtual and the physical settings. A major professional development effort for faculty will be essential to ensure effective learning and teaching in new online, blended, and traditional environments. Ongoing research on both the science of learning and faculty development will be key to education reforms. Society and the research community have much to learn about learning—in classrooms, online, and in blended learning settings. Online education presents an opportunity to significantly reform the quality of learning in higher education. If meaningful learning analytics can be applied to the growing ocean of online data, the nation could undertake learning research at a scale previously unavailable.

It is now becoming possible to tackle long-standing questions of learning science: Does the effectiveness of instructional practices vary for students of different ages and groups? Can the transfer of learning across courses be enhanced? Are there optimal ways to structure, track, and assess a student's learning as it takes place over time, rather than simply to count the number of courses they have taken and the grades they have received? How do noncognitive aspects of learning, including motivation and social learning features, influence student success? Online assessment, if done properly, can reveal much about learning in ways that could drive educational reforms in online and face-to-face education. To achieve such goals, and to improve both online and face-to-face education, it will be necessary to apply systematically what is now known and what is learned in the future about learning science.[28]

Although online learning may already offer new education opportunities, particularly in the blended model, the entry of MOOCs into higher education is in its infancy. Because their potential is only starting to be understood, the business model is not clear. Several features will have to be addressed if sound business models are to evolve.

First, MOOCs will require expensive up-front development. To offer quality courses with interactive features means an investment in development; to simply offer videos of existing lectures completely underutilizes the medium and its interactive and assessment potential. To raise the online technology bar, universities (or, more likely, consortia of universities to save costs and share expertise) will need to consider supplementing their traditional faculties with online development experts. Development of standard "platform" software features will need to be developed that can "snap in" to serve a menu of courses, reduce their costs, and improve performance (for example, through standard features for the assessment of students). Significantly, the up-front costs potentially can be spread over a much wider group of students, and across universities, significantly lowering the cost per course per student. Most courses and course elements can likely remain in the market for extended periods with modest updating—they don't have to be reoffered each year like a lecture course. Schools can also arrange to borrow (or license) each other's best courses, so that schools that can meet the up-front development costs can provide online material for others. So economies of scale for online education should be available. Working out a sound pricing model will be a work in progress for some time to come.

At this time, MOOC courses are freely available to viewers. If a student wants a certificate, assessment will be needed and a modest charge can be imposed depending on the course population—but at what level? Georgia Tech's collaboration with Udacity for an online master's degree in computer science suggests how MOOC pricing options may evolve. Georgia Tech will charge students seeking credit for its respected computer science program a price closer to a community college: approximately $134 per credit, compared with the normal rates at Georgia Tech of $472 per credit for in-state students and $1,139 per credit for out-of-state students. The program is expected to take most students three years to complete and to cost around $7,000. Income will be split 60-40 between Georgia Tech and Udacity.

Clearly, differential pricing within an institution is now being introduced for online versus face-to-face (or blended) courses. Will there be popular "blockbuster" courses that (like blockbuster Broadway shows) can charge a premium? If more of the content and lecture teaching load is picked up online, will faculty size decline—and if so, how will research universities cover the range of expertise and the expense of seminar-like approaches that they need to offer? Regardless, universities (and certainly the for-profits) will clearly need to recoup their development costs. Otherwise, this revolution will be stillborn.

The pricing models for nonprofit MOOC providers could prove advantageous for experimentation, because, at least for well-endowed schools, prompt profit recovery does not have to be built in, but will nonprofits be able to keep up with for-profits in incorporating technological advances? EdX has announced an "open source" approach for its software platforms, posting its code and inviting the software community to contribute improvements in a "commons" development model. Textbook publishers are entering online education as well, creating textbooks that will increasingly be packed with online features, and publishers may also collaborate or compete with MOOC consortia.

Universities are under pressure to reform if the low-cost standard lecture is displaced over time by MOOCs. If they offer improved face-to-face learning, they may have to move to what initially appears to be a more expensive face-to-face model, with more intense faculty mentoring and seminars, in order to realize the potential of personal learning. Can universities recoup these costs against their MOOC offerings? As they do so, they will be going up against a tradition that online offerings should be free. They will also be going up against for-profits that will not face carrying costs for big campuses and research facilities. And there is the additional problem of what to charge if a university offers lifelong learning opportunities. Or, if one university develops a course, and another uses it in a blended model, what does the first university charge the second? EdX has two approaches to cost recovery for its university partners: lower-cost "self-service," where a school or its faculty members develops an online course (to edX standards) but uses the edX system for its distribution, and "edX supported," where edX charges more as a course design partner, contributing technological know-how to course construction, as well as handling online distribution.

To return to the cost question concerning the blended model, its more personalized approach suggests that it may require a more enriched atmosphere; online courses and materials may offset some costs, but will that be enough? Given the cost pressures on universities enumerated above, there will be pressures to avoid this blended environment and just concentrate on the cost-saving aspects of online learning (more or less the way telephone answering machines and word processing were used to eliminate receptionists and secretaries, respectively). Part of the challenge facing universities is that they may feel they must defend their old-fashioned large lecture tools for cost reasons, even though blended approaches may be needed to optimize learning. So blended learning options must be better understood and blended approaches adapted into cost ranges that universities can afford, even if it turns out that MOOCs can provide some cross-subsidies.

Fortunately, important research work is ongoing on ways to significantly improve the learning process in large, 300-student courses through better ways of teaching subject expertise and discourse than the standard lecture.[29] If this reform is coupled with the self-pacing and continuous assessment features of supporting online materials,[30] which in effect become significantly enriched textbooks, this blended approach could be an economically manageable step. But if costs can't be driven down, the learning value may not be sufficient to enable lesser universities to survive and provide good education. So there are downsides and dangers here, with the likelihood of winners and losers, as is the case with most innovation-based transformations.

Adding to the economic complexity are unresolved issues of intellectual property. The Bayh-Dole Act's award of patents to universities for the research they conduct has encouraged the translation of innovative research into implementation. But this patent approach is not applicable to the world of MOOCs. Textbook royalties have motivated some faculty. But who owns a MOOC, the university or the faculty that produced it? How will the answer to this question affect tomorrow's university and professional identities?

Overall, a very different business model for online versus face-to-face higher education is likely for a very different cost structure. While efforts continue apace to start MOOCs, online backers are still shooting in the dark as to the business model. A blended model of online and face-to-face would be optimal, and could be both interesting and disruptive. It offers the possibility of both significantly lowering student costs and improving the overall quality of education. But work will be required to make it affordable.

Will Higher Education Resist Blended Learning?

One bottom line appears to be that universities that are largely lecture-based and have only a limited funding base for online development costs and reform of face-to-face educational methods may be in for a rough ride as they try to shift to new models of online and face-to-face education. Increased student throughput offers one solution, but some schools may have difficulties attracting or housing sufficient students to be able to expand in this direction. The point here is that online-only education is not perfect. There are limits to its ability to facilitate learning, but it is going to be pretty good, particularly in providing and reinforcing content and information. If lower-cost online courses with interactive and assessment technical features go head to head in competition with less learning-efficient live lectures, online may win. And the lifelong learning potential for online education will provide an extra advantage. But a blended learning model is clearly preferable from an educational perspective.

At the moment, most universities are doing only the minimum. They are tolerating the evolution of a parallel universe of online courses led by a few schools, and leaving their existing campus-based course delivery system intact. Only a few have started to recognize what they need to do to optimize learning: to develop a new, blended model that includes a new, more dynamic role for faculty in face-to-face learning that uses the unique strengths that only they can muster in expression, in written analysis, and in learning-by-doing research.

To make this model affordable, universities will need to examine the evolving research on how to make it work in large classes. Asking higher education, which has been historically averse to innovation, to pursue two simultaneous major education reforms—online and blended—is asking a lot. While some may suggest that faculty, once they see learning improvements available for their students, will introduce blended online and face-to-face reforms on their own initiative, the reality is that advances in learning science to significantly improve teaching have been well understood for over a decade, and yet there have been almost no university teaching reforms to date.[31] Faculty remain oriented to a university rewards system focused on research, not teaching.

So there is increasing risk that higher education will tolerate MOOCs but will resist a blended learning model that requires faculty teaching practices to change significantly, especially if they are expected to learn major new skills without any alteration in their other responsibilities. Already there are cries from unionized faculty about MOOCs violating academic freedom.[32] Challenges from faculty against MOOCs as infringing on their intellectual property rights—is a MOOC course like a copyrighted textbook?—may be on the way. These are not purely Luddite responses; there are real questions here.

To offer the best education, reform of higher education arguably needs to embrace both revolutions—online and blended. Higher education would embrace a system in which online education does what it is good at (providing content and information, enhancing data visualization, offering continuous assessment) and face-to-face education does what it is good at (fostering discourse and argumentation, written analysis, mentoring, training students for research, making conceptual leaps). It would extend J. C. R. Licklider's vision to a human-online symbiosis[33]—the right blend of students, teachers, and teams with online capabilities—that could catalyze a new generation of stronger learning.

A Complex Legacy and Complex Potential Disruption

Research universities constitute a curiously complicated legacy sector. The structure of the research university embodies a set of cross-subsidies and externalities, both positive and negative, which are being exposed, disaggregated, and disrupted by the advent of the MOOC. The cost of higher education is at the same time an investment in increased future income, a consumption item for the student and his or her future intellectual and cultural life, and a social investment—a positive externality—in an educated and uplifted citizenry and in increased scholarly knowledge and communication. As we have pointed out earlier, education tuition subsidizes the university contribution to research, which as things now stand is insufficiently compensated by federal overhead allowances.

In a research university, the faculty is compensated and promoted primarily on the basis of their research. This research is also the basis of the reputation of the university and is an important input to the tuition it can charge. There is even a feedback loop here, since the demand for admission to a university increases with increased tuition ("perverse demand"). Most faculty members therefore have little incentive to invest time in better teaching methods. Conscientious teachers, for their part, find that good teaching by traditional methods leaves little time for experimentation with new methods and may require relief from teaching obligations—an investment on the part of the university—if they are to undertake such experimentation.

Research enriches teaching and hence education, but as we have observed, the extent to which it does so is not the basis for faculty compensation and promotion. So teaching tends to get short shrift, or to be left to adjuncts, part-timers, and graduate students (who are in essence volunteers, low-wage workers, and low-paid apprentices, respectively). The upshot is that there has been within most universities little interest in or money for research in improved teaching, and hence no supply of innovations in education and no change agents within universities to overcome the obstacles to the implementation of these innovations were they to become available.

The legacy pressures in universities may resist blended learning reforms even as they are starting to work with online delivery. Here, education presents special characteristics. In some other sectors, a disruptive technology can just move into implementation and avoid a confrontation with the sector. Widespread Internet access, for example, enabled air travelers to go around and avoid travel agents to make their own travel plans and so transformed airline reservations. A problem with true blended learning is that the higher-education service sector is not facing a purely technological challenge that it can ignore, where the technology could operate as a stand-alone disruption. In other words, the classroom can't remain exactly the same, with students simply directed to watch a video in their spare time; the nature of the classroom experience needs to change. Instead, the optimal learning model combines service (classroom) and technology (online), which require higher education to undergo internal reforms in its service side, the classroom. While banking could accept ATM machines and insurance actuarial software programs as "paradigm compatible," the blended model appears to be "paradigm incompatible" because it will require significant change in the classroom.

So the legacy sector features will lead to resistance not just to MOOCs but to the blended model as well. We recount these features here to show how closely they fit the legacy model. There remain *powerful vested interests* in higher education—particularly faculties and the academic departments they control—that are reluctant to adopt innovative education reforms like blended learning that oppose the existing teaching paradigm and threaten their existing business models. The pressures discussed above of *public habits and expectations* that are attuned to existing education approaches may operate to enable a legacy institution of higher education to maintain its *established infrastructure and institutional architecture* and its high-cost, *"perverse" price and demand structure* that equates high cost with educational quality.

Optimal online and blended learning requires continuing innovation and an R & D effort behind it, but as we have pointed out earlier, higher education conducts almost no R & D on education and learning as applied to its own classrooms[34] and so has been *averse to innovation* and may continue to avoid R & D on education reforms that could improve learning. Higher education's *established knowledge and human resources structure*, particularly self-perpetuating faculties and academic departments oriented to their own needs and resistant to change, and its difficulty in mustering the *collective action* required to implement innovative reforms, continue to constitute barriers to blended learning. This is still the case even as higher education adopts MOOCs as, in effect, a sideline that is less directly threatening to current education practices. Despite the evolution of MOOCs, this legacy sector resistance could result in an incomplete and imperfect revolution in education.

Are there *change agents* that could drive higher-education blended and online reforms despite these legacy pressures? The multiple cost pressures discussed above certainly could *induce* change. This may work for online courses, but unless online can offset the costs of the blended courses and cost-saving ways are found to introduce these courses—which may be possible—then the cost pressures work against the more expensive blended model.

Surprisingly, the major change agents to date have come from within universities: small groups of faculty drawn from a field already prone to disruptive innovation. Certain better-endowed universities, led by strong computer science departments, have pushed online reforms. The two for-profit MOOC offerers to date have spun off of Stanford's computer science faculty, and MIT's president, Rafael Reif, himself a computer scientist, along with its computer science faculty, created the nonprofit MOOC, with Harvard as a cofounder. Computer science faculty at these schools saw the new online opportunities made possible by advances in technology, particularly its ability to reach to global learners, and the edX founders committed major funding. The MOOC offerers subsequently began to see the importance of the blended model.[35] They increasingly understand the risks as well as benefits of an online-only approach, and are seriously looking at the blended approach.[36] However, can a core group of major universities drive optimal blended learning changes, on their own campuses as well as elsewhere?

Applying lessons from the defense technology sector in chapter 8, there is no education equivalent to DARPA undertaking R & D on innovative learning science for both optimal face-to-face and online teaching reforms. And there is no equivalent of a secretary of defense with authority to drive innovation opportunities over legacy barriers in the highly decentralized sector of higher education. Instead, the initial change agents are universities operating, unlike DARPA, on the inside not the outside of the higher education system. As a result of these change agent issues, the jury is out on the possibility of a sector-wide shift to blended learning.

The sadder scenario would be that Christensen's "steamship" analogy, in which pure steam prevailed over the steam-sail blend, may eventually prove accurate over an extended period of time. If a strong, blended learning model does not evolve in universities to optimize a combination of online and face-to-face learning, then the potentially disruptive technology revolution embodied in online education just might eventually prevail, even if it alone can't offer optimal education.

HEALTHCARE DELIVERY

The existing paradigm of health delivery in the United States involves a complex system of mixed public and private payers. This has given rise to powerful vested interests—including a rigid system of professions and institutions—that are well positioned to fight any rationalization of the system. Together, they support a tariff structure that favors sophisticated medical procedures over nonmedical measures to improve public health or promote healthy lifestyles, and a fee-for-service system that rewards doctors and hospitals for expanding services, especially equipment-intensive, high-tech procedures, rather than for performance.[37]

Medical expenses are truly enormous; they absorb about one-sixth of the total annual output of the US economy, and the federal government estimates total US healthcare expenditures will pass $3 trillion in 2014 and $4.8 trillion by 2021.[38] A major motivation for healthcare reform comes from the fact that the resulting system provides the United States with relatively poor public health for too much of its population: around 15% of citizens have limited access to care. To be sure, spectacular medical advances have multiplied in recent decades, so that a plethora of vital new procedures and path-breaking medicines are available; the system is therefore facing a backlog of innovations that it must accommodate and amortize, complicating the conflict between performance and fee-for-service.

The steady increase in the share of GNP devoted to healthcare is reminiscent of Baumol's Cost Disease, but actually stems from a different underlying cause. Since much of the recovery of fees depends on employment-related health insurance and from government entitlements (through Medicare or Medicaid) that guarantee payment, pricing in the system is relatively unconstrained. There is no limit to the demand for a product that costs the user little or nothing, and no limit to what its provider can charge until whoever is actually paying the bill reaches its limits to pay. Since this is the case for healthcare, it is not surprising that high costs are straining the capacities of employers and insurance companies to pay.[39]

The huge medical cost of the baby boom demographic bulge also may eventually threaten the federal government's fiscal stability. Market and political motivations to reform the system are lacking because most people are satisfied with the care they now receive and are shielded from its cost by the third-party payment system and by cost-shifting to government. On the positive side, the expense and inefficiencies built into the health delivery system have become significant motivations for reform. A further motivation for reform—although one that receives much less attention—is the fact that much medical technology has never been subjected to objective tests of effectiveness.

Resistance to IT-Based Innovation

A wide range of innovative applications of information technology (IT) to health delivery are at or near techno-economic readiness. These include technologies for digitizing healthcare, standardizing medical reporting, improving communication among different actors in the system, and building databases to evaluate performance and efficiency. Also in the works are instant transmission of complete medical histories and of precision digital test data such as advanced imaging, and ways to obtain immediate real-time results of many tests, along with better ways to compare real-time actual performance against standards of care and best practices and to perform precision remote robotic surgery and other services through online connections. Longer term, "big data" and analytics promise new ways of developing capabilities for personalized medicine.[40]

Although the IT innovation wave transformed productivity in a number of economic sectors, its entry into healthcare delivery in the United States has to date been limited. IT innovations have been implemented successfully through the Veterans Administration, and in single-payer systems in Scandinavia and the United Kingdom, so that we do have information on their potential. In the United States, several systems have been implemented at pilot scale or in limited markets. In the framework we have set forth earlier, these experiences have constituted niche markets in which bugs are being worked out prior to full-scale implementation. Such full-scale deployment has been hindered by a lack of standardization of reporting formats and harmonization of payment procedures and by the absence of uniform state regulations (or in most states, any regulations at all) that would make it possible to achieve *network economies*.

More important, performance and efficiency are not adequately rewarded in the existing US fee-for-service model of healthcare delivery. The incentives for doctor and hospital actors in the system are tilted toward performing more and more services, systemically driving up compensation and therefore costs.[41] Institutional and professional resistance to IT-based performance and efficiency reforms has been significant and continuing.

Aside from the lack of performance incentives, the existing system resists transparent benchmarks for medical outcomes and efficiency so that medical consumers and employer providers too often fly blind through the system. An IT-based technology incursion that would enable a transparent measurement and benchmarking system has not been adopted because the fee-for-service delivery model does not offer the level of economic rewards needed to implement it. The situation exemplifies the mismatch between producer incentives and social goals that is typical of a legacy sector.

Legacy Sector in Health Delivery

Healthcare delivery exhibits many legacy sector features:[42] it (1) is subject to *"perverse" prices* and a *price structure* that has increased its prices at a significantly higher rate than overall inflation, creating a mismatch with the broader social goal of a healthy public at affordable cost, and that rewards medical procedures more than nonmedical measures (such as advising on healthier behaviors and lifestyles) that might be more effective both for the individual patient and for the general population; (2) is based on an *established infrastructure and institutional architecture* consisting of a mix of institutional actors and providers that resist change; (3) contains *powerful vested interests*, particularly professions and the faculties they control, as well as insurance companies, that defend the existing delivery paradigm and resist innovations that threaten their business models; (4) is *sustained by public habits and expectations* attuned to existing delivery approaches; (5) is based on an *established knowledge and human resources structure*: particularly professions and their supporting faculties oriented to existing systems and resistant to change; and (6) has been *averse to innovation*, as an industry that has conducted only very *limited R & D* on possible reforms in systems of health delivery that could improve efficiency and outcomes.

Health delivery is also characterized by the market imperfection of an inability to muster *collective action*. It is very difficult to organize collective efforts around health delivery because the system is highly decentralized, scattered among many thousands of providers and institutions. Even hospital "systems" that include public institutions remain quite decentralized, with regulation falling among the fifty states and a range of federal agencies that are not well coordinated. The decentralized nature of health delivery institutions means that reforms adopted in one or even some are hard to spread to the others and hence to expand to full scale.

Furthermore, innovation in the healthcare delivery system is impeded by *governmental and other institutional* obstacles. The federal government funds some 40% of the healthcare system through coverage for the elderly (Medicare) and the poor (Medicaid), the two most expensive medical populations. Thus far, it has attempted partial rationing of innovation by limiting access to some procedures under Medicare and Medicaid, rather than through competition based on cost and performance. Despite occasional forays into reform, the political system has not proved to be able to restructure the fee-for-service model that is sustained with political support from the elderly, the hospitals, and the medical professions.

IT-based health innovations face another problem: they require investment and therefore place unsustainable costs on healthcare providers, who are already under pressure from insurance companies to reduce fees and increase patient throughput in the name of "productivity," whereas the benefits of these investments are likely to redound to their patients and to insurance companies, neither of whom will accept the costs. This is an impediment to innovation due to the market imperfection of *nonappropriability*. Also impeding innovation in the health sector is the need to achieve *network economies* that can be achieved only in the presence of large-scale networks, and that therefore require the adoption of standards or other requirements to ensure the interoperability of the subnetworks through which information is to be communicated.

Developing New Medicines and Medical Devices

Unlike the situation for health delivery systems, it is tempting to assume that because the biotech sector appears so successful, improved pharmaceuticals and devices for use in hospitals and by physicians can readily overcome impediments to *paradigm-compatible* innovations that slot nicely into the existing system and face only the usual problems of the "normal innovation" model: the need for research support and venture capital to bridge the valley of death.

But there is a distinction between the systems for developing medicines and for delivering services. The former has been robust. New medicines can sometimes help drive down delivery costs by reducing the need for services. For example, while several decades ago AIDS appeared to be a new plague that would force the nation to double or triple the number of hospital beds, medical research has led to treatments that made AIDS into a manageable chronic disease, and the need to build and staff all those additional hospitals has not materialized.

However, the two systems—developing medicines and delivering health services—don't necessarily match up readily. While there is an innovation system for developing new medicines, led by the National Institutes of Health (NIH) and the Food and Drug Administration (FDA), there is only a very limited system for developing improved methods for delivering health services, and NIH and FDA are not focused on these problems. The technology for digitizing the back-office operations of hospitals and private physicians is the province of private providers that don't support linking the emerging systems into coherent networks.

Even paradigm-compatible innovations in medicine face a series of hurdles. First, bringing a new drug through development, clinical trials, and FDA approval costs approximately $1 billion, an investment that clearly qualifies for *lumpiness*.[43] This means that biotech and pharma companies must develop drugs and devices that satisfy a very large market; non-"blockbuster" drugs are commercially unattractive. Although technological advances promise progress on "personalized" medicine—individualized drugs and devices that will fit individual needs—to date, the existing economic model has hindered rather than incentivized this approach. Innovation impediments and accompanying major development costs due to *lumpiness* also affect drugs for diseases of the developing world and those that benefit small populations. They also affect investment in vaccines, new contraceptives, and new antibiotics, as well as other remedies that immediately cure a disease or condition or that involve low profit margins or large potential liabilities. These categories of drugs do not offer prospects for blockbuster status and therefore do not fit into the existing paradigm.[44]

Second, although the NIH at $30 billion a year is the nation's largest basic research organization, it is organized around a biological model for drug development, and generally does not support work on innovation for devices, practices, or information systems. A growing research model that promises a new generation of medical advance, the "convergence" model of integrated, cross-disciplinary research combining life sciences, physical sciences, and engineering,[45] is limited by organizational problems at NIH and the FDA. Neither is well organized to support nonbiological research directions, despite their promise; if these opportunities are to be realized, new approaches to peer review, education, and cross-institute and agency collaboration and research processes will need to be tested and adopted by NIH, and the FDA will have to examine and revise its evaluation capabilities and procedures.[46] Indeed, these organizations themselves show many of the features of legacy sectors.[47]

Thus, *governmental and other institutional* impediments in the area of drug, device, and systems innovation exist in the health sector, even apart from the problems in the health delivery system discussed above. Other impediments to innovation arise due to *economies of scale*: innovations of potentially important reach, for example for small patient populations or Third World diseases, face limits in their ability to scale up within the current blockbuster market structure. Other major issues are connected with the challenges of developing a system of evidence-based medicine and undertaking the research on cost-effectiveness criteria that are needed to measure and assess the successes and failures of medical interventions in meeting public health goals, and in this way to provide the analytic tools and standards to support a shift away from a fee-for-service system to one of performance-based medicine.[48]

There are *change agent* issues for innovation in the healthcare delivery and the next generation of personalized and convergence-based medicines and devices. Change agent challenges remain in all these areas. The identity of a possible change agent depends on the specific area in which innovation is needed. There is no DARPA equivalent pressing R & D from outside the system,[49] and there are major institutional barriers limiting NIH and FDA in these areas. Concerning innovative medicines and devices from convergence research, a number of major research universities are working on these issues, and there is some NIH-, DARPA-, and NSF-supported research.[50] Innovative biotech firms could bring such convergence-based medicines to markets. Innovations in healthcare delivery, however, lack support to research and implementation, although there is some federal support for research on the comparative effectiveness of different treatment regimes.[51] Personalized medicine, for its part, lacks an economic foundation because of the prevalence of the blockbuster drug model.

In summary, although the biotech sector has been a model of successful innovation, and medical research has received far more federal research investment than almost any other sector, there are structural and organizational challenges to innovation in both healthcare delivery and the next generation of pharmaceuticals and medical devices. Even the 2010 Affordable Care Act has only a limited focus on the innovation system for healthcare delivery.[52]

THE CONTEXT OF SERVICE SECTOR INNOVATION

IT and online technologies have transformed several legacy service sectors. Online, for example, after much delay is entering the entertainment business. First to transform was music. While the iPod was a quality MP3 player device, its real power was in joining that device to a highly efficient, low-cost, searchable software system to provide much better, on-demand access to music. To cross the hardware and software in the device, Apple's Steve Jobs literally reorganized the music recording and sales system.[53] Now, online videos are starting to reorganize the movie business through YouTube access and with, for example, Netflix's online, on-demand access system, which are driving structural changes in the film industry.

Another example of IT-driven transformation is in financial services. IT and online capabilities enabled high-speed, largely automated transactions, which in turn were tied to innovations in software and mathematics that enabled a long list of new investment instruments. In a relatively brief period, these developments created for the first time a truly global financial services system, which constituted an innovation wave. This major innovation, however, came a cropper because there was no built-in negative feedback to push back against the many highly profitable excesses and indeed scandals that emerged during the boom that preceded the Great Recession.[54] In both entertainment and financial services, the IT and online-related innovation entry was achieved in significant part because it was *paradigm compatible*.

Higher education also has now entered a potentially transformational change through online education technology, and there is a strong argument that education can significantly improve if a blended learning model evolves as technological advance is tied more directly to the service. It remains to be seen whether cost issues, combined with the legacy pressures that remain in this sector, will allow the blended model to evolve. The major change agent to date has been a group of relatively wealthy major universities experimenting with online models; it is not clear if they will extend their efforts toward implementing the blended model.

Healthcare delivery is still further behind the innovation curve. There have been dramatic innovations in medicine, particularly as a result of the biotech innovation wave. But in health delivery, legacy barriers have limited the entry of online and other IT-based service delivery options. There is no DARPA equivalent in health delivery—an R & D entity outside the system to drive change. While scientific advances have enabled breakthrough medicines, the major source of funding for health-related research, the NIH, is still oriented to biology-only, drug-only development, and doesn't view its mission as encompassing a wider range of technologies or the health delivery system. So it is a step removed from the innovation task in healthcare delivery.

Bringing IT advances to the health delivery system remains a systemic challenge, as we have discussed. And there are challenges on the innovation side, where new advances could reduce disease and care delivery costs. For example, there remain potentially available a remarkable new suite of technologies, such as engineered devices linked to online evaluation tools also tied to drug delivery—"labs on a chip." The convergence research model is particularly promising, suggesting new generations of devices that combine drug delivery with engineering. While genomics (itself enabled by a convergence of supercomputing and biology) promises techniques like genome editing to resolve genetic issues related to diseases, the task of nanoscale entry into the cell to deliver therapy requires a convergence model combining medicine, engineering, and materials science. But there is institutional resistance to these IT and convergence approaches to innovation because NIH, FDA, and the research systems they support are not organized to embrace them. Developing the innovation agents and accompanying outside change agents to alter this legacy sector remains a challenge.

8 Innovating in the Defense Sector

The defense sector has often led US technological advance. Yet historically, militaries have often been the most conservative of organizations, always seeking to refight the last war, suppressing innovation in the name of discipline and reliability, and therefore famously subject to technology surprise—the Maginot Line and Pearl Harbor being good examples. The US military, like all others, exhibits these legacy sector tendencies. However, in the late 1970s, after almost three decades of Cold War, a remarkable effort began in the US Defense Department to introduce transformative technologies. That process contains important lessons for innovation organization within legacy sectors.

THE REVOLUTION IN MILITARY AFFAIRS

When Harold Brown became defense secretary and William Perry undersecretary for defense research and engineering (DR&E) in the Carter administration in 1977, the nation faced a major Cold War dilemma. Starting under Eisenhower and Kennedy, the United States had developed superiority in nuclear weapons and their missile delivery systems that offset Soviet advantages in conventional forces in Europe. However, by the mid-1970s, that advantage had faded, with the United States and Soviets in rough parity in these systems. With its deterrence threat eroding, and the army's capability in decline as a result of the terrible pressures of the Vietnam War, Perry and Brown were deeply concerned about the possible outcome of a possible conventional warfare confrontation in Europe. Concern about mutual destruction blunted the ability to use nuclear weapons as a deterrent, and the Soviets had built a three-to-one advantage in force levels, tanks, armored fighting vehicles, and artillery in Europe. As Perry later put it, "We thought they had a serious intent to use them, to send a blitzkrieg down the Fulda Gap [the anticipated route of the Soviet ground invasion of Western Europe then thought possible]."[1] This imbalance in conventional forces could have forced the United States into a situation where it would have had to employ nuclear weapons, with all of their devastating consequences.

In the 1973 war between Egypt and Israel, US defense experts saw the rapid attrition in Israel's US-equipped, highly capable air forces as they faced a Soviet-equipped Egyptian force with Soviet air defenses. The Israelis lost more than 100 combat aircraft—much of their front-line capability—in 18 days.[2] The analysts, including Perry and Brown, realized that the United States and NATO could not cope with such a rapid attrition rate in their European forces. Since equaling Soviet force levels in Europe was not feasible, Perry and Brown developed an "offsets" theory as the basis for a new US defense strategy.[3] They decided to achieve parity and therefore deterrence in conventional battle through systematic technological advance in order to offset the Soviet advantage in force levels. They began a process of translating advances in computing, information technology, and sensors, which had been initiated and long supported by investments in defense research, through the Defense Advanced Research Projects Agency (DARPA) in particular, into three areas of advance: stealth, precision strike, and unmanned aerial vehicles (UAVs).

In the late 1970s, Soviet military leaders thought that their superiority in conventional arms in Europe was assured. But in the 1980s, Soviet military theorists were becoming concerned that the new generation of precision weapons and delivery systems would lead to a late 20th-century "Revolution in Military Affairs" (RMA).[4] As they saw, the United States was working to put this transformation in place; arguably these technological advances helped lead to the conclusion of the Cold War. Mikhail Gorbachev announced the withdrawal of Soviet forces from Eastern Europe in December 1988, and the Berlin Wall was torn down in November 1989.

The 1991 Persian Gulf War (Desert Storm) provided startling evidence of US progress. The US-led coalition was up against an Iraqi force of comparable size with a Soviet air defense system, but was able, as Perry later put it, "to win quickly, decisively and with remarkably few casualties."[5] The small number of F-117 stealth aircraft, for example, flew only 2% of the aircraft sorties in the 43-day war but struck 40% of the strategic targets with an 80% hit rate.[6] Perry concluded that his "offset strategy" had become a "force dominance" strategy—allowing the force with precision strike capabilities to dominate the battlefield.[7]

In 1990, the Pentagon's famed director of net assessment, Andy Marshall, a man about as close to Yoda as the DOD will ever employ, began urging the DOD to see the transformation it was undertaking as a possible "dominant operational approach."[8] He directed a major study by Lt. Col. Andrew Krepinevich, which was circulated in the DOD in 1992 and concluded that a military revolution was occurring that would fundamentally alter "the character and conduct of military operations" as completely as the blitzkrieg, strategic bombing, and aircraft carriers had done in the years leading to World War II.[9] This US-led RMA in turn led to an operational doctrine of "network-centric warfare."[10] Krepinevich also saw in this report that low-intensity, nonconventional warfare would be the prevailing pattern following the Cold War, with nonpeer "street fighter states"[11]—as indeed the lengthy conflicts in Iraq and Afghanistan proved to be—but also saw the relevance of precision strike capabilities in this type of conflict.

How did this RMA come about? Although this revolution suggests the power of the DOD's innovation system, it is also possible to characterize much of the DOD as a legacy sector. The existing paradigms within the DOD are averse to the risk of innovation. In many cases, this group of precision-strike capabilities was seen as threatening to vested technologies[12] and capabilities within the military, to the officers that had spent their careers developing and using them, and to the organizations and the firms in the defense industry that depended on the earlier technology. In each case, these technologies faced difficulty in obtaining needed investment and support, just like disruptive technologies in civilian firms that are organized around older technology—picture clunky electromechanical calculating machines at the advent of electronic calculators, or mainframe computers at the advent of desktops. Still, in each case, the DOD found a way around these legacy challenges, in ways that we explore below.

THE DEFENSE DEPARTMENT'S SYSTEMS APPROACH

The innovation system used by the defense sector has led most of the major innovation waves of the 20th century: aviation, electronics, nuclear power, space, computing, and the Internet.[13] All of these advances involved substantial challenges to a then-prevailing paradigm within the military. The Defense Department has achieved these technological advances through a "connected" or systems approach,[14] operating at each stage of the innovation process: R & D, prototypes, demonstrations and test beds, follow-on engineering and incremental advances, and initial market creation. This approach corresponds to the *innovation organization* model we have developed in chapter 3 of this book, in that it deals explicitly with the legacy features of the military as they affect each stage of innovation. To understand the need for this approach, we need first to understand the innovation system by which the DOD manages *paradigm-consistent* innovation.

Paradigm-consistent advances are a particular focus of the individual military services and are managed in accordance with the *extended pipeline* model. For each stage of the process, the DOD has created a set of institutions and functions that make possible this systems approach: (1) at the breakthrough R & D stage, the DOD often uses DARPA, which supplements the more traditional R & D agencies of the military services; DARPA acts within the *extended pipeline* model (reviewed in chapter 3); (2) at the prototype/demonstration/test bed stage, it uses the services, including their system of Federally Funded R & D Centers (FFRDCs) and service laboratories; (3) at the engineering and incremental advances stage, for its technologies and the platforms that use them, the DOD uses the services' development and procurement programs, based on the DOD's technology "requirements" system; (4) for initial market creation (or its equivalent in the single-market situation of defense procurement), the DOD uses its services-based procurement programs. While the handoffs between these DOD institutions and functions are rarely smooth, the system is nonetheless comparatively integrated. The DOD periodically supplements this system with efforts to launch technologies through civilian markets—an approach in which DARPA has played a particularly important role, notably in the IT sector.

This, then, is the outline of the way the extended pipeline model in the DOD is supposed to work, via a system of integrated innovation handoffs. In practice, however, this system can break down, particularly when a particular innovation requires links between the military services—the army, navy, and air force—and hence involves the central management functions of the Office of the Secretary of Defense. Such innovations are likely to be at least to some extent disruptive.

Despite its best efforts to create a system that can smoothly incorporate disruptive technology, the DOD is, after all, a half-trillion-dollar annual economy dating from 1789, and is dominated by its services, which have the characteristics of vested interests defending existing paradigms, as we have seen them in other legacy sectors. The services use a variety of means to ensure that dominance, including cost structures, institutional architecture, and established knowledge/human resources structures. In this way, the DOD has developed many of the significant features of a legacy sector, which we now explore.

DEFENSE AS A LEGACY SECTOR

These legacy sector features are reviewed below:

1. Concerning politically *powerful vested interests*, reinforced by public support: the services have vested interests in their existing missions and capital platform commitments, so they defend their existing paradigms. They have networks of contractors, veterans, and their own public support organizations, which lobby Congress to ensure that their historic shares of DOD spending remain intact. These support groups defend existing service paradigms and resist disruptive innovations that threaten their established service "business models."

2. Concerning *cost structures* that create a mismatch between the incentives of the services and the needs of geopolitical security: the power of the services as vested interests is locked in place in particular by the levels of long-term contracted expenditure—the cost structure—to which they commit the DOD through the budgeting process. These long-term spending commitments by the services generally match the established priorities and *vested technologies* for their force structure and supporting platforms—carriers in the navy, tanks and ground force support in the army, strike and bomber aircraft in the air force—so that it is hard to shift funding to a disruptive new function that will sacrifice spending on their core priorities. In other words, they tend to be locked into their established paradigms; this structure amounts to a cost structure that

creates a mismatch between DOD spending and changing geopolitical security missions.

3. Concerning established *institutional architecture:* the services contract for defense technologies by assuming the lead role within the DOD (although with sign-off from the secretary's staff). This limits the DOD's ability to bring on critical, "out of the box" technologies when it needs them. In other words, the services dominate not only the budgeting and DOD cost structure but also the decision process on technology acquisition. In this way, they tend to lock in their favored technologies. This established service infrastructure and institutional architecture imposes hurdles or other disadvantages to pursuing disruptive technologies.[15]

4. Concerning *established knowledge and human resources structures* oriented to the services' needs: the services have military academies, training systems, and an elaborate system of service specialties. The latter tend to be particularly problematic for introducing change; for example, naval aviation, submarine, and surface fleet leadership are separate cadres, each contending for overall service leadership and for their share of procurement funding. Senior navy leadership is under pressure to accommodate each internal group. The other services tend to have comparable problems. Thus, the leadership of each service is preoccupied with satisfying the needs of its own contending in-service baronies; this makes it even harder to accommodate the priorities of the other services. Thus, the services tend to have knowledge and talent bases organized around existing paradigms.

In addition to the barriers formed by established technological/economic/political/social paradigms, the DOD faces critical "market imperfections."[16] Concerning *split incentives*, the services are often reluctant to bring on new defense technologies that fall outside the way they define their current missions, that could disrupt their existing programs, and whose benefits would be shared between services, which forces them to, in effect, "cross-subsidize" the other services. This is institutionally analogous to the reluctance of state regulatory boards to authorize investments in the electric grid that might benefit utility customers in other states. The air force, for example, may prove reluctant to develop an advance that may also benefit naval aviation—the incentives are split, so that cross-service development is complex and difficult. Another example is the air force's reluctance to invest in ground support to the army, which led the army to invest in helicopters.

Concerning *collective action*, each service budget is separate, so that shared or "joint" cross-service procurement simply doesn't exist for defense programs. While joint operations between services and a system of joint theater commanders have evolved in the DOD over time, procurement is still by service. This means that technologies that benefit multiple services are particularly difficult to stand up. The DOD also has problems involving *network economies* (where new entrant technologies require new networks because they don't fit existing DOD and service networks), *lumpiness, economies of scale,* and *transaction costs.*

These characteristics have helped lead to a series of major challenges to today's defense innovation system: (1) problems in linking innovators (such as DARPA research teams) with service-led implementation; (2) lack of clarity among services on the security threats that the nation faces, which creates corresponding difficulty in developing department-wide technology strategies (for example, the United States currently faces a complex mix of monolithic and distributed threats that both strategists and services have had a hard time sorting out and don't necessarily match long-standing service missions); (3) defense business practices that curtail innovation, resilience, and adaptability (for example, "Lowest Price, Technically Acceptable" (LPTA) procurement requirements that sacrifice long-term value for short-term price gains); and (4) too long an innovation timeline (platform procurements can take twenty-five years or longer, which limits experimentation and the ability to move technological advances into procurement programs). These problems translate into competitive challenges. China, the upcoming peer competitor, currently has some nine jet fighter programs ongoing compared to one in the United States, and dozens of UAV programs against fewer than 10 in the United States.

Against this background, we can now explore the legacy sector problems faced by three of the major sets of technologies behind the DOD's Revolution in Military Affairs. We will examine how these structural obstacles and "market imperfections" work out in practice and how strong change agents within the defense establishment have been able, at least in these cases, to use the *innovation organization* model to overcome them.

STEALTH AIRCRAFT

Air superiority has been a fundamental doctrine of US defense since World War II.[17] However, by the late Vietnam War, Soviet air defense systems were making US aircraft ever more vulnerable. This forced the air force to employ vast air armadas of mixed-purpose aircraft, undertaking jamming and electronic countermeasures, chaff dropping, and radar attack, so as to protect a smaller number of attack aircraft that were actually undertaking the strike mission. As early as 1974, discussions began between the DOD's office of the director of defense research and engineering (DDR&E) and DARPA about the need to develop a "Harvey" aircraft (named after the invisible rabbit in the play and film) that would have a greatly reduced radar, infrared, acoustic, and visual appearance. The then DDR&E, Malcolm Currie, sent out a memo inviting DOD organizations to develop radical new ideas for such an aircraft. These ideas became known in DARPA, borrowing a term from antisubmarine warfare, as "stealth," and DARPA began to pursue a research agenda around it.

In 1975, a Lockheed engineer, Denys Overholser, located a research paper by Pyotr Ya. Ufimtsev, a physicist at the Russian Institute for Radio Engineering, titled "Method of Edge Waves in the Physical Theory of Diffraction"[18] and realized that a computer program could be developed from these concepts to design geometric shapes that would minimize the radar cross section of an aircraft. The Soviets had allowed publication of Ufimtsev's paper, not recognizing that there might be military applications of his work. Lockheed created the computer program and brought it to DARPA. DARPA staff understood the importance of the findings, but DARPA director George Heilmeier insisted that if the concepts were going to become an aircraft, the air force would have to take the lead in developing it because developing and buying aircraft was not a DARPA role.

Currie supported the stealth approach and used contacts he had built up in the air force leadership to try to bring them on board. However, a major Institute for Defense Analysis retrospective study found that

Air Force support was highly uncertain, as the Air Force saw limited value in a stealthy strike aircraft, given the severe operational limitations that [meant it] would be relatively slow and unmaneuverable, giving it limited air-to-air combat ability, and it would have to fly [only] at night—a far cry from the traditional Air Force strike fighter. There were also competing R & D priorities, most notably the Advanced Combat Fighter program (which eventually became the F-16).[19]

Currie was able to get the air force to go along only by securing extra funding for the project, so that stealth development would be in addition to existing air force R & D efforts, and, in particular, would not curtail the F-16 program.

William Perry, who succeeded Currie in leading DR&E, continued to press the stealth program forward because it fit perfectly with his "offsets" strategy. Lockheed's noted "Skunk Works" won the development contract for what became the F-117 strike fighter. The Skunk Works used its famous skills in experimentation, flexible problem-solving, and strong engineering and collaboration to push the F-117 successfully from idea to breakthrough reality.[20] Northrop, the other defense contractor working in the stealth field, embarked on a follow-on project that became the B-2 stealth bomber. To retain support from a still skeptical air force, defense secretary Harold Brown made development of stealth aircraft "technology limited" as opposed to "funding limited." In other words, the funding for this secret program was open-ended and was to continue unless a technological barrier emerged.[21] In Desert Storm, the F-117 enabled the United States to obtain air dominance at the outset of the conflict despite being up against the same type of Soviet air defense system that had created such difficulty for US-built aircraft in Vietnam.

Because the services had limited interest in such a radical and different concept that potentially made many of their existing and upcoming platforms obsolete, stealth overcame the service legacy sector barriers listed above (from *powerful vested interests*, to *cost structure*, to *institutional architecture*, to *established knowledge/human resource structures*, to *collective action*) only because of DARPA's highly innovative organizational and technical capabilities, which operated outside the established defense service hierarchies according to the *innovation organization* model. DARPA, in turn, required support from the highest levels of the DOD's civilian leadership, including Secretary Brown and the DDR&Es, and from a separate funding stream. Thus, a series of change agents came to bear on the problem, led by DARPA but linked to the DOD senior leadership and to Lockheed, a major defense contractor. The air force, however, did embrace the technology over time. Interestingly, initial attempts to introduce stealth technology into navy shipbuilding – Lockheed's Skunk Works developed the "Sea Shadow" – failed because of navy opposition for reasons very similar to the air force's concerns.[22]

PRECISION STRIKE

The mix of defense capabilities known as precision strike developed as part of the DOD's focus on the RMA, responding to the confrontation between Cold War forces in Europe. Faced with much larger Soviet forces, William Perry formulated precision-strike objectives as the capability to "see all high value targets on the battlefield at any time; make a direct hit on any target we can see; and destroy any target we can hit."[23] While armies before the RMA had relied on the massed force of as many individual weapons as possible and a few overwhelming nuclear weapons, precision-strike doctrine focused on the ability both to see and to select critical high-value targets and to cripple them rapidly in order to break down the enemy's operating capabilities, without major casualties on either side and without significant civilian casualties.[24] While the wars Clausewitz wrote about were between mass armies inflicting mass casualties on a massive scale, the RMA used precision strike to scale this way back.

To achieve precision strike required "joint" efforts between services. Air force and navy weapons systems would have to work in intimate coordination with army systems. This coordination is never easy between rival stovepipes, and, as noted earlier, weapons procurement itself remains service controlled. Again, the DOD's efforts began with DARPA working initially outside the service R & D systems. The "Assault Breaker" R & D program was envisioned to break up any Soviet charge through the Fulda Gap, and was led by a series of related DARPA technological development efforts over many years.[25]

Over time, the technologies contemplated in Assault Breaker were modified and evolved into the DOD's "1997 Joint Warfighter S&T Plan."[26] The precision-strike system came to include JSTARS, a large aircraft packed with powerful radars to "see" much of the battlefield and acquire and track ground targets. These were tied to Army Tactical Missile Systems (ATACMS) that could hit mobile targets well behind battle lines, as well as to a range of other precision-guided missiles and aircraft-launched precision "submunitions" (smaller weapons carried in a missile warhead) and "smart bombs"—all linked to a "Battlefield Control Element" (BCE) to collect and integrate battlefield information.

In summary, the Joint Warfighter S&T Plan entailed a combination of technologies for surveillance, targeting, and precision-guided munitions, all resting on earlier DARPA-led advances in information technology. Again, there was service resistance at a number of stages in the implementation process. Leadership from the Office of the Secretary of Defense was required to build and mount the operating systems, and was crucial in pressing for more service "jointness." The retrospective Institute for Defense Analysis study found the following:

Perhaps even more important than the testing and developing of specific technologies [led by DARPA] was the conceptual breakthrough in getting the Services to work together across the barriers of roles and missions to attack the Warsaw Pact tank threat. This cooperative approach was resisted by . . . the Services, but facilitated by parts of the Army because they understood that the Service needed to work more closely with the Air Force to meet the European threat. . . . The Services had other priorities. The Army continued developing and deploying tanks and helicopters and many in the Service did not want to invest in the new missile technology. So too the Air Force. The larger Service had more important acquisitions: the F-15 and F-16, for example. When competing with Service programs, even good new ideas will not get through the system without a powerful advocate—and for a Joint concept as sweeping as Assault Breaker the advocate had best be the Secretary of Defense.[27]

Precision strike thus resulted from the promotion of innovation by DARPA, combined with pressure from the secretary's office, according to the *innovation organization* model. Together the two organizations constituted the change agent required to get around the legacy sector problems—from *powerful vested interests* to *cost structures* to *collective action* problems—that afflict the defense establishment.

UNMANNED AERIAL VEHICLES

The idea for unmanned aerial vehicles (UAVs, often called drones) began and went through limited development stages in both world wars as attack devices before the advent of guided missiles. While there were early Cold War efforts by the navy and air force, with some remotely piloted vehicles (RPVs) used in Vietnam, the air force shut down its UAV efforts in 1976 and shifted focus to cruise missiles. Work on a navy antisubmarine rotor aircraft ("Dash/Snoopy") was undertaken in the late 1960s. These devices were used on ships and by marines in Vietnam but the program was subsequently terminated.[28] Despite this early history, today's UAVs are pervasive on the US battlefield and in counterterrorist operations. They undertake a wide range of roles: reconnaissance (using cameras, sensors, and radar), electronic intelligence gathering, long-term surveillance, target designation, communications relays, and now, carrying on-board weapons, attacks on specific targets. The US military is approaching the point where it will have more UAVs than manned aircraft.

Starting in the mid-1970s, DARPA played a key role in developing the enabling technologies that lay behind later UAV success. It funded R & D in sensors, radar, signal location systems, controls, lightweight and low-visibility airframe structures, long-endurance propulsion, and new operating concepts. In the 1980s, working with a highly innovative designer, Abraham Karem, and his small company, DARPA also funded a critical UAV technological development program that built and tested the Amber UAV. After initial flight demonstrations, Navy Secretary John Lehman, a UAV advocate, provided support for the program.

However, Amber was terminated in 1990, rejected by the services as not meeting their durability requirements. But the prototypes for Amber pushed the state of the art, developing critical technologies that were fundamental to subsequent development. This was an example of DARPA pushing outside the box of its R & D role and undertaking product development traditionally left to the services. DARPA played a significant role in the development of other UAV prototypes during this period, and the navy learned lessons from Israeli drones, which were adopted as the "Pioneer UAV" for spotting ship gunfire.[29] But UAVs weren't being developed or produced at a pace where they could make a difference—they weren't scaling up. Frustrated with service failures in developing UAV technologies, Congress intervened in 1988 and forced the consolidation of service UAV programs into a joint project office, a reform that led to a third generation of UAV technology.[30]

Taking advantage of the remarkable performance of RMA technologies in the 1991 Gulf War as a demonstration of the power of advanced technology to transform the battlefield, the Defense Science Board, the leading DOD technical advisory body, called attention to military problems that could be resolved by improved UAV capabilities. And in the subsequent Clinton administration, the trio of defense and intelligence agency leaders, Secretary of Defense William Perry, Undersecretary of Defense John Deutch, and CIA director James Woolsey, pushed together for a renewed UAV effort. In cooperation with DARPA, a new "Advanced Concept Technology Demonstration" (ACTD) process was created under Deputy Undersecretary for Advanced Technology (and later DARPA director from 1995 to 1998) Larry Lynn, to streamline and accelerate defense technology development and management, but with early cooperation with service users. In effect, Lynn, Perry, and Deutch created a new process—essentially an innovation organization model—that was outside of the services but involved them in implementing new defense technologies, using UAVs to test the approach.

Two deployed UAVs, Predator and Global Hawk, resulted, both of which proved highly successful. Predator proved its worth in Bosnia, then in Kosovo, in Iraq no-fly zones, and in Afghanistan, where it was also armed with Hellfire missiles, becoming an attack as well as a surveillance system. Global Hawk was developed by DARPA (using its unique "Other Transaction Authority"[31] to waive traditional acquisition laws and requirements in order to speed development) and initially deployed in Afghanistan as a highly sophisticated reconnaissance tool.[32]

The Institute for Defense Analysis study reached several conclusions about the on-again, off-again UAV experience:

As occurred with [precision strike and stealth], successful demonstration of the technology for RPV/UAVs did not lead to early acceptance and deployment of the vehicles. . . . There were often differences between the expectations of the DARPA [program manager] and those of the Services on performance (unprepared field versus prepared airstrip) and the level of development (proof of principle versus the need for extensive engineering) needed to transition a program. These differences had an impact on the ability of the system to successfully continue into a deployed system. . . . The systems did not fit within the existing force structure and did not have strong service champions. Without better planning they could not survive the budget battles. The developments often did not fit with existing [Service] operations and doctrine.[33]

When UAV programs started, DARPA's role was to transition the technology to the services after the proof-of-concept stage, with DARPA doing the R & D and the services and industry doing the engineering and development. Then, with the Amber project, DARPA undertook to actually do the development, but the handoff to the services still proved difficult. The creation of a new technology transition mechanism, the "Advanced Concept Technology Demonstration" (ACTD) in the secretary's office, which used DARPA's highly flexible procurement authority and built-in service participation, made possible a more extended process. In effect, a new organizational mechanism was created outside the existing system as a change agent that finally succeeded in getting around the legacy sector problems between the services and efforts in the secretary's office to push innovative technologies, a clear example of the effectiveness of the *innovation organization* model in the military.

THE ROLE OF DARPA

Given its important role as change agent in advancing innovation despite the legacy features of the defense sector, DARPA requires a further examination. Created in 1958 by Eisenhower as a unifying force for defense R & D in light of the stovepiped space programs of the separate military services that had helped lead to America's *Sputnik* failure, DARPA became a unique entity, set up to address what we now call the legacy sector problems of the military, specifically the deficiencies in R & D collaboration between the military services. This was a particularly interesting model, very different from the basic research agencies that presidential science advisor Vannevar Bush advocated at the end of World War II, as typified by the National Science Foundation.

DARPA embodied a return to an earlier World War II "connected science and technology" approach, in which the innovation actors from private, academic, and government sectors collaborated, working at all stages of the innovation process from research through implementation. DARPA's aim was a "right-left" approach: decide the technologies you require from the right side of the innovation pipeline, then nurture breakthrough scientific advances on the left side of the pipeline to get there.[34] This approach is critical to the implementation of the *technology challenge* model, which calls for pursuing breakthrough technological challenges with potential transformative effects.

DARPA, probably the most successful of the postwar and Cold War science and technology agencies, led the information technology revolution[35] and a long series of other major advances.[36] As it came into its own in the 1970s and 1980s, DARPA was a counterweight to the Vannevar Bush postwar swing toward pure basic research. It operated not only in the basic research space but also further down the innovation pipeline in the development and prototyping spaces and has tried, as we have seen in the examples above, to hand off its technology advances to military procurement for initial product implementation. In this way, it is at the same time the leading example of the "extended pipeline" innovation model, and as we have seen in the preceding examples, when it confronted legacy sector issues, an excellent example of the operation of the "innovation organization" model.

Despite being tied to a security mission, DARPA and the DOD played a key role in the 1990s information technology innovation wave and the accompanying resurgence of the US economy. DARPA deliberately stood up most of its contributions to the IT revolution through the civilian sector. It recognized that the military, while strong at the initial breakthrough technology stages, had much more difficulty in mustering the money for ongoing development, incremental advances, and driving down the cost curve that an emerging civilian IT sector, mobilized around the profits from an irupting innovation wave, could invest. This approach enabled the DOD to gain access to IT technologies with more rapid incremental improvement at a much lower cost through the civilian economy than if it had operated on its own. So in IT, DARPA played the role of innovation sponsor, enabling the DOD to subsequently leverage IT technologies it needed off investments at scale from the private sector.

DARPA also incorporated another important feature. "Great group" innovation theory[37] posits that innovation involving complex technologies occurs through face-to-face collaboration in highly talented groups, and no longer by solo inventors. Groups that can accomplish breakthrough innovation advances (such as Oppenheimer's group at Los Alamos, the Rad Lab group developing radar in World War II, the transistor group at Bell Labs, Xerox PARC's desktop computing group, and the Mac group at Apple) appear to follow a number of common organizational methodologies, approaches, and principles that constitute "rulesets." Warren Bennis and Patricia Biederman examine a series of such groups and posit that achieving innovation requires a competitive challenge, met through deep collaboration, remarkable talent in a range of complementary fields, strong leadership, devotion to a mission, and other core organizational principles.[38]

Behind these "great groups" lies a supporting "innovation ecosystem" (or "innovation environment") based at the institutional level and above the personal, face-to-face group level. Both the groups and the ecosystem are required for innovation to occur. DARPA has operated at *both* the institutional and personal levels of innovation. Itself an institution, it plays a supporting role in promoting institutional innovation but has consciously fostered great groups as well.[39] DARPA has been both an innovation actor, in the sense that it has directly promoted innovation, and an innovation enabler, in the sense that it has promoted and encouraged great groups and even new institutional arrangements conducive to innovation. DARPA became a bridge organization connecting the two organizational elements behind innovation, both the institutional and the personal, unlike any other R & D entity previously stood up in government.

Other DARPA characteristics enhance this ability to operate at both the institutional and the personal innovation organization levels. The following list is largely drawn from DARPA's own descriptions of its organizing elements; together they define the ruleset by which DARPA operates.[40]

- *Small and flexible.* DARPA consists of only 100–150 professionals; some have referred to DARPA as "100 geniuses connected by a travel agent."
- *Flat.* DARPA is a flat, nonhierarchical organization, with empowered program managers.
- *Right-left challenge model.* DARPA uses a challenge-based, "right-left" research model.
- *Entrepreneurial.* DARPA emphasizes the selection of highly talented, entrepreneurial program managers, often with both academic and industry experience,

who serve for a limited (three- to five-year) duration, which sets the timeframe for DARPA projects.

- *No laboratories.* DARPA research is performed entirely by outside performers, with no internal research laboratory.
- *Acceptance of risk.* DARPA projects focus on a "high-risk/high payoff" motif, selected and evaluated on the impact that they could make on achieving a demanding capability or challenge.
- *Seed and scale.* DARPA provides initial short-term funding for seed efforts that can be scaled up to significant funding for promising concepts, but with clear willingness to terminate nonperforming projects.
- *Autonomy and freedom from bureaucratic impediments.* DARPA operates outside the civil-service hiring process and standard government contracting rules, which gives it unusual access to talent, plus speed and flexibility in contracting for R & D efforts. Although largely outside the bureaucracy, it tries to maintain a lifeline back to senior DOD administrators for support on technology implementation.
- *Hybrid model.* DARPA often puts small, innovative firms and university researchers together on the same project so that firms have access to breakthrough science and researchers see pathways to implementation.
- *Teams and networks.* At its best, DARPA creates and sustains highly talented teams of researchers—great groups—highly collaborative and networked around the challenge model.
- *Acceptance of failure.* At its best, DARPA pursues a high-risk model for breakthrough opportunities and is very tolerant of failure if the payoff from potential success is great enough.
- *Orientation to revolutionary breakthroughs in a connected approach.* DARPA is focused not on incremental but rather on radical innovation. It emphasizes high-risk investment, moves from fundamental technological advances to prototyping, and then hands off the production stage to the armed services or the commercial sector
- *A technology visioning process.*[41] Defined as creating an image of how a technology is likely to develop in the future and what a successful technology would look like (as opposed to taking incremental steps), this occurs at the front of DARPA's research-nurturing process.

Despite the organizational principles enunciated in this ruleset, DARPA is part of the defense innovation system; it is an entrepreneurial innovator within the DOD. To foster implementation, it must still rely on the military services, and must face the legacy pressures they can embody, for the follow-on stages.

INNOVATION AT THE DEFENSE DEPARTMENT

The stories of the three core breakthrough technologies behind the Revolution in Military Affairs illustrate the fact that the defense sector has many of the attributes of a legacy sector. However, the important point is that the DOD has found a way to put revolutionary technologies into place and bring on significant innovation. It has taken the technology covered wagons east!

The DOD turned out to have two major advantages in managing change in its change-resistant, entrenched legacy sector. First, it developed DARPA, a unique innovation entity aimed not only at great technological advance but also at innovation as a system and trying to solve profound puzzles surrounding implementation. DARPA operates outside the pressures of the military legacy sector and was created and designed in response to *Sputnik* in order to bring innovative change to a Defense Department affected by legacy problems. In effect, DARPA (and its allies) came to play the role that Hyman Rickover and his group played for atomic submarines[42] and that Bernard Schriever and his group played for inter-continental ballistic missiles.[43]

Second, DARPA alone was not enough. Unlike other legacy sectors, the DOD has an official, the secretary of defense, who must by law be a civilian and who can exercise authority to force change. If the secretary sees the need for a technology shift, he or she can muster the power, despite all of the legacy sector checks in the system, to direct it. DARPA has been successful when it ties its technological advance to a senior defense leader in the Office of the Secretary who is prepared to override legacy pressures. Of course, the DOD faced additional pressures for change—to meet national security needs and eventually to pass the practical test of actual warfare, but these two characteristics remain central. There are important lessons here for other legacy sectors: DARPA is a *connected* innovation agency that uses both the *extended pipeline* and the *innovation organization* models, that is outside the legacy system, and that is linked to a source of power that can direct change. This combination has allowed DARPA to be a vital "change agent" in the defense sector's ability to innovate.

CHANGE AGENTS AND META-CHANGE AGENTS

Transformative innovation in the military is not induced solely by strategic necessity or economic incentive; there is a visible hand. Although the elements needed for implementation of a significant innovation may be present on the landscape, a *change agent* is required to pull them together and catalyze change. These change agents can be individuals or organizations or both. Like innovation itself, change agents function at both the institutional and the personal, face-to-face level. And leadership—what we have called "meta-change agents" or "innovation enablers"— is needed to establish the change agents within the organization and then to allow them to carry out their work.

The DOD in the past has been able to initiate change through (1) competition between services (for example, through competing missile programs), (2) struggles between competing groups within a service (such as between "brown shoe" carrier aviators and "black shoe" battleship sailors in the navy), or (3) through directives from defense civilian leadership (such as through the DARPA-led advances noted above). In each approach, change agents were critical.

DARPA led the efforts for the technological advances leading to UAVs, precision strike, and stealth, and served as an institutional change agent. Its "challenge model" of organizing its R & D around breakthrough technology challenges was vital to this role. But additional actors at higher levels of the DOD were also critical. William Perry, allied with DARPA in two different tours of duty at the DOD, guided a series of major innovation efforts though the department. He served as a *meta-change agent* or *innovation enabler* as well, helping to get a change agent system started by putting in place the structures and policies to help enable the change agents to do their jobs. As we have seen, navy secretary John Lehman, defense undersecretary John Deutch, and deputy undersecretary Larry Lynn also played key roles in UAVs, and Malcolm Currie as DDR&E supported stealth as well as GPS and smart weapons in the 1970s. All played roles as change agents.

These conclusions apply to legacy sectors in the civilian world, mutatis mutandis, as well. These sectors need a strong research capability, change agents capable of effecting the resulting innovations, and meta-change agents to establish and support them within the organization and enable them to do their work. Without all three, it is hard to see how innovations, particularly in legacy sectors, can emerge out of the innovation pipeline.

LESSONS FROM THE IMPLEMENTATION OF INNOVATION IN DEFENSE

The stories of the three core breakthrough technologies behind the Revolution in Military Affairs illustrate that the defense sector has many of the attributes of a legacy sector. However, the important point is that the DOD has found a way to still put these revolutionary technologies into place and bring on significant innovation. Unlike most legacy sectors, where breakthrough and disruptive innovations languish, the DOD has actually implemented them.

As we have noted, the DOD turned out to have two major advantages in finding ways to change its legacy sector characteristics. First, it developed DARPA, which promotes innovation from outside the military services and sees innovation as an element in a system that must also consider the challenges of implementation. Second, DARPA has found ways to ally itself with defense leaders—meta-change agents—who can press its technology visions into realization.

A key lesson from DARPA's ability to bring innovation into a defense sector with deep legacy characteristics has been the importance of critical innovation institutions that embody both *connected science and technology*—linking scientific research to implementation stages—and *challenge* approaches—pursuing major mission technology challenges. As we have discussed above, innovation requires not only a process of creating connected science and technology challenges at the *institutional level*, but also must operate at the *personal level*. The critical stage of innovation is face-to-face, not institutional, so while institutions where talent and R & D come together are required, personal dynamics, usually embodied in "great groups," are a necessity.

The DARPA "right-left" research model can be important to reaching the innovation stage, where program managers contemplate the technological breakthroughs they seek to have emerge from the right end of the innovation pipeline, and then go back to the left side of the pipeline to look for proposals for the breakthrough research that will get them there. This process tends to lead to *revolutionary breakthroughs* that could transform a technology sector. A *technology visioning* process at the outset of the effort appears to be a particular key. The approach seeks *high-risk but high-reward* projects. These points about front-end innovation will be elaborated on below.

Second, DARPA alone, although it has played an institutional change agent role, has not been enough. Unlike most legacy sectors, the DOD has an official, the secretary of defense, who must by law be a civilian and who can exercise authority to force change. If the secretary, or the other senior officials who work with him or her, see the need for a technology shift, they can muster the power, despite the extensive legacy sector checks in the system, to direct it. DARPA has been successful when it ties its technological advance to a senior defense leader in the Office of the Secretary who is prepared to override legacy pressures and be a *change agent.* The agent can be an individual, typically part of an institution, such as the secretary's office or DR&E, or an organization. Of course, the DOD faced additional intense pressures for change—meeting national security needs and the ultimate test of armed conflict—but these two characteristics, a strong front-end innovation linked to change agents, remain central.

There are important lessons here for other legacy sectors: a "connected" innovation agency, using the "extended pipeline" model that is outside the legacy system, and linked to a source of power that can direct change—a change agent— has proved to be vital to the defense sector's ability to innovate. The long-standing perspective on DARPA has been that its successes have been in the "frontier" sector; it is rightly acclaimed for its foundational role in the IT revolution. But there is a less understood perspective on DARPA that is the other side of the coin: it has brought disruptive, radical innovation into a legacy sector, the military.

So DARPA doesn't belong only in the "extended pipeline" model. It also has developed features that have enabled it to innovate in the legacy defense sector. This means that it also represents key features of what we term the "innovation organization" model. Legacy sectors use political, technological, economic, and social system barriers in their defense against disruptive innovation. The innovation organization model recognizes that there are many institutions and mechanisms operating within an innovation system, particularly in legacy sectors; this mandates a fuller evaluation of the potential for innovation, of the obstacles to these innovations, and of the policies that could facilitate them. DARPA and its senior department allies have found ways, which we have delineated above, to impose this richer mix of considerations. This mix of strong front-end innovation capability, linked to change agents and backed by meta-change agents and innovation enablers, provides basic lessons for innovation in legacy sectors that go far beyond defense and apply directly to other key parts of the economy. We shall return to this this theme in chapter 11 after we explore the international dimensions of the legacy sector model.

9 Enabling and Disabling National Innovation Environments in Europe, China, and India

Most countries are not concerned about driving covered wagons west. Unlike Americans, they don't always identify the idea of innovation with the design and commercialization of new industrial products.[1] Nor have they based their economies on the development of radical new products the way Americans have. In short, they don't have covered wagons, and if they had had them, they might never have driven them west in the first place.

Although much of the US economy is in what we have called legacy sectors, the recent IT and biotech innovation waves have created a general impression that the US economy is generally open to new products and to radical innovations, so that American readers are likely to consider the legacy sectors that we discussed in previous chapters to be exceptional cases. The reality is that the frontier sectors in the United States, which scale gradually, still constitute a modest percentage of the US economy as measured by their total contribution to GDP, as compared to the significant majority of the economy that can be readily categorized as in legacy sectors.[2] But for deep cultural and historic reasons, the frontier sectors create the appearance of operating at a larger scale in the United States.

The overall economies of most other countries display many of the systematic obstacles to innovation, defended by entrenched vested interests and stacked in favor of incumbents, that we have used to define the idea of a legacy sector. This is not to say, however, that other countries do not innovate or that Americans have nothing to learn from them. On the contrary, we have been learning from other countries, and they from us, for centuries. Today, the national innovation environments of China and Germany have many of their strengths in just those areas where the American system is weakest, and are doing their best to increase their overall competitiveness by shoring up their own weak spots. So we shall now explore how our conceptual framework can illuminate these strengths and weaknesses, and what the new perspective made possible by this comparison can teach us about the American environment for science, technology, and innovation.

INNOVATION ENVIRONMENTS, CONTEXTS, AND SYSTEMS

To begin this quick journey, we need to recall our earlier discussion of the environment for innovation, an idea that we introduced very briefly in chapter 1. We can define the national innovation *environment* (or if you prefer, the national innovation *ecosystem*)[3] as consisting of the national innovation *system* plus the national innovation *context* in which it operates. It's time to explore these concepts in more detail.

The national *innovation system* is defined as a set of public and private institutions and policies established for the purpose of encouraging, facilitating, and supporting research, innovation, and the development of technological capacity.[4] It includes publicly and privately owned scientific and technological research and development laboratories, science and engineering education at all levels from elementary school to the Ph.D., technical support organizations like institutions for standards and metrology (the science of measurement), geological and other natural resource surveys, consulting and engineering firms, disciplinary and cross-disciplinary organizations of scientists, engineers, and health professionals, and the policies and funding arrangements that support all of the above, including for technology transfer and for the protection of intellectual property. Depending on the country, this system may be supported by government, by private industry, by nongovernmental organizations, or (most commonly) by some combination of the three.

In economic theory, the role of government intervention in promoting innovation is justified by the need to correct for the various imperfections in the market for technology that result in suboptimal levels of investment. The implicit assumption is that government will step in whenever market imperfections inhibit innovations that would otherwise take place. In practice, however, resources are inevitably limited. Even the wealthiest countries are forced to make choices about the areas of science and technology that they wish to emphasize. In addition, many governments, including that of the United States, support the development of technology they deem to be strategic, taking on risks the private sector is reluctant to assume. The national innovation system inevitably reflects this strategic emphasis even as it seeks to encourage research and innovation throughout the economy.

The national *innovation context* exerts at least as powerful an effect on the speed and direction of innovation in a given country as does the more obvious and better studied national innovation *system*. Key elements of this context include culture (especially attitude toward competition, cooperation, risk, novelty, entrepreneurship, and the importance of family, social class, gender, sexual preference, and national origin), religion, social structure (including social mobility and the relations between researchers and businesspeople), the economic perspectives of the political system, macroeconomic policy (including possible controls on the prices of energy and other basic commodities), the system of banking and finance, industrial structure, business climate, trade and exchange rate policy, labor and environmental policies, immigration laws, bankruptcy and real estate law, the functioning of the legal system, the state of physical infrastructure and connectivity, and even the definition of innovation—radical versus incremental—implicit in the policies that support the innovation system.[5]

The national innovation context and the national innovation system are closely interrelated. Much of the national innovation system in any country is designed to support innovation in areas where the country is already strong, that reflect existing political and market support or into which it is well positioned to move on the basis of existing strengths. These areas reflect comparative advantage that has already developed within the prevailing innovation context and may indeed have gained their strength from the past policies and programs of the national innovation system. The national innovation system thus reflects prevailing conditions and sentiment, and may therefore not be available to encourage innovation when it is needed in areas that are not in tune with prevailing paradigms. To the extent that all or part of a given national innovation system reflects an economic structure that is no longer in sync with larger goals, we could even say that it itself reflects some of the characteristics of a legacy sector, a thought to which we shall later return.

The national innovation system also includes public policies, programs, and institutions specifically intended to help overcome known deficiencies in the national innovation context. In the public sector, these might include subsidized venture capital intended to overcome the risk aversion of the financial system, measures to encourage the participation of disadvantaged groups, or measures to encourage collaboration among competing firms on "precompetitive" research—that is, research on problems that are common to many firms in an industry but will not lead directly to proprietary products. In the private sector, business can contribute to the innovation system over and above its own proprietary research, for example by setting technical standards or by its contribution to precompetitive research. Even so, and as we have seen, the problems addressed by these measures are typically deeply rooted in a country's culture and social and economic structure and are difficult to overcome, so that policy measures to overcome them are in effect "pushing on a string." Subsidized venture capital, for example, may be ineffective in stimulating entrepreneurial activity if entrepreneurship and risk-taking are inhibited by legal, social, or cultural factors.

When a national innovation context presents obstacles to innovation, it forms an important part of the paradigms that characterize legacy sectors. More constructively, a national innovation context can stimulate and encourage innovation across an economy—or it can encourage innovation in some sectors and discourage it in others. The national innovation context also has a strong influence on the direction of innovation and, at a more basic level, on the choice of technology that is applied throughout the economy. The strength and effectiveness of policies for the protection of the environment, of public health, and of worker health and safety, to cite three examples, affect the willingness of industry and government to invest in available technologies for these purposes, and in the longer run, to invest in research and innovation to improve these technologies. Labor laws affect the willingness of employers to hire and train workers, and hence the availability of a skilled workforce and the choice between labor- and capital-intensive technology. The overall business climate and the rate of growth of the economy affect the willingness of firms to expand and hence to invest in new capital equipment embodying newer technology. The six country cases we explore in this chapter display the importance of the national innovation context and its interaction with the better known national innovation system.

THE INTERNATIONAL INNOVATION SYSTEM AND THE VALUE CHAINS WITHIN IT

National innovation systems have increasingly become pillars of support for an *international innovation system* that facilitates the flow of information, ideas, education, skills, technical services, people, equipment, and capital, including venture capital.[6] The international R & D collaboration that is an essential feature of this international system provides the basis for the globalization of technological capacity for research and of the development and production of innovative products.[7] It also facilitates the spread of the results of basic and precompetitive research, the financing of which is still largely dominated by national innovation systems.

The international innovation system is dominated by multinational corporations (MNCs), which in the aggregate carry out over half of all of the world's research and development (predominantly development). Multinationals are important for the development and engineering of new products, as well as for their unique integrating function. Unlike university or government laboratories, they can tap into and integrate world knowledge, enter the innovation process at any point, and translate an idea into a product and carry it through to production and commercialization, locating the necessary operations wherever they find it convenient to do so. (Foundations and aid agencies do some of this, but only to a limited extent and in special cases.) In this way, they operate with the features of the later stages of the extended pipeline model discussed in earlier chapters, except that they do not do much basic research, so generally have a more incremental than radical innovation approach.

As we have seen in chapter 4, this international flexibility is a critical contributor to the problems of the US manufacturing industry. Conversely, as we shall shortly discuss, it is of key importance to developing countries like China and India that are upgrading their manufacturing capability to more profitable products and more advanced technology. To understand the evolving innovation systems in the four economies we evaluate below, we need to understand the nature of the value chains that help sustain them.

As we have already discussed in the specific context of manufacturing, much of the international innovation system in many industries derives from the globalization of the *innovation value chain* as a result of the relatively easy separation of research and new product development, on the one hand, from production and process innovation, on the other, across what we have earlier called the *engineering fault line*. A similar process of globalization has taken place in the *innovation value network* or *industrial ecosystem* of support institutions like consulting firms, equipment suppliers, and technical services.

Both of these are examples of the "unbundling" of tasks—the separation of once-unified tasks into component parts, each of which can be located in a different place. In the academic literature, this is known as the "organizational decomposition of the innovation process."[8] A different unbundling, that of the production of goods, allows the easy separation of once-unified production processes into their component parts—a critical factor in the export of production jobs to emerging economies and hence to the employment problems of the United States and other advanced countries, as discussed in chapter 4.

The concept of the value chain was originally applied to the links that connect the producers of raw materials with the consumers or users of the finished final product of which they form a part, which we may call a *production value chain*.[9] The decentralized production value chain for coffee, for example, starts with the growers of coffee beans and extends through the processors (roasters, grinders), transporters, and finally to the retailers and coffee shops.[10] Innovation can take place at any link in this chain, for example through improved agronomy, food technology, or transportation technology, and can also take place in the definition and marketing of the product (as, for example, the promotion of Colombian coffee and the invention of the Starbucks "experience") or in the organization or the structure of the value chain itself. Other value chains are vertically integrated entirely within the structure of a multinational corporation. Whether the production value chain is integrated or decentralized, the location of its elements—and the jobs that they create—is determined by a number of criteria, two of the most important of which are proximity to markets and the relative capability of different possible locations to carry out the various tasks and steps in the production process.

The concept of the value chain can be applied to the innovation process. Here the geographic patterns are analogous to those of the production value chain. As described in chapter 4, the innovation value chain begins with research and proceeds to invention, product development, prototyping, demonstration, pilot production, and finally to full-scale manufacturing process and innovation.[11] The location of each innovation process is determined by the geography, technical capacity, and business climate of different potential locations, by the characteristics of the production process (tacit or codified, easy or difficult, labor- or capital-intensive), and by the proximity to prospective markets. If innovation and production are closely linked, they will by definition have to be located together; if not, at least for some product lines (including commodity goods and IT goods), they can be separate. This is the case whether the value chain for innovation is decentralized among nominally independent entities or is vertically integrated within the organization of a multinational corporation, in which case the MNC can locate innovation and production wherever it likes, together or separately.[12] Indeed, more than half of the

R & D carried out by MNCs takes place away from the country in which its headquarters are located.

The international innovation system is important to producers in developing countries that want to upgrade their participation in the value chain. It creates space for suppliers to innovate, first in production processes, later in components of a standard product, and still later as a manufacturer of original equipment. The lead company sets the product standard up to the point at which the supplier makes the fateful decision to strike out on its own and to produce under its own brand name, at which point it is itself responsible to innovate in response to changes in markets and technology. This process of technology transfer and absorption, followed by indigenous innovation and movement up to the more profitable links in the value chain, was critical to the development of the manufacturing sectors of Korea and Taiwan, and is now being followed by China and several of the smaller countries of Southeast Asia. It is also the pattern, mutatis mutandis, for the development of the Indian IT sector.

STRONGLY ENABLING AND DISABLING INNOVATION CONTEXTS: SCANDINAVIA AND RUSSIA

We now return to the national innovation *environment* in order to consider two extreme examples, taken from opposite ends of the spectrum of economic liberalization, that illustrate the critical importance of the national innovative *context*.

Innovation in Scandinavia

The small, open economies of the Scandinavian countries provide an innovation environment that demonstrates the synergy that can obtain between a favorable innovation context and a truly enabling national innovation system. In these countries, both private industry and the general public understand that their economy is constantly subject to the pressures of international competition, so that continuing innovation is necessary to meet international standards of performance, quality and price. The Scandinavian labor force is generally accepting of technological change and willing to adapt to a changing global environment. They recognize that innovation is good for the society as a whole, even if individual jobs are temporarily lost or changed.

This willingness to accept change is an important cultural element of the Scandinavian innovation context. It is in part a function of the safety net created by the welfare state, of the high level of trust in institutions, and of the strong social cohesion characteristic of the relatively homogeneous Scandinavian societies. It is reflected in a number of public policies that reinforce this context. "Flexicurity" policies make possible a flexible labor market that allows firms to take on workers in the knowledge that they can be let go if things do not work out. On the labor side, these policies are reinforced by a welfare state that provides generous unemployment benefits and "active labor market programs" to help the unemployed find jobs.[13] This system reduces the costs and hence the potential opposition to the creative destruction of firms at the same time that a strong safety net reduces the risks inherent in any new venture to both individuals and to employers—the opposite of the vested interests that obstruct disruptive innovation in legacy sectors in other countries.[14]

The Scandinavian innovation *system* is likewise strong. Scandinavian governments are committed to high levels of R & D funding, which in turn tend to spur complementary investments in R & D by industry.[15] Scandinavian education systems are famously strong, especially for primary and secondary education. Tertiary education, though solid, varies in quality across the different countries and universities, as does its links to private industry.[16] Even so, the idea of the "triple helix" of collaboration between government, universities, and industry is ingrained in the Scandinavian system. It is recognized that close cooperation among these groups is key to innovation.[17] While the Scandinavian economies appear in general to have avoided many of the characteristics of legacy sectors as set out in chapter 5, particular sectors in particular countries can still be subject to various legacy market imperfections, from lumpiness to split incentives to network economies.

Innovation in Russia

Conversely, a grossly unfavorable innovation context can defeat almost any national innovation system and create a disabling innovation environment. Innovation faces almost insuperable obstacles in kleptocracies like those of contemporary Russia,[18] many of the former Soviet republics, and the dictatorships that preceded (and mostly survived) the Arab Spring—more or less independent of the strength of the innovation system as measured, for example, by the level of government support to research and development. The entire economies of these countries display legacy characteristics, posing obstacles to innovation that dwarf those encountered in legacy sectors in the United States—all stoutly defended by entrenched vested interests closely linked to the government.

The dominant feature of the Russian innovation context is a stifling business climate. Regardless of official efforts to build "innovation cities,"[19] there is not much point for a budding entrepreneur to work day and night on an innovative technology (or indeed on anything else) if they know that the economic system excludes anyone without the proper political connections or that the government is likely to stifle their business, once it is successful, with a thicket of mutually contradictory regulations and an endless series of trumped-up inspections violations—or worse, if the local government, perhaps in league with organized crime, is likely simply to seize their assets, an extreme form of the obstacles to innovation from *government regulation*.

The actions of this carefully designed, predatory kleptocracy have put all businesspeople, no matter how prominent, on notice that their money and assets are subject to confiscation whenever the rulers decide they need them.[20] A defining feature of this corruption is its short-term outlook, born in part from the perception of an uncertain long-term outlook and in part from long tradition dating back more than a century. In Russia, corrupt officials prefer a quick payoff even though it forces a firm into bankruptcy—killing off the goose that lays the golden eggs rather than caring for it as an investment.[21] As we shall shortly see, corruption plays an important role in the People's Republic of China, too, but with a very different impact on the growth rate and innovation environment in that country.

The communist economies of the old Soviet empire and of Maoist China are iconic examples of such disabling innovation systems. In brief summary, the tenets of Marxist economics, the dominance of the military-industrial complex, the system of centralized planning, the preferential allocation of investment capital to state-owned enterprises, and the operation of production facilities to meet physical production targets rather than to satisfy consumer demand, the fixation on the use of domestic raw materials and on technological self-reliance (reinforced by extensive restrictions on technology exports from the West), Stalinist gigantomania[22] and determination to dominate nature,[23] and Maoist revolutionary anarchy and dogmatic attachment to small-scale technology—all combined to create an environment that provided few incentives for innovations to improve efficiency or quality, in classic examples of disabling innovation contexts that vitiated the substantial Soviet investments in research.[24]

The assumptions of Marxist economics directly affected the innovation context of communist countries and the choice and implementation of technology in Russian and Maoist Chinese factories. Of these assumptions, two of the most important were the absence of value attached, first, to human capital and, second, to natural resources, including the environment. Surprisingly in the "worker's paradise," Soviet industry invested little in worker training (Lenin was a Taylorist and regarded the worker as an extension of the machine) or in the creation of a safe and healthful workplace. On the contrary, demanding physical labor under difficult conditions in polluting factories was the hallmark of the heroic Soviet worker.

The Marxist assumption that resources and environment were free goods prescribed a *perverse price structure*—or more precisely, the absence of a pricing structure—that led to a systematic misallocation of resources in order to maximize production, regardless of input costs or environmental damage—resulting, among other things, in the creation of some of the most dangerous factories and most polluted places on earth.[25] When the Soviet Union fell, its focus on energy-intensive heavy industry, combined with the Marxist emphasis on the production of tangible objects rather than services, left the states of the former Soviet Union and its satellites in Eastern Europe stuck with obsolete plant just as the world economy was evolving resource-conserving, information-intensive industry, a damaging long-run consequence of these perverse incentives.

These economic distortions were complemented by counterproductive *organizational and institutional* obstacles to innovation. The Soviet military-industrial complex—which produced most consumer durables in addition to strictly military hardware—had first claim on natural and human resources and, like the military everywhere, was largely immune to cost or environmental limitations. Below a handful of strong universities and technical institutes for R & D, engineering education was fragmented into small subspecialties ("ball-bearing engineers"), leading to a *human resources structure* organized around existing technologies.

On the research side, the separation of research into specialized technical institutes separate from the higher education system blocked the creation of strong research universities (and accompanying "learning by doing" research education for graduate students) that is so critical to research-based innovation in most OECD nations.[26] And the separation of research from production ignored the difficulties of technology transfer and the need for the direct involvement of researchers in the adoption of technology by industry. The communist system thus left an economy-wide legacy from which China and the independent states of the former Soviet Union are endeavoring to escape, but which created a variety of powerful *vested interests* that pose major obstacles to reform.

Today's Russian innovation *context* displays legacy characteristics in particularly dramatic form. These include *perverse subsidies and prices* that neglect externalities, particularly environmental externalities, a *governmental and institutional architecture* that limits innovation through governmental controls and failures, an *established knowledge structure* embedded in problematic R & D organization, and an *aversion to innovation* because of its historic defense orientation, as well as a series of market imperfections. (The countries of Eastern Europe inherited a somewhat similar legacy[27] but benefited from the opportunity to join the European Union and have followed a different trajectory.)

The cultural aspects of the innovation *context* are likewise a problem. A national culture inherited from the communist regime—and in many cases from czarist times—still embodies a general distrust of business and a tradition of central allocation of resources for technological showpieces rather than for profitable innovation. Intermittent government repression discourages creative people from remaining in the country. Another old tradition, that the prospect of earning income from a business is a privilege granted by government rather than the right of a citizen, has led to weak protection of intellectual property. On the economic side, the dominance of investment in oil and natural gas, together with an exchange rate set by energy exports—a phenomenon known to economists as "Dutch disease"[28]—has discouraged private investment in relatively risky investments in technological innovation (although recent fluctuation in energy prices shows that energy investments have risks of their own). In the innovation system, the separation of Russian research institutions from universities and industry continues to have deleterious effects on innovation.[29]

A QUICK TOUR OF FOUR NATIONAL INNOVATION ENVIRONMENTS: GERMANY, FRANCE, CHINA, AND INDIA

Against this background, we are now ready to examine the national innovation environments of France, Germany, China, and India, countries chosen both for their intrinsic importance and for the variety of stimuli and obstacles to innovation that they illustrate. Our analysis is based on secondary sources and the authors' personal experience in these countries. It uses the conceptual framework based on the ideas of innovation environment and legacy systems that we have developed in this and earlier chapters.

As we shall see, the national innovation contexts of these four countries pose obstacles to the kind of path-breaking product innovations that constitute American comparative advantage. The same incentives that affect the rate and direction of innovation can also pose obstacles to efforts to increase employment (France) or to protect the environment (China). On the other hand, they are well suited to innovations in manufacturing (in Germany and China) and in the development of modern infrastructure (France and China).

National authorities in these countries are well aware of the strengths and weaknesses we shall discuss, and have put in place a variety of policies and programs in their innovation systems intended to increase their competitiveness and help overcome existing obstacles to radical product innovation. In particular, European countries have made efforts to establish a regional innovation environment through the European Union (EU) that would be intermediate between the national and global systems described in an earlier section of this chapter. This system is intended to supplement the work of national systems by promoting agreed strategies for establishing a regional framework for innovation: harmonized standards, "enabling technologies," and common policies for competition, trade, investment, education, and training.[30]

EU research programs encourage and facilitate the creation of international research networks and cross-border collaborations, and facilitate the sharing of risks of projects too large for any single country to undertake. They typically provide relatively small amounts of money, which are, however, valued for their flexibility by researchers and research administrators, much of whose budgets are tied up in salaries and other fixed expenses. The effect of these programs is to overcome the *lumpiness, economies of scale*, and *network economies* inherent in much of today's research and development.

The EU has publically recognized that the main obstacles to European regional innovation system are actually issues of innovation context and legacy paradigm of the kind we have discussed: "poor availability of finance, costly patenting, market fragmentation, outdated regulations and procedures, slow standard-setting and the failure to use public procurement strategically," and is starting to address them.[31] The European Commission promotes the idea of a "Fifth Freedom for Europe," the freedom of knowledge, by removing barriers to knowledge circulation.[32] The Commission attributes these barriers to "cultural differences between the business and science communities; lack of incentives; legal barriers; and fragmented markets for knowledge and technology"[33]—again, issues concerning the innovation context rather than the innovation system as the latter is traditionally defined.

The EU programs embody the principles set forth in the Lisbon Agenda, a plan laid out in 2000 by the European Council to increase the competitiveness of the European knowledge-based economy by the end of the decade. The Agenda included no enforcement mechanism, instead relying on peer pressure to induce the individual countries that agreed to the Agenda to carry out its recommendations. The Lisbon Agenda raised European consciousness and stimulated discussion of the issues surrounding competitiveness and entrepreneurship. Even so, countries found it difficult to enact and implement the many necessary reforms, first because some of the goals, such as the target of innovation intensity (R & D expenditure divided by GNP) of 3%, were unrealistically ambitious except in Germany, and second, because many of the elements of the national innovation context that are addressed in the Lisbon framework are deeply embedded in national culture and identity—a problem that persists today and to which we shall return.[34]

The German Innovation Environment

As we have explained in chapter 4, the German innovation environment is especially effective in its support to globally competitive, family-owned manufacturing firms that feel substantial loyalty to the regions in which they are located, that are relatively free of short-term pressures from capital markets, and that dominate specialized niches in capital goods industries by virtue of superior quality.[35] Our review of the German innovation environment focuses on this part of German industry, since this has been the aspect of greatest interest to international readers. These innovative small and medium-sized firms are supported by a rich "industrial ecosystem"—in our terms, an innovation system—of applied research institutions, skilled workers, trade associations, unions, vocational schools, university programs and curricula, university-industry collaborations and technical advisory committees. However, this network has not been able to exploit new technological opportunities in sectors like information and communications.

The German innovation *context* is a mixture of economics and culture that is equally favorable to large, small and medium-sized manufacturers. On the economic side, as we discussed in chapter 6, German manufacturers benefit from the fact that the country shares the euro currency with the weaker economies of southern and Eastern Europe, making its exchange rate cheaper and hence more favorable to exporters than it would have been if Germany still had its own currency—a *perverse price* for foreign exchange from the point of view of the United States and the rest of Europe, although perhaps not for Germany.[36]

On the cultural side, Germans have a strong tradition of appreciation for the importance of manufacturing, backed by a traditional emphasis on craftsmanship and cooperation, even among competing firms—a *public expectation* opposite to that regarding the manufacturing sector in the United States. The institutional expressions of this tradition are: a *Kurzarbeit* program that provides subsidies to firms to encourage them to retain skilled workers at reduced working hours during economic downturns;[37] laws that make it easy and advantageous to pass ownership down from generation to generation and hence reinforce a long-term planning horizon; locally owned, regionally focused financial institutions with a long time horizon and a clear understanding of the needs of small-scale manufacturers and of their importance to the local economy;[38] and the requirement by law that one-third to one-half of the supervisory boards of private firms consist of union representatives, a structure that maintains and reinforces the strength of these unions and ensures political support for major programs of vocational education, apprenticeships, training, and retraining. (Despite these strong programs of vocational training and apprenticeship, Germany has begun to suffer from skill shortages, a problem exacerbated by relatively strict limitations on the immigration of skilled workers.)[39] This structure, however, creates *vested interests* that make it difficult to restructure firms so as to increase productivity.[40] Until recent reforms, strong labor legislation made it difficult to fire workers, creating additional strong motivation for private investment in worker training and skill formation but also leading to a reluctance to hire additional labor, although the effect of this reluctance on training and employment has been mitigated by the continued strength of the German economy.[41]

All of these characteristics form part of an enabling innovation context that underpins and reinforces German skill at incremental process innovation in manufacturing and in the rapid "repurposing" of technology—that is, the application of a technology that was developed for application in one industry to solve problems in a completely different industry—for example, by adapting technologies originally designed for shipbuilding, robotic coating systems, and the manufacture of automobile components to various applications in the renewable energy industries.

On the down side, German culture tends to be conservative and to prefer well-established products, an example of *public habits and expectations* favoring incumbent technology and discouraging breakthrough innovation. It is also *risk averse*, a characteristic whose institutional expression takes the form of banks that are reluctant to finance start-ups and other risky ventures, although they continue to support innovative small and midsize manufacturers.[42] There are some signs of change: Berlin is becoming an active hub for start-ups and may become an emerging exception to this generalization. According to the concepts we have developed in our previous analysis of legacy sectors, this would count as an *imperfection in capital markets*—or in the words of chapters 2 and 5, a "financing system geared to incumbents and reluctant to extend risk capital to disruptive, new entrant technologies."

The cultural dimension of the German innovation context also includes limited tolerance for the risks of entrepreneurship and a tendency to punish failure; a failed businessperson is unlikely to find support for a second try. These features of German culture pose major obstacles to the development of radical new products—a problem highlighted in our previous discussion of legacy sectors as a *"public habit and expectation attuned to existing technology."* A variety of permitting issues, somewhat analogous to those that arise in the United States, pose obstacles to the deployment of renewable energy technology—a *"regulatory hurdle . . . [for] new entrants."*

The German innovation system reinforces the strengths of the German innovation context and makes some efforts to overcome its weaknesses. Its greatest strengths are in the strong industrial associations and research consortia that provide a venue for interfirm collaboration, and strong university programs in manufacturing engineering and in research collaboration with industry. At the apex of this system stands the Fraunhofer Gesellschaft, a set of sixty large (300–400 employees each), well- and stably financed institutes that carry out high-quality, short-term, immediately applicable research, financed by contracts with industry with cost-sharing by government, that encourage collaboration between university and industry and between large and small firms.[43] The Fraunhofer institutes focus their efforts on industries that are already well established in Germany, rather than on newer and riskier high-tech areas.

Through the Fraunhofer institutes, complemented by a regional manufacturing financing system that enables rapid scale-up of innovative production and a strong system for workforce training, Germany has been able to systematically advance its strong manufacturing sector. Its innovation system focuses on incremental advances at the engineering stage and is weaker on radical innovation, but it continues to use its collaborative system to translate production and related innovation into employment. Unlike the United States, Germany has built a strong public-private collective capability across its manufacturing sector that serves as an international model that substantially overcomes the market imperfection around *collective action*.

The R & D in most German small and medium manufacturers is located in Germany, close to their main production facilities, so as to encourage interaction between producers and researchers. In these industries, the participation of German SMEs in the *international innovation system* often takes the form of R & D facilities established alongside manufacturing operations that are located near large overseas markets in order to take advantage of the close links between R & D and manufacturing.[44] The back-and-forth technology transfer transactions of German windmill manufacturers with their Chinese counterparts, described in a subsequent section of this chapter, illustrate another pattern of active participation by German small and medium-sized manufacturing firms in the international innovation system. Like their counterparts in other countries, large German MNCs, such as Siemens, BMW, Volkswagen, and Daimler-Benz, participate actively in the international innovation system through subsidiaries and manufacturing and R & D facilities all over the world. The Fraunhofer Gesellschaft, although based primarily in Germany, maintains seven branches in the United States, in part in order to keep track of technological developments there, as well as branches in China, Austria, Portugal, and Italy, another example of German participation in the international innovation system.[45]

German funding for higher education and research is generous and stable even during economic downturns, as evidenced by the €11 billion in stimulus to education, science, and technology provided during the 2008 economic crisis.[46] Until recently, research money was awarded to German universities largely on the basis of tradition and institutional prestige rather than open competition, an element of the national innovation system that constituted an adverse *institutional architecture* that discouraged discoveries that might lead to radical innovation. The main institutions for research in Germany are the Max Planck Institutes for basic research and the Helmholtz Association, which funds and encourages multidisciplinary research on "grand challenges."

German universities tend to be overcrowded—perhaps because of the tradition of free tuition—underresourced, and hampered by rigid institutional and career structures. Professors are civil servants and until 2002 were paid according to their age rather than on the quality of their teaching and research.[47] The requirement of the *Habilitationsschrift*, a sort of second Ph.D. thesis—in our legacy sector terms, an "established *knowledge and human resources structure*"—until recent reforms tended to discourage creativity and originality among aspiring university professors but was defended by many older faculty who had come up through the system and in this sense formed a *vested interest* defending an entrenched paradigm.

German authorities are well aware of the problems we have described and have enacted a number of reforms under the Lisbon Framework to free up labor markets and increase the availability of venture capital. These labor market reforms have relaxed regulations on worker dismissal and on short-term and part-time work, and have changed unemployment benefits to make it more worthwhile to work. These reforms were enacted under the leadership of Chancellor Gerhard Schroeder and are said to have been an important factor in denying him reelection. However, Germany continues to face skill shortages, particularly in innovation-intensive industries, and will need to increase labor force participation by women and older workers and to attract high-skilled immigrants—and to assimilate immigrants of all kinds more effectively into mainstream society and especially into the educational system—in order to overcome these shortages.[48] University reforms have loosened some of their rigidities, especially reliance on the *Habilitationsschrift*.

In sum, the German innovation context, especially cultural appreciation for manufacturing and a tax structure and local or regional banks attuned to its needs, and the German innovation system, especially the Fraunhofer institutes, reinforce each other to create an environment that favors small and medium-sized manufacturing industry. On the other hand, other aspects of the German innovation context—in particular the risk aversion of capital markets, combined with structural rigidities in universities and other parts of the innovation system—constitute elements of a legacy system that discourage the formation of start-ups based on radical innovations in most parts of the country. The result is a high-wage, globally competitive, export-oriented manufacturing sector but only the recent beginnings of progress toward a vigorous start-up culture.

The French Innovation Environment

The French innovation environment supports the efficient management of engineering-oriented infrastructure but fails to encourage entrepreneurship and product innovation. The French innovation system has been making persistent but so far largely unsuccessful efforts to compensate for this weakness.

Like its German counterpart, the French innovation *context* discourages risk and punishes failure through cultural norms that are sometimes translated into law. Bankruptcy, for example, is considered a disgrace.[49] Unlike its German counterpart, the French social context emphasizes French nationality and proper family and alumni connections in decisions regarding hiring and promotion. Social attitudes, traditions, and university and laboratory politics—including ideological opposition from left-wing unions—tend to discourage collaboration between universities and industry and hence pose an obstacle to the commercialization of successful research results. Again referring to the characteristics of legacy sectors set forth in chapters 2 and 5, these constitute *public habits and expectations attuned to existing . . . institutions."*

The strong hand of government and the system of *grandes écoles* described in ensuing paragraphs result in an innovation system that excels in engineering- and management-intensive infrastructure suited to top-down management, as exemplified by French success in nuclear energy, the metro, fast trains, and internal waterways. Past public investments in "national champions"[50] have left a legacy of strength in aviation, telecommunications, armaments, and nuclear power, even though many of these industries were originally chosen for their prestige and their contribution to security and great power status, rather than for their prospective economic competitiveness, and even though some (like computers) were notable commercial failures.[51] Reflecting this strength, banks tend to prefer to lend to businesses that sell to infrastructure and other sources of public procurement, an imperfection in capital markets that discourages investment in many kinds of technological innovation. This amounts to a legacy problem in *financing support*.

The French governmental structure is strongly centralized in Paris. Despite periodic efforts at "devolution," regional governments remain relatively weak, a fact that hampers public efforts to address environmental issues, which are typically regional rather than national in scope. This is an example of an *institutional architecture* that imposes regulatory hurdles or other policy disadvantages, in this case to effective environmental management and the development and implementation of technology for this purpose.

French small and medium industry tends to be relatively weak, the more so because the expansion of any given firm is discouraged by numerous laws and regulations that take effect when a firm hires as many as 50 employees.[52] Inflexible labor laws and other regulations protect the way of life of people who are already inside the system, but make it hard to create jobs for those outside it, resulting in high unemployment among youth and minorities. These laws also make it extremely difficult to fire workers who hold "contracts of indefinite length" (*contrats de durée indéterminée*—that is, regular employees, as opposed to temporary workers). French courts frequently hold that the mere prospect of increasing profitability does not constitute sufficient grounds to lay off an employee, a ruling that discourages hiring and thus presents *perverse incentives* to employers.[53] French unions are extremely strong in such critical places as education, nationalized industry, and the transport system and exercise an effective veto over attempts at reform in these areas by calling paralyzing strikes when their interests are threatened. While German unions have been more integrated into the innovation elements of firms and training, French unions have had a more adversarial effect. As in Germany, limitations on immigration exacerbate looming shortages of skilled workers, while nonportability of pensions discouraged worker mobility until recent reforms.

All these constitute an "established . . . *institutional architecture* that imposes . . . disadvantages to new entrants" and that "create(s) a mismatch between the incentives of producers and broader social goals"—in this case greater employment and the growth of small firms into larger ones. These are defended by "politically powerful *vested interests*, reinforced by public support, that defend the paradigm and resist innovations." In France, these obstacles are a result of the legal framework rather than being created by perverse subsidies, as is frequently the case in the United States.

The French innovation system reinforces the top-down, government-led, engineering-oriented orientation of the innovation context. It is dominated by an elitist system of higher education, at whose apex stand the *grandes écoles*, especially the École National d'Administration (ENA), the École Normale Superieure (ENS), the École Polytechnique and the École des Mines. The last two are schools of engineering-oriented administration that shower resources on a relatively small number of carefully chosen students. Upon graduation, the alumni of these schools become members of the close-knit elite of French government and industry. These institutions are oriented toward management in government and industry but (with the exception of the ENS) not toward research, so that their graduates tend to choose careers in business and government rather than in science.[54] Once they have attained executive positions, these graduates tend to under-invest in research compared to their counterparts in other advanced countries.[55] Public trust in these highly trained technocrats, once nearly absolute, still gives them great power to overcome widespread public hostility to technologies like nuclear power.[56]

French universities, like their German counterparts, are overcrowded and underresourced. Faculty jobs are badly paid but secure and high in prestige. Once a faculty member has attained a given rank, his or her pay is determined primarily by seniority rather than merit, so that there is little incentive for research, for collaboration with industry or even for good teaching.[57] Most French research is carried out in the laboratories or with the support of the National Center of Scientific Research (CNRS), since, as we have pointed out earlier, neither most French universities nor the *grandes écoles* are particularly oriented toward research.[58]

The CNRS research institutions and university faculty associated with them offer job security that allows researchers to undertake long-term, multidisciplinary projects and makes possible excellent research in such fields as biotechnology, informatics, infrastructure management and engineering. On the other hand, this security led in the 1960s and 1970s to a civil service mentality and a certain institutional stodginess and weak cooperation with industry that afflict public-sector laboratories worldwide, including in the United States, resulting in a widespread failure to follow up on patents based on successful research.[59] The result was an *"established knowledge and human resources structure"* that was relatively inefficient in supporting the broader goal of innovation, despite substantial public support to research and development. These problems were all the more serious because, as we have seen, French industry tends to underinvest in research and to depend on the government laboratories of the CNRS (and also, for example, CNES, CEA, and EU support) for technical innovation—an extreme form of the pipeline model we have previously set forth. (Surprisingly for a US audience, much of French industry also depends on an extensive system of embassy-based science attachés for much of its overseas technological intelligence.)

The French have long been well aware of these problems. Starting in the 1980s, French technology policy has made a major effort to remove the bureaucratic rigidities of the CNRS system and to improve the relations between the CNRS and French industry, for example by making it easier for CNRS researchers to work with French firms and to spin off innovative firms that take advantage of the results of CNRS research. These efforts had disappointingly little effect, in large part because of the effects of the innovative context set forth earlier.[60]

More recently, French authorities have enacted a number of reforms to increase the flexibility of their labor markets and to stimulate competition and entrepreneurship under the Lisbon framework.[61] Of these, probably the most important have been the billions of euros (as of 2011) in seed funding, venture capital, and other investment for small and medium enterprises, and the establishment of the Carnot Institutes, which are selected national applied research organizations to which substantial extra funding is awarded in proportion to the amount they earn from contract research with industry.[62]

In sum, the French innovation environment is well suited to the management of top-down, engineering-intensive infrastructure. Despite the best efforts of its policymakers, however, it is hampered in its efforts to make a transition toward growth-oriented, innovation-intensive small and medium industry by a legacy innovation system characterized by elitist engineering-oriented education, underinvestment in and relative lack of interest in applied research on the part of private industry, and government laboratories oriented to basic research—all this despite the best efforts of its policymakers to encourage collaboration between researchers and industry. These efforts are further hampered by a national innovation context characterized by legacy elements, including a cultural aversion to risk and intolerance of failure that is reflected in the lending policies of banks, by laws that discourage the growth of small industry, and by the efforts of vested interests in faculties and labor unions to defend long-standing rigidities in the structures of universities and labor markets, respectively.

The Chinese Innovation Environment

The Chinese innovation environment illustrates the important role of the innovation context, even in a country that is growing extremely rapidly, increasing its technological capacity in manufacturing and manufacturing-related innovation, and making major investments in its national innovation system. China has built a remarkable growth rate sustained for three decades, in part because it has been bringing innovations into nearly all sectors of its economy. Chinese national policy calls for continued major investments in education, research, and development, intended to allow its industries to move up their respective value chains and to make the country a powerhouse in radical product innovation.[63]

Even so, China retains numerous characteristics that are typical of legacy sectors, most of which are leftovers from the Maoist era of genuine communism, as opposed to the present system of "communism with Chinese characteristics." They are thus legacies in the most literal sense! The objective of cutting-edge technological leadership, however seriously entertained by top national leadership, is undercut in many important industries by the incentives that are perceived by entrepreneurs, who face mixed messages resulting from a three-dimensional cat's cradle made up of personal relations, deliberately ambiguous regulations, and what can still be conflicting policies at national and provincial levels.[64]

The Chinese innovation *system* benefited from major early investments in education at all levels that have brought literacy levels up to those of the advanced countries and provided the educated workforce for the labor-intensive manufacturing industry that sparked the early expansion of the post-Mao Chinese economy. These included major investments in new universities and in education at all levels, including a huge program of overseas scholarships and fellowships. China has also made major investments in research and development intended to make the country into a major center of product innovation based on the latest cutting-edge technology. Remarkably for a country at its stage of development, most of the investments in research and development take place in industry (although largely at state-owned firms) rather than in government laboratories. There are generous incentives, administered locally, for selected strategic industries. Thousands of innovation centers, many of them established jointly with industry, employ a wide variety of strategies and approaches to the encouragement of innovation and the building of technological capacity. Development support by provincial governments now exceeds the central government's R & D support.

Chinese industry has achieved world-class capability in the scale-up of manufacturing, both for sophisticated information technology products and for reverse-engineered but often redesigned, low-cost, reduced-quality products for domestic and regional markets. The effect has been to commodify what were once advanced, high-end products like motorcycles, substantially reducing not only manufacturing costs but also design and engineering costs and profit margins. The rapid growth of Chinese industry has attracted an industrial ecosystem of supporting services, suppliers, distributors, and sources of information that supports a large number of manufacturing clusters throughout the country—at some cost to the corresponding US ecosystem, as discussed in chapter 4.

The experience of the Chinese wind turbine industry, as documented by Lewis, provides an excellent example of the innovation systems at work within the country, and shows that increasing numbers of Chinese manufacturers are capable of participating as equals in the *international innovation system*, collaborating on equal terms in the back end of the innovation process, with their counterparts in developed countries.[65] Like most of the products manufactured by Chinese companies, modern wind turbines for electricity generation were first developed overseas. While these European companies manufactured the first turbines installed in China, Chinese entrepreneurs soon became aware of this developing market and sought to capitalize on its growth. Aided by requirements for domestic procurement in the large Chinese market for wind energy and by substantial government support to research, and beginning by mastering technology acquired from foreign companies, Chinese firms have been able to develop several new designs specifically adapted to the Chinese market, including offshore installations, turbines optimized for the varying climatic conditions throughout the country, and lower cost, higher reliability models with a locally manufactured "direct drive" replacing the traditional gearbox.[66]

From there, several Chinese manufacturers have upgraded their technological capacity to the point where they have become full collaborators on research and design with established companies in developed countries. They sell technology to European firms and even purchase foreign companies and capably merge them and their technology into their own operations, sometimes setting up subsidiaries for research and development in order to take advantage of the networking and other advantages of established overseas clusters.

The wind turbine technology demonstrates a typical experience within the Chinese national innovation system. Chinese firms have been extraordinarily successful at recognizing an opportunity to produce a promising product, integrating foreign technology and reengineering the product to reduce costs and suit the needs of local and similar foreign markets. This process has led to new, low-cost manufactures in such diverse fields as motorcycles, household appliances, artificial lenses for cataract victims, and medical electronics—products that emerged from improvements in manufacturing process. Thus China has proved adept at *manufacturing-led innovations*, in the terminology we developed in chapter 3, and in this way has been able to blur the line between product and process innovation. Its ability to form regional collaborations in manufacturing sectors for rapid production scale-up is an example of a *collective action* capability that is still a problem in US legacy sector manufacturing, as we have discussed in chapters 4 and 6.

These experiences show that Chinese firms are working hard to catch up to the product quality and manufacturing technology of market leaders in advanced countries, and that many of them may be expected to make every effort to move up the value chains in manufactured products, especially in industries in which product innovation is closely tied to manufacturing processes, as is the case for many capital goods. While the progress made in China in advancing the design and application of wind energy technology has been remarkable, it does not represent a case of radical product innovation, and its profit margins are correspondingly lower. The core technology in this and in the other cases we have cited (and many others) did not originate in China. This pattern, however, is showing signs of change, and there are signs of a stirring of a more US-style entrepreneurship and start-up culture,[67] although focused on lower risk areas.

The effectiveness of the Chinese innovation system is shaped by the larger innovation *context*, which is dominated by the facts of China's enormous population, huge and rapidly expanding domestic market, relatively high productivity, and new physical infrastructure, as well as its history of low wages, undervalued exchange rate, and casual attitude toward the environment. These constitute attractions to overseas investors and multinational corporations that smaller countries cannot hope to match, even granted that China's manufacturing wages are rising and that its business climate seems to be becoming increasingly difficult because of problems like intellectual property theft. China now ranks 96th in the International Finance Corporation's 2014 report on the ease of doing business in different countries. There are intermittent signs that at least some factories are displacing to countries in Southeast Asia or even back to the United States, but there are still major advantages to locating production facilities close to what is still (even with a somewhat lower growth rate in recent years) the world's fastest-growing market.[68]

China has also become competitive in industries linked to infrastructure, such as electric power generation and distribution, railroads, hydroelectric dams, telecommunications, and connectivity, all of which have grown with extraordinary rapidity in the past four decades and many of which constitute neglected legacy sectors in the United States. Some of these skills, like those involved in tunneling and information technology, have been shaped (or in Ruttan's terminology, *induced*) by the particular demands of mountainous geography and authoritarian government, respectively.

The Chinese *national* innovation system is intimately tied to the *international* innovation system. First, many of its most innovative companies are owned by foreigners, in most cases based in Taiwan, whose economy has essentially become integrated with that of the mainland. As was the experience in Taiwan and earlier in Korea and Japan, many Chinese firms began as high-volume, low-margin component manufacturers or assemblers of "original equipment"—products of standard design manufactured on contract to be sold under the brand name of another, better-known firm. Many of these are now moving up what might be called the *value-added ladder* to become producers of products under their own brand names for local or international markets.

Second, China sends more students overseas than any other country. It has more than 500,000 tertiary-level students abroad, compared to 200,000 from India and 50,000 from the United States.[69] It further benefits from extensive research collaboration with foreign universities and from investments and scientific, technological, and commercial collaboration with the huge overseas Chinese diaspora.

Third, the size of the Chinese market has made it possible for the Chinese government to put heavy pressure on foreign investors to transfer technology and to overlook a weak intellectual property regime and even the brazen theft of technology. The government has long pressured and indeed required overseas investors to establish research and development laboratories in China. These laboratories began as Potemkin villages but evolved into real centers of innovation as the cost-effectiveness of Chinese scientists and engineers became apparent. Foreign firms investing in China, to be sure, do not always transfer their best and most advanced technology, and do their best to ensure that they retain competitive advantage in strategic technologies, especially in the conception of new products and in the overall management of their supply chains, but are not always successful in doing so. Finally, China maintains an impressively extensive program of semiofficial industrial espionage targeting a broad range of military and high-tech industry—a link to the international innovation system that is no less important for the fact that it is nominally covert.

More broadly, China has benefited by being something of a free rider on the international system, a fact with important implications for its innovation *context*—although to be sure, other countries are in an equally questionable position.[70] It long maintained an artificially low exchange rate by dint of an implicit bargain with the United States, whereby it invested much of its export surplus in acquiring US debt and other dollar-denominated assets even when these could be readily seen to be declining in value. It is the world's largest emitter of carbon dioxide, the United States being number two and the market for much of China's carbon-intensive exports. Like many other governments, again including the United States, it is notably uncritical of the governments of the countries from which it obtains its natural resources, many of which have questionable human rights records. It controls access to many of its domestic markets contrary to World Trade Organization rules, and as noted earlier is weak in its protection of the intellectual property rights of foreigners—although this may be gradually changing as more and more Chinese companies have their own intellectual property to protect.

The Chinese macroeconomic environment is a critical feature of its innovation context. The historic pattern of systematic purchase of assets denominated in dollars, intended to sustain an undervalued exchange rate, favored exporters— who are typically manufacturers—at the expense of firms, including those in service industries, that produced for the domestic market. This discouraged domestic consumption. Although most administratively controlled prices have now been phased out, the subsidized cost of energy and capital to favored enterprises encourages a high rate of capital investment and (given the ample supply of labor) a lower wage bill, again favoring manufacturers, which are generally more capital- and energy-intensive than service industries.

Again referring to the characteristics of legacy sectors laid out in chapter 5, these have create a "tilted" (nonlevel) playing field caused by *prices* that provide *perverse incentives* that favor "existing technologies, and that create a mismatch between the incentives of producers and innovators and the goals of the larger society"—in this case, additional consumer goods for the domestic Chinese market, a livelier service sector, energy conservation, lower carbon dioxide emission, a healthier environment, a better allocation of resources and hence a better life for the Chinese people.[71] (These subsidies are also perverse from the point of view of US manufacturing, a point developed in chapter 6.)

Given the lingering limitation on exports imposed by the recent world recession, it would make obvious sense for Chinese policymakers to shift their emphasis to satisfying the needs of the domestic market, and this is indeed the stated intention of Chinese economic policymakers. However, such a shift poses technical difficulties and besides would require standing up to political pressure from exporters, who by now constitute a powerful *vested interest*.[72]

The reputation of Chinese exports—and indeed of all Chinese products—is also tainted by intermittent scandals resulting from poor quality or outright adulteration. China's spotty record in the latter area reflects not only the intense competitive pressures to cut costs, to which all Chinese firms are subject, but also the pervasive corruption at many levels of its government and industry. Chinese corruption, while at a level somewhat comparable to that of Russia, has until now had a somewhat different effect on technological innovation, in large part because of the different incentives facing officials in the two countries, and the time horizons deriving from these incentives.

As Wedeman has shown, Chinese corruption differs from its Russian counterpart in important respects. First and most important, unlike Putin's Russia, the post-Mao Chinese government did not begin with an entrenched corrupt bureaucracy and was not deliberately set up to be kleptocratic and parasitic on the economy but rather to win legitimacy for the government by delivering rapid growth. On the contrary, Chinese corruption began small—too small to block economic reform—and increased only after the rapid expansion of the overall economy opened up new opportunities. Second, while Chinese corruption remains a serious and pervasive problem, it has been prevented from spiraling out of control by periodic anticorruption campaigns that, while imperfect, have been sufficient to create significant risks even for highly placed officials.[73]

Third, the promotion of Chinese officials within the huge Chinese bureaucracy depends largely on the economic performance of the area under their jurisdiction. These officials are not expected to be honest, but are expected to keep their corruption within bounds, and certainly short of the point where it would interfere with economic growth or with "harmony"—that is, with the stability of Communist Party rule. Officials are thus motivated to take the long view, and to provide a favorable climate for the businesses from which they can derive a steady income rather than shoot for a Russian-style quick killing.[74] Here they fit the model of the "stationary bandit" in the framework proposed by the late Mancur Olson, by which he meant a rational kleptocrat who encourages economic growth so that in the long run, he or she will have a bigger economy from which to steal.[75] The overall result is a high but stable level of corruption, combined with an economic and political climate that is relatively favorable to private business, certainly as compared to that in Russia; these limits helped make possible China's extraordinary rates of growth.

The Chinese people are enthusiastic savers. Savings amount to more than half of GNP[76]—in large part because of a weak safety net and the one-child policy, which led to a dearth of children to support parents in their old age. But most Chinese savers are forbidden to invest overseas—that is, to export capital—but instead are required to place their savings in domestic accounts whose interest rates are kept at a lower level than would obtain in a free market, sometimes even at negative "real" (i.e., inflation-corrected) interest rates.[77] Government-controlled banks then make the resulting relatively cheap investment capital preferentially available to inefficient, state-owned firms controlled by members of the political elite or their families, or to private firms that are closely tied to them.[78] The result is a large Chinese market for new industrial plant and capital equipment, much of which uses the latest technology—although the protected firms that make much of this investment do not always use the equipment with the highest efficiency, a situation reminiscent of post–World War II Argentina. The result is a *financing system* that actually favors innovation, but not necessarily in the areas where it is most needed or can be used most efficiently.

Other private firms that lack these political connections have historically been left to scramble for investment capital from informal sources that typically demand very high returns, creating a "dual economy" in which capital-rich and capital-starved firms exist side by side, a pattern familiar to students of the developing economies of the 1970s.[79] Foreign banks are free to lend to privately owned firms and to conduct business in local currency, but their share of Chinese capital markets is still quite small. This imperfection in capital markets exemplifies a *"financing system* geared to incumbents and reluctant to extend risk capital to disruptive, new entrant technologies" that is characteristic of a legacy sector (although when central authorities instruct state-owned enterprises to invest in clean energy or environmental technologies, they do it in a big way).[80]

The favoritism in the financial system is reinforced by the Chinese system of residency permits (*hukou*), which imposes strict limits on rural-urban migration and in this way gives a substantial advantage to state-owned or politically well-connected firms that can offer *hukou* permits to prospective skilled or professional employees, another regulatory obstacle to new firms that lack such connections. On the other hand, the situation of private firms is substantially alleviated by their favorable return on assets as compared to that of state-owned enterprises, a fact that enables them to finance their expansion from retained earnings rather than from borrowing.[81]

To compound the overall financial picture, artificial corporations known as "local investment companies" enable local governments to borrow, at low interest rates and without effective controls, in order to finance infrastructure projects. Some of these are sound investments, whereas others are "roads to nowhere." The overall result is a potential investment bubble in housing, roads, ports, airports, railroads, energy, and telecommunications, reminiscent of the one that preceded the recent financial crisis in the West.

The protected status of state-owned firms leads to a peculiar paradox. We have already mentioned that a large proportion (76%) of Chinese research and development is financed by industry and might therefore be supposed to be closely related to commercial objectives.[82] This statistic, however, is somewhat misleading, as 45% of this R & D is financed with public money by state-owned enterprises, some of which are under little competitive pressure to use the results of the research that they themselves have financed.[83] As a consequence, the results of Chinese industrial research are less likely than they would otherwise be to be followed up into actual innovations, so that Chinese industry in the aggregate is not getting its money's worth for its investments in research and development.[84]

It is therefore a mistake to judge China's technological prowess solely from input statistics like research and development expenditures and patents, the more so since patent production is the subject of an explicit government target that puts pressure on researchers to patent an invention regardless of its quality or value. On the other hand, the level of expenditure and the quality of innovation management is sufficient that real innovation, focused on development, does occur in both public and private sectors, although not as much as it would if these resources were better allocated and managed—a situation somewhat analogous to problems faced by the legacy side of the US military discussed in chapter 8.

Another important feature of the Chinese innovation context is a certain tension between national policies to encourage research and development by private firms, on the one hand, and local realities, on the other. Firm managers are aware of national incentives for research and the design and development of new products. However, they are also aware that these policies may be couched in deliberately ambiguous terms, so as to provide flexibility in interpretation and to allow policymakers to experiment and learn what works out in practice.[85] Besides, these policies are frequently closely tied to the personal preferences of particular officials, who are likely to change jobs every few years, leaving investments in long-term projects begun under their sponsorship high and dry. It therefore often makes more sense for firms to invest in shorter term projects involving process innovation rather than longer term development of potentially more profitable, radically new products. The end result is an "established *institutional architecture* that imposes . . . disadvantages favoring existing technology or discouraging new entrants" and "create(s) a mismatch between the incentives of producers and broader social goals," another characteristic of a legacy sector.[86] This situation may be resolving itself as local authorities provide an increasing proportion of support to R & D, but this support still comes predominantly at the development stage, not at the research stage.

The Chinese semiconductor sector provides an example of a related problem. China has a history of state planning and industrial policy organized around strategic industries. However, at the leading edge of innovation in advanced, competitive sectors, more flexible, market-oriented policies may be necessary.[87] China has a new 2014 strategy to upgrade its semiconductor industry to push it toward the threshold of world-class innovation. However, the strategy has limited ability to undertake flexible policy adjustments and is still more a top-down industrial policy directive than the more market-driven approach that may be needed to reach the innovation frontier in this sector.[88] This also amounts to an issue of *institutional architecture*.

An area in which the incentives of producers are misaligned with broader social goals, one which national policymakers are now committed to address, is the huge problem of air and water pollution, which between them may cost China some 4-6% of GNP annually, depending on the study.[89] Outdoor air pollution resulted in an estimated 1.2 million premature deaths in 2010,[90] and the Chinese Ministry of Environmental Protection rated 57% of China's urban water supplies as "relatively bad" or worse.[91]

Until about 10 years ago, provincial officials could be confident from their own past experience—and from the low level of priority assigned to environment in otherwise high-sounding official pronouncements—that their prospects for promotion were tied to their economic growth performance, and that poor environmental indicators would hardly count against them.[92] This is an example of the legacy sector characteristic of *perverse incentives*, although in this case the incentives are political and careerist rather than economic. National policymakers are now committed to address these crises in public health, and have incorporated a variety of measures of environmental performance into the criteria used to evaluate officials in China's huge bureaucracies—a major step forward. These criteria, however, are not driven so much by explicit environmental or public health objectives, as by the goal of "social stability"—that is, the quieting of widespread public dissatisfaction with existing air and water pollution and the resulting threat to the regime's hold on power.[93]

Whatever the motivation, the result is a major and very desirable increase in local investments in water purification and in air pollution controls, as well as the equally desirable shutdown of outdated and polluting facilities, although there is a long way to go in all these areas. However, it has also led to a variety of efforts by local officials to game the system and in this way to appear to meet both economic and environmental targets by such devices as faking data, cheating on tests of environmental performance, pretending to shut down obsolete plants, shutting down or improperly managing installed antipollution equipment, or even cutting off electric power in order to reduce emissions.[94]

The Chinese early-stage innovation system also faces major challenges. While R & D continues to grow at the central government level,[95] and is exceeded by R & D (primarily late-stage applied research and development) at the provincial level, there are problems in the system. Maoist rule and the Cultural Revolution profoundly damaged the quality of Chinese universities; though rapidly expanding, their foundational research base has not fully recovered. Strong governmental investments in R & D and the emphasis at the top universities on hiring faculty with strong international training are reactions to this problem. Chinese science officials understand fully the importance of strengthening their early-stage research system to bolster front-end innovation capacity because they want the gains from the full range of innovation, not only manufacturing-led.

Even so, a tradition of outstanding basic research is a long-term project and has only to date reached some academic areas. China's research agencies are often understaffed compared to their OECD counterparts, creating significant problems in grant evaluation. China only recently developed a system for indirect cost recovery by universities; partly as a result, corruption has been an issue in its university and research institute R & D system.

While China is encouraging entrepreneurship and venture funding, these efforts focus on lower risk efforts to implement technologies that have already been implemented elsewhere and that have proven that they can create markets. Breakthrough innovation is still rare—in part because of an aversion to risk taking. After all, why should firms risk breakthrough innovation when so many innovations proven elsewhere can still be implemented in China? This in turn pushes research in universities more toward applied objectives than toward more basic work that could result in breakthroughs. Not surprisingly, 61% of China's R & D is focused on manufacturing.[96]

As is the case in France and Germany, the Chinese government is well aware of these problems, and at the national level at least, has announced steps to address them. The recently concluded Third Plenum of the 18th Central Committee of the Communist Party of China announced that "the market will be more decisive in setting prices and allocating resources,"[97] and that there was a need to "promote urban-rural equity, [and to] better manage urbanization to promote productivity in areas that are under-urbanized," a reference to the *hukou* system mentioned earlier. It further asserted that competition is good among banks, between domestic and foreign enterprises, and between provinces, and that privately owned firms should be considered on par with state-owned enterprises.[98] It also announced a five-year plan to combat corruption, which if carried out should have a favorable effect on both the business climate and the environment. The governor of the People's Bank of China, Zhou Xiaochuan, pledged in March 2014 to allow market forces to take a greater role in deposits and interest rates by 2016.

China's R & D officials recognize that its R & D system needs systematic strengthening; they are concerned that with wages rising and growth slowing, they will need more early-stage innovation over time to complement their present focus on production and manufacturing-led innovation. Like Taiwan and Korea, they want to seek a wider range of gains from their innovation system beyond those accruing from manufacturing-led innovation; like R & D leaders in those nations, they understand well the need to strengthen their early-stage breakthrough innovation, although they have deeper challenges in achieving this than do those two countries.

The measures needed to carry out all of these stated policies would constitute badly needed reforms. However, as we have noted earlier, they threaten a number of politically powerful *vested interests* and hence the stability of the regime. Restrictions on immigration to megacities will remain, although with some modifications. State-owned enterprises continue to be favored, despite the fact that private firms are more profitable than state-owned enterprises, a gap that has been growing. Recent severe crackdowns on Chinese journalists and human rights advocates demonstrate that the Chinese government intends to deal with these issues by itself without the debate that in more open countries is a source of pressure for reform. Chinese authorities are thus aware of the need for reform at many levels and are making statements that indicate willingness to effect important change. It remains to be seen whether this awareness will translate into effective action and what the practical effect will be of any resulting policy measures on Chinese innovation.

In sum, the Chinese national innovation environment has been an important underpinning of its dramatic economic growth. China has benefited from the many favorable aspects of its innovation context: a huge market, controlled corruption, and modern infrastructure in key parts of the country. It has invested heavily in its innovation system, especially in education, and in research and development intended to allow firms to move up the value chain to more profitable and more technology-intensive products, and has developed particular skill in manufacturing and manufacturing scale-up for both cutting-edge and low-tech products.

As a complement to its national innovation system, China participates actively in the international innovation system. It sends more students overseas than any other country and collaborates extensively with researchers all over the world. MNCs or foreigners, in most cases based in Taiwan, control many of its most innovative companies. It encourages foreign investment and indeed frequently requires investors to transfer technology, even when they know that it is likely to be stolen. It operates an extensive program of semiofficial industrial espionage.

Even so, the Chinese context retains legacy characteristics as detailed above, some of them literal legacies of the old Maoist communist system, and some derived from the decades of dramatic, export-led growth: a low interest rate that penalizes savers, and cheap capital and other incentives that favor manufacturing exporters and especially state-owned enterprises. These measures powered the rapid growth that has been essential to Chinese political stability and are defended by powerful vested interests. However, they constitute perverse market distortions that led until recently to the accumulation of declining dollar-based assets and now hamper the necessary transition to a more sustainable growth trajectory that would increase the supply of consumer goods and improve the environment and health of the Chinese people. From the purely US point of view, they also constitute artificial incentives that encourage the offshoring of US manufacturing facilities.

The Indian Innovation Environment Then and Now

The evolution of the Indian innovation environment since India gained its independence in 1948 illustrates in extreme form the dominant role of the innovation context, even in the presence of a reasonably active innovation system. The first president of independent India, Jawaharlal Nehru, had great faith in the promise of science and technology and made sure to establish the basis of what we would call today a national innovation system.

Nehru's oft-quoted words well express his commitment to science and technology:

It is science alone that can solve the problems of hunger and poverty, of insanitation and illiteracy, of superstition and deadening custom and tradition, of vast resources running to waste, of a rich country inhabited by starving people. ... Who indeed could afford to ignore science today? At every turn we have to seek its aid ... the future belongs to science and those who make friends with science.[99]

One of Nehru's first acts as president was to secure support for seven world-class science and engineering institutes, the Indian Institutes of Technology, each funded and sponsored by a different advanced country, as well as a number of management institutes. He also founded the Council of Scientific and Industrial Research (CSIR), a chain of 29 applied research laboratories (the number has since grown to 41), as well as well-funded programs of space science and nuclear technology.[100] Although the overall effort in science and technology was relatively small, amounting to less than 0.5% of GNP throughout the 1950s, it represented a serious commitment to the development of science and technology in what was then one of the poorest developing countries.[101]

At the same time, however, Nehru was an English-educated socialist with a deep distrust of private industry and an equally deep commitment to national self-sufficiency. At the center of Nehru's policy—and hence of the national innovation *context*—were high tariffs and a variety of nontariff barriers that insulated local industry from foreign competition, and a strict licensing system that insulated it from domestic competition as well. In the legacy sector terminology of chapter 5, these amounted to an impediment to innovation derived from *government policy*, since the lack of competition eliminated the incentive to improve technology.

Nehru's vision was that government-owned industry would occupy the "commanding heights" of the economy, demonstrating proper methods of management to private firms that were presumed to be in need of this tutelage—a concept parallel to the role President Franklin Delano Roosevelt envisaged for the Tennessee Valley Authority vis-à-vis private utilities in the United States in the 1930s.[102] Nehru envisaged keeping private industry on a tight leash, granting firms licenses to produce only specified amounts of specified products—so many matches or so many shirts per year—so as to avoid "unnecessary" production and the resulting "waste" of resources. Once a company had such a license, it was protected from "wasteful" competition, both foreign and domestic—but also from the spur to increased productivity and product quality (and hence improved technology) that would have resulted from such competition. As a result, the Indian economy became known informally as the "license raj"—a sobriquet that lasted until about 1990. The companies thus protected—whether publicly or privately owned—prospered, grew, and became comfortable, politically powerful and protective of their favored positions. Nehru also reserved a list of several hundred products for small-scale businesses, also protecting them from competition and hence the pressure to improve their technology.[103]

The result was a general lack of demand for improved technology throughout Indian industry. Why would a firm invest in new technology if it could make guaranteed profits making the same inferior product in the same old way? And in the absence of such demand, why should they hire the graduates of the IITs, or cultivate good relations with the research laboratories of the CSIR? As a result, and with important but limited exceptions, virtually the whole of Indian industry displayed a number of the characteristics of a legacy sector as set forth in chapter 5: *regulatory obstacles* and a limiting *institutional architecture* within an all-encompassing set of market imperfections defended by politically powerful *vested interests* in private and publicly owned industry. With their opportunities at home limited by a constrained *knowledge and human resources structure*, small wonder that IIT graduates emigrated in droves to Silicon Valley, where they flourished, and that even the researchers in the CSIR laboratories themselves became largely cut off from their presumed clients in industry. As a result, Indian industry—and even the researchers in the CSIR laboratories themselves—remained largely ignorant of technological and market developments outside India.

There were, to be sure, notable exceptions to these generalizations—impressive development of local technology by such dedicated innovators as Anil Malhotra in offshore oil drilling, M. M. Suri in heavy industry, Y. Nayudamma in small-scale leather technology, and J. R. D. Tata in cars and trucks, not to mention impressive technological development in the specially favored, high-prestige programs of Vikram Sarabai in space technology and Homi Bhaba in nuclear technology.[104]

Even so, the general picture is clear. An unfavorable innovation context—a *dis*abling environment, if you will—largely defeated the Indian investments in its innovation system, up to and until the liberalization of the Indian economy that began around 1990. This clear historical demonstration of the power of the national innovation context—and its potential for *dis*abling rather than *en*abling innovation—was a harbinger of the less extreme versions of the same phenomenon that we have seen in contemporary China and Europe.[105]

A good deal has changed in India since the days of the license raj, although it still lags behind China in important respects. On the contextual side, Indian macroeconomic policy is relatively stable, a fact that facilitates planning on the part of investors.[106] It has substantially liberalized its formerly notoriously high tariffs, although its average tariff level is still half again as high as China's.[107] In the innovation system, the CSIR has made dramatic strides in effecting close relations with Indian industry, beginning with the major reforms under R. A. Mushalkar. Research by private firms has increased and now constitutes more than half of the overall Indian expenditure for research and development, with over 250 laboratories established by foreign-based multinational corporations.[108]

The most dramatic and best-known development in Indian technology is the explosive growth of the Indian software and IT services industry, which was made possible in large part by the high quality of the best Indian engineering graduates and by the liberalization of telecommunications regulation in the Indian states of Maharashtra (capital Mumbai, formerly Bombay), Tamil Nadu (capital Chennai, formerly Madras), and Delhi. These radical reforms greatly improved communications service and connectivity—an illustration of the key role of innovation context. While the license raj had curtailed innovation in India's manufacturing sectors, the regulatory opening in information technology changed the innovation context and allowed India to create a new model of IT-services-driven innovation that contrasts with China's more traditional model of low-cost, manufacturing-driven innovation. (Chinese IT is also strong in emulating OECD technologies, but its civilian applications are focused largely on the domestic market.)

India participates vigorously in the international innovation system, supplying about 5.7% of the world total of overseas students in higher education—a figure, however, that is much lower than that of China. It further benefits from its links with the large diaspora of Indian engineers and managers, most famously in Silicon Valley. It is a major exporter of software and software services. India has further established itself as an "innovative developing country" (the phrase is from Mushalkar) by such "poor man's innovations" as low-cost CAT scanners, computers, cataract surgery, and water purification systems.[109]

Even so, Indian technological development is still hampered by aspects of its innovation context: limited foreign investment (especially prior to 2005), a difficult business environment, a low level of mass education, and poor physical infrastructure, especially for transport and energy.[110] Nonagricultural import tariffs were reduced in 2007, but remain very high. Difficult customs procedures, pervasive corruption, and weak intellectual property protection remain significant barriers. The broad economic reforms of 1984 and 1991 abolished restrictions on most industries, but licensing remains for the atomic energy, defense, and alcoholic beverage industries: a *governmental barrier* to competition and hence to innovation. The slow-moving political system and cumbersome bureaucracy, protected by *vested interests*, typical of legacy systems, have hampered many of the efforts to continue implementing these reforms. In addition, the heavy-handed, government-controlled legacy *financial system* remains an inefficient allocator of capital resources.

Informal remnants of the license raj have also played a role. In a telling example, the minister of railways refused as late as 2004 to import sorely needed parts, insisting that they be built in India and citing the ultimate authority of the Hindu god of machines over the railway system—an extraordinary example of *public habits and expectations*![111] The "inspection raj" that has recently emerged (in which inspectors "discover" fabricated violations that they offer to ignore in exchange for bribes) also threatens efficiency.[112]

On the innovation system side, the graduates of top Indian universities and technical institutes rank with the best in the world, but their number is very small—perhaps 7,000 per year in a country of 1.3 billion population. Most Indian universities are of relatively poor quality, and their faculties use their political influence to resist the creation of private universities that might offer competition, another legacy problem of *vested interests* that perpetuate an *established knowledge structure*. The general quality of basic primary and secondary education is very low, as illustrated by an illiteracy rate of 37%, a fact that hampers the development of a high-productivity industrial sector.[113] This is further complicated by restrictive labor legislation that discourages hiring by making it difficult to fire workers in order to improve productivity.[114]

In sum, the history of the "license raj" of pre-1990 India in suppressing technological innovation in India, and the contrasting effect of the liberalization of communications in making possible the explosive growth of the Indian software industry, together show the decisive influence of disabling and enabling innovation context, respectively. The license raj displayed many of the characteristics that define legacy sectors in the United States, but was especially stifling in overregulation, perverse incentives, low-quality universities except for a few top schools, underinvestment in private-sector R & D and risk-averse banks—all defended by vested interests in industry and universities that benefited from the freedom from competition and by bureaucrats defending their turf.

Economic liberalization, combined with reforms in the innovation system, especially in the CSIR, has made it possible for India to take advantage of its top-tier institutions of higher education and to increase its participation in the international innovation system through collaboration in research and IT-based industry. It has become a world-class supplier of software and software services and an "innovative developing country" specializing in low-cost innovations for developing country markets. Even so, it lags behind China in economic growth and technological development.

LESSONS FOR THE US INNOVATION ENVIRONMENT

This quick tour of national innovation environments on two continents illuminates some of the strengths and weaknesses of alternative approaches to science and technology, and provides a broad perspective on the characteristics of the American innovation environment. By comparison to the countries we surveyed, we can see that Americans benefit from their generally favorable innovation context: the continental size of their largely unregulated market, the strength of their higher education, the flexibility of their markets for capital and labor, their pride in individualism and entrepreneurship and acceptance of the possibility of failure, their taste for novelty, their willingness to reward merit, their distrust of monopoly, their relative indifference to family, religious or social background, and their openness to disruption, to criticism, to immigration, to risk, and to bankruptcy without stigma—all of which have made the United States a magnet for talent from all over the world and the world center of radical product innovation. While not always appreciated by the public, these enduring and compelling strengths are at the core of American competitiveness in high-technology markets and are hence central to its economic, military, and geopolitical strength.

As we have earlier observed, other countries have tried to emulate these strengths, and indeed a major concern of US policymakers is that they will succeed to the point where they threaten American competitiveness, especially in fields like capital goods where manufacturing and product innovation are closely linked. Fears about China are particularly pronounced, so that it may be some relief to know that the Chinese innovation environment has its weaknesses and obstacles in addition to its substantial and increasing strengths.

From the point of view of radical product innovation, the entire economies of the countries whose innovation environments we have examined display the characteristics of a legacy sector, sometimes in a form that seems extreme by American standards. These countries have often found that the obstacles to innovation are deeply rooted in their culture and social structure and are hence difficult to overcome, so that policy measures to address them are in effect "pushing on a string." In the words of a British member of Parliament (in a somewhat different context), "We could have all these benefits as well, if all we did was change every single piece of our social structure."[115]

At the same time, Americans can gain from the broader perspective provided by a comparison of their own innovation environment with those of other countries. Germany, France, and China display strengths precisely in those areas where the United States is weakest: in infrastructure and infrastructure management, in niche-market "Main Street" manufacturing, and in manufacturing scale-up—all of which are areas of critical importance for technological competitiveness, for employment, and for economic growth. While countries like Germany, Korea, Taiwan, and now China have achieved success with manufacturing-led innovation, and are now addressing issues in the strength in their breakthrough innovation capability, the United States faces the opposite side of that coin and has only started to think about its weakness in manufacturing-led innovation. As we have seen, innovation in the above areas in the United States is blocked or at least severely hindered by a variety of deep-seated and entrenched structural obstacles that deserve increased attention by policymakers and indeed more discussion in the political arena.

The US national innovation system has evolved along with its innovation context and reflects many of its essential characteristics. Investment in research and development has tended to lag in legacy sectors, as exemplified by the relatively low federal budgets for research in transportation, nonindustrial agriculture, healthcare delivery systems, and advanced production technologies and processes. Private-sector investment in these fields has also lagged, in large part because there does not seem to be much prospect of implementing even the most promising of ideas if they do not fit with prevailing sectoral paradigms. In some fields, most prominently in energy, even the technology itself has become ensnared in political polarization—the Right backing nuclear energy and fossil fuels, the Left backing renewables and conservation, with only occasional efforts to bridge the gap.

What is more, certain elements of the US innovation system have developed their own signs of inflexibility and unresponsiveness to newer demands. For example, as noted in chapter 7, the internal organization of the National Institutes of Health, with 27 separate institutes and centers, results in the fact that this $30 billion dollar entity, which is the largest public program of health research in the world, has resisted calls for increased translational research to convert research findings into useful medicine, and for research on medical devices and bioengineering. While there are significant advantages to the US system of numerous, decentralized R & D agencies allied to particular missions—the preferences of no single official or agency can dictate the priorities of the entire scientific establishment, for example—this system makes it very difficult for the United States to mount a unified and coherent cross-disciplinary, cross-agency R & D effort in areas like nanotechnology and advanced manufacturing.

More generally, the overall American system of public support to research and innovation itself displays some of the characteristics of a legacy sector. We emphasize again that this system is the envy of the world and has created the technical basis for many of the most competitive sectors of the US economy. The problem lies in the fact that it and its intellectual and political underpinnings now get in the way of efforts to address some of the nation's most pressing problems in the critical legacy sectors we discuss in this book—not to mention other areas we do not consider in any detail, for example, "evidence-based medicine," aspects of the environment, and the general area of technology assessment.

WHAT HAVE WE LEARNED ABOUT NATIONAL INNOVATION ENVIRONMENTS?

Our quick world tour of innovation environments in different countries provides a new perspective on the problem of legacy sectors in the United States.

First, the innovation context matters—probably just as much as the innovation system, although it's hard to make any kind of quantitative comparison. Culture, law, politics, finance, and economics all affect innovation, not just laboratories, start-ups, and IP regimes. Together, a country's national innovation system and its innovation context make up an environment in which different kinds of innovation can either flourish or perish.

Second, the features that characterize legacy sectors in the United States derive mostly from the American innovation context, rather than from its innovation system.

Third, the contextual obstacles to innovation in the countries we surveyed include many of the features that characterize legacy sectors in the United States, but go beyond them to include trade and exchange rates.

Fourth, context can help, hurt, or shape the speed and direction of innovation. What's good for radical innovation may create a complex catch-up problem for small-scale manufacturing or infrastructure, and vice versa.

Fifth, an innovation system can only go so far in compensating for obstacles presented by context. If contextual obstacles are too severe, policies to overcome them are "pushing on a string."

Finally, the US innovation system is still the envy of the world—but others are studying it and emulating it. The United States has much to learn from the innovation environment of other countries. Even though they may not be as good as the United States at radical or breakthrough innovation, they can excel at manufacturing-led innovation, scale-up, or infrastructure management—areas where US performance is lacking.

10 Exporting Inappropriate Paradigms in Agriculture and Energy

We now turn to the analysis of an international economic sector, agriculture, and use it as a case study to explore the limits that legacy sectors in developed countries can impose on other economies.[1] This is followed by a similar review of the international energy sector. We move, then, from examining legacy sectors as national economic challenges to viewing them as transnational ones. In this way, we add an international dimension to our conceptual framework, and to the concept that implicitly underlies the regime defined and enforced by the World Trade Organization (WTO) and by the Trade-Related Aspects of Intellectual Property Rights (TRIPS) regime in areas other than agriculture. This system is universally accepted among advanced industrial countries as the basis of the globalized knowledge economy and is enshrined in WTO and TRIPS. We will review this system and use the two legacy sector examples, industrial agriculture and fossil fuel energy, as case studies.

Within the constraints of the WTO system, each sovereign country is entitled to evolve its own national innovation system and its own domestic paradigm. Any country may make investments in its innovative system and therewith in its dynamic comparative advantage. Once a new product is developed, WTO rules make it difficult for other countries to restrict it from being imported, with largely theoretical exceptions for products deemed to have detrimental environmental or public health effects. The system of intellectual property rewards innovation by protecting the resulting monopoly and the consequent economic rents of the innovator.

The international market in technology leads to an inherent conflict between intellectual property rights, which are essential to encourage vital private investment in innovative technology, and the global environmental, public health, or other benefits that would accrue from the widespread implementation of disruptive innovations in many legacy sectors. This conflict admits of no clean universal solution but must be addressed case by case. In agriculture, development assistance agencies, private foundations, nongovernmental organizations, and even some multinational corporations have undertaken to make available innovative technology to farmers who otherwise could not afford them. In infectious disease, major programs of research and technical assistance have long been underway.[2] In energy, programs of international collaboration are taking shape on the implementation of technology and to some extent on precompetitive research (research that does not lead directly to proprietary commercial products).[3]

The impact of the international market for technology on developing countries is mixed. The "Gang of Four" (Korea, Singapore, Taiwan, and Hong Kong) made the necessary investments in dynamic comparative advantage during the 1970s and 1980s and are competitive in the new knowledge economy. Likewise, China, India, and perhaps Brazil and Mexico are on their way to becoming "innovative developing countries."[4] Gulf states could, if they so choose, use their oil money to finance and benefit from innovation. A few other developing countries—Thailand, Malaysia, Turkey, and Chile, perhaps—are also within range. But the challenges for smaller and the least developed countries are much more serious because markets and technology are moving so fast, and because some of the methods used by the Gang of Four are now forbidden by the WTO (although China evades WTO restrictions because of the allure of its huge market for foreign investors).

The result is *asymmetric technological capacity*, in the sense that most developing countries are technology takers and have no choice but to accept technology from advanced countries and hence to import paradigms that evolved in advanced countries under quite different circumstances.[5] This works well if the needs of a developing country are the same as those of advanced countries, directly or with minor modifications. Occasionally, as in the specific case of cell phones, developing countries have not only leapfrogged legacy landline technology but also built on imported technology to make world-class innovations to suit their own needs and situations, as for example in mobile finance.

Even so, the export of paradigms from developed countries can result in the importation—sometimes at the insistence of the importers—of ill-suited technologies like expensive high-tech hospitals that can't be sustained over time, rather than the development of needed innovations like well-designed rural clinics. With important exceptions, some of which are described in Chapter 9, developing countries have historically lacked sufficient technical and innovative capacity—or sufficient motivation—to strike out on their own to develop technologies not based on or adapted from models from advanced countries, or even to choose to import technologies from smaller exporters whose situation is closer to their own (a choice that may require resistance to political pressures and to temptations to corruption in public procurement).

The international technology market in developing countries involves important additional market imperfections. Capital goods specifically suited to conditions in developing countries require economies of scale in manufacture, which may be difficult to achieve if their market is scattered across many countries and if innovative firms in developing countries lack the expertise and infrastructure for worldwide marketing. Moreover, the combination of lack of market power and lack of technical and innovative capacity results in important areas of "orphan technology"— technologies like malaria vaccines that would answer a critical social need, but that have limited commercial markets and are therefore dependent on public-sector intervention by governments, private foundations, non-governmental organizations, or development assistance agencies based in advanced countries.

The situation is brightened by a number of promising developments. The research arms of bilateral and multilateral assistance agencies, including the specialized agencies of the United Nations, have long sought to overcome these obstacles. More recently, their efforts have been complemented by new technologies and new actors. The revolution in information and communications technology has provided disruptive technologies in finance, education, health services delivery, small business creation, and all aspects of logistics and coordination, as well as a new vehicle for global marketing of products of all kinds.[6] Advances in basic science have made possible promising cures or vaccines for some previously neglected tropical diseases.

The rise of India and China, which have large markets compared to those of other developing countries and the innovative capacity to develop products to satisfy them, has helped to create markets for efficient, low-cost products suited to the needs of poor people. The Tata Nano automobile and the low-cost electrocardiograph are pioneering examples. The evolution of massive, online courses (MOOCs) described in chapter 7 could bring new access to higher education in the developing world. A growing number of public-private partnerships are now aimed at orphan technologies at the "bottom of the pyramid," especially in public health and education but also in raising the productivity of scattered small-scale producers.[7]

Despite these positive developments, the obstacles to innovation in developing countries remain important. The combination of entrenched paradigms in legacy sectors in advanced countries, corruption, asymmetric technical and managerial capacity, lack of market power in developing countries, and assorted imperfections in both domestic and international markets, all taken together, inhibits the development and spread of innovations that could make important contributions to global humanitarian, development, and environmental problems. We explore these considerations as they apply to agriculture and energy, using our newly expanded conceptual framework.

INDUSTRIAL AGRICULTURE

Before turning to an international perspective, we will examine the *innovation environment* for industrial agriculture in the United States, which as we have discussed in chapter 9, includes both the *innovation system* and the *innovation context*. Turning first to the context, US agriculture is characterized by a strong *technological/economic/political/social paradigm* in support of large-scale, mechanized, input-intensive industrial agriculture—big subsidies and resulting *perverse prices*, strong *vested interests*, a well-established *value network*, strong public *habits and expectations*, and a well-established *knowledge structure*—all of which reinforce the effects of the vast land and water resources and continent-sized market in favoring large-scale industrial, input-intensive agriculture. The US Department of Agriculture at the federal level has supported this model with subsidies and low-cost lending and price supports. This model has its severe critics, who argue that it has generated grain, produce, and meat of declining nutritional quality, that nearly a billion people are overweight and a similar number are hungry, and that high-volume factory food production systems have created new risks for food-borne illness.[8]

The *innovation system* in support of US agriculture includes R & D and extension programs, and the educational and research functions of the land grant colleges that the US Department of Agriculture (USDA) helps support at the state level. This system has helped overcome the problem of *collective action* facing the fragmented US agricultural sector, which is characterized by a vast number of small, thinly capitalized, still largely family-owned farms,[9] at least as this problem applies to industrial agriculture. However, "sustainable" agriculture—low-input agriculture that minimizes environmental disruption and resource use and has largely been, to date, smaller in scale—generally has not benefited directly from this paradigm.

In addition to the weight of historical development favoring industrial agriculture, sustainable agriculture suffers from a number of inherent problems. First, sustainable agriculture—which implies much lower resource inputs and greater environmental compatibility—is subject to many alternative definitions.[10] Sustainable can incorporate "organic" agriculture, which, generally speaking, can be characterized, defined, and labeled as constituting "practices that foster cycling of resources, promote ecological balance, and conserve biodiversity; synthetic fertilizers, sewage sludge, irradiation, and genetic engineering may not be used."[11] However, various standards for the definition of "organic" agriculture disagree on whether any use of chemical pesticides, inorganic fertilizer, bovine growth hormone, or genetically modified crops is to be allowed. Other possible definitions would require free-range livestock, much more efficient water irrigation, minimum energy use, minimum environmental footprint, or local production that minimizes transport between the sites of production and consumption.[12] Moreover, although there are signals that this is changing,[13] sustainable agriculture in the United States did not benefit in the past from many of the services of the US Department of Agriculture and the land grant research system, which supply a scale of support that largely overcomes the collective action problem for American industrial farmers.

In contrast, most organic producers of whatever stripe have been small in scale and ill equipped to carry out research.[14] The result is that organic and sustainable farmers have been forced to establish themselves as an upscale, high-cost niche market. This niche sector is expanding rapidly from a low base but despite the high hopes of its devotees, does not show clear signs yet of becoming a truly disruptive technology that can reach a scale to challenge the strongly entrenched, prevailing paradigm of high-input, large-scale industrial agriculture.[15] Indeed, the most promising sign that sustainable and organic agriculture may be "mainstreamed" into the prevailing paradigm is its adoption by large-scale farmers.[16]

The remarkable success of industrial agriculture, coupled with the Green Revolution in developing countries, has been that it has scaled production to more than meet population growth;[17] the continuing expansion of the world population and of the industrialization of the developing world will require gains in food production at an accelerating pace for the foreseeable future. With world population projected to reach 9 billion by 2050, agricultural production must increase by some 70% to meet the demand derived from this growth in population.[18] This is a remarkable challenge, since little additional arable land remains to expand food production, and there are dramatic potential threats from water scarcity and climate change.

However, these can be potential *forcing mechanisms* lurking in the wings that may induce a different kind of agriculture in the United States and other countries. Water availability is a growing world problem, including in the United States; climate change may accelerate this problem and disrupt current world food production patterns over time.[19] The recent sharp drop in energy prices shows that energy costs are subject to dramatic shifts—and what goes down can also go up, a fact that provides an additional threat to industrial scale farm equipment and to the production of the fertilizer that is pervasive in US agriculture.[20] In other words, limits on the heavy resource inputs required by industrial agriculture may in time induce the adoption of more sustainable technology, in this way disrupting the legacy sectors in US agriculture and at the same time providing a technology better suited to the needs of developing countries, as we shall discuss further in the following section.[21]

However, there are limits to what these emerging currents may be able to change. One problem is that plant research at the USDA (and in NSF's plant genome program) is organized around plant species that are already in production. People depend on a dozen plant species, primarily grains such as rice, wheat, and corn, for most of their calories, and current agricultural research is organized around these species.[22] Yet understanding the molecular, genetic, cellular, physiological, and biochemical science behind plant growth in a much larger range of species could provide new potential food sources.[23] Broadened research on new food sources could prove important due to the stresses that world agriculture will face from reduced arable land, pests, high salt, drought, and the needs to increase yield and reduce food waste.

In a good example of the legacy sector characteristics of *established institutional architecture* and *vested interests*, research is largely locked into current agriculture industry agendas. In addition, only a small part of the USDA's research is competitive; most is locked into an entitlement program for land grant schools, many of which do not have leading molecular biology and genomics capabilities. These deep innovation organization problems have been recognized in a 10-year research plan from plant science research experts[24] and recent National Academies and President's Council of Advisors on Science and Technology (PCAST) reports.[25] USDA leaders are attempting to move past some of its research structure problems by founding an independent foundation to seek nongovernmental grants to support research areas it is limited in supporting.[26]

Another problem lies in the fact that agricultural production cannot be viewed as a stand-alone sector. Rather it is embedded in a complex food system that integrates agricultural produce and its industrial production model into an even larger food production and delivery system, which also has the characteristics typical of a legacy sector and tends to lock in its legacy features. This larger food system includes farms and their agricultural practices, processed food production, the international agricultural trading system, food transport, and consumer health and nutrition delivery. Only five agribusiness firms, for example, control the majority of the world's seed base. [27]

The global interconnectedness of food processing can make the food system vulnerable, leading to increased food security risks due to shifts, for example, in the availability and price of fossil fuels for transport or unexpected weather and climate patterns.[28] The system is also characterized by perverse subsidies that can disrupt markets and access, and with a notorious pesticide "circle of poison" that can affect consumer health.[29] The global network of agricultural transport for both processed and unprocessed food leads to trade-offs between the efficiency of transport and food quality, such as plants bred for delayed ripening but of reduced nutritional value. Increasingly efficient transport also facilities the global spread of disease (usually bacterial).

The linkage of agricultural production with this larger, closely integrated system may curtail the "forcing" (i.e., *inducing*) mechanisms that were described earlier as offering the promise of more sustainable agricultural practices. The problem lies in the fact that the most profitable economic segment of the food industry is based on value added to crops through processing and packaging foods. The price pressure on the commodities that go into food manufacturing is even greater than on produce that moves directly to grocery stores. For this reason, the combined agriculture and food industries have shown limited interest to date in longer range research aimed at a broader agricultural base—for example, by supporting broader research into new plant species, varieties and techniques that we may need to feed a growing world population and meet the water, climate. and related stresses that global agriculture will face in the future.

THE INTERNATIONAL MARKET IN AGRICULTURAL TECHNOLOGY

Let's turn now from the United States to the international picture. Industrialized countries have their own systems of agricultural education, research, and extension, and agricultural policies that support their own domestic paradigms, reflecting societies accustomed to food (*public expectations*) and a well-established market system of processing and distribution of agricultural products. All advanced countries subsidize their agriculture in one way or another, in order to ensure their cheap food for their population and also to stimulate exports. These subsidies (*perverse pricing*, at least from the environmental point of view) are heavily defended by farmers and agribusiness (*vested interests*), which are overrepresented politically in most advanced countries one way or another. These subsidies are complemented by research, extension, and other institutions that provide necessary innovative capacity and technical services.

Many poor developing countries by default practice organic agriculture, largely because they can't afford industrial inputs such as fertilizer, pesticides, mechanized irrigation, and heavy equipment. Many farmers in developing countries would seek, if they were affordable, more such industrial inputs because they could increase yields. Farmers in developing countries, like farmers everywhere, suffer from *collective action* problems, but the institutions serving them are in general much weaker than those in advanced countries. Research and extension institutions are much less effective—an aspect of the *asymmetric innovative capacity* discussed earlier—and when they do exist are typically patterned on those of the advanced countries. Besides, technology for sustainable agriculture tends to be more locality specific than industrialized agriculture, and hence would put much heavier requirements on these researchers and extension workers to respond to local conditions and hence to collaborate with farmers. Thus, higher yield but sustainable technologies appear somewhat elusive for the developing world.

This means that most poor developing countries have limited opportunities to develop innovative, sustainable technologies that protect their environment, which by and large is more sensitive to unsustainable practices than that of temperate zones.[30] This situation is exacerbated by an overall underinvestment in developing country agriculture and agricultural research,[31] and by the imperfections in the global market for agricultural products—most especially derived from the subsidies to and protective tariffs around developed country agriculture that encourage dumping of surplus production into export markets.[32] The well-known result of these subsidies is to reverse the classical comparative advantage in agriculture that should be enjoyed by tropical countries, and hence to depress investment in these countries in agriculture and hence in agricultural research.[33]

The upshot of this situation is that the input-intensive system of agriculture that characterizes advanced country agriculture has been exported to the developing countries in modified form. The first stage of this paradigm export was the Green Revolution,[34] in which internationally supported research laboratories (which helped to overcome the problems of both *asymmetric innovative capacity* and the need for *collective action*) transferred and adapted technology for high-yielding varieties of cereal grains, including wheat and rice, based on selection and hybridization techniques that were already in widespread use in Japan and the United States.[35] These crop development efforts to suit local production conditions were coupled with modern management efforts, large-scale production of hybridized seed, irrigation techniques, synthetic fertilizers, and pesticides.

The Green Revolution resulted in dramatic benefits: greatly increased yields and much lower food prices than would otherwise have been the case, initially in Mexico, Pakistan, and India and then more broadly in Asia and Latin America.[36] This arguably avoided the widespread starvation in India that had been authoritatively predicted,[37] and may have saved a billion lives worldwide from starvation.[38] At the same time, it put stresses on tropical environments in the form of erosion, chemical pollution, and water stress that might have been avoided had there been more understanding of and attention to sustainability from the beginning.[39]

The point here is not to offer criticisms of the Green Revolution, on which there is an ample literature, but to point out that it was based on an advanced country paradigm, which in retrospect was adopted because the need to raise developing country yields in the light of increasing population was urgent and because no alternative, less input-intensive technology was available for transfer. Indeed, the use of fertilizer and pesticides in developing countries was so low in the 1950s that it was thought urgent at the time to increase them, and understandably so. The research and extension capabilities in Mexico, India, Philippines, and many other developing countries improved dramatically, based on the model from the United States, Great Britain, and France, and reflecting their national agricultural paradigms. In many countries, the use of fertilizer and pesticides was subsidized, a practice that still continues even now that the dangers of overuse of these inputs are well understood and the resulting low prices provide *perverse incentives.*

The export of this paradigm has been further complicated by the recent impact on developing countries of two issues of foreign origin: the modest rise in food prices caused by competition for land use induced by subsidies to food crops, especially corn,[40] and the export to developing countries of the largely European controversy over genetically modified (GM) crops. In the latter case, European risk/benefit calculus—one perhaps appropriate to an affluent region with ample food supplies—has been exported to countries where GM crops could make a major contribution to agricultural productivity.[41] Critics point out correctly that existing GM crops benefit mostly large industrial farmers in advanced countries—but this is a matter of the choice of research objectives, itself a reflection of an entrenched paradigm. If researchers were to be tasked with, and given adequate resources for, applying GM techniques to sustainable agriculture, the resulting technology could be quite different. Here the *lumpiness* of research on GM crops poses major obstacles to agricultural researchers in developing countries,[42] as the cost of a single commercial GM crop exceeds the entire budget of the Consultative Group on International Agricultural Research (CGIAR), the major network of international laboratories devoted to agricultural research for developing countries.[43]

The impact of intellectual property (IP) protection on the availability of GM crops suited to the needs of developing country agriculture is more complicated. The Green Revolution, as noted above, was based on food crop varieties adapted by publicly funded international research laboratories from varieties developed by government and university laboratories in Japan, the United States, and Europe, and placed by them in the public domain. The large commercial seed companies raised no objection to this system. Nor did governments raise objections to the international exchange of genetic material, which was correctly perceived to be of universal benefit. GM crops, in contrast, are mostly developed by private companies and are subject to IP protection. Private foundations exist to facilitate the donation of these IP rights to developing country laboratories.[44]

There are, to be sure, possibilities for increased sustainability at minimum cost within the prevailing paradigm of high-tech industrial agriculture. Networks of cheap sensors and radio frequency identification (RFID) in plants and soil could make possible far more efficient delivery of dosages of nutrients and water appropriate to particular plants and field areas.[45] Coupling techniques of drip irrigation with a sensor system that delivers water based on the needs of different parts of fields could increase the efficiency of water use. Small-scale, semiautonomous robotics responsive to field sensor networks could replace some of the current energy-intensive, large-scale mechanized equipment, enabling harvesting to occur when the network indicates that particular plants are ready, not on a fixed preset calendar date. Costs for some of these technologies can be driven down and their operation and maintenance simplified, so as to make them relevant to developing countries.

As with energy, there is no single technological silver bullet. Different countries and different geographic and climatic regions will require different approaches to conservation and agricultural technology. Any new agricultural technologies must still go through the cycle of research, development, prototyping, and test beds to demonstrate efficiencies and costs and make possible enough early deployment to drive down its costs so as to be competitive with industrial agriculture. At the low end of the technological scale, agricultural researchers in developing countries are devoting increasing attention to the contributions of individual farmers to indigenous innovation through new methods of participatory research and extension.[46] Even so, the problems of *asymmetric technological capacity*, *perverse incentives*, *collective action*, and *lumpiness* in the legacy agricultural sectors of both the developed and developing world remain; until they can be overcome, a transformation to greater sustainability will remain elusive.

THE FOSSIL-FUEL-BASED ENERGY ECONOMY

Our discussions of energy in chapter 6 set forth the characteristics of the technological/social/economic/political paradigm that underlies the fossil-fuel-based energy economy in the United States and by extension in all advanced countries.[47] In this paradigm, as have seen, *perverse prices* create producer incentives that are misaligned with the broader environmental need to conserve energy and minimize carbon dioxide emissions, as well as with the geopolitical and economic need to minimize the importation of petroleum. Both of these social needs apply worldwide, in the sense that it is in everyone's interest that everyone else apply carbon-dioxide-minimizing and energy-conserving technology, no matter where on earth they live.

The international market in energy technology thus leads to the tension, previously mentioned, between the desire of innovators and innovating nations to realize the gains of IP rights, on the one hand, and global environmental and security externalities, on the other. Intellectual property rights are essential to encourage private investment in innovative energy producing and energy-using technology. On the other hand, the existence of global externalities implies that a free exchange of innovative technology would be desirable to encourage the implementation of technologies that minimize carbon dioxide emissions and petroleum imports.[48]

At a minimum, these global externalities justify a substantial program of international collaboration on precompetitive research and technology implementation, and in fact some efforts at such programs are underway. Innovative crossover efforts are underway in countries that do not share the impediments of American paradigms, as, for example, the financing of production by provincial Chinese governments of US-developed advances in energy technology that can be developed into profitable products for subsidized markets both in China and in Europe, but that the United States is not prepared to commercialize at scale itself.[49]

These projects dramatically illustrate the impediments to US manufacturing that are discussed at length in chapter 6, and the tension between the need to promote US competitiveness and the need to address global environmental problems.[50] While a major objective of US innovation policy is to benefit from its own innovations rather than shifting the gains from the markets that they create to China, in effect these projects constitute pilot projects for technologies that could be potentially disruptive back in the United States, should market imperfections and other obstacles somehow be removed. Either way, the implementation of these technologies would greatly benefit American consumers and the global environment—although at the potential cost of competitive disadvantage of American producers.

On the other hand, the world cannot count on China or any other country to take up the slack in developing and launching technologies in those cases in which subsidies for sustainable technology are lacking and deeply entrenched obstacles in a global legacy sectors paradigm make it unlikely that there will be a near-term commercial market. The recent reduction in subsidies to renewable energy in Germany, Australia, and other countries raises concern that this situation may arise—unless ongoing projects intended to drive down solar and wind energy costs enables them to competitive with fossil fuel without subsidy, at least in some markets.[51]

The absence of carbon charges or other incentives for carbon-saving technology poses obstacles even at the stage of research collaboration, especially when large sums of money are involved, as is the case for demonstration projects of *lumpy*, engineering-intensive technologies like carbon capture and sequestration and enhanced ("hot rocks") geothermal. While there is significant focus on a technology push strategy for new energy technologies in a number of countries, there is a risk that firms and countries could slow the investment in technology development and implementation and in the time commitment of their best technical people in such large-scale technologies, which will be economic only if carbon charges or other restrictions on carbon dioxide emissions come into more widespread use.[52]

The situation is further complicated by the rise of China as a major manufacturer of hardware for renewable energy,[53] and increasingly as a major investor in research and technology development in this and related areas.[54] Efforts to launch collaborative research at the precompetitive level have been hindered by the recent recession in advanced countries, and by the political complications associated with the rise of China as an economic and possible geopolitical competitor.[55] On the positive side, China and the United States announced in November 2014 bilateral carbon dioxide reduction targets.[56] It remains to be seen how these issues will play out in the context of specific individual collaboration projects.

GLOBAL IMPLICATIONS OF DOMESTIC PARADIGMS

It is a standard observation in the study of the transfer of technology that imported technology embodies cultural values essential to industrial modernization: workforce discipline, acceptance and support of productivity gains, and understanding of the economic value of time. By way of contrast, the older literature on "appropriate technology" also frequently noted that such imported technology was often overly capital-intensive or difficult to maintain because it was developed to correspond to the factor endowments of developed countries, which it was frequently argued were inappropriate to developing countries.[57]

The literature of the time, however, did not take explicit note of the fact that in some sectors at least, technology in advanced countries embodies other, less desirable characteristics: lack of cost consciousness, for example, and profligacy in the use of natural resources and environment, stemming from their having been treated in effect as free goods. In such cases, technology may be "inappropriate" to both the exporter and the recipient! Indeed, it is common to acknowledge this fact indirectly in the form of the wistful hope that the developing countries might avoid repeating the mistakes of the developed countries, and instead "leapfrog" over legacy technologies and follow a more sustainable path.

Continuing resource exploitation and the rapid growth of automobile markets in emerging nations are examples that suggest that this is likely to remain a hope rather than a reality. With occasional exceptions—cell phones being the most prominent example—this hope has by and large not been fulfilled. As we have seen earlier, agricultural research in developing countries has historically focused on technologies requiring the increased application of fertilizer and pesticides (although starting from a very low base), on the assumption that attention to environmental issues could be postponed. Energy policies in emerging nations have focused on increasing the supply of fossil-fuel-based electricity, rather than on supplying energy in forms better suited to conservation or to specific end-uses.[58] Builders in tropical countries have constructed "modern," glass-walled, air-conditioned skyscrapers, even in desert countries with distinguished traditions of attractive, energy-conserving architecture.

The reasons are not hard to find. First is the familiar problem of "orphan technology"—technologies for which there is a need but no market. Poor countries and poor people do not offer large enough commercial markets for products like malaria vaccines, which therefore depend on the benevolence of rich countries and private foundations. This is not a market failure. It is, after all, the way markets are supposed to work. They need enough customers with money to pay in order to allow products to be made at sufficient scale to be profitable.

But important imperfections in the international market for technology are also involved here. Developing countries have lacked the technical and corresponding innovative capacity—and perhaps as importantly, the institutional and political strength—to strike out in new directions, although some emerging economies have shown that it is possible to break out of this box. Importation of high-tech equipment makes for attractive photo-ops, and in addition is popular with exporting countries and often their development assistance agencies—and not incidentally offers superior opportunities for corruption. "Advanced," imported technologies have the prestige of the foreign, and have the extra advantage of having been shown to work in their countries of origin—a version of the *first-mover advantage*. More generally, these nations point out, why should we take the chance of trying out a new approach, when we can follow a well-worn path blazed by the countries that have already developed? Why have we the responsibility to conserve resources for the benefit of humankind, they ask, when our predecessors in development—the currently "advanced" countries—have not done so?

The technological/economic/political/social paradigms in innovative countries thus have global as well as domestic implications. As we have seen, technological trajectories in legacy sectors peculiar to their country of origin may affect the choice of technology all over the world. This technological lock-in may be problematic not only because it limits access to new, more appropriate technological paradigms in developed nations but may be even less appropriate to the differing needs of the developing world.

The dramatic rise of China and India raises both problems and opportunities. These countries combine growing investments in research, development, and innovation with large domestic markets that offer attractive commercial possibilities for products suited to the needs of the poor as well as to those of a growing middle class.[59] For these countries, and especially for China as the world's leading manufacturing center, "orphan technology" is at least as much a commercial opportunity as the sign of a social problem. China especially is emerging as a formidable competitor, vigorously seeking markets for low-cost products in both advanced and developing countries, as well as for potentially disruptive products like equipment for the generation of renewable energy.

From the developing country point of view, this may be a big advantage, as these new actors are likely to be major sources of technology aimed at poor people—technologies that have hitherto been "orphaned" by the lack of a commercial market of paying customers.[60] On the other hand, the world is in great need of innovative technology in legacy sectors like agriculture and energy, where both the development and large-scale implementation of innovation are often stymied by entrenched paradigms that have been exported worldwide. Here developing countries need to build the capacity to identify technology that has been developed in countries unaffected by these strictures.

There are sustainability reasons for the United States and other advanced countries to engage in cooperative, precompetitive research and technology implementation, and in efforts to overcome established technology paradigms in areas like sustainable agriculture, renewable energy, or infectious disease, where continued innovation serves everyone's interest. However, it is overly optimistic to expect that such international collaboration will overcome the many obstacles to widespread implementation of sustainable technologies in these and other legacy sectors in the absence of substantial change in one or another underlying technological/economic/political/social paradigm. The question for the future is whether a US or other developed world paradigm in these and other complex established legacy sectors will be entrenched as a global paradigm and hence as a permanent obstacle to badly needed innovation, or whether disruptive innovations begun and tested in places free of these strictures will come to flourish. These places may develop, in turn, their own paradigms and their own strictures, of course, but this will be a future story.

We have started in previous chapters from a vision of legacy sectors as national or sectoral phenomena, looking at a series of US sectors and their legacy characteristics. We then turned in the preceding chapter 9 to a review of the innovation environments of six quite different nations, where embedded legacy features tend to act both to *en*able and to *dis*able innovative capacity. This chapter adds a further dimension—that the characteristics of a legacy sector in one nation can be visited upon another, a significant potential problem in the relationship between developed and developing countries. This provides an additional impetus for developing the policies necessary to tackle the deep problem of bringing innovation into a legacy sector, a topic that we address in the next chapters.

11 Innovation Dynamics, Change Agents, and Innovation Organization

Prescribing policy for widely varying legacy sectors is a monster challenge. After all, energy is different from manufacturing, which is different from health. But are there commonalities—common policy approaches—that can cut across sectors? The upcoming chapters on policy are a search for these policy commonalities.

We begin with an elaboration of the five underlying models of the dynamic of innovation that must be brought to bear on legacy sectors, expanding on points that we summarized briefly in chapter 3. We follow with a discussion of the overall innovation policy context and then with a review of imperfections and market failures common to legacy sectors, setting forth possible approaches to overcoming or circumventing each. We then elaborate on the "innovation organization" model in some detail and show how it can be used to advance the ideas of leading innovation theorists.

RETURNING TO THE FIVE MODELS OF THE DYNAMICS OF INNOVATION

To move innovation into complex, established legacy sectors, we need a working theory of the dynamics of innovation. We must understand how technological innovation takes place in economic sectors in response to technological developments and market opportunities, and how public policy operates to affect this process. Unless we understand the ways innovation typically enters the economy, we will not be able to extend innovation theory so that it can apply to legacy sectors. This section is particularly focused on the fifth model, "innovation organization," an overarching model key to grasping legacy sector innovation. But since it incorporates the other models, we need to elaborate as well on the series of more basic and partial models of the innovation process that were first briefly explained in chapter 3.

The pipeline model: The US conception of the origin of innovation typically begins with basic research. According to the "pipeline" model of the dynamic of innovation associated with Vannevar Bush[1] (which can also be termed the "linear" model), research intended to advance the frontiers of knowledge—driven, ideally, by curiosity about the operation of the natural world—will, in the aggregate and over time, lead to "radical" or "breakthrough" inventions that create "new functionality." They make it possible to do entirely new things: model weather patterns five days in advance, play video clips on a handheld device, or visually and orally navigate on a smartphone through any city in the world. Results emerging out of the research stage provide a "technology push" that can then be translated into commercial products; these will be transformed into profitable innovations and give rise to economic growth. The assumption is that commercialization and widespread deployment can be on autopilot. The marketplace will take over from the researcher, implementing the technology without further government intervention.

US basic research tends to take place in federally funded universities and research institutes, whereas product development takes place in private industry.[2] The bulk of federal R & D agencies in the United States—the National Science Foundation, the National Institutes of Health, the Energy Department's Office of Science, to cite three prominent examples—follow Bush's design and invest in basic research.[3] Compared to the situation in many other countries, the US system works well: the basic research funded predominantly by government has led to dramatic follow-on technological advance.[4] Even so, this institutional separation gives rise to a difficult-to-finance gap between the proof of concept in a university laboratory and development of a commercializable product that is attractive to the venture capitalist and industry. This gap between research and late-stage development has become known as the "valley of death" where most new technologies die, whether intended for legacy or nonlegacy sectors alike.[5]

The emphasis on radical innovations embodying new functionality is well suited to an American temperament oriented to opening new frontiers—to bringing on the "next big thing." As we have discussed, Americans are less good at dealing with the obstacles to innovation created by long-standing, entrenched, pervasive, and efficient "legacy" technologies, like an energy sector based on fossil fuels.

The induced innovation model: Federally funded research leading to radical or breakthrough technologies is not the only driver of innovation. Industry, of course, has a profound role. To deal with the industrial role in established, complex technology legacy sectors, we need additional conceptual tools. The theory of *induced innovation* (sometimes referred to as "market pull" or "demand pull") was offered by the late Vernon Ruttan, who observed that innovators spot established or niche markets susceptible to the entry of new technology and then move to fill them.[6] This kind of innovation typically takes advantage of incremental or secondary as opposed to radical technological advances and is led by industry. The model can also be applied to explain the overall direction of technological change in a country, geographic region, or industry.

In its simplest original form, the theory of induced innovation states that innovation tends to minimize the use of relatively expensive inputs and maximize the use of inexpensive ones.[7] As a result, a change in the price of a key input like energy, whether through pure market forces or a change in government policy, can affect the direction of innovation. At first, this can occur through modest technology adjustments, like selling smaller cars, or the introduction of "inducible" technologies that are ready for implementation but have lacked competitiveness because of pricing or other external factors and could be quickly implemented if these were to change. If the price changes are expected to be enduring, more expensive energy will lead to the development and introduction of new, energy-efficient products based on existing technologies and, in the still longer run, to a change in the direction of applied research. Alternatively, a firm may spot a market niche not well served by existing technologies—for example, a niche for specialty LED lighting, or a market opened by a new regulatory requirement or a change in demographics—and launch a technology in that niche.

The induced innovation model assumes that a technology can sooner or later enter the marketplace more or less automatically once the appropriate market incentives are well established. This is not always the case, especially when the technology in question is not technically ready for implementation or faces competition from established technologies, such as those dependent on fossil fuels. Obstacles to innovations that are based on the results of long-term research may appear at the classic valley of death between proof of concept and first product. Others may appear at a later stage, when the product is ready for market launch at scale, a time that is especially critical for innovation in legacy sectors. In particular, as we have seen, induced innovation in legacy sectors is typically hampered or blocked by price structures, market imperfections, and other obstacles that favor and help entrench incumbent technologies.

The extended pipeline model: Neither pipeline nor induced theories of the dynamic of innovation fully encompass what more recent scholarship has been teaching about the role of government in innovation.[8] Current conservative political mythology portrays incompetent government relentlessly hampering a dynamic private sector, through such devices as high taxes and excessive regulation. It is true that the state can play such a role if it forms part of a disruption-resistant technological/economic/political/social paradigm. However, in many cases the opposite takes place: the state can serve not only as technological initiator and change agent at the research stage, as captured in the pipeline model, but also in all of the follow-on stages. In such situations, the private sector, which is inherently risk-averse and short-term in its outlook, invests only after entrepreneurial government has made the high-risk, longer-term investments.

The role of government in research, development, prototyping, demonstration, test beds, and often initial market creation is increasingly well understood by at least some experts as a result of the success of the IT sector.[9] Microprocessor advances, personal computing, supercomputing, the Internet and the Web, cloud computing, broadband and mobile communications, and robotics—economic sectors now producing many billions of dollars in revenue annually—all had their origins in federal support.[10] For example, nearly every technology that makes Apple's iPhone so "smart" was government funded: GPS, the Internet, the touch-screen display, and the voice-activated command system of Siri.[11] The Defense Department in particular has played a critical role in the advance of IT.[12] Biotechnological and pharmaceutical advances are also beneficiaries of this governmental role.[13]

We call this model, whereby government participates not only in R & D, but also in the later stages of the innovation process, from early-stage research through the customer role in market creation, the *extended pipeline*. Like the pipeline, it is a "technology push" model. Government's role here is not simply the modest one of intervening in cases of market failure, as envisioned in classical and neoclassical economics and summarized in chapter 2, but one of shaping and creating markets.[14] It has operated across the full spectrum of innovation advance, and has enabled private-sector entry that takes place only after government has assumed the initial risk.

However, this governmental role is not well understood by either the public or by politicians, a fact that operates as a brake on the understanding of both future opportunities for innovation and on the reaping of the full rewards of contemporary innovation-driven capitalism. It should be emphasized that this "extended pipeline" system now operates predominantly through the Defense Department, which led most of the Kondratiev innovation waves of the 20th century, from aviation to electronics, nuclear power, space, computing, and the Internet and which tends to operate at the innovation frontier, not in legacy sectors. The governmental role in medicine, in industrial agriculture, and in aerospace provides other examples of this kind of active involvement, as suggested in chapters 6, 7, and 10. The "extended pipeline" theory is not a new theory on its own, but is rather a variation on and an extension of the "pipeline" theory ascribed to Vannevar Bush, intended to overcome the front-end-only limitations he imposed on it and to capture the reality of a deeper governmental role than was previously understood.

The manufacturing-led model: The fourth model of the dynamic of innovation, another "technology push" model that is not explicit in the innovation literature, we can term *manufacturing-led*. Innovation in the United States is generally associated with the front end of innovation: R & D through prototyping; manufacturing is usually not understood as part of the innovation process.[15] This is an inherently disconnected view; innovation must be looked at as a system, stretching from early-stage research through to production and market introduction. This contrasts with the perspectives of Germany and Japan, which have cultures emphasizing engineering, artisanship, and quality, and histories of innovation and success in production.[16] Both see production as being at the core of innovation and have run major trade surpluses in manufactured goods, in contrast to the major deficits in the United States.[17]

Innovative approaches are pervasive at the production stage and can take many years to bear fruit. Deep challenges must be resolved: designing a product that will optimally fit to a potential market, carrying out engineering design, overcoming problems of production and component cost, determining and forming production processes, creating efficient production systems, developing and applying new production and product business models, educating the production workforce in the new system, building a supply chain, financing production scale-up, and then scaling up production to fit evolving market conditions and reducing all these steps to a routine.

These are highly creative processes that are required to take place, by ensuring that manufacturing requirements are fully integrated, ideally when a product is first being designed, but at least by the outset of production at scale, and in either case entailing extensive engineering and science. Often the initial concept of the innovation itself must be completely rethought and reworked to fit production, cost, and market needs. In addition, many firms find that because there is so much "learning by building," the first production plant must often be written off because the second plant can be made much more efficient than the first by applying lessons drawn from the initial production experience. The front-end R & D begins the innovation process, but the subsequent stages through initial production at scale are just as critical, not only for incremental technology advance but also for radical or breakthrough innovation. In sum, much innovation is "manufacturing-led"; this must be regarded as a key approach to innovation and a model in its own right. It is a critical aspect of "technology push" but also serves the incremental and secondary advances of induced, "demand pull" innovation.

The United States has excelled at manufacturing in the past, inventing in the second half of the 19th century a production paradigm around mass production to serve a continent-sized economy.[18] But following the creation in the postwar period of a powerful front-end innovation system, US innovation has tended to become front-end loaded, emphasizing R & D as opposed to its previous focus on production. Since today's innovation system must also embrace the back end—the prototype, demonstration, test bed, and initial production phases—the United States has a problem, as we have reviewed in chapter 4. China, which now exceeds the United States in manufacturing net output, emphasizes the back end of innovation, particularly production, even as it works to build its front-end R & D system. Although many have assumed that China has achieved its production leadership through lower wages and costs, the studies we have reviewed earlier suggest that it is able to scale up production volume rapidly through advanced processes that are integrated across regional firms and tied to system efficiencies and cost savings.[19]

Just as there are limits to front-end innovation, there are limits, too, to manufacturing-led innovation. Asian economies like Taiwan and Korea have emphasized this manufacturing-led stage, but are now competing with lower-cost economies in areas that are increasingly dominated by commodity goods and face slowing growth. In other words, they grasped the back end but overlooked the need for stronger front-end innovation, while the United States did the opposite. The lesson seems to be that strengths on both front- and back-end innovation are complementary. While the United States retains a strong front-end innovation system, it has not understood the need to extend its view of its innovation system to include production. So it has failed to grasp the importance of manufacturing-led innovation, although this remains an important innovation model.

Innovation organization: The last model of the dynamic of innovation is the most far-reaching. Innovation requires not only a supply of technology (as captured in the pipeline and extended pipeline models) and a corresponding market demand for that technology (as captured in the induced and the manufacturing-led models), but also active organizational elements that are properly aligned to bring the two together. This fifth model is not spelled out in the innovation literature.[20] It stretches beyond the other four models to reach not only technology supply and market demand, but also the entire innovation system, from front end through to implementation.

In decentralized sectors in which there are many private firms, as exemplified especially by manufacturing but also by many high-tech fields, there must be a chain of institutions, from research through to implementing firms, with links connecting them, to enable new technologies to evolve to meet radically new requirements or to translate radically new capabilities into practical applications—in the jargon, to enable technology push to meet up with and satisfy market pull.

This leads us to a fifth model for the dynamic of innovation: the concept that "innovation organization" is required to form a new technology and to link up—and if necessary to orchestrate—the disparate institutions and firms needed to launch it, overcoming any institutional or policy obstacles that come up on the way. This innovation must be anchored in both the public and private sectors, because these sectors are otherwise inherently disconnected. The innovation organization model combines the first four innovation models but also moves beyond them to overcome or circumvent the obstacles in the innovation environment and to identify and facilitate the work of the change agents that confront them. This function is particularly important in legacy sectors, in which these obstacles are particularly problematic. It is implicit in the other four models but deserves to be explicit in its own right. We elaborate in the next two sections below on this and other elements of the innovation organization model.

THE CHANGE AGENT

Whatever the model, innovation doesn't just happen. Even if the elements for an innovation system are assembled, someone or something must serve as the catalyst for change. We call that person or organization the *change agent*. Change agents, like innovation itself, must operate at both the institutional and the personal, face-to-face level. And as usual in human affairs, there is no substitute for leadership.

We explored the concept of change agent in the defense sector in chapter 8, focusing on the role of leaders in the secretary of defense's office allied to an innovation agency, in that case DARPA. The change agent, whether an institution or an individual allied to an institution, must be a policy orchestrator, pulling threads of policy options together to effect change and drive the innovation. The agent, therefore, must have available "inducible" or at least potential technological innovations, the policy instruments to push them, and the ability to identify, access, combine, and deploy both the innovations and the complementary policy instruments needed to exploit them.

The change agent takes a different form depending on which kind of model the innovation process is following. In the pipeline model, as we have seen, there is a major institutional gap between basic research organizations, which pursue discovery, and industry, which pursues the later stages of implementation. There are few bridges across this gap;[21] the key job of the change agent is to find one. In this case, the change agent is likely to be industry, particularly a small firm or entrepreneur prepared to pursue a radical innovation from research to a commercial product, sometimes with the aid of a technology transfer office in a university or government laboratory. As an example, many early software advances were supported by federal research. The critical computer language for what became desktop computing, which was both simpler to program with but able to reach sophisticated levels, was BASIC, developed by Dartmouth researchers from an NSF grant. But it took Bill Gates, Paul Allen, and their Microsoft "Microkids" team to apply BASIC to early microcomputers, from the earliest Altair through the IBM PC, making Microsoft's application of BASIC (and the MS-DOS operating system that used it) effectively the industry standard.[22]

The induced innovation model is inherently less ambitious and more connected. Here the change agent is industry. A firm sees a market opportunity, typically for an incremental or secondary technological advance, and moves to meet it. This is the story, for example, of Boeing's 787 Dreamliner. While jet aircraft were nurtured and sustained for decades by the military, the 787 applied a series of incremental advances to reduce weight, improve performance, and cut fuel consumption so as to fill a market need of the commercial airlines.

The manufacturing-led innovation model is exemplified by Japan's adoption of its famous quality manufacturing paradigm in the 1970s and 1980s based on ideas by Edward Demming. Japan's industrial leadership cadre were the change agents. Demming's principles were implemented most famously in the "Toyota system," which led to a production renaissance in Japan, allowing the nation to capture leadership in the auto and consumer electronics sectors.

The extended pipeline is an attempt, as we have discussed, by federal R & D agencies, largely in the defense sector, to reach further down the innovation pipeline past basic research toward implementation. Here the change agent can be the agency, best exemplified by the DARPA model, in which empowered program managers press to get their technology implemented and in this way act as change agents. Typically, the agency uses the "island-bridge" model, explained below, which develops the innovation in protected isolation from bureaucratic pressures, but uses a bridge to a senior decision-maker to press the advance. This is the story recited in chapter 8 of DARPA's developing stealth, UAVs, and precision strike innovations with backing from senior DOD leaders.

Whereas the initiative and creativity of program managers/change agents are critical to the operational successes of DARPA, their success depends critically on the support and effectiveness of the senior managers of the organization, who also act as change agents. To carry this idea still farther, one may consider William Perry, who, allied with DARPA, guided a series of major innovation efforts though the Defense Department (as discussed in chapter 8), as having been in this sense a *meta*-change agent—a person who helped get this whole kind of change agent system started. These meta-agents put in place the structures and policies that enable the direct change agents to do their jobs. Other defense sector examples of meta-change agents include Malcolm Currie, a director of defense research and engineering in the 1970s who supported GPS, stealth, and smart weapons, early DARPA director Jack Ruina, who guided its early contributions, and J. C. R. Licklider, the first Information Processing Techniques Office director at DARPA, who was the visionary of personal computing and the Internet. Others who might rate as *meta-meta*-change agents include President Dwight D. Eisenhower for putting DARPA in place, and Herbert York, its first chief scientist, for envisioning its initial structure.

ELEMENTS OF INNOVATION AND INNOVATION ORGANIZATION

We now set forth in more detail a series of elements that are explained in the innovation literature and are key to our understanding of the operation of the "innovation organization" model.

Linkages between innovation actors: Richard Nelson provided an initial insight: innovation proceeds "through the work of a community of actors," which includes R & D performers and technology implementers.[23] It includes public and private sectors, from R & D agencies to implementing firms. This community amounts to a social and economic system, and proceeds through the development of "routines"[24] along technological pathways, which, as Brian Arthur explained, become "path dependent" and can lead to technology "lock-in,"[25] allowing a technology to scale.

Paul Romer offers an overall insight: innovation requires "better recipes, not just . . . more cooking."[26] His insight leads us to the point that more inputs don't alone equal innovation; innovation lies in the arrangement of the ingredients, including institutional arrangements and the support systems behind them. His point is that "if we arranged our institutions optimally, growth in the United States could take place at an even higher rate than that to which we have become accustomed."[27] The idea of innovation organization must, therefore, embrace the range of institutions involved in the creation, development, and introduction of a technology, in both the public and the private sectors. It involves, in particular, the system of linkages between these institutions, including the strength of the mechanisms for handoffs between them.

So the linkages between institutions, both public and private, into a *connected science and technology model* become key to Romer's "recipes." This "connected model," the search for which is arguably a central task for innovation organization, takes a nonlinear, systems approach: the course of innovation is determined by the institutional elements that link technology to an eventual market demand.[28]

Technology push and demand pull: William Abernathy and James Utterback introduced the terms "radical" and "incremental" technology advance,[29] which help us see the role of the pipeline and induced models: Radical innovations that introduce new functionality result predominantly from "technology push," while incremental innovations result predominantly from "demand pull." (Secondary innovations can come from either direction.) Innovation organization must include both technology push and demand pull, because for innovation to be introduced into a legacy sector both approaches must operate. Unlike the other four models, one or the other won't do; changing a legacy sector may require radical, secondary, and incremental advances. This requires us to consider both technology-push and demand-pull mechanisms.

Transformative innovation that goes beyond research: As Avery Sen has pointed out, transformative research, heralded in recent years by federal R & D agencies, is not enough. On the contrary, as he notes, *transformative innovation*,[30] which is a different animal, is required in many important sectors—including, as our analysis has shown, in energy, manufacturing, and higher education. Innovation goes beyond research, discovery, and invention to encompass societal and economic entry *at scale*. In the useful formulation of the Council on Competitiveness, innovation is defined as "the intersection of invention and insight leading to the creation of social and economic value."[31]

A *transformative innovation* is defined as a technology or technologies that create or transform an economic sector. We would stretch Sen's definition and propose that such a transformative technology could be a radical technology that creates new capability (such as personal computing), but could also be a discontinuous secondary technology that makes possible a transformative improvement in an existing function, significantly altering a sector (such as turbine engines for aircraft). It could emerge from a research pipeline, be launched from a niche market, or be induced by a change in markets or policies, depending on the situation.

Transformative innovation means looking at both the front and back ends of the innovation system, from research and development through technology implementation.[32] This requires, as we have suggested above, examining the institutional connections between the front end, where federal research support dominates, and the back-end stages, from late-stage development to demonstration at scale through to production, where industry traditionally dominates. But the transformative process is not only about linkages and technology supply and market demand mechanisms. It entails an up-front visioning step to foresee those innovations that can be truly transformative of a sector. As we shall see in the next chapter, an analysis based on the innovation organization model must include this element, as well.

The talent base: Institutions and their linkages are not all that is required for innovation; it also requires integration of talent. Romer in 1990 demonstrated the central importance of "human capital engaged in research" as an innovation input.[33] Sheer numbers of talented science and technology "prospectors" were not enough; they had to be engaged in the innovation system. Bennis and Biederman take this a step further, arguing that "great groups" of talented technologists are key to the innovation stage, and these develop their own interactive rulesets that are key to their accomplishments.[34] Since people innovate, not institutions, the ways in which talent and institutions come together is crucial.[35] Scientists and engineers can't produce innovation standing apart by themselves, but rather require institutional mechanisms. The management of innovation, getting the right combinations for talent and institutions, becomes necessary. Institutions are a major input, but behind them lies their talent and its organization, and the combination requires merging talent management into innovation organization.

Overcoming obstacles within the innovation environment: A fundamental lesson from the evaluation of legacy sectors is the importance of the innovation environment, which includes both the innovation context and innovation system as we have defined them. Lurking within a legacy sector, as discussed in chapter 5, are networks of legacy characteristics and market imperfections that constitute barriers that must be overcome to advance innovation within the sector. While the pipeline and extended pipeline models are focused more on frontier sectors, legacy sector innovation via the innovation organization model must confront these obstacles as well. Thus, unlike the other four models that are descriptive of current approaches to innovation, the innovation organization model goes beyond the definition of the innovation system as it is classically defined and requires consideration of the issues within the full innovation environment.

Strategic systems approach: An additional element that must be included in the innovation organization model is a systems approach; legacy sectors arguably require it. The government-driven, front-end research stages of the innovation system have the potential for innovation in a legacy sector only if the back-end institutional elements and connections are in place. So, especially in a legacy sector, innovation requires a system where clear organizational links are in place to enable handoffs between institutional elements as well as to respond to innovation management. The point is that legacy sectors appear to require systems that encompass a range of transformational dynamics from pipeline to induced, radical to incremental to production.

The basis for basic research and the linear model that goes with it is that curiosity-driven research, including the hope for unanticipated results, is the source of eventual technological breakthroughs. This can, over time, work for frontier innovation. But legacy sectors—and many frontiers—need more systems and strategy. Arguably, bringing innovation to legacy sectors requires a much more conscious approach because of the systematic barriers and paradigms that must be overcome. That doesn't mean that serendipity isn't welcome for innovation in legacy sectors: as Sen notes, "Being strategic does not ignore serendipity; it organizes programs to capitalize on serendipity."[36] Legacy sectors require a strategic vision across the innovation stages, from research through production.

INNOVATION ORGANIZATION AND THE THEORY OF INNOVATION

How does the innovation organization model proposed here fit with the ideas of some of the leading exponents of innovation theory? We consider three pioneers of innovation theory—Schumpeter, Christensen, and Ruttan. In each case, we find that our model builds on the work of these pioneers and extends it to situations on which they did not focus.

Schumpeter, the great advocate for the processes of creative destruction that lie behind the success of capitalism, argued that disruptive innovation is central to economic advance. His theory is Darwinian, of evolution driven by a kind of economic natural selection; his disruption idea amounts to a kind of mutation process that spawns new species created by innovation. Disruptive innovation is central to Schumpeter's theories of how economic expansion occurs: technology-driven innovations build plateau upon plateau in our economy,[37] which amount to a series of economic step functions. But Schumpeter doesn't concentrate on the system that gives rise to the innovations themselves; his emphasis is on the disruptive economic effects of innovations that sweep aside their predecessors. The idea that innovation organization is needed to orchestrate the launch of a paradigm-inconsistent, disruptive innovation in legacy sectors is not part of his perspective.

Christensen suggests that disruptive innovation can never occur by trying to satisfy an existing market, but only by creating new ones.[38] Ruttan's point, that major innovation waves in the 20th century have been driven by war, the Cold War, and the pressures of national security, is complementary: defense innovation has tended to create new sectors. Are Christensen and Ruttan suggesting in their different ways that disruptive innovation requires new frontiers? But what about innovating in legacy sectors that resist innovation? For them, is this a "Mission Impossible"? Christensen typically examines established product and business lines that are displaced by significant product or business improvements, and both he and Ruttan explore the idea of the innovation system. But the range of issues envisioned here within the innovation organization model extends beyond their findings, as does the exploration of the large-scale legacy sector challenges that our model addresses.

Ruttan emphasizes the role not only of defense research but also of defense procurement as a stimulus for the development of new technologies. An issue for legacy sectors is that Ruttan's approach of working through government contractors—which was the way aviation advances, the Manhattan Project, the moon launch, and supercomputing evolved—won't work well by itself. This is because, in the end, the transformative innovation has to occur within the legacy sector, which is generally rooted inside the established economic sector, while the government contractor approach operates outside it. So, even if the government were prepared to contract for a disruptive technology, it would still have to be adopted within the legacy sector. To elaborate, even if the government contracted to build a carbon capture and sequestration (CCS) pilot plant, for example, that contracting step alone would not ensure that the utility sector would subsequently adopt and implement CCS technology; there still have to be policy steps to assure the technology is actually adopted within the affected sector.

To summarize, then, what are the lessons suggested by this exploration of innovation organization? Romer's insight that better recipes are required, not simply more cooking, seems fundamental. Strong innovation institutions with linkages between them are needed, a fact that mandates a "connected" model. To be sure, the strength of each institutional element in the innovation system is critically important—but the institutions must also be linked and connected. This means looking at both the front and back ends of an innovation system, incorporating both technology-push and market demand mechanisms.

When legacy sectors require radical innovation, as many do, a process to envision the development and launch of such technology is needed. The talent behind the innovation institutions is also key, so that management must reach both institutions and talent if the innovation organization approach is to be effective. Although discussion from innovation theorists like Christensen and Ruttan has emphasized product lines and frontier sectors, the entry of technology into the major legacy sectors discussed here presents a particular challenge. It must focus on the private sector since it dominates legacy sectors, and entry via the public sector alone won't work.

While some legacy sectors can be altered by policy shifts to allow induced innovation to operate, most also require active measures to foster the introduction of new transformative technologies, and in most cases these must lead to radical innovations. This requires a systems approach, with a strategic effort across all the elements of the applicable innovation system. To this we add the concept of change agent: a strategic systems approach needs to be complemented by institutions and individuals prepared to press the strategy.

SCALING THE LEGACY BARRIERS ONE AT A TIME

Chapter 5 delineated a series of features and market imperfections that constitute barriers protecting legacy sectors. Each barrier and imperfection suggests policy elements that could lead to its mitigation. We review each below, with accompanying interventions to overcome it. After viewing each standing alone, we shall then return to thinking more broadly about the dynamic of innovation as a system and the consequent need for a systematic approach to introducing innovation into legacy sectors.

1. *"Perverse" subsidies and prices and "adverse" cost and price structures.* These create a price or cost mismatch between innovators and legacy producers, which may get in the way of larger societal needs. Subsidies and tariffs can be repealed or adjusted, or benefits to new entrant technologies can be grown to offset them, but these steps require the consent of the political structure, which may be hard to obtain against entrenched interests. For example, the government's subsidies and support for fossil fuels have outweighed its support for renewable technologies.[39] The resulting cost disadvantages of innovations as compared to established technologies require a potentially more difficult process of bringing in efficiencies and production improvements for innovations to drive down their cost curve; the Energy Department's "SunShot" effort to cut solar costs[40] is an example. Or, to shift to a services example raised in chapter 7, the classroom instruction reforms needed for optimal blended learning, combining online and face-to-face education with more focus on the progress of the particular learner, may be most effective in small seminars, but these will be more expensive than either large MOOCs or large lectures. So this expensive "cost structure" is "adverse" to the optimal educational approach, of seminars and more individualized learning. However, the blended model could also be reworked to function in a less costly classroom of

more than 100 persons to reduce its cost, through more active learning and discourse features.

2. *Established government infrastructure and institutional architecture.* These can also discourage new entrant technologies. For example, the focus of the federal highway trust fund on roads historically discouraged mass transit or high-speed rail options, which were correspondingly hindered from obtaining the supporting financing to build out infrastructure. In a second example, the regulatory control that each state exerts over decisions regarding the location of energy infrastructure discourages locating power lines to connect renewable sources in one state to customers in another. Again, interventions can be made in the political system, but this is often difficult. Restructuring the highway trust fund meant political battles over shifting funding away from roads toward transit, which pitted rural against urban areas. But gradual progress in this direction was made through the Intermodal Surface Transportation Efficiency Act of 1991, where Senator Patrick Moynihan (D-NY), the Senate committee chair and lead author of the legislation, acted as a change agent.

3. *Powerful vested interests.* These can use political or pricing tools against incoming innovators. For example, established airlines used price cutting, their control over airline terminal space and their established computer reservation systems, to block new entrant airline competitors following deregulation in the 1980s.[41] Similarly, legacy electric utilities are attempting to institute "net metering" charges to limit the growth of decentralized generation by small-scale solar and wind installations.[42] Antitrust remedies can be of some use in pricing wars but require that new entrants survive the often interminable litigation. The political power of these interests often can be counteracted only by developing corresponding broad-based political power in the American system of intense, contending interests. For example, the political heft of the corn growers overcame the oil lobby to force, by federal mandate, the blending of corn-based ethanol into transport fuels. In contrast, when electric vehicle start-up Tesla Motors initially tried in New Jersey to use direct marketing as a way to skip the creation of independent auto dealerships, it was blocked by a state regulation pressed by politically powerful auto dealers.[43] In the higher-education sector, it would be wise for promoters of MOOCs to involve university faculty members in developing "blended" models of online education and to use MOOCs to increase the effectiveness of the teaching faculty and hence their prestige and popularity, rather than stimulating their opposition by using MOOCs solely as a cost-cutting tool to save on faculty salaries.

4. *An innovation time horizon* that is longer than the financial system can support. While a strong financial support system has been built for IT and biotech entrepreneurial start-ups and their innovations through venture and angel capital and IPOs, it is geared to time horizons that do not mesh with energy, manufacturing, and other capital goods sectors. These sectors simply lack the longer term capital support system that they require.[44] Reforms to capital availability for longer term risk capital, public and private, are required.[45]

5. *Public habits and expectations.* The public tends to "lock in" to technologies and the infrastructure systems around them. Public habits are therefore hard to move, unless a significant price advantage accompanies an emerging technology. For example, electric vehicles face established transport from fossil-fuel-fed internal combustion engines and their gas station infrastructure; electrics have a significant up-front cost disadvantage and a massive task of infrastructure build-out. A long competition lies ahead. Public subsidies and infrastructure support, to present the public with an alternative menu of options to explore, perhaps organized in municipalities with political constituencies ready for such a shift, could provide a partial answer. The boost to bike riding that some cities are providing, through bike-sharing systems and dedicated bikeways, provides an example of public support through new infrastructure that is enabling a remarkable change in consumer attitudes about transport. For electrics, continuing public support of research to improve battery efficiency and cost will also be required.

6. *Established knowledge and human resources structure.* Whole professions and supporting educational institutions are formed around established technologies; it is difficult to construct parallel systems for a competing technological advance. Online education offers one new route to scale the knowledge base and build supporting communities for new entrant technologies.

7. *Aversion to innovation.* Legacy sectors like fossil energy, higher education, and healthcare delivery often undertake low levels of R & D, exhibiting an adversity to innovation, particularly disruptive innovation. This can be overcome by governmental R & D and by start-up firms working on new products for market niches.

In addition to overcoming these legacy barriers, a series of *market imperfections* adverse to innovation tend to solidify around legacy sectors:

A. *Network economies.* Some legacy sectors tend to organize around network economies, such as the grid or IT operating systems, that create barriers to potential competitors; these can be overcome by governmental action to set standards or requirements. Where these network economies take the form of systems of resources, suppliers, components, and production facilities, it may be possible to assist alternative technologies in assembling a comparable network. For example, contract manufacturing, led by highly specialized producers building efficiencies into a particular kind of production either on or increasingly offshore, can lower direct costs and risks, and offers an alternative pathway for technology producers to having to create their own production facilities. However, this may risk loss of aspects of the firm's innovation capability. To revisit an example noted above, Tesla Motors is trying to overcome its lack of an extensive dealership system for its electric vehicles by direct and Internet sales systems (although it is battling against franchise auto dealers trying to protect their territorial monopolies).

B. *Lumpiness.* In sectors that are characterized by lumpiness, where a minimum investment size and scale is required for entry, public financing can provide a solution for lower-cost technologies in cases in which a public good is arguably involved. This is the course the Department of Energy is attempting to follow in dealing with the major up-front cost of demonstrating carbon capture and sequestration technology to cut carbon dioxide emissions at coal-fired power plants. Given the large sums involved, however, private investment seems likely to await regulatory requirements or other comparable change in policy.

C. *Economies of scale.* Here the purchasing power of the Defense Department can back innovations relevant to military needs. These in many cases can then spin off into civilian sectors, once they have reached the scale and low cost needed to compete on the commercial market. Gas turbine engines in utility power plants, building on decades of defense investment in aircraft engines, are an example.[46]

D. *Nonappropriability* or *split incentives.* These market imperfections occur in sectors where innovation gains accrue to others than the innovator or technology investor. For example, restructuring transaction structures so that the benefits of energy conservation go to landlords who invest in them could encourage investments in energy efficiency in commercial and rental real estate projects. A successful example comes from the provisions of the American Recovery and Reinvestment Act of 2009, which offered financial incentives for healthcare providers to adopt electronic health records (EHR), and also required their "meaningful use" by 2014; as a result, EHR use has expanded, although further improvements are still needed.[47]

E. *Collective action.* Where a sector is composed of numerous, thinly capitalized firms—for example, farmers, builders, or small manufacturers—innovation may require collective action. Creating incentives for collective organization and group financing—for example, through farmers' organizations or for technological collaborations between small and large manufacturers and research universities or manufacturing institutes—is a way to overcome this. The extensive research and extension programs of the US Department of Agriculture constitute a long-standing example of a large and effective government program to overcome a collective action problem. An example from the private sector is the Energy Power Research Institute (EPRI), which was formed after the great northeastern blackout of 1965 left 30 million without power as a collaborative research arm for utilities that generate 90% of US power.[48] As discussed in chapters 9 and 13, German Fraunhofer Institutes, which create collaborations between small, midsize, and major manufacturers with academic engineering experts, cost-shared by government, have notably surmounted a manufacturing sector supply chain collective action problem, spurring innovation in German production.

F. *Governmental regulation and institutional structures.* These factors can either favor or discourage innovation, depending on the situation. Where they tilt toward existing technologies and block new entrants, the political system must be approached. For example, the cartel-pricing-based regulatory system that blocked new entrants to the airline business was eventually changed through aviation deregulation legislation. Building codes, which are balkanized among thousands of local jurisdictions, tend to significantly lag behind new building technologies and limit their entry. This is a significant barrier to technologies for the conservation of energy in buildings, which can be resolved by developing new "model codes" and the political support to implement them. That this can work is shown by the success of the Milbank Foundation in convincing states to adopt standardized principles of evidence-based medicine, but this is a long process requiring persistence and determination.[49]

Each of these efforts, to overcome barriers and market imperfections, treated individually, is piecemeal. Each fix proceeds barrier by barrier. This one-at-a-time approach lacks a strategic focus across the particular legacy sector. Part of this is due to the macroeconomic nature of many of these means to resolve barriers and imperfections—taxes, regulations, laws, pricing structure, finance, and so on—which by nature often cross many sectors, making it more difficult to fashion fixes for a particular legacy sectors, large though it may be.

Although the macroeconomic options are important, an exclusive focus on them tends to gloss over a critical and frequently neglected part of the problem: the need to develop innovative technology, technology that has not been developed precisely because of the absence of incentives for innovation. This is a classic catch-22. Political forces that might have supported such innovation avoid doing so lest they antagonize the vested interests behind established technologies, while researchers can foresee the frustration inherent in developing new technologies that will have to take on powerful incumbents.

To reiterate, these barriers and market imperfections are often heavily defended by those that benefit from them. Given the importance of the industries that they affect, these barriers—and the factors that entrench them—are critical obstacles to many of the innovations needed for future economic growth. Despite its importance, most general innovation theorists ignore this reality.

We see, then, the profound challenge of improving innovation systems and overall innovation environment to address legacy sectors. It involves a clear understanding of the dynamics of innovation and conscious efforts to overcome the many obstacles typical to innovation in these sectors. It can happen—chapter 8 portrayed a dramatic technology transformation in the legacy defense sector. The next two chapters, 12 and 13, detail possible pathways for innovation transitions across legacy barriers. These transitions require a concerted approach that combines the five innovation models, with a particular focus on innovation organization.

But understanding the models alone is not enough. A deeper grasp of the innovation context—a better picture of how innovation works, and of innovation organization—is also required. While the imperfections due to particular legacy sector characteristics can be addressed separately, one by one, this problem commands a more unified understanding and approach. The next chapter takes up this challenge, delineating a broad five-step process and setting forth a series of possible overall policy prescriptions common to the legacy sectors. The following chapter focuses on manufacturing and describes how these policy fixes could play out in that particularly challenging legacy sector.

12 Launching Innovation into Legacy Sectors

We now turn in this chapter to an integrated strategy and framework for bringing innovation to legacy sectors. In previous chapters, we have described in detail the profound challenge of innovating in legacy sectors, as well as its economic and societal importance. We have placed sector after sector under the microscope, from energy to transport, including two massive service sectors, higher education and health. We have traced the compounding effects of decline in the legacy manufacturing sector. We have extended our analysis to international dimensions. We have developed models of the dynamics of innovation, including one that sets forth a new approach to the challenge of optimizing the organization of innovation. We now turn to the need for action: both analysis and policy responses to address the twinned root problems that are the focus of this book: expanding innovation and overcoming "jobless innovation."

We build on the findings of the previous chapter concerning the need to focus on innovation organization, initially at the front end of the innovation system, and then at the subsequent stages of the innovation process, including the linkages between the actors and the role of change agents. We will set forth a five-step process for the analysis and development of strategy and policy for introducing innovation into legacy sectors. This process moves from the research-and-development stage through the launch of the technology into markets, and identifies and examines the gaps between institutions required for the innovation process to work.[1] It tackles the market failures and imperfections in legacy sectors not one by one, fix by fix, but through a generalized overall policy approach. The process we propose is based on experience in analyzing the issues raised by—and the steps needed to stimulate—innovation in manufacturing, a particularly and demanding legacy sector that we shall examine as a case study in the next chapter.

A FIVE-STEP POLICY FRAMEWORK

Innovation in legacy sectors requires linkages between innovation stages and actors—what we have termed *connected science and technology*. The design of any program to stimulate innovation in any legacy sector therefore requires an integrated consideration of the entire innovation process, including research, development, and deployment or implementation, drawing on the two pipeline and the induced and manufacturing-led innovation models. As we discussed in the previous chapter, it also requires analysis of deep systems issues regarding the organization for innovation, because new organizational routines will be needed in both the public and private sectors in order to facilitate integrated policies to support innovation.

We must confront, then, a series of issues. How strong are the overall innovation systems in the sector under examination and the linkages between the innovation actors on both the front and back ends? What are the structural obstacles to innovation? What policies could support particular pathways of technology launch? Would policy change be sufficient to induce technological change without further intervention by the public sector to promote the development of technology? What are the institutional gaps that must be filled, and the mechanisms to fill them, in order to enable deployment at sufficient scale to make a difference, and how can this be accomplished? What critical institutions and individuals can take on the role of change agent so as to lead these efforts, and how can they do so?

Progress through the five steps delineated below—from idea to technology transformation—requires both analysis and orchestration. Who can undertake this? Will the same entity carry through all steps, or are there different mechanisms required for each one? Each step calls for different skills and different organizational positioning, although working from the same playbook. How could they connect? How could this evolve?

Sometimes the transformative ideas may come from the "bottom up"; this approach might involve research experts who see evolving technology opportunities and perform the initial visioning, foundations or agencies to do the initial orchestrating, with the private sector doing the implementing, perhaps, at first, in a market niche. An alternative "top down" approach could feature an agency or innovative firm pressing for transformation, allied with researchers who are developing the required advances in technology, perhaps aided by supportive government policies and test beds or industry standards. Either approach requires each innovation actor to change its conception of its role.

As detailed toward the end of this chapter, the concept of "change agent" is critical here. As suggested in chapter 11, such agents must have available "inducible" or at least potential technological innovations, the policy instruments to push them, and the ability to identify, access, combine, and deploy both the innovations and the complementary policy instruments needed to exploit them. While we will explore all these questions below, in steps 2 through 5, the first step is a prerequisite for reaching these levels: there must be strong innovation institutions on the front end—institutions contemplating not only the research but the follow-on stages toward technology implementation.

Without changes in the incentive structure resulting from institutional or policy change, innovation capable of transforming a legacy sector will not emerge from "induced innovation," which is industry led, since only advances compatible with the legacy sector paradigm are likely to see the light of day as a result of the operation of this model. While the induced model may be need to be applied later on, this reality means that the "pipeline" and "extended pipeline" models, the usual source of breakthrough or radical innovation, will play a particularly critical role in innovation in many if not all legacy sectors.

This means that the task of legacy sector innovation will often be particularly dependent on the front end of the innovation system. This will not always be the case: electronic medical records, buildings, and the electric power grid, for example, may require largely incremental systems advances to make substantial improvements in their respective sectors—"inducible innovations," in our terminology—once the obstacles to their deployment have been removed. In other areas, like driverless cars and carbon capture and sequestration, steady advances in technology will ideally be accompanied by careful design of policies that at the same time facilitate innovation and deal with unavoidable issues. But many legacy sectors require real technological breakthroughs: for example, energy, defense, manufacturing, and other areas of health delivery, such as convergence-based medical devices. The steps below constitute a kind of "playbook" for considering and undertaking innovation in these legacy sectors.

STEP 1: STRENGTHENING THE FRONT END OF THE INNOVATION SYSTEM

There can be no innovation in legacy sectors without the innovations themselves. Sometimes these innovations can be incremental; often they must be breakthrough, and sometimes there will be some of each. It is not enough to assume that innovations will evolve by themselves; on the contrary, much work in innovation organization and in applying best practices for innovation is required. Strengthening the front end usually will be an essential first step.

To put the horse before the cart, then, we must begin with the issues that arise at the earliest stages of innovation. How strong is the "front end" of the innovation system: the research, development, prototyping, and early demonstration stages? Is it sufficiently strong to create the applicable technologies that the legacy sector will require? What are the candidate technologies that could bring on innovation that should be examined?

The first step of this five-step analysis is therefore *strengthening the front end* of the innovation system. If the obstacles to innovation are visibly high, the interest of researchers and potential change agents will be affected, so that a stronger support system on the front end may prove key. While many may think of the "front end" as encompassing individual inventors or a university research laboratory, its scope is broader, including these but also larger institutional efforts, from industry labs to DARPA and NSF, to the overall systems encompassing R & D efforts. The Defense Department's innovation system, discussed in chapter 8, provides the classic public-sector example of such an overall system. Tesla's efforts to bring on electric vehicles, through innovation in batteries linked to government R & D, in engineering, in production, in new approaches to recharging infrastructure, and in new ways of reaching customers through design and direct marketing, constitute an innovative private-sector example.

Strengthening the front end of the innovation system requires an assessment of the innovative capability for research, development, prototyping, and early demonstration, and of the institutions that support them. Is the system capable of generating the innovations required to bring change to the legacy sector? A series of evaluations is required and may require the implementation of improvements. Here our guide is the "pipeline" or "extended pipeline" models that typically describe the front end of innovation.

This requires an extended discussion. The five models of the dynamic of innovation that we have presented glance only partially at the means and mechanisms by which innovation originates. Yet, as discussed above, this step is crucial. Achieving transformative potential change for a sector from innovation requires a laser focus on the optimal workings of the front end of the innovation process. We have discussed in the previous chapter the importance of innovation organization overall, but we require much more depth of understanding of the techniques and the important historical lessons that apply to innovation organization at the front end of the innovation system. For most legacy sector innovations, there will be no transformation unless we get these early stage lessons right. A series of factors for consideration in this step of transformational innovation are reviewed below:

1. *Form critical innovation institutions.* If R & D is not being conducted at an adequate scale by talented researcher teams, innovations will not emerge. But talent alone is not enough. Talent must operate within institutional mechanisms capable of moving technological advances from idea to innovation. There are two issues here: talent for R & D capability and the ability to incorporate that capability into an innovation system. These *critical innovation institutions* provide the space where research and talent combine, where the meeting between science and technology is best organized. Arguably, there are critical institutions working on scientific and technological advances that can introduce not only inventions and applications, but also significant elements of entire innovation systems.[2] We saw in chapter 8 the vital role that DARPA, with a history of attracting outstanding research talent and of spurring remarkable technology advance,[3] has long played in promoting innovations within a sector that has many legacy features. Since it is the most successful US R & D agency operating in the innovation space, and because it represents more of a "connected science and technology" approach than other agencies, the initial focus below is on lessons that can be learned from the characteristics of the DARPA model.

DARPA was a unique entity, aimed at both avoiding and creating "technology surprise."[4] In many ways, as suggested above, DARPA directly inherited the "connected science and technology" (linking science research to implementation stages) and "challenge" (pursuing major mission technology challenges) organizational models of the Rad Lab and Los Alamos projects stood up by Vannevar Bush, Alfred Loomis, and J. Robert Oppenheimer during World War II. Building on the Rad Lab example, DARPA built a deeply collaborative, flat, close-knit, talented, participatory, flexible system, oriented to breakthrough radical innovation. Its challenge model for research moved back and forth from fundamental to purely applied, from applied to basic, and from applied research back and forth to and from development, creating connected science that linked research, development, and prototyping, with access to initial production. In other words, it followed an *innovation path*—a way to technology implementation, not simply a *path leading to discovery or invention*.

DARPA has been able to achieve a position where it played a role in most of the five steps explored here. Most R & D organizations are not so well positioned. ARPA-E in the Department of Energy, for example, modeled on DARPA but operating in the legacy energy sector, has no links into a governmental procurement system like the DOD's that would enable it to implement its technologies, and so it must be creative about coordinating with potential implementers.[5] As explored in chapter 13, advanced manufacturing requires a series of agencies to collaborate, in addition to public-private cooperation. This means a different organizational solution. The DARPA model remains instructive, however, to the examination of the various bridges that must be crossed on the way to technological innovation.

Innovation further requires not only a process of creating connected science and challenges at the *institutional level*; it must operate at the *personal level* as well. This was suggested in chapter 8 but must be expanded on here. Innovators are people, not just institutions where talent and R & D come together. Analysts have argued that innovation, because it is much more complex than the earlier stages of discovery and invention, requires "great groups," not just individuals.[6] In just this way, and unlike other federal R & D agencies, DARPA operates at *both* the institutional and the personal levels. DARPA became a bridge organization connecting these two institutional and personal organizational elements. ARPA-E, too, has begun to spur significant advances in energy technology in a similar way.[7]

Both DARPA and ARPA-E adopt the DARPA ruleset detailed in chapter 8 for their operations, with variations based on their different missions in defense and energy, respectively.[8] Both DARPA and ARPA-E use a *"right-left" research model*. They contemplate the technology breakthroughs they seek to have emerge from the "right side" of the innovation pipeline, and then go back to the "left side" of the pipeline to look for proposals for the breakthrough research that will get them there. Both agencies use a *"technology visioning"*[9] process that conceives of a technology advance that could have breakthrough and transformative effects, and considers how it could be developed and whether there is a sound developmental pathway. Both use a *challenge-based* research model, seeking research advances that will result in solutions to important technological challenges. Both tend to look for *revolutionary breakthroughs* that could transform a technology sector, seeking *high-risk but potentially high-reward* projects.

Using these tools and concepts, agency program managers develop a vision of a technological advance that could be transformative, and then work back to understand the sequence of R & D advances required to get there. If these appear within range of accomplishment, both agencies have processes that allow very rapid project approvals by the agency directors. This *technology visioning* process is very different from the way that industry typically undertakes by the "stage gate"[10] process, a step-by-step "downselection" (i.e., elimination) of technology options in which considerations of budget and prospective market gain are used to weed out less profitable projects and to decide which incremental advances to pursue. The visioning process is also very different from how other federal R & D organizations work; these place more emphasis on research for the sake of research. The visioning process may well be particularly valuable in the process of bringing transformative innovation into legacy sectors, many of which, as we have seen, suffer from a long-standing under-investment in research.

2. *Use the island/bridge model.* Bennis and Biederman[11] have argued that innovation requires locating the innovation entity on an "island," protecting it from "the suits," the bureaucratic pressures in larger firms or agencies that too frequently repress and unglue the innovation process. But they note that there must also be a "bridge." The innovation group must also be strongly connected to supportive top decision-makers who can press the innovation forward, providing the needed resources.

Lockheed's Skunk Works,[12] Xerox PARC (Palo Alto Research Center),[13] and IBM's PC project[14] exemplify the island/bridge model at the industry level, severing innovation teams from interference from the business side. While the Skunk Works and IBM PC groups also had strong bridges back to "mainland" decision-makers, PARC had no such strong bridges, and its failure to commercialize the personal computer and most of its many other inventions (the laser printer being the only exception), exemplifies the need for such bridges.[15] Rickover's atomic submarine and Schriever's ballistic missile programs exemplify the island/bridge model within the military.

DARPA and ARPA-E represent island/bridge in a federal R & D agency.[16] DARPA has initiated innovation both in frontier sectors, particularly IT, where it operated largely outside the Pentagon's legacy systems, working with and helping to build emerging high-tech firms, but also working within the defense legacy system. It operated as an island there but also used strong links with the secretary of defense and other senior defense leaders to function as a bridge, where top decision-makers pressed technology advances, such as UAVs and precision strike, into the military services. ARPA-E similarly operates as an island as well as a bridge, using its ties to the energy secretary to build cooperation and focus within the department.[17]

There are alternative models to island/bridge. In the "open innovation"[18] approach, firms drop their reliance on in-house R & D laboratories and reach out to groups at other, often smaller, firms through acquisitions, technology licensing, or partnerships, as best exemplified in biotech-pharmaceutical firm relationships, or at universities, linking to public-sector-funded researchers at these institutions and licensing their work or creating collaborations. This is primarily, however, a tool for more mature firms facing global competition and less able to afford in-house R & D, or for their rivals attempting to outcompete them. Robert Rycroft and Don Kash pose a similar model but broaden it, arguing that innovation requires "collaborative networks" at a series of levels that must reach outside the organization for a kind of heightened R & D "situational awareness," to apply a defense term, and can be less face-to-face and more virtual.[19] Neither approach obviates the need for an originating innovation "great group" applying an island/bridge approach.

3. *Build a thinking community.* A prerequisite for ongoing success of the island/ bridge is building a community of thought. In science, it is well understood that each contributor stands on the shoulders of others, building new concepts on the foundations of prior concepts. Ernest Walton and John Cockcroft, for example, working at Cambridge's Cavendish Laboratory, built an early particle accelerator using a circuit based on an innovative voltage multiplier and became the first to split the atom, changing the atomic nucleus of one element (lithium) into another (helium) in 1932.[20] They built on the active work of a host of other contemporary physicists, from Cavendish director Ernest Rutherford, to Ernest Lawrence, Merle Tuve, Peter Kapitza, James Chadwick, George Gamow, and Nils Bohr, to name only a few. The group at the Cavendish was a remarkable "great group" itself but it was also part of a powerful *thinking community* that was constantly contributing ideas to each other. The 40 physicists who attended the 1933 Solvay Conference, half of whom won the Nobel Prize (including Cavendish attendees Rutherford, Walton, Cockcroft, and Chadwick), exemplify such a community.

Building a sizable "thinking community" has also been key to DARPA's success, as a source of contributing ideas but also for talent and political support.[21] Composed of multiple generations of DARPA program managers, and researchers working in a field DARPA has supported, at its best this community becomes a group of change advocates. Building a thinking community around a problem takes time to evolve until it reaches a density and mass at which the development of ideas starts to accelerate. For example, in the field of nanotechnology, physicist Richard Feynman arguably initiated the community with a noted talk in 1959 entitled "There's Plenty of Room at the Bottom," urging work at the smallest scale where quantum properties operate. In 1981, researcher Eric Drexler published the first journal article on the subject, and by 2000 over 1,800 articles using the term *nanotechnology* had accumulated, showing that a thinking community had formed and was starting to accelerate advances.[22]

4. *Link technologists to operators.* Another key organizational feature involves connecting the technologists to the operators. This approach is perhaps best exemplified by the relationship between British scientists and the military on the eve of and during World War II. In the early 1930s the assumption of all, from the prime

minister down, was that "the bomber will always get through"—that there was no adequate defense against bomber aircraft, which could devastate both military and civilian targets virtually at will.[23] With Hitler building 4,000 aircraft in 1935 and with England only a few miles across the Channel from the European mainland, this assumption was an important underpinning of the appeasement policy of the 1930s.

A small group began to investigate whether air defenses could be created. At the behest of the Royal Air Force's (RAF) Tizard Committee, a scientist team, under Robert Watson-Watt, the scientist supervisor of a small defense laboratory, began investigating the radio beam technology that became radar. Even so, the technology did not create an air defense system against the bomber all by itself; extended trial-and-error testing with RAF pilot teams led by physicist Henry Tizard, head of Imperial College, developed the operational routines that enabled the British to maximize the utility of radar technology for air defense and use it to win the Battle of Britain.[24] So it was the constant testing and evaluation with air force operators— fighter interceptor pilots and what became ground control groups—that linked the technologists to the operators, using new but demonstrated technology-based operating systems. Tizard, a World War I pilot as well as a leading scientist, famously spoke the pilots' language from shared experience, and the experimental regimens he helped devise and the RAF implemented between 1935 and 1938, coupled with continuing incremental improvements in the technology to meet evolving operator needs, changed the course of the war.[25]

Along with Tizard, three members of his RAF committee, A. V. Hill, A. P. Rowe, and Patrick Blackett, developed a doctrine for linking scientists and technologists with operators, which became known as operations research.[26] This approach used statistical analysis of operations, looking at a range of changes in technology and in the operations themselves to find optimal solutions to operational challenges. Operations research had World War I precedents in the methods of optimizing antiaircraft artillery developed by Hill[27] and was written up by Blackett in 1941 as a chapter in a short edited book entitled *Science in War,* which advocated its widespread use by the military.[28] As director of Naval Operational Research, Blackett subsequently applied the techniques he helped develop to Britain's war against the U-boats that were threatening to cut off Britain's wartime food and supplies. Research by his team (known as "Blackett's Circus") resulted in dramatic improvements to methods for the optimization of the size and protection of convoys that led to a dramatic reduction in ship sinkings by German U-boats.[29]

The British approach to applying science in World War II was to isolate and protect its scientists from military hierarchies but also to integrate them with military operators when the outcomes of their research appeared promising. Inventing and using operations research analysis, the wartime British science leaders found that their scientists must be informed, involved in, and linked to decision-making—not just on technology but also on related strategy and tactics. The British model for using scientists, then, was to keep them out of uniform, working in separate research centers (ranging from the RAF's radar operational experiments at Biggin Hill and Bawdsey to the code-breaking activities at Bletchey Park) as islands, but with strong ties ("bridges") to the mainland—the service operators.

Henry Tizard, leading the 1940 Tizard Mission that brought vital British microwave radar advances to the Americans before they entered the war, spent two months in discussions with American scientists and military that year, including extensive exchanges with science leaders Vannevar Bush and Alfred Loomis.[30] Tizard and his team explained to Bush and Loomis the organizational model for scientific research that he and other British science leaders had developed during his 1940 mission.[31] Bush and Loomis ended up creating largely the same island/bridge model in the United States, implementing it in such famous projects as the Rad Lab for microwave radar advances at MIT[32] and the Los Alamos laboratory for atomic weapons development.[33] These in turn became central to the subsequent organization of postwar US science.

5. *Change agents.* Innovation will not take place, particularly in thorny legacy sectors, unless there are institutions and accompanying individuals prepared to act as change agents. The identification of possible change agents therefore needs to be considered even at the first step of the analysis of a legacy sector. Who and what institution(s) will undertake to press for the needed change? How might they operate?

The importance of change agents is illustrated by an example we have already cited, the Royal Air Force in the 1930s, which could be viewed as a legacy sector. Like its German counterpart, the RAF was dominated by an emerging air power ethos led by its bomber force, which was not focused on generating defenses against bombers, a task it considered largely hopeless. It took a defense R & D organization, led by defense scientists under Tizard and others, to take on this assumption. To bring on the transformative technological innovation of radar, they built a strong research group, made links to political authorities prepared to support the effort, and created a working testing process with fighter pilot operators. As discussed in chapter 8, DARPA has led similar changes in UAVs, precision strike, and stealth in similar ways. These organizations and key individuals within them functioned as change agents. Without such change agents, it is hard to see how innovations, particularly in legacy sectors, can emerge out of the innovation pipeline.

To summarize the first step of building front-end innovation capabilities to influence legacy sectors, one of the important lessons from DARPA's ability to bring innovation into a defense sector with deep legacy characteristics has been the importance of *critical innovation institutions.* These institutions should attempt to embody both *connected science and technology*—linking scientific research to implementation stages—and *challenge* approaches—pursuing major mission technology challenges.

Innovation requires not only a process of creating connected science and challenges at the *institutional level*, but it also must operate at the *personal level.* The critical stage of innovation is face to face, not institutional, so while institutions where talent and R & D come together are required, personal dynamics, usually embodied in "great groups," are a necessity. The DARPA *"right-left" research model* can be important to reaching the innovation stage, where program managers contemplate the technological breakthroughs they seek to have emerge from the right end of the innovation pipeline, then go back to the left side of the pipeline to look for proposals for the breakthrough research that will get them there. This process seeks *high-risk, high-reward* projects and tends to lead to revolutionary breakthroughs that could transform a technology sector. A *technology visioning* process at the outset of the effort is a particular key.

The *island/bridge* organizational approach for innovation institutions is also important. The innovation team should be put on a protected island apart from bureaucratic influences so it can focus on the innovation process. The strength of the innovation process will also depend on building or forming a solid *thinking community* as a source for ideas and support. Because innovation must span numerous steps from research through initial production, means for *linking technologists to operators* appear to be critical. Finally, *change agents* will be required to move the innovation toward implementation.

These rules apply to the important first step of front-end innovation organization, and can apply to public or private-sector research institutions. Some of the legacy sectors we considered in chapters 6 and 7 have technologies that may be farther along than some of the ones that figure in the stories presented here. But most still require careful attention to the principles of innovation organization reviewed here, and the examples cited of breakthrough innovations like radar, as well as of incremental innovations derived from operations research, are particularly telling. Careful attention to the front end of the innovation system is a prerequisite for innovating in many legacy sectors, which means that the "pipeline" and particularly the "extended pipeline" models will be important in this context.

STEP 2: IDENTIFYING THE LAUNCH PATHS FOR EMERGING TECHNOLOGIES

The second and in many cases the most difficult step in developing and deploying new technology in established legacy sectors is the launching of these technologies into complex and competitive markets for technology.[34] This *point of market launch* perspective is the basis for our argument that any program of government or other support for innovations in these sectors should be organized around the most likely bottleneck to their introduction into the market. This encompasses and goes beyond the long-standing focus of pipeline theorists on the "valley of death" between research and late-stage development.[35]

The second step of this analysis therefore requires identifying launch paths for the technologies that could transform a legacy sector, as suggested in step 1. Once the front-end innovation institutions have been identified and strengthened, this means assessing the most promising technologies that could emerge as innovations in the particular legacy sector, based on the likely bottlenecks in their launch path, and classifying them into groups that share the same likely bottlenecks. Four basic categories of launch path appear possible:

- *Experimental technologies.* This category includes experimental technologies that require extensive long-range research. The deployment of these technologies is sufficiently far off that the details of their launch pathways can be left to the future. Examples in the energy legacy sector would include hydrogen fuel cells for transport, genetically engineered bio-systems for carbon dioxide consumption and sequestration, and, in the very long term, fusion power. An example in the manufacturing area would be research into the "materials genome" to develop a range of new materials that could fit particular manufactured product needs, such as stronger, lighter weight transport vehicles.[36] Because of the dominant role of federal support for basic research, this path depends on continuing government R & D support under the pipeline model.

- *Disruptive niche technologies.* These are potentially disruptive technological innovations[37] that can be launched in niche markets and that may expand from this base as they drive down the production cost curve and become more price competitive. Tesla's introduction of electric vehicles presents an instructive example. Building an attractive and expensive battery-powered sports car for the highest price market, Tesla found a niche that made it possible to launch an initial product and experiment with technology to drive down the cost curve so as to develop more price-competitive models. An example in the healthcare delivery sector was the development by the Veterans Administration of electronic medical records. The VA system constituted an initial niche market where these technologies could be initially implemented, experimented with, and tested. Examples in the energy sector include LEDs and wind and solar used in off-grid electric power. Where government support for technology entry is unavailable, niche market entry becomes a critically important approach.

- *Secondary technologies—uncontested launch.* This group includes secondary (or component) innovations (like an improved battery for a car) that are part of larger technology platforms or systems that will face market competition the moment they are launched, but are consistent with existing paradigms or will likely be acceptable to recipient industries if their performance offers major advantages and their price range is acceptable. The point is that their launch will not be contested by the recipient industry; the new technology will be accepted as long as it can be price competitive. These technologies still must face the rigors of a tilted playing field, such as a subsidy for competing incumbents, or the obstacle of a major cost differential (perhaps due to the lack of economies of scale) without the advantage of an initial niche market. In the air transport sector, an example of a successful introduction of a new secondary technology is that of new carbon fiber composites for airframes with improved weight-to-strength ratios; the potential savings in energy over time from reduced weight offset the higher material costs. Examples in the energy sector include advanced batteries for plug-in hybrids, and enhanced geothermal and on-grid wind and solar technologies.

- *Secondary technologies—contested launch.* These are secondary (or component) innovations that have inherent and unavoidable cost disadvantages but are desirable for broader environmental, safety, or public health considerations, or that can be expected to face economic, political, or other nonmarket opposition from recipient industries or interest groups. Their entry therefore will be contested by the recipient industry that dominates the overall platform where they must land. Because the new entrant technology will disrupt incumbent technologies, it must overcome these obstacles in addition to those facing the technologies in the two preceding categories. Carbon capture and sequestration technology will not be welcomed by utilities that must spend major sums and find the space to adapt current coal power plants, which will also lose significant power production efficiency. More widespread attention to preventive healthcare, to cite an example from a different field, will require that federally regulated healthcare systems give this subject greater recognition and importance. Building efficiencies will require widespread change to and recognition in local building codes. Examples in the energy sector also include biofuels and fourth-generation nuclear power. None of these is likely to emerge without governmental intervention in the form of regulation or subsidies.

To summarize, these four categories divide evolving technologies into different launch pathways, so that relevant policies for each can be designed to support their launch. Without governmental intervention, the most productive route for the introduction of new technologies will likely be through identification of and entry into niche markets. However, many technologies contemplated for legacy sectors are component or secondary technologies that fall into the third and fourth categories above. This complicates the technology launch picture because component technologies will not land in open frontiers, but will land in existing systems or platforms—in "occupied territory," where a governmental role may be critical. Here again, the optimal candidates for the entry of technology into legacy sectors will be for disruptive technologies that can open new frontiers by initially filling niche markets. Depending on the type of innovation, the change agents may be firms prepared to bring the technology into niche markets, or firms willing to press component technologies into platforms by making them competitive with existing technologies, or governmental entities prepared to intervene to level playing fields to encourage new entrant technologies where their launch needs incentives or regulatory actions.

An ongoing technology strategy effort shared by industry, government, and academic research experts could be one way to attempt to undertake and continually update a process of identifying a launch path. Over time, such strategies could be turned into technology roadmaps to guide decisions on technology investments and avoid technology lock-in problems.[38] Sematech, the semiconductor collaborative technology program, has sponsored perhaps the most sophisticated and effective industry technology roadmapping effort in the United States. This roadmap has kept the industry on Moore's Law for decades and stands as a model for this collaborative approach.[39] The roadmap could lead to the identification of a range of incentives suggested in step 3, which could then be identified, altered, and aligned with the technology strategy process. Additional mechanisms, such as translational R & D, technology financing, and technology roadmapping, could then fill the gaps in the innovation system.

The third step of our analysis consists of classifying support policies for encouraging innovation, and then matching these policies to the technology launch groupings developed in the second step of the analysis. Because several generations of technologies may be needed as a sector evolves, for example in new energy technologies, these policy packages should be as technology neutral as possible. This step is more focused on governmental interventions, which generally will be available only when there is an overriding policy concern that brings government in on the side of innovation, such as national security, environment, healthcare reform, or renewable energy. But purely private-sector approaches should be considered as well.

This is the stage at which a number of the legacy sector obstacles that affect a particular sector must be considered. As we noted in chapter 11, particular policies to address particular barriers can be devised. However, these policies will be more effective if the barriers are addressed not only issue by issue but within the context of a much broader approach that includes a set of steps that encompass both the innovation and public policy efforts suggested in this chapter. The next chapter, chapter 13, provides a case study of how legacy obstacles in a particular sector, advanced manufacturing, might be overcome. It incorporates this kind of broad approach and proposes a range of innovation and policy tools. However, the general description of possible incentives and regulatory steps set out below suggests means to surmount any of a number of legacy barriers.

- *Nurturing technology development.* This involves direct government support for R & D over the long term, including support to technology prototyping, demonstrations, and test beds, in what was called in the last chapter "the extended pipeline." This goes beyond the support to research and development, which is incorporated into step 1 and is mandatory for the evolution of almost all innovations before they can be commercialized.
- *"Back-end" incentives.* Incentives (carrots) to encourage technological transition on the back end may also be needed as a technology closes in on commercialization. Such "carrots" can encourage secondary or component technologies facing both uncontested and contested launch, along with incremental innovations in technology for conservation and end use, as well as technologies for manufacturing processes and scale-up. Incentives may also be useful in stimulating some disruptive technologies as they transition from niche areas to more general applicability.

Such incentives may include tax credits of various kinds for new technology products, loan guarantees, low-cost financing, price guarantees, government procurement programs, buy-down programs for new products, and general and technology-specific intellectual property policies. As one example, procurement by the Defense Department, the nation's largest owner of buildings and facilities, could effect cost savings over time by using its facilities as an efficiency test bed, and could at the same time help ascertain the optimal approaches to building technology. However, there are challenges: How can abuses be avoided that may arise in deviating from lowest-cost procurement criteria? How could such procurement be reconciled with the technology-neutral strategy advocated here? Despite potential complications, government procurement may be one of the better levers for lifting a range of technologies out of their "steady states."

- *"Back-end" regulatory and related mandates.* Regulatory and related mandates ("sticks"), also on the back end, may be needed in order to encourage component or secondary technologies facing contested launch. The government's regulatory role already reaches far into the health, transport, and education sectors. Government also mandates regulatory standards for renewable portfolios and fuel economy in the energy sector, as well as other technology-specific standards in the building and construction sectors.

Just as there is no one-size-fits-all R & D program that requires R & D efforts to be tailored to particular technology categories, so particular "carrots" and "sticks" may fit one group of technologies but not another. Loan guarantees may work for major utilities building next-generation nuclear power plants but may be less useful to small firms and start-ups that are deploying new energy or manufacturing technologies, have limited capital, and are less able to meet loan requirements. Analytical work is needed to evaluate the relative economic efficiency of particular back-end incentives or regulations. In the energy sector, a system of carbon charges, such as a cap-and-trade program, can substitute for many (although certainly not for all) of the back-end proposals listed above, both carrots and sticks, because it would induce similar effects.

If governmental incentives or regulatory steps are not available, alternative approaches can be considered. For example, if an emerging technology offers a new functionality—a capability that is not available through existing technologies—it may be able to command a premium price on introduction. So focus should be placed, if possible, on technologies that offer new functionality. Alternatively, it may be possible to build into the R & D stage a focus on lowering production costs, so that the new technology can be more competitive at market entry.

To summarize, the third step calls for aligning governmental policies to fit the launch pathways for paradigm-incompatible technologies seeking entry into legacy sectors. While front-end R & D is important to virtually all such technologies, support for the "extended pipeline" that includes later innovation pipeline stages is significant, as well. Where the government has an overriding policy stake in an innovation direction—for reasons that may range from national security to environment—this may justify further policy interventions. These include both incentives ("carrots") and regulatory limits ("sticks"). If supportive governmental policies are not applicable, then alternative routes can be considered, such as instituting financial mechanisms aimed at the private sector, focusing on technologies that provide new functionality, or building an effort to drive down the production cost curve into the R & D phase.[40]

The fourth step of our analysis consists of a survey of existing institutional and organizational mechanisms for the support of innovation. This is intended to determine what kinds of innovations (as classified by the likely bottlenecks in their launch paths) do not receive federal or other support at critical stages of the innovation process, and what kind of support mechanisms are needed to fill these gaps. This step is based on the fifth of the models of the dynamic of the innovation process described in chapter 11: the innovation organization model.

While step 1 examined the front end of the innovation system to identify possible candidate technologies for innovation within a sector, step 4 looks system-wide, including the back end of the innovation system, all the way through to technology implementation. This can be described as an institutional gap analysis. In energy, for example, we have had difficulty in translating our research into innovation, in financing the scale-up of promising technologies, and in forming an overall strategy for collaboration between the public and private sectors to roadmap the details involved in developing and deploying new technologies at scale. These are all gaps in the innovation system that require attention. Gaps within the innovation system can be created by legacy sector characteristics and imperfections as well; these must be identified and policy approaches selected to overcome them.

As suggested in the last chapter, the optimal approach to bringing innovation into established legacy sectors requires taking advantage of all five models of the dynamics of the innovation process: the pipeline, the induced, the extended pipeline, the manufacturing-led and the organizational models. These interact with each other. The technology-supply approach in the pipeline model will be more likely to produce economic results if it is accompanied by elements of the extended pipeline and manufacturing-led models that move the technology through additional pipeline stages.

The induced innovation model relies on demand-side signals that stimulate continuing incremental advances to drive down production costs; even when they are technically ready, new entrants take time and incremental improvements to move down the price curve to compete with the mature, efficient and cheap technologies that occupy legacy sectors. On the other hand, induced innovation depends on a robust technology supply program, supported by a strong pipeline and extended innovation system, to enable the technologies that are needed to create alternatives and drive down costs to become available within a reasonable time. This is particularly true when the technological transformation being sought is as dramatic as it is with energy. The manufacturing-led model for innovation, for its part, focuses on the back end, requiring creativity on the engineering and process side of product design and production. However, it is very dependent on a strong front-end innovation system for the ideas that this manufacturing-led stage must translate into producible and saleable goods.

The effectiveness of all these efforts requires strong and connected innovation organization. Although their route can be circuitous and overlapping, technologies generally must move through research, development, prototyping, demonstration, test bed and initial production stages, with a series of institutions, public and private, active at each stage, which, in turn, must be connected with each other.

STEP 5: FILLING THE GAPS IN THE INNOVATION SYSTEM

The fifth step in our analysis is the identification and recommendation of new institutional and organizational mechanisms to fill the technology gaps identified in the fourth step above. The extended pipeline model described in the previous chapter is particularly relevant here. Here, R & D agencies should view their tasks as encompassing not only funding important foundational research but also envisioning and finding ways to press identified technologies further down the innovation pipeline. These agencies—acting as or combined with change agents—need to perform a transformational innovation role as well as a transformational research role. The critical question, then, becomes: what is the menu of institutional fixes and policy mechanisms, public and private, by which a technology can emerge at scale? As noted above, legacy sector barriers can also cause gaps in the innovation system—for example, through a failure of collective action that limits the presence of effective actors in the innovation system, requiring policy solutions to strengthen that system.

How might a gap-filling process for an economic sector proceed for steps 4 and 5?[41] Gaps in the innovation system of a particular sector can be examined at any of a series of points. On the front end of the innovation system, more translational R & D could be needed in order to move technologies from research into implementation. Innovative new R & D mechanisms and organizations may be required to help fill this gap. This might require institutional fixes to help fill in the innovation system.[42] Steps 4 and 5 should also include consideration of the change agents, institutional and personal, that will be required to see an innovation through to implementation; without such agents, there will be no change.

THE FIVE-STEP POLICY FRAMEWORK AND ITS IMPLICATIONS

In summary, our five-step framework develops an integrated approach to the development of strategy and policy for innovation in legacy sectors, rather than approaching each sector imperfection and market failure separately. The first step draws on the analysis of legacy sectors in chapters 6, 7, and 8 and calls for an initial focus on strengthening the front end of the innovation system because critical institutions can play such an important role in initiating the innovation. This is a prerequisite for the subsequent steps in most legacy sectors. In the second step, the launch pathways for emerging innovations in a sector are identified and the menu of emerging technologies grouped into them. Once common launch paths are identified, the availability of supportive federal incentives or regulations can be considered and applied. This constitutes the third step. It includes policy measures to overcome barriers in particular legacy sectors. The fourth step looks at the innovation system for a technological sector overall, and analyzes whether there are gaps in the system corresponding to the various stages of the innovation process as it applies to that particular innovation. The fifth step is the logical response to the fourth: it develops the institutional fixes and mechanisms to fill those gaps.

Returning to the models of the dynamics of innovation explained in chapter 11, the first of these five steps draws on pipeline and extended pipeline theory, suggesting that support from the government research pipeline will be important to creating, launching, and enhancing a range of technology options. But since the technology streams will need to land in the private sector at a large scale, the subsequent second and third steps are also informed by induced innovation theory, which concentrates on the policy or demand signals that will induce the private sector to take up, modify, and implement the technology advances that originate from the innovation pipeline. Whether these come from a demand-pricing system like the cap-and-trade scheme proposed for carbon-based energy, from technology incentives, or from regulatory requirements, these signals will need to be coordinated and, to the extent possible, will need to be technology neutral.

The fourth and fifth steps in our analytic process draw on the innovation organization model: the gaps in the innovation system will need to be filled for the handoff to occur between the application of the pipeline, extended pipeline, and induced models, especially at the points where technology supply push meets market demand pull. The manufacturing-led model of innovation dynamics emphasizes the importance to innovation of the critical back-end stage; without sound capabilities for production (reaching from product design and engineering through efficient manufacturing processes) there is a major gap in the system that must be filled. Part of that gap-filling process will include identification of institutional and individual change agents that can press the innovation through to implementation.

THE ROLE OF THE CHANGE AGENT

The role of the change agent is key. Making it through the five steps explored here—from the idea through to its implementation—requires orchestration. Different legacy sectors will require different approaches. There may be situations where the same entity can carry through all five steps of the framework we propose. As reviewed in chapter 8, DARPA was able to undertake most of these steps in a critical series of defense technology transformations, although even it required alliances with senior defense leaders, who joined in as change agents. Other situations will call for a series of separate mechanisms, one or more for each step. In the case study of the legacy manufacturing sector explored below, each step calls for different skills and different organizational positioning, so that a series of complex collaborations will be required, with a number of change agents. Whether the approach in a particular sector is more unified or more collaborative and linked, we suggest that institutions and change agents will need to operate from the same general "playbook," one that includes the five steps identified here.

As suggested in the introduction to this chapter, sometimes the transformative technologies may come from the "bottom up," pushed initially by researchers with a vision, or sometimes from "top down," pressed by an overall institutional authority, whether in the public or private sector, or even by stakeholders who are not directly involved in the innovation process but perceive an urgent need for change. Different legacy sectors and the technologies that could alter them may lend themselves to different approaches. Both top-down and bottom-up approaches require the innovation actors in the legacy sector's innovation system to change their conception of their role. They must grasp the role of change agents, and must also understand "the playbook." As noted above and suggested in chapter 11, such agents must have "inducible" (or at least potential) technological innovations near to hand, have access to the policy instruments to push them, and the ability to identify, access, combine, and deploy the innovations and the complementary policy instruments needed to exploit them. Meta-change agents can help, as noted in chapter 11, by creating the structures and systems that support, mentor, and protect the hands-on change agents who are working on particular innovation challenges, in this way enabling them to succeed.

There are commonalities among the obstacles thrown up by legacy sectors, but there are also differences among them and differences between the policies they require. The path through these obstacles will need orchestration by change agents, but the kinds of change agents required will vary to fit different legacy sectors and different innovation challenges. The legacy defense sector is different from the legacy manufacturing sector and requires different innovation organization approaches and correspondingly different agents. However, there are commonalities as suggested above. The five steps suggested here lead to a change agent playbook that we believe can cross legacy sectors, stimulate innovation, and overcome the obstacles they face.

This proposed new unifying conceptual framework has implications beyond theory; it also leads to a different logic and new tools for the practical design of technology policy. It suggests a systems approach to policy, moving beyond the historic focus in the United States since the end of World War II on the pipeline theory that emphasizes the earliest stages of innovation, to a broader look at all of the stages, with accompanying policies for each. It further leads us to consider standard governmental policy packages of incentives and support across common technology launch areas, so that some technological neutrality is preserved and the optimal emerging technology has a chance to prevail, ideas that we shall pursue in greater detail in chapter 13. Particular technologies can then qualify for these packages, based on their launch requirements. Our current policy approach tends to offer unique policy designs for each technology challenge, often based on the political clout behind that particular technology; our new analytic framework proposes a larger and broader perspective on innovation, leading to policies aimed across legacy sectors, not simply at specific technologies.

The next chapter offers a case study of a particularly complex legacy sector, manufacturing. It shows in a more concrete way how a variety of change agents might work with the common five-step framework outlined here for launch of innovation into legacy sectors. It also suggests that the demands of the manufacturing sector require new approaches to incentives and support that could provide a model for other sectors.

13 Case Study

*Applying the Policy Framework
to Advanced Manufacturing*

We now make the policy framework set out in the last chapter concrete by applying it to a case study: advanced manufacturing. As discussed in chapter 6, this
is a sector with profound legacy sector characteristics. There will be no single
"silver bullet" approach; legacy sectors are not only established but complex and so
demand a mix of policies. Manufacturing presents not only a legacy sector challenge, but, as noted in chapter 11, it turns out to be significant to the overall innovation process itself. This is a particularly important exercise in the United States
because of its neglect of one of the five models of the dynamics of innovation,
"manufacturing-led" innovation. Is there a pathway with a chain of connected
policies that conceivably could transform the US manufacturing sector and that
can be found by applying the identified policy steps from chapter 12?[1] The lessons
from the case study arguably can be translated internationally, as well. We examine each step below.

APPLYING STEP 1: INNOVATING ON THE FRONT END OF THE SYSTEM

We begin with the issues that surround innovation in manufacturing. First, what
candidate technologies could bring on innovation and should be examined? Then,
how strong is the "front end" of the innovation system: the research, development,
prototyping, and early demonstration stages? Is it sufficiently strong to create the
technologies that the applicable legacy sector will require?

Technological Advances That Could Create New Manufacturing Productivity Paradigms

Manufacturing has already begun a process of technological transformation. In the past quarter-century, manufacturing has moved from labor-intensive, mechanical processes to information-intensive processes. Unlike education, healthcare delivery, and government, sectors that have resisted the IT revolution, manufacturing embraced it early on, leading to increases in productivity. This IT-intensity trend will continue and accelerate as new advances in IT come to bear, including the use of advanced computer simulation and modeling in product design, IT systems embedded in products at every stage of the production system and product life cycle, continued IT-derived efficiency gains in supply chain management and the distribution system, and more flexible manufacturing to allow unique, customer-driven designs.[2]

US manufacturing could compete with low-cost, low-wage, increasingly advanced-technology economies, as noted in chapter 4, through major productivity gains that more than offset these cost advantages. At the core, then, must come innovations in manufacturing technologies and related processes. Are there new manufacturing technologies that the United States, taking advantage of its continuing leadership in innovation, could bring into its manufacturing sectors? Could it undertake a technology revolution comparable to the one Japan introduced starting four decades ago around quality manufacturing? The following areas of advance offer such transformative possibilities:

- **"Network-centric" manufacturing:** a continuation and acceleration of existing IT intensity in manufacturing, which includes a mix of advanced IT, radio frequency identification (RFID), and sensors in every stage and element of the production process, from resource through production through product life cycle, with new decision-making tools from "big data" analytics, along with advanced robotics, supercomputing, and advanced simulation and modeling. In addition, software is now a major component in complex products; the high cost and complexity of software has become an inhibitor in efficient production. Integrating software development at the outset with design and new systems for hardware/software integration also appear to be key to this new approach to production.
- **Advanced materials:** creation of a "materials genome,"[3] the ability, aided by supercomputing, to design all possible materials with designer features, to fit new materials precisely to product needs for strength, flexibility, weight and production cost. In addition, evolution of new biomaterials from synthetic biology, exploration of biofabrication and lightweight everything.
- **Nano-manufacturing:** fabrication at the nano-scale and the ability to embed nano-features into products to raise the efficiency and performance of products.
- **Mass customization:** production of one item or of small lots at the cost of mass production, for example through 3D printing/additive manufacturing and connected computer-controlled equipment.
- **Distribution efficiency:** driving even 10% out of the cost of product distribution can shift decisions on whether to produce in the United States or abroad;

further IT advances that yield distribution efficiencies, including in the supply chain, could provide this.

- **Energy efficiency:** excess energy is "waste"—a largely nonrecoverable production cost—and US manufacturing has long been overly energy intensive; conservation and energy efficiency technologies and processes could significantly drive down production costs.

This is not an exclusive list; it is illustrative.[4] A selection process for focus areas should be dynamic and ongoing, taking advantage of emerging technology options. Former DARPA administrators Regina Dugan and Ken Gabriel have argued that "the 19th century was about manipulating energy, the 20th century was about manipulating information, and the 21st century will be about manipulating matter."[5] DARPA has been making major investments in advanced manufacturing R & D, which it views as vital to "accounting for time"—sharply cutting the standup time between product conception, prototype, and production, so that the DOD can move away from its slow and expensive system of awarding a contract and then embarking on a decades-long redesign and development process, in which the component technologies must be continually updated before final production. In DOD language, it needs to transition from this current system of "buy, then make" to "make, then buy." If DARPA's initiatives to cut time to production are successful for the DOD, its approaches to erasing time could lead to a sea change for manufacturing in general.

Won't low-cost, low-wage competitors simply implement the same approaches to efficiency? Not necessarily. As Japan demonstrated when it developed the paradigm of quality manufacturing, there is a first-mover advantage that can ensure leadership for a significant period. Offsetting a low-cost, low-wage, competitive advantage with productivity gains levels an essential playing field, and it is a complex task for an emerging economy to shift strategy away from its initial competitive advantage based on low costs and wages that employ large populations without significant disruption.

Strengthening the Front End of Manufacturing Innovation

Won't this require a major new R & D programmatic effort? Such an effort is already underway. Four leading R & D agencies—the DOD, NSF, DOE, and NIST—are already undertaking significant R & D programs directly, not just indirectly, in the advanced manufacturing space. A 2010 survey, updated in 2014, drawn from agency data and program summaries, indicates that these four agencies were investing approximately $700 million a year.[6] This does not encompass the leveraging for manufacturing advances that is possible from other more indirect research efforts, such as on robotics and advanced materials. What is missing is closer industry-university-regional collaboration and cross-agency coordination, which must be coupled with a technology strategy and eventually a public-private roadmapping exercise, as discussed in step 5, below. The 2012 report of the Advanced Manufacturing Partnership called for exactly these steps, which were expanded on in the Partnership's second report in 2014.[7] So the foundational R & D investment is largely in place and ready to be called on.

The elements called for in step 1, as delineated in chapter 12, will be required. "Critical innovation institutions" will need to be engaged; strong agencies like DARPA, NSF, DOE, and NIST already undertaking manufacturing work offer a substantial foundation for this effort. Should a new agency be created? The problem is that the manufacturing challenge is inherently crosscutting and requires collaboration among existing agencies rather than a separate entity disconnected from their missions. While in federal government practice the term "interagency" has often proved an inherent contradiction, the White House Office of Science and Technology Policy has statutory authority to create interagency collaboration by naming National Science and Technology Committees for interagency efforts.[8] These can work; the cross-agency National Nanotechnology Initiative[9] is a possible model.

Between the participating agencies (and likely within each), "connected science and technology," the technology "challenge" model, and "technology visioning" will be required, organized around collaborative manufacturing technology strategies. Overall, "thinking communities" and "linking technologies to operators" will be required as well, as delineated in chapter 12. This group of agencies will also need to embody an "island/bridge" approach. Both the necessary collaborations and the follow-through on advances will require connections between the agencies and decision-makers who can help put their findings into effect. The problem is whether they can build collaboration across agencies around advanced manufacturing paradigms that would also incorporate these characteristics. This question is explored, as an innovation system gap, in more detail in step 5 below.

Could Technological Innovation Work?

If the front-end institutions can be strengthened and focused on new paradigms, could these efforts at technological innovation translate into significant efficiencies and gains in manufacturing productivity? In other words, could the new technologies become the basis of new paradigms for the entire manufacturing sector? There are numerous historical precedents, such as the way technologies for interchangeable machine-made parts led to mass production in the 19th century. More recently, Japan's quality manufacturing paradigm and IT-intensive manufacturing have had comparable effects.

Is there a current example that illustrates how this could work? Tonio Buonassisi, Doug Powell, Alan Goodrich and colleagues have closely examined the cost structure of crystalline solar photovoltaics;[10] for this technology to be competitive with other electricity-producing technologies for residential and commercial uses, it needs to continue to cut production costs dramatically. Major R & D efforts are underway to do this on a pathway that resembles what Moore's Law did for semiconductor efficiency and performance. As noted in earlier chapters, DOE calls its program "SunShot," implicitly comparing it to the "moon shot" of the 1960s. If achieved, these cuts can lead to a major economic sector.

Innovative applications now being explored and within range of implementation ("line of sight" innovations) will move this technology far down the production price curve; breakthrough innovations now in the research stage could advance it well past the goal line of international competitiveness. Buonassisi, Goodrich, Powell, and colleagues indicate that if the United States is able to sustain its R & D efforts and continues to press these innovation efficiencies for the rest of this decade, it can offset the advantages in production costs that China currently enjoys in solar PVs and enable the United States to be competitive in this sector, even if the technological advances were to be simultaneously transferred to China.[11] Their analysis thus indicates that an innovation-intensive approach could at the same time drive down production costs for all producers and change the current imbalance in production costs between the U.S. and China.

A particularly critical issue for advanced manufacturing in the United States will be who will be the *change agent*. The Obama administration, led by the president, has pressed initiatives to support advanced manufacturing. Presidential leadership can be vital in putting talent and resources on a problem, and this president has done that. Using the concepts we developed earlier, if this advanced manufacturing focus endures, he could be considered the "meta-change agent." But a president cannot focus on pressing the innovation initiative on a day-to-day basis. Effective day-to-day, hands-on leadership is also needed from the president's National Economic Council staff, the White House Office of Science and Technology Policy, and an interagency program office that has been set up.

The president also convened the Advanced Manufacturing Partnership (AMP), a collaboration among top leaders in industry and universities focused on developing common policy responses to manufacturing innovation needs. While AMP recommendations have led to important policies, including (as discussed below) the creation of manufacturing institutes, coordination has not yet emerged among R & D agencies on advanced manufacturing research tied to technology strategies developed with industry and university experts for promising technologies for advanced manufacturing. Although the prototype and test bed stages can be assisted by the institutes, there has not yet been identified an institution or coordinated institutional effort that will nurture and press the needed technologies forward on an ongoing basis to feed into the institutes and eventually into implementation by industry. Industry leadership will also be critical in this effort. In short, the role of change agent is not yet filled on the front end of the innovation system. Thus the classic problems of interagency coordination and industry ownership and collaboration remain as major issues.

In conclusion, if the United States wants to compete with low-cost, low-wage, increasingly advanced-technology competitors in production, strategically and systematically investing and applying its comparative advantage in technology innovation will be critical. Technological innovations that could transform production appear to be available, and a series of R & D agencies are engaged, although a more concerted cross-agency, "connected science and technology" effort will be required.

The United States did not lead the last manufacturing revolution. Japan did, around the quality model,[12] and US manufacturing had to play catch-up. So there is no reason to assume that the United States will necessarily lead the next revolution in manufacturing. Other high-cost developed nations, led by Germany and Britain, are already exploring advanced manufacturing.[13] China has a comparable "Strategic Emerging Industries" plan intended to make its leadership in production in critical manufacturing sectors secure.[14] So competitors are adopting new competitive models; the United States must understand its competitors' approaches if its own are to be successful. It has much to learn from them.

There is a substantial argument that advanced manufacturing technologies such as those cited above will emerge somewhere in the world and become pervasive over the next decade and a half. Just as survivor US firms had to launch "lean" manufacturing in order to compete with Japan's quality manufacturing model of the 1970s and 1980s, US firms will either implement these advanced technology paradigms or will fail. How these advances reach the mass of US manufacturing—the 300,000 small and midsize manufacturers that lack integrated R & D capability—is particularly problematic and is discussed in step 5.

If these new manufacturing technologies could be implemented, what would be the implications for overall employment? The efficiency and productivity gains in production that such paradigms could create may lead to fewer jobs on the actual production line. However, as explained in chapters 4 and 6, the key strong point of manufacturing employment is its role as a job multiplier. It supports many more jobs in the value network of resource, supplier, component, distribution, sales, and maintenance firms that are built around the production firm. In addition, the emerging model of firms that tie produced goods to related services, fusing these two, means that an increasing number of service jobs can be tied to production. Here Germany provides an interesting example. By driving innovation into its production sector, it maintains strong overall manufacturing employment—currently 20% of its workforce as compared to 11% in the United States—despite a much higher manufacturing wage rate than in the United States, and so benefits from a correspondingly larger manufacturing job multiplier effect.[15] There is every reason to ensure a healthy US manufacturing sector that can participate in and take advantage of this coming technological revolution.

APPLYING STEP 2: IDENTIFYING THE LAUNCH PATHS FOR EMERGING TECHNOLOGIES
Technology Strategies

Building on a strengthened foundation of front-end R & D, step 2 requires identifying launch pathways to move technologies emerging from that system toward implementation. An ongoing technology strategy effort shared by industry, government, and academic research experts is a way to undertake and continually update a process of identification of launch paths. Over time, such strategies can be turned into more detailed technology roadmaps. These are plans, often coordinated across firms, to match short- and long-term goals for technological advances, with specific technological development solutions to meet the goals; they can guide decisions on technology investments and should help avoid problems of technology lock-in.[16]

As we have seen in the last chapter, Sematech, the semiconductor industry's collaborative technology program, is a model for this collaborative roadmapping approach. Two relevant efforts in the Department of Energy also bear noting. The SunShot Initiative noted above,[17] an effort led by DOE but involving industry and academic experts, has attempted to define technology pathways to drive down solar costs so as to be able to compete with fossil fuels, and has been making steady progress. DOE has also initiated government-wide effort to coordinate disparate energy programs and initiatives, the Quadrennial Energy Review (QER),[18] as well as a Quadrennial Technology Review (QTR) effort, first issued in 2011[19] and revisited in 2014. Although the report development teams omitted direct participation by industry or academic experts, these experts have advised the efforts, and the QER is at least attempting to get the government's energy act together across agencies.

Technology strategies, the step preceding a technology roadmapping effort, have been attempted for aspects of advanced manufacturing in the second phase of the industry-university-government collaboration convened in 2013 by the president, known as the Advanced Manufacturing Partnership 2.0.[20] Preliminary strategies were developed in 2014 in three advanced manufacturing fields: advanced sensing; controls and platforms for manufacturing, visualization, information, and digital manufacturing; and advanced materials manufacturing.[21] These three pilot strategies have amply demonstrated the value of a collaborative industry-university-government strategic effort, probably the first serious attempt since Sematech to undertake such an effort. As gauged by the interest the pilots have commanded across sectors, they indicate that experts from a range of companies and universities can find common ground and develop sophisticated approaches that can drive significant public and private investments in the hundreds of millions. For example, a manufacturing institute with major public and private cost sharing has recently been created in digital manufacturing; it is applying major elements of the pilot strategy in that area. Another institute encompassing the sensing-control pilot strategy has been proposed by the DOD, which will also require major industry cost sharing to complement federal and state funding. And advanced materials manufacturing is a possible topic for a future institute; existing institutes with major industry and regional government cost sharing already embody composite and lightweight metal advanced materials. Such strategies need to be ongoing; for this approach to be meaningful, a permanent and ongoing strategic development process, incorporating the involved federal agencies, will be required.

Selecting New Manufacturing Technologies That Apply across Manufacturing Sectors

Manufacturing is a sector in itself but there has been increasing sectoral overlap for complex, high-value goods. For example, most cars still have internal combustion engines but also hold from 30 to 60 processors and ever more intricate software systems to run them. An aircraft is a complex system, combining aeronautical design, turbine engines, electronics, advanced materials, software, and information technology. Improvements in one sector therefore translate into the production of complex goods by other sectors.

Generally, it would be important in pursuing technological advances and translating them into launch pathways to create as much synergy as possible. The strategic selection of innovations for emphasis for launch, then, should be focused on transferability across sectors. A matrix should be prepared, therefore, comparing technology options against the sectors to which they apply, and selecting for focus technologies with payoff across sectors. The technologies listed in step 1, above, translate well into a range of industrial sectors, as suggested in the matrix in table 13.1.

Additional variables that cut across sectors and should be considered when priority technologies are selected include the maturity of the technology embedded in the paradigm and the time it may take to translate it into implementation, the readiness of relevant sectors to undertake that translation, the market demand, US national security needs, and the ability of an enhanced sector to translate into economic benefits for the United States.[22]

Examining Advanced Technology, Process, and Business Models

A new generation of advanced manufacturing technologies alone will not be transformative. To foster the launch pathways, there must be a realization that it is not workable just to develop new technologies without accompanying new processes and business models to enable them to be implemented. Although new

Table 13.1 Industry Sectors and Relevant Advanced Manufacturing Technologies

Manufacturing Technology	Sector						
	Bio/ pharmaceutical	Aerospace	IT/ electronics	Heavy equipment	Digital search, network	New energy	Transport
Network-centric	X	X	X	X	X	X	X
Advanced materials	X	X	X	X		X	X
Nano manufacturing	X	X	X	X	X	X	X
Mass customization	X	X	X	X	X	X	X
Distribution efficiency	X	X	X	X		X	X
Energy efficiency	X	X	X	X	X	X	X

advanced manufacturing technologies will be a first building block, the launch process requires that there be accompanying new production processes to make the equipment embodying the technologies and to adapt the technologies into the production system so as to realize the efficiencies they make possible. Firms adopting the new technologies and processes will need new business models in order to ensure that these new approaches are creating, delivering, and capturing economic value. The new advanced manufacturing technologies and processes have to work economically, with significant and demonstrable economic gains flowing to implementing firms. Otherwise they will never be adopted. These process and business model features must be built into a technological R & D effort along with the development of the technology itself. Technology development is not all there is to a manufacturing technology launch.

In summary, a technology strategy developed by industry, academic, and agency experts, and updated based on ongoing developments, will be important to the identification of launch pathways for emerging advanced manufacturing technologies. Selecting areas of technology where there are payoffs across a number of manufacturing sectors is a way to further identify, refine, and optimize these launch pathways. It will bring more talent into the launch task. Finally, the process of identification of a launch pathway must include an understanding, not only of the potential significance of the particular advanced manufacturing technology under consideration, but also of whether efficient production processes and business models are available to support its launch.

APPLYING STEP 3: MATCHING SUPPORT TO LAUNCH PATHS

Step 3 calls for matching policies for technology support to the prospective launch pathways of the emerging technologies. As detailed in the previous chapter, these can be available not only from government, but also from other sources, and can take the form of "carrots"—incentives. While "sticks"—regulatory requirements—appear more suited to energy technologies, such as carbon capture and sequestration, some could also reach the more general manufacturing sector. For example, industrial emissions are a major source of carbon dioxide emissions (some 19%);[23] it is such a serious problem that DOE is has significantly enlarged its Clean Energy Manufacturing Initiative,[24] and is second only to the DOD in sponsoring new advanced manufacturing institutes to create more efficient production systems. The Environmental Protection Administration already regulates emissions in a number of industrial segments, and further major efficiency savings in some additional industries could be regulated, if they offer significant reductions and "carrots" are not working.

"Carrot" (and possibly in the future "stick") approaches can be undertaken to overcome some of the legacy sector barriers in this sector identified in chapters 4 and 6. As discussed in the previous steps, there are a series of advanced manufacturing technologies—from additive manufacturing to advanced materials—that could transform manufacturing and that, with additional work, are readied for implementation, that is, for technology launch. But relevant legacy obstacles must be overcome. For example, financing support for the innovation is a significant issue in the manufacturing sector. There is a particularly problematic area in advanced manufacturing, where incentives are needed: financial support for small and mid-size manufacturing firms and start-ups for scaling up product production. While other legacy obstacles are discussed in step 5, we focus on financing here because it is so tied to the technology launch process.

Financing Production Scale-Up

As discussed in chapter 6, large US production firms have used offshoring of production to low-wage, low-cost nations as a way to avoid the costs and risks of undertaking innovation in production.[25] But advanced manufacturing technologies and processes are also likely to be outside the reach of both the small and midsize manufacturing enterprises (SMEs) that undertake the majority of US manufacturing, and the entrepreneurial start-up production firms that represent the next generation of technological advance. The lack of financing for implementing production advances is a root cause of the decline in this sector.[26]

The problem faced by SMEs in innovating in production is being exacerbated by structural shifts in the US financing system, briefly noted in chapter 6, away from local banking. For start-up and entrepreneurial firms engaged in production, their support system of venture and angel capital is on a time horizon for investment that is around five to seven years. While that time period fits well with the IT sector, it does not work well for many other sectors, including manufacturing for goods such as in aerospace, energy, complex pharmaceuticals, and capital goods generally, where the production scale-up process may take 10 years or more.[27] So in addition to the traditional "valley of death" problem between R & D, these firms face a "mountain of death" problem for production scale-up, as well: the five- to seven-year time horizon of the VC/angel investment system does not work well for the 10 years or more yardstick of manufacturing and comparable sectors. Increasingly, they shift initial production to contract manufacturing firms abroad organized to undertake the financing and production risk.[28]

What are the "workarounds" for this "mountain of death"?

Public-Sector Incentives

The Advanced Manufacturing Partnership effort referenced above has identified a number of federal program incentives that could reach this problem. Although none fits perfectly and most are limited in scale, a mix of these could help. There are federal industrial *financing programs* that could be applied to manufacturing scale-up.[29] For example, Title III of the Defense Production Act allows the DOD to build plants and supply production equipment, through purchase and purchase guarantees in the $8-20 million range, to manufacturers of defense products, to enable commercial-scale production. The program can be used to create or maintain production capabilities, reduce the cost of advanced technologies, and strengthen the competitiveness of the defense manufacturing base. The Small

Business Administration (SBA) 7A Loan Program is a widely used lending program for up to $5 million; the Certified Development Company 504 Loan Program allows loans up to $4 million for buildings or building improvements. The Commerce Department's Economic Development Administration (EDA) provides grants to state revolving loan funds for small-firm capital projects. The SBA and EDA programs, however, do not meet adequately the levels of financing needed for production financing. The Department of Energy has a loan program available to renewable energy companies and advanced technology vehicle production, if an SME or start-up is working in those areas. None of these or other financing mechanisms exactly fit the scale-up problem, but some or a mix of them may assist small manufacturers.

Tax incentives are also relevant. The R & D tax credit provides research and particularly development support and can assist large manufacturers, but start-ups generally lack the revenue to take advantage of the credit, and SMEs usually don't perform traditional R & D. However, the New Market Tax Credit creates community development entities that can provide investment capital in low-income communities, and could help SME production in those areas. There are also some *public-private financing* models. For example, the SBA's Small Business Investment Company (SBIC) program can provide financing for SMEs averaging between $1 million and $10 million, and would cover production scale-up. This level of assistance can help some firms with some technologies and processes; however, higher financing levels would increase its utility for this purpose.

Private-Sector Incentives

On the back end of the innovation system, incentives for VC and traditional commercial lending to provide production scale-up financing could in principle be legislated, but given budget pressure and congressional logjams this is unlikely in the near term. Corporate venture funds could play a larger role in supporting SME suppliers and complementary technologies. Those banking institutions that remain interested in SME industrial lending could adopt a centralized information system. In the longer term, new kinds of financial instruments might evolve. Some experts are looking at new tools that would allow much larger investor pools to be assembled around broad portfolios of new technology firms; larger funds and a portfolio approach to manage risk could enable debt financing to better reach areas like R & D and potentially production scale-up.[30] Meanwhile, test beds (discussed below under manufacturing institutes) could be key: if the efficiency, cost savings, and productivity of new advanced manufacturing technologies can be fully demonstrated for small and midsize manufacturers, they may be able to obtain loans because higher investment certainty is provided.

These "workarounds" for the "mountain of death" problem of the 10 years or more time horizon are not only important to existing small or midsize firms, but they are also vital for start-ups. If the innovative start-ups outside the IT sector must continue to offshore the risk and cost of production to contract manufacturers abroad, this has major implications, as we have seen, for US manufacturing in the future: it may thereby be losing production capability for the next generation of goods, with corresponding damage to the tie between innovation and production, further affecting innovation capacity. So resolution of this production scale-up financing issue is important if the United States is to adopt advanced manufacturing with its corresponding competitive advantages.

APPLYING STEP 4: GAP ANALYSIS OF THE INNOVATION SYSTEM

Growth economics has identified and developed two core factors that make direct contributions to innovation: R & D supporting technological and related innovations and the talent base behind this R & D.[31] However, these alone are not enough if innovations are to be implemented and scaled into the economy. As we discussed in chapters 11 and 12, a dynamic system for "innovation organization" that connects these factors and the innovation institutional actors that incorporate them, tying them to implementation stages in industry, is also key.[32] As noted, the innovation organization model is anchored in both the public and private sectors, and links up—and if necessary orchestrates through change agents—the disparate institutions and firms needed to launch innovation, overcoming any institutional and policy obstacles, including legacy barriers, that arise on the way. So the model provides the connecting tissue for the R & D, the talent, the institutional actors, and the implementation stages, with the policy framing to overcome barriers. Step 1 focused on strengthening institutions that carry out early stage innovation. But the analysis must be more encompassing, reaching all the stages of innovation. To create this dynamic system, it is critical to perform a gap analysis of the system, identifying system gaps and weaknesses that must be filled. A series are identified below.

Gaps between the Breakthrough Federally Funded R & D System and the Industrial Focus on Production Advances

Dan Breznitz and Peter Cowhey have argued that the United States needs to better link the two systems of innovation it maintains.[33] The first, the *novel and breakthrough product/technology innovation* system, includes university research supported by R & D agencies—the "pipeline" system as we have termed it here—and uses "technology push" to implement its advances. We have discussed improvements to the front end of the innovation in our earlier discussion of step 1. The second, the *process and incremental innovation system*, emphasizes engineering enhancements to products and technologies, including the way they are produced, distributed, and serviced. This system is dominated by industry.[34] Breznitz and Cowhey describe this at the industrial sectoral level; we describe it more broadly. There is a division in the US innovation system into innovative front-end and legacy back-end parts, as we pointed out at the beginning of chapter 1 of this book. This is a larger point—we put this division into the broader context of legacy sectors that affect much of the economy, which generally suffer from a disconnect between front- and back-end; this is a significant issue affecting the introduction of innovation into legacy sectors. Both parts of the system are vital, and our current pipeline technology policy model, which dominates US discussions, pays great attention to the former and little to the latter, which includes the production stage. The first system rarely is brought to bear to assist the second.

Manufacturing has historically fallen into the second category. It has been viewed as dominated by industry and engineering processes—although, as has been demonstrated repeatedly over the decades, from US mass production to Japan's quality production, it can be novel and breakthrough as well. It has never been the focus of a major federal R & D effort. This is part of the reason why the United States continues to innovate technologies and yet the product evolution occurs abroad.[35] Suppose the United States worked to unify its systems, and brought the remarkable innovation talent in the first to support the second, as well as the first? This reform in "innovation organization" is an important part of what we must accomplish if we to implement new manufacturing technology paradigms. It is a key gap in the existing innovation system.

More concretely, what would we fill this gap with? As noted above under step 1, four leading federal R & D agencies active in advanced manufacturing research are already undertaking some $700 million in R & D that directly bears on this field.[36] If indirect areas are included, the number is significantly higher. For example, advances in materials, advanced computer simulation and modeling, robotics, and nanotechnology have important ramifications if translated into manufacturing as well.

Gaps between Federal R & D Agencies Supporting Advanced Manufacturing R & D

The lead manufacturing R & D agencies—the DOD, DOE, NSF, and NIST—have begun some collaboration.[37] Deep collaboration across agency seams with truly interagency R & D efforts, funding, and programs, as opposed to information exchanges across agency walls, has not been fully achieved in the highly decentralized US R & D model, even in the noted attempts at cross-agency work in the National Nanotechnology and High Performance Computing initiatives.

That level of integration may be too much to expect in as varied and complex a sector as manufacturing, but it should be possible to better organize and coordinate agency R & D in advanced manufacturing and move it into the emerging manufacturing institutes—for a stronger R & D feed-in process. In other words, unless they are better connected to the results coming out of the R & D system—a stronger feed-in—these institutes may become isolated over time from the technology opportunities they were created to exploit. In addition, strong ties with work in industry must be created if the gaps between the two innovation systems identified above, novel/breakthrough and incremental/engineering, are to be closed.[38] The lessons of a unified R & D effort that includes R & D, process, and business models, identified in step 2 above, must also be considered and applied. This may be critical if the relatively modest direct manufacturing R & D efforts in federal agencies, as well as the far larger indirect efforts (such as more general research in advanced materials or nanotechnology) are to launch new advances in advanced manufacturing technology onto factory floors.

The gap analysis should also evaluate the resources of the Department of Defense. As described in chapters 8 and 11, the DOD operates at all stages of the innovation system. It performs the research, the development, the prototype, the demonstration, and the test bed, and often creates the initial market for new technologies through its procurement system. It can operate as an integrated innovation system;[39] that systemic role may be needed for advanced manufacturing. The DOD's contracting role makes it a major actor in advanced manufacturing.

It also has a major stake in maintaining US technological leadership through manufacturing. A 2013 Defense Science Board study[40] found that the shift of manufacturing from the United States to China and other nations is a leading threat to the US military advantage. This shift of manufacturing to foreign nations also affects US defense technology leadership by enabling new players to learn a technology and then gain the capability to improve on it. An additional threat to defense capabilities from offshore manufacturing is the potential for compromise of the supply chain for key weapons systems components. The report also found that the rise of technically and economically strong foreign adversaries will challenge US superiority in speed, stealth, and the precision of weapons systems, and other countries are likely to develop counters to some or all of the foundation technologies on which the United States has come to rely.

Manufacturing, then, is not an abstract problem for the DOD; it is a central element of US world security leadership.[41] Gains in production efficiency and productivity also will be key to the DOD's ability to control its procurement costs, and because of the relationship between R & D and design with production, to its future technological edge. The DOD, because of the inherent strength of its connected innovation system and its corresponding ability to fill gaps, will need to be a central agency partner with the private sector in any advanced manufacturing strategy.[42]

The technology push from the federally driven, R & D pipeline part of the innovation system will be needed for the transformation of manufacturing, just as it has been needed for innovation in many fields—from space to nuclear power to computing to the Internet. But the seams between agencies need to be better managed in this field; otherwise the needed scale of research over a range of technologies cannot be assembled. Our highly decentralized system of diverse federal mission-driven R & D agencies has many advantages, but in those cases in which crosscutting collaboration is required, decentralization can be a barrier to innovation. For example, the Department of Energy has started manufacturing institutes in power electronics and composites because of their potential in energy and production efficiency. But the DOD has long performed research in these areas, and fields defense technologies that could benefit greatly from advances in them. Connective tissue is needed between these DOE and DOD efforts, along the lines of more coordinated R&D described above, but also through a network of the different agency-supported institutes discussed below. In the field of advanced manufacturing, then, mechanisms for the organization of innovation that enable technological advances to get across the seams that separate the different agencies would close a critical gap in the system.[43]

Gaps in the Incentive System to Meet Production Scale-Up Financing

As discussed in detail in step 3 above, there is a significant gap because of the weak financing system for manufacturing; this financing system obstacle creates a gap in scaling up production that should be filled, with possible incentive mechanisms summarized in the previous step. In addition, the decline in the manufacturing ecosystem, discussed in chapter 4, led to a corresponding decline of the support and knowledge transfer systems for SMEs, which presents a major problem to scaling-up innovations. There is a need for what Gary Pisano and Willy Shih would call a new kind of manufacturing "commons"[44] through which small and large firms can collaborate and share costs and risks in rebuilding that ecosystem. This includes gaps in the linkages and between small and large firms key to stronger supply chains, and gaps in workforce training, particularly for SMEs.

Gaps Created by the Hollowing Out of the Manufacturing Ecosystem and the Cross-Firm Supporting Infrastructure

Chapter 4 discussed the emigration of multinational firms offshore and the corresponding offshoring of important portions of their production capability. While once larger firms and the smaller firms in their supply chain orbits shared best practices in production and processes, in production innovations and in workforce training, this system has hollowed out. This in turn, as described in chapter 6, left many SMEs, as Suzanne Berger has termed it, "home alone." Pisano and Shih term this, as noted above, the failing of the manufacturing "commons" that historically supported industrial firms. Germany's model is relevant here, particularly its network of innovation organizations that help firms collaborate, with each other and with engineering schools, to bring new ideas and processes to small, midsize, and large firms alike through its Fraunhofer Institutes.[45] These institutes emphasize development, prototyping, demonstration, and test bed stages, so firms can test out new technologies. Is this a model that the United States could emulate?

Manufacturing in the United States is not a national system. It is a collection of regional systems, based in industrial sectors with connected clusters spread throughout the country. An advanced manufacturing effort must be organized around that regional reality. It can't simply be an R & D program run at the national level, but must include additional stages and connect to the regions where manufacturing is organized and advances must be implemented. The Fraunhofer system provides lessons for this regional organizational challenge.

In addition, while R & D conducted by government and universities can take a technology from basic research through proof of concept and early stage technology development, it usually does not advance to the later stages of technology demonstration and system and subsystem development. There are seams between each of these innovation stages, which are usually performed by different actors in the institutional system for innovation. All these seams between the stages as well as those between the institutions must be crossed.[46]

While large firms may have the capability to undertake those later stages, the 300,000 small and midsize manufacturers that form the bulk of the US manufacturing sector are not organized or funded to do so. So the United States has had a problem of connecting with regions and has a problem with transitioning technology from development to later stages, particularly for smaller firms. This mass of smaller firms must be risk averse to survive. They lack resources to undertake R & D, testing, and evaluation and lack capital to implement new technologies. Unless the new advanced manufacturing technology paradigms delineated in step 1 are fully tested and costed out, their efficiencies demonstrated, and their reliability proven, they will simply not be adapted to actual factory floors. And smaller firms must be able to demonstrate their efficiencies and cost savings in order to obtain financing to install them. While the advanced manufacturing technologies may be particularly helpful to small and midsize firms, they can also help large firms transition to new advanced technologies. This hollowing out of the manufacturing ecosystem creates a major innovation system gap in this sector.

Gaps from the Lack of a Change Agent in the Front End of the Advanced Manufacturing Innovation System

The lack of a cross-agency R & D agenda, coordinated with shared industry-university-government technology strategies, were noted above under step 1, and are directly related to the lack of a change agent. No institution or institutional effort has yet come forward to close these gaps—to serve as an advanced manufacturing change agent. But there is a larger problem here apart from these front-end problems. Manufacturing is major legacy sector and one of the largest elements of the economy. Industrial and governmental shifts to drive a production transformation of more scope than simply the front end of this innovation system are required. Change agents from industry and government are needed to take on this larger task.

Gaps in Obtaining Workforce Talent to Staff an Advanced Manufacturing System

New paradigms in manufacturing will require an ever more skilled workforce, yet a manufacturing skills gap may be developing. As we noted in chapter 6,[47] there does not appear to be an emergency in workforce skills availability.[48] However, smaller and more innovative firms that require higher job skills appear to be facing problems. Coupled with the aging demographics of the production workforce, this signals issues ahead. If the United States wants to move toward new production paradigms, there may be an emerging gap in manufacturing skills. A root cause of the problem may be manufacturing's image. A survey of engineering and science undergraduates found limited interest in manufacturing as a career;[49] job loss and offshoring in manufacturing over the decade 2000–2010 may be contributing to this perception.[50] The problems manufacturers, particularly SMEs, now have in providing strong skills training may also be discouraging entry of new talent.[51] Skills training must be improved and also constitutes an emerging gap in the system.

To summarize the results of step 4 of this analysis, US manufacturing innovation includes the following gaps: gaps between the federal R & D system, which generally supports more breakthrough or radical innovation, and the industrial system, which supports advances in production processes; gaps between the federal R & D agencies supporting manufacturing research (where the defense R & D system in particular could play a role); gaps in the incentive system for financing production scale-up; gaps in the support infrastructure between manufacturing firms; and gaps in educating and training the workforce for an advanced manufacturing economy. Steps in filling these gaps are reviewed below.

APPLYING STEP 5: FILLING THE GAPS IN THE MANUFACTURING INNOVATION SYSTEM

We tackle below this series of manufacturing innovation system gaps with a corresponding series of ways to fill them. While previous discussions enable a brief summary for gaps 1–3, gaps 4–6 require more elaboration.

Gap 1

The *gaps between the breakthrough federally-funded R & D system and the industrial focus on production advances* could be addressed by collaborative technology strategies developed by industry, agency, and university experts in areas that present potential technology paradigms. This technology strategy approach is detailed in step 2, above. Such strategies could detail launch paths for new advanced manufacturing paradigms, and inform and help link both the federal R & D relevant to advanced manufacturing and industry efforts on manufacturing processes. Over time, the strategies could become actual technology roadmaps.

Gap 2

The *gaps between federal R & D agencies supporting advanced manufacturing R & D* also need to be filled so these largely disconnected efforts can be better coordinated and shared. How could this system work more in tandem? As discussed in step 1, coordination among the diverse group of federal R & D agencies could be organized under the White House Office of Science and Technology Policy, which is charged with this coordination responsibility, using its authority to create an interagency collaborative committee. These efforts, in turn, could be linked to the technology strategies described above, developed between industry, university, and agency experts. As noted in step 4, the Defense Department, which has its own mechanisms for coordination across its R & D organizations, as well as a more integrated innovation system that stretches from research through initial production, has particular capabilities that could be applied here.

Gap 3

Ways to fill the *gaps in the incentive system to meet production scale-up financing needs* were discussed under step 3. To summarize briefly, there are some existing federal programs for business financing through the Defense Production Act, the Small Business Administration, the Treasury, and other agencies that could be adjusted to help SMEs and start-ups with production scale-up. Private-sector financing options could evolve, as well.

Gap 4

Gaps are created by the hollowing out of the manufacturing ecosystem and the cross-firm supporting infrastructure. We explored the gap created by the hollowing out of the manufacturing in step 4, but what are approaches to fill it in more concrete terms? Arguably, a new kind of regional infrastructure is needed, tying regional manufacturing firms, small and large, with the results of research and into test beds where new manufacturing technologies can be proven. While German industry differs in many ways from US industry, the Fraunhofer institutes may offer a model for closing a significant and growing gap in the US manufacturing ecosystem.

We earlier described how the Advanced Manufacturing Partnership, called into being by the Obama administration as an industry-university consortium, proposed a network of manufacturing institutes[52] where teams of industrial and academic experts from a range of fields can work on these intermediate stages of advanced technologies relevant to regional firms.[53] A series of these institutes are forming, cost-shared among federal agencies, state governments,[54] and private companies, bringing firms into industry-led collaborations with regional research universities. Competitive selections have been held around potential new advanced manufacturing technologies, including additive manufacturing, digital manufacturing, lightweight metals, power electronics, and composites. The institutes emphasize the stages of technology development, prototyping, demonstration, and especially test beds. Area firms participate and bring in their workforces for training on the implementation of the technology onto the factory floor, potentially cooperating with area community colleges on curriculum for the new production paradigms. The focus is on the translation of technologies into manufacturing applications, with attention to new industrial processes and the information needed to organize new business models around them.

While the manufacturing institutes must be embedded in regional economies, they will be developing important lessons that must be transferred to firms, small and large, nationally. The additive manufacturing institute, for example, is headquartered in Youngstown. Ohio, but this potential new technology effort has lessons for industries far beyond Ohio. An institute network[55] to disseminate best practices and results from individual Institutes across to other Institutes and outside the institutes is needed, as recommended in the second and final Advanced Manufacturing Partnership report issued in 2014,[56] to translate this regionally based model into nationwide effects. The manufacturing institutes, individually and combined into a network, have potential for filling gaps created by the hollowing out of the US manufacturing ecosystem. They may also prove to be an important distribution mechanism, enabling new manufacturing paradigms to spread through small, midsize, and large manufacturing firms as well as start-ups.

Gap 5

Gaps emerge from the lack of change agents in advanced manufacturing. The gaps in the front end of the advanced manufacturing innovation system were noted above under step 1. As discussed, the lack of a cross-agency R & D agenda, coordinated with shared industry-university-government technology strategies, is directly related to the lack of a change agent. But there is a larger change agent problem. In addition its front-end challenges, manufacturing has numerous legacy sector characteristics, as we have discussed. Within the overall sector, is there a force that will act as a change agent, affecting front and back ends? As noted above and in chapter 6, major manufacturing firms are multinational and can go abroad for lower wages and costs. They don't have to take the risks and expenditures of implementing advanced manufacturing. Small and midsize manufacturing firms and production start-ups are too decentralized and too small to be able to lead a shift to advanced manufacturing. These are unlikely to be change agents. Meanwhile, the president has stepped forward to try to take on the manufacturing challenge, driven by the economic consequences of the decline in manufacturing and the national anxiety about this decline—which translates into a political driver. Can the president and his staff act as the meta-change agent, or what is the same thing, the champion? Since the administration is coming to an end, can this federal role become an enduring political force that can act as the change agent over an extended period?

The administration is developing an agenda to implement the lengthy recommendations of the Advanced Manufacturing Partnership's 2014 report; its officials have recognized their term is ending and have made this a priority for action.[57] Plans for a total of fifteen manufacturing institutes are rapidly being implemented, and hundreds of millions are being spent on new workforce training and apprenticeship programs. Congress at the end of 2014 passed bipartisan legislation to authorize the Advanced Manufacturing Institute program, including a network to better coordinate and connect the growing number of institutes, and required a national advanced manufacturing strategy.[58] Mechanisms to coordinate manufacturing R & D across agencies, to develop further technology strategies, and to set up a permanent advisory committee with industry and university expert input are all planned. Senior administration officials in the White House and in the agencies are specifically charged with implementation responsibilities; this is a personal priority of the president. Governmental action—and potential change agents—to push for manufacturing innovation are now further along than ever before, and there is strong companion interest in the industrial sector, as evidenced by the remarkable level of work and dedication that went into the Advanced Manufacturing Partnership reports[59] and the willingness of industry to cost-share manufacturing institutes. But will this effort be enduring? The "corporate welfare" attack is always lurking in the political system because the public and the political system have only a limited understanding of how the innovation system actually works. So the jury is still out.

There is an additional change agent force that could come to bear. The Defense Department has a major stake in the nation's strength in production, which is deeply tied to the nation's security strength. Fortunately for the US manufacturing industry, major defense contracting firms cannot shift production abroad; they are stuck in the United States. If they want to stay competitive and to be able to offer their government customer more affordable goods, they may need to shift to advanced manufacturing. Defense firms have already expressed strong interest in the manufacturing institutes proposed to date, and the great majority of these have been proposed and supported by the Defense Department.

Since the defense sector remains an important part of the US manufacturing sector, it is possible that the leading defense contractors could serve as the required change agents, ready to press for change. However, within the Defense Department civilian and military leadership, focused as they are on short-term security issues, there is only limited understanding of the importance of strong manufacturing to strong defense. For innovation in advanced manufacturing to become a reality, the change agent gap must be filled on both the front and the back ends of the production innovation system.

Gap 6

One major gap remains: the *gap in obtaining workforce talent* to staff an advanced manufacturing system. Advanced manufacturing will require a renewed and more skilled workforce, but there are problems in training and with the image of the sector, that has discouraged the entry of the talent that will be needed. Advanced manufacturing and production innovation calling for high skills and technology challenges, as well as the new "Maker Movement" growing in schools and colleges,[60] may help alter the image problem, but skills training must still be improved.

The nation's 1,500 community colleges have become the major providers of technicians, and this role can be further rationalized. Programs are afoot to build ties between industry and community colleges for standardized curricula for skills training at community colleges that would lead to skill certifications with widespread acceptance throughout industry.[61] Such national curricula, linked to industry needs along with project-based learning tied to industry internships and apprenticeships, could be important. Stackable credentials adapted to lifelong learning are another way that community colleges are offering employers ways to evaluate job candidate competencies and updated skills and are increasingly being recognized nationally. The administration has been providing significant funding to new skills and apprenticeship programs, and NSF's Advanced Technology Education (ATE) program is bringing new advanced manufacturing curricula and programs to community colleges.[62]

At the professional level, undergraduate engineering students receive only limited manufacturing content. Yet unless engineers become fluent with advanced manufacturing technologies, these technologies simply won't translate to industry. For example, nanofabrication is being performed at research benches, but until it reaches the factory floor it cannot be transformative; skilled engineers are traditionally the translators. New technical master's degrees in manufacturing could help; in effect, these could become professional degrees, like MBAs, but ones that signal practical expertise in production.[63] As important would be for universities and the Accreditation Board for Engineering and Technology (ABET, the engineering school accrediting system) to develop online curricula around advanced manufacturing technologies and processes that would educate both new and current engineers and technicians. Online courses appear particularly suited to skills updating and to lifelong learning when the learner already has foundational skills.

There is also an overarching issue in US education regarding technical talent. As described in chapter 7, US college graduation rates have stagnated in recent decades, while other nations have been sharply increasing their rates, eroding this historic US comparative talent advantage.[64] Since manufacturing is a dominant employer of engineers and scientists in the US innovation workforce, this affects its access to the future STEM workforce.

There are numerous training and education solutions, but unless workforce skills are updated, advanced manufacturing paradigms cannot be implemented at scale. And there are overall technical talent problems in the education system that require addressing, as well.

SUMMARY OF MANUFACTURING POLICY RECOMMENDATIONS

To summarize the policy recommendations in this section, table 13.2 lists the six major gaps identified above in the manufacturing innovation system, and ways to fill them, drawing on the five-step approach.

How well will these six ways to fill the policy gaps for manufacturing address the legacy sector characteristics identified as problematic for this sector in chapter 6?

Concerning the *cost structure* problem, whereby US-made goods face competition from lower cost goods from abroad and face currency valuation problems that improve the positions of competitors, an effort, discussed in steps 1 and 2, to develop and launch innovative advanced manufacturing technologies and processes, accompanied by new business models, could help drive down costs and drive up efficiencies, helping US goods to compete.

Concerning an *established infrastructure and institutional architecture*, the thinning out of the manufacturing ecosystem could be addressed by the manufacturing institutes described in step 5, with the corresponding rebuilding of the manufacturing "commons." This could be particularly beneficial to manufacturing SMEs but could also help large firms strengthen their supply chains.

Concerning *an innovation time horizon that is substantially longer than the financial system is prepared to support*, the problem of production scale-up financing

Table 13.2 Six Gaps in the Manufacturing Innovation System and Ways to Fill Them

	Gap	Possible system solution	Policy step
1.	Links between federal R & D and industry production and processes	Technology strategies developed by industry, university, agency experts around possible new manufacturing technologies	See *step 1*, innovating on the front end of the system, *step 2*, identifying the launch paths for emerging technologies, *step 4*, identifying the innovation system gap, and *step 5*, filling the gap.
2.	Coordination between federal R & D agency research in advanced manufacturing	Create an interagency coordination mechanism around possible manufacturing technology paradigms using authority held by the Office of Science and Technology Policy	See *step 1*, innovating on the front end, *step 2*, identifying launch paths for emerging technologies, *step 4*, identifying the innovation system gap, and *step 5*, filling the gap.
3.	Financing of production scale-up	Improve the available federal financing mechanisms and explore private-sector financing options for scale-up	See *step 3*, matching support to launch paths, *step 4*, identifying the innovation system gap, and *step 5*, filling the gap.
4.	Hollowing out of the manufacturing ecosystem and the cross-firm supporting infrastructure	Form manufacturing institutes for collaborations on new paradigms for manufacturing technology among large firms, SMEs, start-ups, and universities, with cost-sharing support from federal, state, regions, and industry	See *step 4*, identifying the innovation system gap, and *step 5*, filling the gap.
5.	Change agents	Identify change agents both on the front end of the innovation system and the back end from industry and government to press manufacturing technology advances to implementation; the Defense Department could play a role.	See *step 1*, innovating on the front end of the system, *step 2*, identifying launch paths for emerging technologies, *step 4*, identifying the innovation system gap, and *step 5*, filling the gap.

Table 13.2 *continued*

237 Case Study: Advanced Manufacturing

	Gap	Possible system solution	Policy step
6.	Obtaining workforce talent to staff an advanced manufacturing system	Community college curricula tied to industry-wide standards, internships and apprenticeships, stackable credentials, professional manufacturing master's degrees, and online engineering courses	See *step 4*, identifying the innovation system gap, and *step 5*, filling the gap.

for SMEs and start-ups could be addressed through the establishment of long-term financing facilities, as noted in the discussion in step 3.

Concerning *powerful vested interests* that are pervasive in the manufacturing sector, as described in chapter 6, many multinationals have limited incentives to explore advanced manufacturing paradigms because they can send their production processes offshore, avoiding the risk and cost of introducing innovation into their production system.[65] The multinationals won't oppose the policies being proposed because these policies don't threaten them; the problem is how to move them to actively support these policies. The collaboration with the SMEs on which they depend for advanced manufacturing technologies and the federal cost sharing offered through the manufacturing institutes could be an incentive to many to alter this strategy. However, further change agents from industry and government will be required. This is a key problem.

The inattention to manufacturing innovation is *sustained by public habits and expectations.* US R & D agencies, for example, have avoided manufacturing because historically most focus on the "pipeline" model—a breakthrough research model and the front end of the innovation system. The proposals in steps 1 and 2 for more collaborative R & D efforts between agencies and for industry-university-agency technology strategies, along with their participation in manufacturing institutes described in step 5, could help overcome this pattern. The unified services-production model that appears increasingly attractive to firms could help renew interest in production because a scalable services model as we discussed in chapter 6 could be tied to it.

Concerning the *established knowledge and human resources structure* that fails to focus on production innovation, the workforce training and education changes noted in step 5 could help mitigate this problem.

A number of the market failures that afflict other legacy sectors also afflict manufacturing. Concerning *collective action,* US manufacturing, as we have seen, is increasingly decentralized, with capabilities moving offshore, leaving SMEs "home alone." The role of manufacturing institutes (step 5) in restoring a more collaborative infrastructure between firms for new advanced manufacturing technology paradigms could be an important contribution. Concerning *lumpiness*, where new advanced manufacturing technologies require significant investment, the shared efforts in the R & D system, through joint technology strategies, and in the institutes, outlined in steps 1, 2, and 5, could offer solutions. The scale-up financing proposed in step 3 could also assist.

The *split incentives* problem, where large firms with the resources to develop manufacturing innovations don't have to do so because they can lower production costs by shifting abroad, can be addressed by the institutes model proposed in step 5, as well as through the benefit of more collaborative R & D in steps 1 and 2. The *economies of scale* problems in introducing new manufacturing technologies can be eased by the collaborative approaches suggested in steps 1, 2, and 5.

Drawing on the underlying framework developed in chapter 11 on the dynamics of innovation, we see that the "innovation organization" model is critical for the innovation approach suggested in this manufacturing case study. It requires innovation institutions that are connected through each innovation stage, from research through initial production—what we have termed "connected science and technology." Manufacturing requires operating at both the front (R & D) and back ends (demonstration through initial production) in its innovation system, taking advantage of the pipeline, the extended pipeline and the induced models of the drivers of innovation.

In sum, the five-step analytic process proposed here for innovation in legacy sectors suggests solutions for some of the deep problems affecting the US manufacturing sector, improving its ability to innovate its way out of its present decline. Since the United States has been weak in "manufacturing-led" innovation, improved performance in this legacy sector appears particularly important to its innovation system in general. The overall process outlined in this case study provides organizational lessons that could apply to other sectors and, indeed, to other nations, depending on their innovation environment.

It could also help to address the problem of "jobless innovation," identified as a major issue at the outset of this work. If innovation in manufacturing could be implemented at scale, there are ramifications for overall employment. Innovation–driven productivity and efficiency gains might lead to fewer jobs on the actual production line. However, as explained above, and in chapters 4 and 6, a critical aspect of manufacturing employment is its role as a job multiplier. It supports many more jobs in the complex and rich value network of resources, R&D, supplier, component, distribution, sales, service and maintenance firms that flow into and out of the production stage. If manufacturing is pulled out of this value chain – if factories close – the input and output parts of the chain are snapped and the chain is disrupted. But if manufacturing expands, the value chains grow with accompanying employment. In addition, the emerging model of firms that fuse produced goods to related services, means that an increasing number of service jobs will be further tied to production. Could the production-stage jobs themselves go up, aside from the manufacturing related jobs? The experience of Germany, which has 20% of its workforce employed in manufacturing as compared to 11% in the US, suggests that a strong production sector can produce growth in both manufacturing and manufacturing-related employment – but this is an open question for the US. The point of the analysis in this chapter is that treating manufacturing as a legacy sector links the problem of legacy sectors to that of jobless innovation and points the way to a strategy for both. Finally, the important role of manufacturing in the innovation process—as expressed in the "manufacturing-led" model of the dynamic of innovation—also means that it is not only a sector but is key to innovation throughout the innovation system.

14 Conclusions

Turning Covered Wagons East

Frederick Jackson Turner, historian of the American frontier, argued that the always-beckoning frontier was the crucible shaping America society.[1] He retold an old story, arguing that it defined our cultural landscape: when American settlers faced frustration and felt opportunities were limited, they could climb into covered wagons, push on over the next mountain chain, and open a new frontier. Even after the frontier officially closed in 1890, the nation retained more physical and social mobility than other societies. While historians debate the importance of Turner's thesis, they still discuss it.

The American bent for technological advance shows a similar pattern. Typically, Americans find new technologies and turn them into innovations that open up new unoccupied territories—they take covered wagon technologies into new technology frontiers. Information technology is a prime example. Before computing arrived, there was nothing comparable: there were no mainframes, desktops, or Internet before Americans embarked on this innovation journey. IT landed in a relatively open technological frontier.

This has been an important capability for the United States. Growth economics has made it clear that technological and related innovation is the predominant driver of growth.[2] The ability to land in new technological open fields has enabled the US economy to dominate nearly all the major Kondratiev waves of worldwide innovation since the mid-19th century.[3] Information technology and biotech are the newest chapters in this continuing story.

While the United States has been successful at standing up technologies in open fields to form new complex technology sectors, it has not been as good at taking its covered wagons back east. It finds it hard to go back over the mountains to bring innovation into the already occupied territory of established, complex legacy technology sectors. In typical American fashion, it would rather move on than move back. Americans find it easier to launch biotechnology than go back and fix the healthcare delivery system.

Of course, the story is more complicated than Turner's frontier thesis about American culture. It's hard to reverse the covered wagons and go back to occupied territory. Over time, established technology sectors develop characteristics that resist change. The underlying technologies themselves become cost-effective and the phenomenon of "lock-in" sets in. Firms go through Darwinian evolution; the leading technological competitors survive, expand, and become adept at fending off new entrants. They build massive infrastructure that is resistant to competitive models, and they form alliances with government to obtain subsidies, typically through the tax system, to tilt the playing field toward their model.

In other words, legacy sectors, often themselves the result of earlier waves of innovation, erect a technological/economic/political/social paradigm that is very difficult to unseat;[4] they plant a series of sophisticated minefields to protect their model and resist its disruption. This pattern applies to highly complex sectors of the economy where technologies are a factor; examples are energy, healthcare delivery, transport, construction and physical infrastructure, education, and agriculture. Legacy sectors also have their own infrastructure, and are supported by established technologies, economic models, public policies, public expectations, and patterns of technical expertise and training. Each of these sectors is defended by its own such paradigm.[5]

To be sure, the United States is not the only nation to experience the economic and political barriers protecting complex established legacy sectors. Japan's economy would be stronger if it could bring more IT-driven retail efficiencies to a nation of small shops or to pursue larger scale agriculture, not simply small family farms. We have examined some of the legacy barriers in the German, French, Russian, Chinese, and Indian economies. The frontier thesis aside, innovation in these established, complex legacy sectors becomes even more difficult once technological lock-in has set in.

THE UNIFYING FRAMEWORK FOR ANALYZING THE DUAL PROBLEMS OF LEGACY SECTORS AND JOBLESS INNOVATION

To aid the reader, we offer a systematic statement of the conceptual framework that underlies the analysis and the findings that we have set forth and their accompanying policy recommendations. This exposition is deliberately spare and condensed, since each of the ideas it sets forth is documented and covered in detail in earlier chapters and each of the concepts we have introduced is defined in the glossary that follows this chapter.

Successful innovation requires both a change agent—an actor or combination of actors who see the innovation from idea through to implementation—and an enabling (or at least a non*dis*abling) context of external factors that affect the speed and direction of innovation. In the United States, we tend to take this enabling environment for granted and to concentrate our attention on the nature of the change agent and the difficulties faced by particular breakthrough innovations. This leads to a special focus on the "front end" of the innovation system: the institutions, policies, and financial arrangements specifically concerned with research and related innovation, especially those that encourage and support basic research and its translation into breakthrough innovation.

In the legacy sectors that are the focus of this book, however, it is the innovation context that is critical. Legacy sectors are found in diverse parts of the American economy: energy, agriculture, construction, health services delivery, education, transportation, manufacturing, and the military, to name only those explored in this book. Their characteristics are detailed in chapter 5. They share common structural obstacles that have prevented innovations from disrupting long-standing and strongly entrenched paradigms that span economics, established technologies, politics, law, culture, and even popular psychology, and are staunchly defended by vested interests that profit from the existing structure. "Sustaining" innovations consistent with this paradigm—improvements in coal combustion, say, or in fossil-fuel-based electricity generation—face no special problems over and above those that confront all innovations. But innovations that run counter to the paradigm are a different story.

We turn first to the nature of this paradigm, and then turn to the requirements for innovation in affected legacy sectors. The features common to the obstacles to innovation in legacy sectors include such market imperfections as *network economies, economies of scale, lumpiness, nonappropriability (split incentives)*, the need for *collective action*, and *government regulation or institutional structure*. These are explained in detail in chapter 5.

All innovations benefit from market imperfections like the protection of intellectual property and other first-mover advantages, but face obstacles as a result of a variety of market imperfections, such as nonappropriability due to "leakage" of technology by such means as theft or evasion of IP, departure of key personnel, and so on. Innovations that seek to disrupt legacy sectors, in contrast, face numerous additional obstacles, which reinforce a form of technological lock-in analogous to the familiar QWERTY effect at the level of individual technologies, or to the dominant design at the level of the product. These obstacles not only hinder the implementation of new technology, but also discourage research and development, since neither prospective researchers nor possible funders of technological development foresee profitable applications for their ideas.

This is not a problem as long as the older technology, and the paradigm that supports it, provide satisfactory results. The difficulty arises when new requirements arise that were not important when the old paradigm evolved, as for example "externalities" like safety, reliability, job creation, security, or environmental sustainability. These objectives may not be well aligned with the incentives to producers that are inherent in the old paradigm, which after all evolved under quite different circumstances. To return to the title metaphor of this chapter, disruptive innovators in legacy sectors must therefore "drive covered wagons east," enter "occupied territory," and confront the structural obstacles that hamper innovation in these critically important parts of our economy and that disruptive innovations in other sectors have managed to avoid.

The broad idea of a techno/economic/political/social paradigm that we use in the book is familiar, not only from Thomas Kuhn's work on the role of paradigms in the history of science, but also from the literature on the "Kondratiev cycles" that punctuate successive 50-year periods of the history of technology. In the Kondratiev model, a paradigm based on a new and superior cluster of technologies overcomes the obstacles that favor its predecessor by dint of its technological superiority and the superior returns it offers to investors. The cluster of iron, steam, coal, textiles, and railways, for example, set the tone for industry in the first half of the 19th century; this was succeeded by electricity, chemistry, oil, and mass production by the early 20th. In contrast to the paradigms that characterize successive Kondratiev cycles, the paradigms that support legacy sectors—fossil-fuel-based energy, for example—may survive repeated Kondratiev cycles and repeated challenges from possible alternatives.

This is further complicated if the need for innovation is driven by an externality like environment, in which case a potentially disruptive technology in a legacy sector is likely to be a secondary or discontinuous innovation that must compete at scale and on price more or less from the beginning with well-established technologies that fit in with the old paradigm, as for example in the competition between wind energy and fossil fuels. In the best case, potentially disruptive technologies may be able to establish themselves in market niches where difficulties can be ironed out and economies of scale can begin to be achieved—as has begun to happen, for example, with solar photovoltaics, LEDs, and advanced battery technologies. Even when this is possible, however, the expansion of the new technology to full scale is likely to involve major difficulties as long as the incentives of producers are out of line with those of the larger society.

The upshot is that, contrary to the experience with previous Kondratiev cycles, the obstacles to innovation in many present-day legacy sectors are so well defended and of such long standing that it is unlikely that they will be overcome simply by virtue of the superiority of a technology or a new Kondratiev cluster. Besides, the need for innovation in these sectors often arises, not only from market forces, but also from "externalities" like environmental sustainability. For this reason, it is unlikely that technological advance, taken by itself, will be sufficient to disrupt existing paradigms. The obstacles that it faces are too strong to be overcome solely by the support to research and development that constitutes the major American instrument for the encouragement of innovation.

In sum, while support to research, development, and innovation is still essential, policies that align the incentives of producers with larger social objectives and functional needs will also be needed if disruptive innovation in legacy sectors is to occur. There must be both a reasonably enabling innovation environment and a supply of innovative ideas ready for implementation—or at least ready for development and scale-up—once efforts to overcome the obstacles to innovation are seriously underway. Moreover, change agents must be ready to think through and facilitate not only research and development, but the entire innovation process, up to and including market launch, together with any policy or other measures needed to level the playing field vis-à-vis incumbent technology.

INNOVATION MODELS AND CHANGE AGENTS FOR LEGACY SECTORS

This brings us to the requirements for the change agents that are needed to develop innovations for legacy sectors and to bring them to scale when conditions are ripe. We first distinguish five models that describe different dynamics of the origin of innovation, depending on the nature of the driving force and the institutional form of the change agent. Although innovation can result from a complex interaction of any or all of these five, some innovations can be adequately described using only one of them. Any of these models can be used as the basis for interventions intended to stimulate innovation in legacy sectors if they are combined with appropriate policy and institutional change.

Broadly speaking, the two basic drivers of innovation are technology push and market pull—or to further oversimplify, the supply of science and technology and the market demand for improved technology. Both supply and demand are necessary if innovations are to be introduced into legacy sectors, but neither will be effective without substantial intervention from government or some other entity that is not motivated primarily by private profit.

The "induced" innovation model describes the origin of innovations developed in response to market forces, and applies to most secondary and incremental innovations. In this case, the change agents are entrepreneurs or firms who recognize a market need and develop new technology or put together existing technologies in such a way as to satisfy that need. As we have seen, induced innovation will not work by itself for disruptive innovations in legacy sectors, which are after all defined by the fact that the incentives for producers in the private sector—and hence also for prospective researchers there—are not aligned with new, broader objectives, such as environmental sustainability or improved safety or reliability. These incentives must change if market forces are to lead to the needed innovations.

The next three models of the dynamics of innovation apply to innovations that emerge from "technology push": the increase in scientific understanding and the march of technological progress. These variants result from the institutional separation between the sources of scientific and technological advance, on the one hand, and the firms that translate these advances into practical and marketable products, on the other. The former originate primarily in university, government, or industrial laboratories or from the work of inventors. The result of this separation is that the supply and demand for improved technology do not always meet on their own, but may require either a sort of midwifery, or else a unified change agent that oversees and orchestrates the entire innovation process.

In the first "technology push" model, the "pipeline" model, researchers introduce a technological advance, which is picked up and commercialized over time by the private sector with financing by private capital markets and without outside intervention. The change agent, then, is a composite of the researchers and the companies that commercialize their ideas. As in the pure induced innovation model, interventions based on the pipeline model can be effective in legacy sectors only if they are accompanied by substantial efforts to overcome structural obstacles and are likely to be an inadequate response even if such measures are in place. This is a particularly important point in view of the importance of this model as the underpinning of most of US policy for science, technology, and innovation.

The next three models are identified and defined for the first time in this book. The second technology-push model, "extended pipeline," describes processes that can both anticipate likely obstacles to innovation in legacy sectors and provide alternatives to existing dominant technologies. In this model, one introduced by the defense innovation system, the federal role for the technology push reaches further down the pipeline to cover the entire innovation process from R & D all the way to the actual implementation of the technology. Here the change agent is the Defense Department itself. Other federal agencies and mechanisms, such as DARPA and the Small Business Innovation Research (SBIR) program, have been gradually extending their reach into this domain as well.

The third technology-push model, "manufacturing-led" innovation, focuses on what can be a highly innovative stage: production and related processes, particularly for the initial production of a new technology. This is where the technological idea is translated into an actual product that can enter a market, often involving creativity in both science and engineering. The point here is that the innovation doesn't occur only at the research stage but also at the production stage, which is a critical phase for both technology push and demand pull.

This model is particularly important to the prospects for restoring US capability to innovate, as we have discussed in chapters 4 and 13. Here the historic change agents have been larger corporations, which have supported an industrial ecosystem from which start-ups or small and midsize firms have also benefited. Innovation by this dynamic shows signs of shifting to the Far East, a trend that has given rise to a widespread concern that the offshoring of manufacturing by US start-ups and multinational corporations may create a fault line between development and engineering and in this way lead to a loss of US capacity for manufacturing-led competitiveness and hence to a loss of technological competitiveness. We shall return to this question in the next section of this chapter.

The "innovation organization" model, defined in chapter 11, is the broadest of the five. It approaches the challenge of innovation as a system and focuses on linkage institutions within public and private sectors that can facilitate innovation by bridging the institutional gap between researcher and implementer. It is particularly appropriate to the challenges of legacy sectors; in chapter 13, we have proposed that the United States use the innovation organization model to strengthen the manufacturing ecosystem.

While the other four models describe existing approaches now in use to demand pull and technology push, the "innovation organization" model is new and more encompassing; it includes the system of public and private institutions and mechanisms that implement an innovation, the linkages between them, and the management of that innovation process. It also requires consideration of the institutional and individual change agents that are essential to the enabling of transformation. It thus involves a strategic approach across the innovation system and reaches into the broader innovation environment, in this way building on and encompassing the other four models. In sum, the application of the innovation organization model involves strategies both to overcome the obstacles by which legacy sectors can limit innovation and to support the R & D that can supplant them.

INNOVATION CONTEXTS AND INNOVATION ENVIRONMENTS

The paradigms that characterize legacy sectors in the US economy are special cases of the broader concept of the innovation *context*, a new concept that we define as the sum of the political, economic, legal, and cultural factors that affect the speed and direction of innovation. This context may either encourage innovation or hinder it or both, whether or not it is intended to do so. This complements the more familiar concept of the *national innovation system*, which is defined as the sum of the institutions, programs, policies, and funding arrangements whose specific purpose is to support and encourage research, innovation, and the development of technological capacity. We define the sum of the national innovation *system* and the national innovation *context* as constituting the national *environment* for innovation, another new concept.

In nearly all countries, the *national* innovation system is closely integrated with a globalized *international* innovation system. Besides multinational corporations, which carry out over half of the world's research and development (largely development), the international innovation system encompasses the international patent system, international flows of technology and capital equipment, the international transfer of technology via direct foreign investments, international venture capital, international distance learning and exchanges of students and faculty, international trade in technical services, international collaboration in research and development, international knowledge and information flows via the wide variety of ethnic diasporas, and the broader international flow of information via the Internet and technical publications of all kinds. A major goal of most national innovation systems is to increase the benefits a country gains from participation in this international innovation system, in large part by increasing its participation in the more advanced and more profitable links in global value chains and value networks.

The structural obstacles to innovation in US manufacturing are of special importance because they threaten to undermine the United States' traditional comparative advantage in product innovation. Manufacturing differs from the other legacy sectors explored in this book in that its legacy status is in part the product of the globalization of innovation via the international innovation system. As we have seen, the gap between research in government and university laboratories, on the one hand, and product development and manufacturing in multinational corporations, on the other, has created an "engineering fault line" across which manufacturing jobs have been exported, largely to China and the Far East, in response to the growing markets and increasing engineering, production, and other technical capabilities in that region. This has led to the offshoring of a once robust "manufacturing ecosystem" (or manufacturing value network), which is no longer available to support small and medium-sized manufacturers in the United States, preventing them from expanding and fulfilling their historic role as a source of employment in both manufacturing and related industries.

Whereas the US economy has historically been based on "innovate here, produce here"—at least for the first years that a new product is on the market—the offshoring of manufacturing jobs, even for the latest products, has given rise to a pattern of "jobless innovation." This pattern of "innovate here, produce there" threatens to lead in turn to a new pattern of "produce there, innovate there"—that is, to the offshoring of the innovation process itself. Since technological innovation is the dominant factor in economic growth, this has important implications for innovation-driven job growth in the United States.

International Ramifications

The US national innovation environment is on balance strongly encouraging to innovation. The structural obstacles we have discussed in the US economy, although widespread, are found at the sectoral level. In smaller open economies, like those of Scandinavia, even sectoral obstacles are unusual. In many larger countries, however, the major structural obstacles occur at the national level. In these countries, even major initiatives undertaken by the national innovation system have so far been insufficient to overcome the obstacles thrown up by the broader national context, so that the overall national environment is on balance hostile to the kind of new product innovation in which the United States has excelled. On the other hand, the national innovation environments in these countries are well suited to innovation in other areas: Germany in manufacturing, France in infrastructure, China in the scaling up of manufacturing processes, and India in IT services and software.

The framework that we have developed has important international implications. We have already seen how the international innovation system has given rise to an "engineering fault line" across which manufacturing jobs have been exported. A second implication arises from the fact that most developing countries are risk-averse "technology takers," in the sense that they typically import technology from world markets and use it with at most relatively minor adaptation to local circumstances. (In this, the emerging economies of China and India are becoming important exceptions.) This imported technology may be directly applicable to local needs—cars, buses, computers, cell phones, medical equipment, and cures for at least some tropical diseases are examples. They do occasionally give rise to important local innovations, like the mobile finance that has transformed much of African commerce and is even being transported into the Americas. But imported technology (high-tech hospitals, for example) may also be inappropriate to local needs—and besides may reflect constraints imposed by paradigms that are inappropriate even to the exporting country.

Two trends mitigate this picture from the point of view of developing countries. First, as we have seen, different technology-exporting countries display different strengths and suffer from problems created by different paradigms. For this reason, their exports reflect different strengths and different constraints, a fact that widens the choices available to technology importers. Second, China and India have emerged as "innovative developing countries." China in particular has developed world-class capabilities at designing and manufacturing lower-cost versions of standard consumer goods and capital equipment, so as to be able to meet the needs of Asian and African consumers as well as those of its own huge domestic market—a partial solution to the old issue of "appropriate technology."

Policy Solutions

The end result, from both the US and the international perspective, is that measures to help overcome the structural obstacles to innovation in entrenched legacy sectors require efforts to deal with foreseeable problems in both policy and technology well before they are encountered. On the policy side, this means willingness to confront serious political and institutional issues that block innovation. On the technical side, it means attention to the entire innovation process—beginning with strong support to the "front end" of research, development, and prototyping (which is now threatened by budget cuts) but also extending to the "back end" of manufacturing and market development, which are not regarded as subjects for innovation in an American outlook that is very much oriented to front-end research and development. On the contrary, the obstacles in these sectors are usually too strong to be overcome simply by the support to R & D that constitutes the major American instrument for the encouragement of innovation.

This new approach to innovation in legacy sectors thus requires attention to both technology and policy. Linkage organizations and the kind of integrated innovation management across sectors encompassed in the "innovation organization" model are likely to be needed in order to foresee and help overcome both the technical and the structural obstacles at all stages of the innovation process. On the technical side, research and development on new technology and its scientific underpinnings are essential to demonstrate that alternative and even transformative approaches to existing technologies are technically and economically feasible. On the policy side, policies are needed that reflect new requirements and that realign the incentives of producers and the activities of the national innovation system with the goals of the larger society. These policies may encounter strong resistance from vested interests that profit from the structural obstacles and market imperfections that defend the present paradigm.

Improving the innovation system to address legacy sectors is a major challenge. It requires a concerted approach based on a combination of the first four innovation models discussed above, but has a particular emphasis on the fifth, innovation organization, a model that encompasses and integrates the other four. While the imperfections due to particular legacy sector characteristics can be addressed separately, the complexity of the challenge demands this more unified approach. We propose a menu of overall policy prescriptions common across legacy sectors, delineating a five-step process.

Here we draw on the analysis of particular legacy sectors in chapters 6 through 8. Except in those cases (such as aspects of buildings and health delivery) in which policy change is likely to induce the necessary innovations without further public-sector intervention, we should begin by focusing on strengthening the front end of the innovation system—the first step—in order to initiate a transformative innovation and in this way to show that greatly superior alternatives to legacy technologies are indeed possible.

We identified a series of fundamental rules for optimal organization of the front end of innovation, particularly in legacy sectors. These include "form critical innovation institutions," apply a "connected science and technology" approach, use the "island/bridge model" to protect the innovation group from bureaucracies but link it to the decision-makers who can help bridge their results into implementation, "build a thinking community" to gather the best ideas from many collaborators, and "link technologists to operators" so that the direction the innovation takes is informed by its potential users. But more is needed than an improved front-end system; the challenge of innovation in legacy sectors is forbidding enough that committed institutional and individual change agents are required to press innovation through from idea to implementation.

The second step requires identification of the launch pathways by which emerging innovations can enter a sector and the technologies can be fitted to an optimal path. In a third step, supportive governmental policy incentives, regulations or private-sector supports appropriate to the particular launch pathway can then be developed and applied. The fourth step requires looking at the overall innovation system for a technology sector, and an analysis of possible gaps at each innovation stage. The fifth step responds to the analysis: develop the institutional fixes and mechanisms to fill the gaps. Among those gaps will be the need to identify change agents as well as innovation-forcing mechanisms. Identification of these steps amounts to an effort to get away from the assumption that innovation occurs in a mysterious "black box" and to develop a practical approach for nurturing and implementing innovation in legacy sectors.

Legacy sectors like those addressed in chapters 6 through 8 of this book—energy, the long-distance electric grid, industrial agriculture, transportation, manufacturing, health delivery, higher education, and part of the military—pose a broad challenge to innovation policy, both in the United States and abroad. These sectors share structural obstacles to innovation that have not received adequate attention from the makers of US science and technology policies, and have serious implications for the US economy and for the economies of virtually all advanced economies. A better understanding of these common features on the part of policymakers—and on the part of the scientific and technological community and the general public—should make it easier to develop a unified approach, based on our proposed five-step process for addressing structural obstacles in these and other legacy sectors.

What's New Here?

The book, to summarize the key points here, has undertaken an ambitious innovation policy agenda. It creates a new, unified, systematic approach to innovation policy, focused on overcoming two deep problems in the US innovation system: expanding economic growth and raising the rate of creation of well-paying jobs.

First, it introduces, defines, and develops the new concept of disruption-resistant *legacy sectors* and sets forth a conceptual framework with which to address this neglected problem. Because US innovation policy historically has focused on "the next new thing," it has missed "the next old thing." In other words, because US innovation is organized around innovation in frontier sectors, it is missing a major potential area for introducing needed disruptive innovations in the legacy sectors that constitute most of the economy. In this way, it misses a chance to accelerate economic growth and to address pressing environmental and other policy problems.

Second, the book extends previous theories drawn from across several disciplines to establish a new framework for understanding how these legacy sectors resist disruptive innovation: the *technological/economic/political/social paradigm*. We identify features common to legacy sectors and use them to create a set of tools for analyzing legacy sectors. We then apply these tools to a series of such sectors in the US economy, including energy, the electric grid, construction, auto and air transport, manufacturing, higher education, healthcare delivery, and industrial agriculture. We also use them to derive new insights into the process of disruptive innovation in the military.

Third, we use this new analytical toolset to explain legacy characteristics in *national innovation environments* (another new term that encompasses both the well-established idea of *innovation systems* and a new concept of *innovation contexts*) in six countries of Asia and Europe. These innovation environments have a major effect on *enabling and disabling innovation* in those countries. In this way, our toolset helps not only to explain the patterns of innovation in a series of major economic sectors but also to understand the strengths and weaknesses of national innovation environments as well. This crystallizes an idea that has received only passing mention in most of the literature in the field of innovation policy.

Fourth, the book identifies manufacturing as a major legacy sector; using the legacy paradigm framework makes it possible to understand manufacturing in new ways. It further shows that manufacturing is a critical driver of the innovation process. This is especially important in view of the major emphasis that advanced manufacturing is now receiving in US policy. By failing to consider measures to counter the tendency of US-based companies to send production offshore, particularly measures consistent with the traditional American emphasis on free markets and free trade, the United States is giving up important parts of its innovation capacity. The book shows that manufacturing is critical to an innovation system, and sets forth a new vocabulary for describing the consequences of the near-exclusive focus on R & D that has been the basis of US innovation policy. "Innovate here, produce here," which we also call *full-spectrum innovation*, in which the United States took gains from its strong innovation environment at every stage, is being replaced by "innovate here, produce there." This threatens to create a problem of *jobless innovation*, and in turn threatens to lead to "produce there, innovate there." The book goes on to identify strategies to bolster advanced manufacturing.

Fifth, the book adds to previous models of the dynamics of innovation, identifying three new drivers, and in this way sets the stage for its recommendations on how to introduce innovation into legacy sectors. Traditional theory ascribes innovation either to a *pipeline model* in which *technology push* results from federally supported basic research, or to an *induced model* in which new products emerge largely from incremental advances by industry to meet a *market pull*. These do not adequately describe the full dynamics of innovation, so we add three additional drivers: the *extended pipeline model* in which innovations are nurtured not just from research but all the way to market launch, the *manufacturing-led model* for innovations that emerge through creative enhancements in engineering and manufacturing processes, and the *innovation organization model* in which innovation requires the creation of linkages between innovation institutions and measures to address the structural obstacles that block disruptive innovation in legacy sectors. This fifth model incorporates and integrates the other four models so as to provide the basis for measures to overcome the *technology lock-in* imposed by legacy paradigms.

Sixth, the book introduces a new vocabulary to fill in the interstices between existing theories. In addition to the concepts summarized in the previous paragraphs, these include *"full spectrum" innovation* (innovation that stems not only from support to R & D, but also to all stages of the innovation process), *"elephant" technology* (technology subject to the market imperfection of lumpiness), *"inducible" technology* (technology that is likely to be rapidly developed and implemented in response to a change in markets or incentives), *innovation value chain* (the value chain that links the actors involved in all the stages of innovation from research and ideation to final production), and *"normal" innovations* (innovations that do not need be introduced into a legacy sector and hence do not face the structural obstacles inherent in its paradigm). Many other new terms are listed in the glossary.

Finally, the book defines a five-step process for addressing the deep policy challenge of bringing innovation to legacy sectors through interventions based on the *innovation organization* model. It argues that successful innovation in legacy sectors requires a strategic and systems approach to institutions and policies that stimulate research and innovation, as well as policy measures that address the structural obstacles to innovation in these sectors. It also requires *change agents*—actors, institutional and individual, who overcome all obstacles and see the innovation through from idea to implementation, and equally important, an *enabling* economic, political, legal, and cultural *innovation context*.

THE ISSUE OF THE PIPELINE MODEL

It is thus urgent that we re-examine the pipeline model that has dominated American thinking for decades, even though policies based on this model have led to American world dominance in reaping the benefits of innovation. We can no longer assume that basic research alone leads inevitably to innovation, economic growth, and high-paying jobs. We need a broader understanding and a unified approach to the problems of legacy sectors and jobless unemployment, based on the principle that attention is needed to all stages of the innovative process and to both technological and structural obstacles.

Books and papers in the innovation literature bemoan the deficiencies of the pipeline model, and many of them make efforts to introduce concepts to fill in one or another of its deficiencies. Some deal with the obstacles inherent in the pipeline process, most notably the "valley of death" between research and late-stage development. Others, like the induced innovation model, describe external market forces that affect the direction of innovation. Still others describe the "supply side" institutions needed to develop innovations among the actors in the innovation system.

In grappling with the problem of introducing innovation into legacy sectors, we have built on these efforts to develop a unifying conceptual framework for describing both the internal and external forces that affect the speed and direction of innovation, at both the national and international levels. Here we have stood on the shoulders of pioneers like Thomas Kuhn, Vannevar Bush, Chris Freeman, Richard Nelson, Carlota Perez, Vernon Ruttan, Suzanne Berger, and Clayton Christensen, all of whom are amply credited in our text and notes.

Even so, grappling with legacy sectors has turned out to be a much larger task than we originally anticipated; much of this is new territory and has required erecting a new idea framework. We have found it necessary to define more than 20 terms and concepts, many of which are enumerated above, that we believe to be new to the innovation literature, and to expand a number of others beyond their original meanings. Many of these, like "extended pipeline," fill in gaps between concepts already developed elsewhere in the literature; still others, like "innovation environment" and "innovation organization," provide a superstructure for better understanding of the international and contextual influences on innovation. These terms were developed to try to move beyond the traditional U.S. understanding of innovation as tied to the pipeline model, toward a broader understanding of the elements of innovation organization needed to accelerate innovation in legacy sectors.

THE POLITICS OF INNOVATION ORGANIZATION

We turn now briefly to the domestic politics of this "innovation organization" model. Grounding innovation policy on a basis broader than the pipeline model will not be an easy task. From the strictly political point of view, the pipeline model is a relatively easy sell. It fits with public experience with the role of science in winning World War II and the Cold War, in defeating numerous infectious diseases, and in powering the information revolution. This model undergirds US front-end innovation strength and is supported by a solid constituency of researchers, universities, federally funded laboratories, federal agencies, and research-oriented industries. However, the recent deep cuts in support to research scheduled to endure for a decade due to budget sequestration show that this constituency is far from all-powerful. These cuts over time will constitute a major danger to the traditional base of US technological competitiveness. So this foundational model, for the first time since it was created after World War II, is starting to come under attack.[6]

There are long-standing extensions to the pipeline model in US practice: federal support to applied and translational research in defense, as discussed, and also in aerospace, healthcare, and agriculture, all of which also benefit from strong political support. But this support has historically not extended to nondefense manufacturing, which as we have seen is a legacy sector in need of public support in order to restore a fading industrial ecosystem. And despite these exceptions, the principle that government supports basic research and leaves commercialization to private industry is firmly lodged in public consciousness.

Applying the innovation organization model to legacy sectors, as we have recommended in a range of cases, will require an active role for government in supporting innovation and will call attention to major political issues: the size and role of government, the desirability of collaborations between government and private industry, and the use of incentives and regulation to achieve societal objectives. Since public funding now appears to be declining for the long-standing pipeline model, it will be doubly difficult to expand public support to the extended pipeline, manufacturing-led, and innovation organization models.

But failing to confront these issues incurs costs of its own: a major limitation on our ability to address problems that afflict major portions of our economy: the problems of technological competitiveness and jobless innovation that we have set forth at the beginning of this book, not to mention the issues of environment, climate, public health, and security that we have encountered along the way. These problems are not subject to purely technological fixes but require attention both to research and to development, on the one hand, and to proactive consideration of a range of measures of policy and innovation organization that are needed to anticipate and deal with structural obstacles, on the other. Given this need, could ways be found to complement and expand beyond measures based on our front-end-focused, pipeline model?

Americans and their political representatives are insufficiently aware of the fact that that, in addition to our strong front-end system, our favorable innovative context, together with the entrepreneurial role of the government in developing technology in collaboration with industry, lies at the core of the technological strength of our economy. Both our economic competitiveness and our military and geopolitical power are derived from this technological strength.

In other words, there is little public understanding of how the US innovation system actually works. Nor do the practical realities behind our technological competitiveness receive much attention in political discussion. This problem is further reinforced by a negative economic and policy doctrine dating from the 1920s[7] that, with the well-defined exceptions of national security, health, space, and agriculture, major public support to innovation beyond the research stage is intrinsically unworkable or constitutes governmental interference in private-sector roles or unacceptable "corporate welfare."

Policies based on the pipeline model have yielded major gains[8] and remain foundational for the overall US innovation system, but success of the pipeline model is only part of a larger story of why innovation is deserving of support. And because of the rise in healthcare costs and because congressional forces give priority to protecting tax and entitlement expenditures favored by party ideologies and constituencies, federal research is slipping into a lower priority.

IDEAS MATTER

Ideas matter here. The dominant narrative of the pipeline model of innovation, with its long history in the scientific community, has obscured the collaboration between government, the academy, and industry that has given rise to many of our most important technological innovations, of which the Internet is only one of the most recent examples. As we have seen, the lack of understanding about how research and innovation work makes it more difficult to mount programs to develop and implement disruptive technologies in legacy sectors, despite their potential importance to US economic growth and employment, as well as to other societal objectives like environment, public health, and security, because to stimulate the development and implementation of these technologies would require attention to the entire innovation process and to the broader structural legacy obstacles that it must overcome.

The neglect of the complexities of the innovation process thus strikes at the heart of American technological competitiveness and hence at the heart of its economic, military, and geopolitical power. This way of thinking, abetted by vested interests that benefit from existing paradigms, stands in the way of any effort to address legacy sectors with reforms that are necessary to competitiveness, sustainability, and future economic growth. The problems are serious enough that it may be possible to overcome the legacy thinking in the political system.

As we have seen, in legacy sectors government can be both part of the problem and part of the solution. But there is no avoiding an active role for government, often in collaboration with industry, if critical issues of innovation are to be addressed. If we rely on technology push alone to solve these problems, we deny ourselves at least half of the policy instruments we need. This is a luxury we can no longer afford.

To return to the two deep issues set out at the beginning of this book, since economic growth is predominantly driven by technological and related innovation, the United States needs to move beyond its narrow focus on innovation in frontier sectors if it is to achieve a more robust growth rate. If it could introduce further innovation into the substantial portion of the economy that can be characterized as legacy sectors, this would begin to create new growth opportunities. As set forth in chapter 1, the legacy sectors reviewed in this book alone constitute 30% of US GDP, and other sectors that fall into the legacy category readily bring the total towards two-thirds of GDP. The dimensions of this problems require developing theory and policy for understanding and overcoming the barriers to innovation that legacy sectors erect through the technological/economic/political/social paradigms we have tried to delineate.

There is a second major step that needs to be undertaken. Because the United States has increasingly followed an "innovate here, produce there" model, it has distributed outside the US economy much of the gains from its innovation capability. To more fully realize these gains, it needs to rebuild the "manufacturing led" aspects of its innovation system. If it does not do so, it will continue to miss many of the gains that it could otherwise reap from its strong front-end-oriented innovation system.

Manufacturing is not only a significant stage in the innovation process. It is also, as discussed in chapters 4 and 6, a legacy sector with resistance to innovation. The limited ability of the manufacturing sector, especially small and midsize firms, to innovate and in this way to achieve fuller gains from innovation is a root cause of the pattern of "jobless innovation" into which the United States has fallen. It is thus critically important to address the legacy barriers hampering the manufacturing sector and thus to restore it and its innovative capacity, an approach that we discuss in some detail in chapter 13. Addressing the problems of legacy sectors, and especially those of the manufacturing sector, requires thinking beyond the pipeline model.

Turning technology-laden covered wagons east is difficult but essential; the United States needs to introduce higher growth into legacy sectors. As a core feature in that effort, it is urgent that it re-examine and extend the pipeline model that has dominated American thinking for decades, even though it has led to American world dominance in reaping the benefits of innovation. We can no longer assume that basic research alone leads inevitably to innovation, economic growth, and high-paying jobs. We need a broader understanding and a unified, strategic approach to the problems of legacy sectors and jobless innovation, based on the application of an "innovation organization" model. And we must apply the principle that attention is needed to all stages of the innovative process and to both technological and structural obstacles to innovation. Much is at stake.

List of Abbreviations

ABET	Accreditation Board for Engineering and Technology
ACTD	Advanced Concept Technology Demonstration
AMP	Advanced Manufacturing Partnership
ATACMS	Army Tactical Missile Systems
ARPA	Advanced Research Projects Agency
ARPA-E	Advanced Research Projects Agency - Energy
BARDA	Biomedical Advanced Research and Development Authority
BASIC	Beginner's All-Purpose Symbolic Instruction Code
BCE	Battlefield Control Element
BEA	Bureau of Economic Analysis
BTU	British thermal unit
CIA	Central Intelligence Agency
CCS	carbon capture and sequestration
CGIAR	Consultative Group on International Agricultural Research
CNRS	National Center of Scientific Research (France)
CSIR	Council of Scientific and Industrial Research
DARPA	Defense Advanced Research Projects Agency
DDR&E	Director, Defense Research and Engineering
DOD	Department of Defense
DOE	Department of Energy
EDA	Economic Development Administration
EPRI	Energy Power Research Institute
EHR	electronic health records
ENA	École nationale d'administration
ENS	École normale supérieure
FDA	Food and Drug Administration
FERC	Federal Energy Regulatory Commission
FFRDC	federally funded research-and-development center
GDP	gross domestic product
GM	genetically modified
GNP	gross national product
GPR	ground-penetrating radar
GPS	Global Positioning System
HRJ	hydrotreated renewable jet [fuel]
IARPA	Intelligence Advanced Research Projects Activity
IIS	international innovation system
IIT	Indian Institutes of Technology
IT	information technology

INS	inertial navigation system
IP	intellectual property
IPO	initial public offering
ITIF	Information Technology and Innovation Foundation
ITS	intelligent transportation systems
JSTARS	joint surveillance and target attack radar system
LDC	less developed country
LEDs	light-emitting diodes
LIDAR	light detection and ranging
MOOC	massive open online course
MNC	multinational corporation
MS-DOS	Microsoft Disk Operating System
NASA	National Aeronautics and Space Administration
NERC	North American Electric Reliability Corporation
NIH	National Institutes of Health
NIS	national innovation system
NIST	National Institute of Standards and Technology
NSF	National Science Foundation
OECD	Organization for Economic Co-operation and Development
OEM	original equipment manufacturer
PARC	Palo Alto Research Center
PV	photovoltaic
R & D	research and development
RAF	Royal Air Force
RAM	random-access memory
RFID	radio-frequency identification
RMA	Revolution in Military Affairs
RPV	remotely piloted vehicle
SBA	Small Business Administration
SBIC	Small Business Investment Company
SBIR	Small Business Innovation Research
SME	small and midsize enterprise
STEM	science, technology, engineering, and mathematics
STS	science, technology, and society
TRIPS	Trade Related Aspects of Intellectual Property Rights
UAV	unmanned aerial vehicle
USDA	US Department of Agriculture
VA	US Department of Veterans Affairs (formerly the Veterans Administration)
VC	venture capital
WTO	World Trade Organization

Notes

CHAPTER 1

1. Bureau of Economic Analysis (BEA), Value Added by Industry Group by Percentage of GDP (table 5a) (2013), http://www.bea.gov/newsreleases/industry/gdpindustry/gdpindnewsrelease.htm.

2. Carl Dahlman, *World under Pressure* (Stanford, CA: Stanford University Press, 2012), chapters 3 and 5; National Science Board, *Science and Engineering Indicators 2014* (Washington, DC: National Science Foundation, 2014), 4-25-4-30.

3. Barry Jaruzelski and Kevin Dehoff, Beyond Borders: The Global Innovation 1000, *Strategy & Business* 53 (Winter 2008), 9, http://www.strategyand.pwc.com/media/file/Beyond-Borders-Global-Innovation-1000.pdf.

4. Suzanne Berger and the MIT Task Force on Production and Innovation Economy, *Making in America* (Cambridge, MA: MIT Press, 2013).

5. Erik Brynjolfsson and Andrew McAfee, *The Second Machine Age* (New York: W.W. Norton and Company, 2014); Erik Brynjolfsson and Andrew McAfee, *Race against the Machine* (Lexington, MA: Digital Frontier Press, 2011).

6. See, for example, Susan Helper, Timothy Krueger, and Howard Wial, Why Does Manufacturing Matter? Which Manufacturing Matters?, Brookings Institution, Washington, DC, February 7, 2012, 9-10, http://www.brookings.edu/~/media/Files/rc/papers/2012/0222_manufacturing_helper_krueger_wial/0222_manufacturing_helper_krueger_wial.pdf.

7. David Autor, David Dorn, and Gordon Hanson, The China Syndrome: Local Labor Market Effects of Import Competition in the United States, *American Economic Review* 103, no. 6 (2013), 2121-2168, http://economics.mit.edu/files/6613.

8. Thomas Piketty, *Capital in the Twenty-First Century* (Cambridge, MA: Belknap Press of Harvard University Press, 2014).

9. David Autor, Skills, Education and the Rise of Earnings Inequality among the "Other 99 Percent," *Science* 344, no. 6186 (May 23, 2014), 843-851, http://www.sciencemag.org/content/344/6186/843.full; Claudia Goldin and Lawrence Katz, *The Race between Education and Technology* (Cambridge, MA: Harvard University Press, 2008).

10. The concept of the complex sector, as discussed here, is broader than that of complex technology introduced by Robert W. Rycroft and Don E. Kash, Innovation Policy for Complex Technologies, *Issues in Science and Technology*, Fall 1999, http://www.issues.org/16.1/rycroft.htm, and is closer to Christopher Freeman's idea of technology clusters that dominate innovation waves. Christopher Freeman, Innovation and Long Cycles of Economic Development, paper presented at the International Seminar on Innovation and Development in the Industrial Sector, Department of Economics, University of Campinas, São Paulo, Brazil, August 25-27, 1982, http://www.globelicsacademy.net/pdf/JoseCassiolato_2.pdf; Christopher Freeman, John Clark, and Luc Soete, *Unemployment and Technical Innovation* (London: Pinter,

1982). It also has features in common with the idea of a "socio-technical system" as developed by Frank W. Geels, Technological Transitions as Evolutionary Reconfiguration Processes, *Research Policy* 31, nos. 8–9 (Dec. 2002), 1257–1274, although we place more emphasis on the economic and political underpinning of the sectors. The idea of such a sector also has features in common with the idea of "dominant design," introduced by William J. Abernathy and James M. Utterback, Patterns of Innovation in Technology, *Technology Review* 80, no. 7 (1978), 40–47, based on Raymond Vernon's product cycle theory in International Investment and International Trade in the Product Cycle, *Quarterly Journal of Economics* 80 (1966), 190–207. Once such a paradigm has set in, the emphasis shifts away from innovation in the overall system toward component innovation in technologies that can be launched on existing platforms. While Clayton Christensen's concept of disruptive innovation in *The Innovator's Dilemma* (Cambridge, MA: Harvard Business School Press, 1997) tends to focus on particular technologies in particular industrial sectors, the concept of a complex legacy sector here attempts to embrace more broadly major economic sectors, and in chapter 9 we extend a legacy analysis to national innovation systems and contexts.

11. See, for example, Joseph Berk, *Systems Failure Analysis* (Material Park, OH: ASM International, 2009).

12. System-of-systems engineering evolved out of Defense Department applications to integrate networks of new and old systems to meet evolving program requirements. See, for example, Mo Jamshidi, ed., *System of Systems Engineering* (Hoboken, NJ: John Wiley & Sons, 2009).

13. Vernon Ruttan, *Is War Necessary for Economic Growth?* (New York: Oxford University Press, 2006).

14. The Advanced Manufacturing Partnership (AMP) was formed to develop and follow up on the recommendations in President's Council of Advisors on Science and Technology (PCAST), *Ensuring American Leadership in Advanced Manufacturing* (Washington, DC: Executive Office of the President, June 2011), http://www.whitehouse.gov/sites/default/files/microsites/ostp/pcast-advanced-manufacturing-june2011.pdf. See also the second AMP report, PCAST, *Accelerating U.S. Advanced Manufacturing* (Washington, DC: Executive Office of the President, Oct. 2014), http://1.usa.gov/1u4Ibl7.

15. John Alic, Daniel Sarewitz, Charles Weiss, and William Bonvillian, A New Strategy for Energy Innovation, *Nature* 466 (July 15, 2010), 316–317.

16. The term "agent" implies a conscious act; we would not use the term to describe an impersonal change, like a fluctuation or secular change in a market price, that could also induce a technological innovation.

17. William B. Bonvillian, Advanced Manufacturing Policies and Paradigms for Innovation, *Science* 342 (Dec. 6, 2013), 1173–1175.

CHAPTER 2

1. Portions of this material were presented as a paper at the 2011 Atlanta Conference on Science and Innovation Policy, September 15–17, 2011, and posted online with other conference papers through the IEEE.

2. Charles Weiss and William B. Bonvillian, Complex Established "Legacy" Systems: The Technology Revolutions That Do Not Happen, *Innovations* 6, no. 2 (2011), 157–187; William B. Bonvillian and Charles Weiss, Taking Covered Wagons East: A New Innovation Theory for Energy and Other Established Sectors, *Innovations* 4, no. 4 (2009), 289–300. The authors thank the editors of this journal for permission to draw from these articles here.

3. This issue is detailed in chapter 3. See, for example, W. Brian Arthur, Competing Technologies, Increasing Returns, and Lock-in by Historical Events, *Economic Journal* 99, no. 394 (March 1989), 116–131.

4. As detailed in chapter 3, we distinguish between the dominant design of *products*, as defined by James Utterback, *Technological Innovation for a Dynamic Economy* (New York: Pergamon Press, 1979), from the larger paradigm that is the hallmark of the legacy *sector*.

5. This issue is discussed in detail in chapter 3. See generally, Carlotta Perez, *Technological Revolutions and Financial Capital: The Dynamics of Bubbles and Golden Ages* (Cheltenham, UK: Edward Elgar, 2002); Robert D. Atkinson, *The Past and Future of America's Economy: Long Waves of Innovation that Power Cycles of Growth* (Cheltenham, UK: Edward Elgar, 2004).

6. Charles Weiss and William B. Bonvillian, *Structuring an Energy Technology Revolution* (Cambridge, MA: MIT Press, 2009), 6, 29–30, 38.

7. As noted in the preface, the reference is to hypothetical technology pioneers who, having driven their metaphorical covered wagons westward to the new frontier, go back over the mountains to the eastern United States whence they came, to insert their technologies into the legacy sectors they earlier left behind.

8. By public intervention, we mean intervention by any entity not motivated by private profit—that is, government, intergovernmental, or nongovernmental organizations, private foundations, or even individual philanthropists.

9. Bonvillian and Weiss, Taking Covered Wagons East.

10. Weiss and Bonvillian, *Structuring an Energy Technology Revolution*, 34, 37–55.

11. Brian Arthur, Competing Technologies, Increasing Returns and Lock-in by Historical Events.

12. Perez, *Technological Revolutions*.

13. Melissa Schilling, *Strategic Management of Technological Innovation*, 2nd ed. (New York: McGraw-Hill, 2005), 86–87.

14. Kenneth Arrow, Economic Welfare and the Allocation of Resources for Invention, in *The Rate and Direction of Inventive Activity: Economic and Social Factors* (Washington, DC: National Bureau of Economic Research, 1962), 609–626, http://www.nber.org/chapters/c2144.pdf.

15. Lewis Branscomb and Philip Auerswald, *Between Invention and Innovation: An Analysis of Funding for Early-State Technology Development* (NIST GCR 02-841; Washington, DC: NIST, November, 2002), Part I: Early Stage Development, http://www.atp.nist.gov/eao/gcr02-841/contents.htm.

16. Suzanne Berger, *How We Compete: What Companies around the World Are Doing to Make It in Today's Global Economy* (New York: Doubleday Currency, 2005), 59–92, 251–277.

17. Douglas K. Smith and Robert C. Alexander, *Fumbling the Future* (Lincoln, NE: iUniverse 1999); Warren Bennis and Patricia Ward Biederman, *Organizing Genius: The Secrets of Creative Collaboration* (New York: Basic Books, 1997), 63–86. The exception was the laser printer, which Xerox did market.

18. Schilling, *Strategic Management*, 86–97.

19. Vernon Ruttan, *Technology, Growth and Development: An Induced Innovation Perspective* (New York: Oxford University Press, 2001).

20. Geoffrey A. Moore, *Crossing the Chasm: Marketing and Selling Technology Products to Mainstream Customers*, rev. ed. (New York: Harper Business, 1999).

21. Vernon Ruttan, *Is War Necessary for Economic Growth?* (New York: Oxford University Press, 2006); Jonathan Zittrain, *The Future of the Internet and How to Stop It* (New Haven, CT: Yale University Press, 2008).

22. Clayton Christensen, *The Innovator's Dilemma: When New Technologies Cause Great Firms to Fail* (Boston, MA: Harvard Business School Press, 1997).

23. Frederick Betz, *Strategic Technology Management* (New York: McGraw-Hill, 1993), 20–22.

24. Bennis and Biederman, *Organizing Genius*, 96–218.

25. William B. Bonvillian, The Connected Science Model for Innovation: The DARPA Model, in *21st Century Innovation Systems for the U.S. and Japan*, ed. Sadao Nagaoka, Masayuki Kondo, Kenneth Flamm, and Charles Wessner (Washington, DC: National Academies Press, 2009), 206–237, http://books.nap.edu/openbook.php?record_id=12194&page=206.

26. Rick E. Yannuzzi, In-Q-Tel: A New Partnership between the CIA and the Private Sector, *Defense Intelligence Journal* 9, no. 1 (2000), 25–38; Glenn Fong, The CIA in Silicon Valley: In-Q-Tel & the Search for a New Government-Industry Partnership, paper presented at the annual meeting of the International Studies Association, Honolulu, March 5, 2005, http://www.allacademic.com/meta/p71327_index.html.

27. See IARPA program description at http://www.iarpa.gov/.

28. See Biomedical Advanced Research and Development Authority (BARDA) program description at http://www.phe.gov/about/barda/Pages/default.aspx.

29. See Homeland Security Advanced Research Projects Agency (HSARPA), http://www.dhs.gov/st-hsarpa.

30. William B. Bonvillian and Richard Van Atta, ARPA-E and DARPA, Applying the DARPA Model to Energy Innovation, *Journal of Technology Transfer*, October 2011, sections 1, 3, and 4(B); William B. Bonvillian, Will the Search for New Energy Technologies Require a New R&D Mission Agency? *Bridges* 14 (July 2007), http://www.ostina.org/content/view/2297/721/.

31. This argument builds on the paradigm concept used by Perez, *Technological Revolutions*, 15ff.

32. A perverse subsidy as originally defined is a subsidy that encourages behavior contrary to public policy, for example for overgrazing or deforestation. See Norman Myers and Jennifer Kent, *Perverse Subsidies: How Tax Dollars Can Undercut the Environment and the Economy* (Washington, DC: Island Press, 2001). These subsidies are technically market imperfections, since they shift prices, and hence supply and demand, away from what they would be in the absence of the subsidy.

33. These imperfections may also hinder innovations that do not face the full panoply of a legacy sector. Mobile telephony, for example, spread more rapidly in Europe and the Far East than in the United States in part because the early adoption of agreed technical standards facilitated the achievement of network economies. For the same reason, radio frequency identification tags (RFIDs) required industry-wide standards for their acceptance. See, generally, Rob Atkinson, RFID: There's Nothing to Fear Except Fear Itself, speech at the 16th Annual Computers, Freedom and Privacy Conference, May 4, 2006, 3, http://www.itif.org/files/rfid.pdf. Examples of the need for collective action to support innovation are found in such disparate industries as organic agriculture, home building design, and municipal waste collection.

CHAPTER 3

1. We discuss three of these models in detail in Charles Weiss and William B. Bonvillian, *Structuring an Energy Technology Revolution* (Cambridge, MA: MIT Press, 2009), 16–34.

2. Vannevar Bush, *Science: The Endless Frontier* (Washington, DC: Government Printing Office, 1945), http://www.nsf.gov/od/lpa/nsf50/vbush1945.htm.

3. Donald E. Stokes, *Pasteur's Quadrant: Basic Science and Technological Innovation* (Washington, DC: Brookings University Press, 1997), 1–25, 45–89.

4. Robert Buderi, *The Invention That Changed the World* (New York: Simon and Schuster / Touchstone, 1997).

5. National Research Council, Science and Telecommunications Board, *Funding a Revolution, Government Support for Computing Research* (Washington, DC: National Academy Press, 1999), 85–157, chaps. 4, 5; Mitchell Waldrop, *The Dream Machine: J.C.R. Licklider and the Revolution That Made Computing Personal* (New York: Viking, 2001).

6. Vernon W. Ruttan, *Technology Growth and Development: An Induced Innovation Perspective* (New York: Oxford University Press, 2001).

7. Vernon W. Ruttan, *Is War Necessary for Economic Growth? Military Procurement and Technology Development* (New York: Oxford University Press, 2006).

8. William B. Bonvillian, The New Model Innovation Agencies: An Overview, *Science and Public Policy* 41, no. 4 (July 2014), 425–437.

9. William B. Bonvillian, The Connected Science Model for Innovation, in National Research Council, *21st Century Innovation Systems for the U.S. and Japan* (Washington, DC: National Academy Press, 2009), 206–237, http://books.nap.edu/openbook. php?record_id=12194&page=206; Weiss and Bonvillian, *Structuring an Energy Technology Revolution*, 26–28; Richard R. Nelson, *National Systems of Innovation* (New York: Oxford University Press, 1993), 3–21, 505–523.

10. The term "agent" implies, as noted in chapter 1, a conscious act; we would not use the term to describe an impersonal change, like a fluctuation or secular change in a market price, that could also induce a technological innovation.

11. James Womack, Daniel Jones, and Daniel Roos, *The Machine That Changed the World* (New York: Free Press, 1990).

12. Although Vernon Ruttan was a leading theorist of the induced model, in his last book he turned to an exploration of what we call here the extended pipeline model. Ruttan, *Is War Necessary*.

13. See, for example, Dale Jorgenson, U.S. Economic Growth in the Information Age, *Issues in Science and Technology*, Fall 2001, http://www.issues.org/18.1/jorgenson. html (the role of IT and semiconductors in 1990s growth).

14. Lewis M. Branscomb and Philip E. Auerswald, *Taking Technical Risks: How Innovators, Executives, and Investors Manage High-Tech Risks* (Cambridge, MA: MIT Press, 2001). See also Lewis Branscomb and Philip Auerswald, *Between Invention and Innovation: An Analysis of Funding for Early-State Technology Development, Part I—Early Stage Development*, NIST GCR 02-841, November 2002, http://www.atp.nist.gov/ eao/gcr02-841/contents.htm. These authors and others point out that innovation in the so-called pipeline model does not really occur linearly, that the stages are in fact much more interactive, and thus that the term *pipeline* itself is a misnomer. Nonetheless, the term is so widely used that we use it here, recognizing that it does not accurately capture the complexity of the relationship between innovation stages.

15. Stokes, *Pasteur's Quadrant*.

16. Branscomb and Auerswald, *Between Invention and Innovation*.

17. See http://oldcomputers.net/appleii.html (prices at introduction of early Apple computers).

18. Bonvillian, Connected Science Model.

19. Ruttan, *Is War Necessary*.

20. William B. Bonvillian and Richard Van Atta, ARPA-E and DARPA: Applying the DARPA Model to Energy Innovation, *Journal of Technology Transfer*, October 2011, sections 2, 4.

21. See, generally, Matthew Hourihan and Matthew Stepp, *Lean, Mean and Clean: Energy Innovation and the Department of Defense* (report) (Washington, DC: ITIF, March 2011), http://www.itif.org/files/2011-lean-mean-clean.pdf; William B. Bonvillian, Time for Plan B for Climate, *Issues in Science and Technology*, Winter 2011, 55–56, http://www.issues.org/27.2/bonvillian.html (regarding energy role of defense procurement).

22. Thomas S. Kuhn, *Structure of Scientific Revolutions*, 3rd ed. (Chicago: University of Chicago Press, 1996).

23. The term *paradigm* goes back to Plato (*Timaeus* 28A). The original meaning is "a typical example or pattern of something, a pattern or model." Definition from Oxford English Dictionary (OED), http://www.oed.com/view/Entry/137329?redirectedFrom=paradigm#eid).

24. Kuhn, *Structure of Scientific Revolutions*.

25. See, for example, Christopher Freeman and Carlotta Perez, Structural Crises of Adjustment, Business Cycles and Investment Behavior, in *Technical Change and Economic Theory*, ed. Giovanni Dosi et al. (London: Pinter Publishers, 1988), 46; and Carlotta Perez, quoted in Wolfgang Drechsler et al., eds., *Techno-Economic Paradigms: Essays in Honour of Carlota Perez* (London: Anthem, 2009), 2. See generally Daniel Smihula, The Waves of the Technological Innovation of the Modern Age and the Present Crisis, *Studia Politca Slovaca* 1 (2009) 32–47, www.ceeol.com.

26. Carlotta Perez, *Technological Revolutions and Financial Capital: The Dynamics of Bubbles and Golden Ages* (Cheltenham, UK: Edward Elgar, 2002), 15–16. Economist Joseph Schumpeter suggested the term "Kondratiev wave" in his honor in 1939.

27. Perez, *Technological Revolutions*, 24–25.

28. Perez, *Technological Revolutions*, 11.

29. Perez, *Technological Revolutions*, 14.

30. Robert D. Atkinson, *The Past and Future of America's Economy: Long Waves of Innovation That Power Cycles of Growth* (Cheltenham, UK: Edward Elgar, 2004), 3–40.

31. Joseph A. Schumpeter, *Capitalism, Socialism and Democracy* (New York: Harper, 1975), 82–85.

32. Perez, *Technological Revolutions*, 26.

33. Perez, *Technological Revolutions*, 155.

34. Perez, *Technological Revolutions*, 165.

35. Perez, *Technological Revolutions*, 12. See generally, Weiss and Bonvillian, *Structuring an Energy Technology Revolution*, 268 n. 14.

36. Timothy J. Foxon, Technological Lock-in and the Role of Innovation, in *Handbook of Sustainable Development*, ed. G. Atkinson, S. Dietz, and E. Neumayer (Cheltenham, UK: Edward Elgar, 2007), 140–152.

37. James Utterback, *Technological Innovation for a Dynamic Economy* (New York: Pergamon Press, 1979).

38. Here we distinguish between a linear *value chain* that connects initial inputs to a final product, and a multidimensional *value network* of supporting vendors, distributors, and other services.

39. Clayton M. Christensen, *The Innovator's Dilemma: When New Technologies Cause Great Firms to Fail* (Boston, MA: Harvard Business School Press, 1997). "Disruptive innovation," according to the website of its originator, Clayton Christensen, "describes a process by which a product or service takes root initially in simple applications at the bottom of a market and then relentlessly moves up-market, eventually displacing established competitors." http://www.claytonchristensen.com/disruptive_innovation.html.

40. W. Brian Arthur, Competing Technologies, Increasing Returns, and Lock-in by Historical Events, *Economic Journal* 99, no. 394 (Mar. 1989), 116–131. See, also, Mitchell Waldrop, *Complexity* (New York: Simon and Shuster 1992), 15–54.

41. Robert Parkinson, The Dvorak Simplified Keyboard: Forty Years of Frustration, *Computers and Automation*, November 1972, 18–25, http://infohost.nmt.edu/~shipman/ergo/parkinson.html. The software to convert the keyboard on your computer to the Dvorak layout can be obtained if you want to relearn how to type.

42. John Graham, No Time for Pessimism about Electric Cars, *Issues in Science and Technology* (2014), 31, 33–40, http://issues.org/31-1/no-time-for-pessimism-about-electric-cars.

43. See generally, Weiss and Bonvillian, *Structuring an Energy Technology Revolution.*

CHAPTER 4

1. Robert D. Atkinson, *The Past and Future of America's Economy: Long Waves of Innovation That Power Cycles of Growth* (Cheltenham, UK: Edward Elgar, 2004); Carlota Perez, *Technological Revolutions and Financial Capital: The Dynamics of Bubbles and Golden Ages* (Cheltenham, UK: Edward Elgar, 2002). See prior discussion in chapter 3. This chapter draws from William B. Bonvillian, Reinventing American Manufacturing: The Role of Innovation, *Innovations* 7, no. 3 (2012), 108–118; the authors thank the journal editors for permission to use this material.

2. Dale Jorgenson, U.S. Economic Growth in the Information Age, *Issues in Science and Technology*, Fall 2001, http://www.issues.org/18.1/jorgenson.html.

3. Robert M. Solow, *Growth Theory: An Exposition*, 2nd ed. (New York: Oxford University Press, 2000) (Nobel Prize Lecture, December 8, 1987), http://nobelprize.org/nobel_prizes/economics/laureates/1987/solow-lecture.html.

4. This *innovation value chain* is distinct from the value chain for established products that is discussed in chapters 2 and 3.

5. Vernon W. Ruttan, *Is War Necessary for Economic Growth? Military Procurement and Technology Development* (New York: Oxford University Press, 2006), 21–32.

6. Charles R. Morris, *The Dawn of Innovation: The First American Industrial Revolution* (New York: Public Affairs, 2012).

7. Vannevar Bush, *Science: The Endless Frontier* (Washington, DC: Government Printing Office, 1945), http://www.nsf.gov/od/lpa/nsf50/vbush1945.htm.

8. Ruttan, *Is War Necessary.*

9. Atkinson, *Past and Future*, 3–40. See, generally, Perez, *Technological Revolutions*, 3–46. The quality manufacturing wave, discussed below, was led in the 1970s–1980s by Japan.

10. Ruttan, *Is War Necessary*; Janet Abbate, *Inventing the Internet* (Cambridge MA: MIT Press, 1999).

11. Suzanne Berger, *How We Compete: What Companies around the World Are Doing to Make It in Today's Global Economy* (New York: Doubleday Currency, 2005), 251–277.

12. Greg Linden, Jason Dedrick, and Kenneth L. Kraemer, Innovation and Job Creation: The Case of Apple's iPod, *Journal of International Commerce and Economics*, May 2011, 229–230, http://pcic.merage.uci.edu/papers/2011/InnovationJobCreationiPod.pdf. The article found that Apple's iPod employed twice as many people outside the United States as inside the United States although the bulk of wages from the iPod went to the United States: $746 million versus $318 million, with engineers and professionals earning $488 million of the $746 million. Only 30 iPod production jobs were in the United States versus 19,160 in Asian nations, led by 11,715 in China.

13. National Science Board, *Science and Technology Indicators 2012* (NSF, Jan. 17, 2012) (NSF *Indicators*), figure 4-16, http://www.nsf.gov/statistics/seind12/c4/c4s8.htm.

14. NSF *Indicators 2012*, Figure O-2, http://www.nsf.gov/statistics/seind12/pdf/overview. pdf. According to *Indicators 2012*, the largest global science and technology (S&T) gains occurred in the so-called Asia-10—China, India, Indonesia, Japan, Malaysia, Philippines, Singapore, South Korea, Taiwan, and Thailand—as those countries integrate S & T into economic growth. Between 1999 and 2009, the US share of global research and development (R & D) dropped from 38% to 31%, whereas it grew from 24% to 35% in the Asia region during the same time.

15. Gregory Tassey, Rationales and Mechanisms for Revitalizing US Manufacturing R & D Strategies, *Journal of Technology Transfer* 35, no. 3 (June 2010), 297, http://www. nist.gov/director/planning/upload/manufacturing_strategy_paper.pdf.

16. NSF, *Indicators 2012*, figure 4.2, http://www.nsf.gov/statistics/seind12/figures.htm.

17. Tassey, Rationales and Mechanisms.

18. As discussed further in chapter 13, the United States in effect maintains two innovation systems, severing its production system from its earlier stage R & D system, as suggested in Charles Weiss and William B. Bonvillian, *Structuring an Energy Technology Revolution* (Cambridge, MA: MIT Press, 2009), 13–26. Similarly, Dan Breznitz and Peter Cowhey argue that the United States maintains two separate systems of innovation and needs to link them better. Dan Breznitz and Peter Cowhey, *America's Two Systems of Innovation: Recommendations for Policy Changes to Support Innovation, Production and Job Creation* (San Diego, CA: Connect Innovation Institute, Feb. 2012). The first system in the Breznitz-Cowhey formulation is the *novel and breakthrough product/technology innovation* system, which includes university research supported by R & D agencies—the "pipeline" system as we have termed it here—and uses "technology push" to implement its advances. The second, the *process and incremental innovation system*, emphasizes engineering enhancements to products and technologies, including the way they are produced, distributed, and serviced. Manufacturing has historically fallen into the second category. We here extend this argument to treat manufacturing as a legacy sector and link it to other legacy sectors that are similarly isolated from the breakthrough system. See also Bonvillian, Reinventing American Manufacturing (linkages between front-end and back-end innovation systems are needed in manufacturing); William B. Bonvillian, Advanced Manufacturing Policies and Paradigms for Innovation, *Science* 342 (Dec. 6, 2013), 1173–1175 (application of its innovation system required for US advanced manufacturing).

19. Bureau of Labor Statistics (BLS), Current Labor Statistics (CES); President's Council of Advisers on Science and Technology (PCAST), Advanced Manufacturing Partnership, Capturing Domestic Competitive Advantage in Manufacturing (May 2012) (AMP Report), 9–10.

20. BLS, CES (manufacturing employment), http://data.bls.ces. See detailed review of manufacturing job loss in ITIF, Worse Than the Great Depression: What the Experts Are Missing about American Manufacturing Decline (March 2012), 4–9, http://www2.itif.org/2012-american-manufacturing-decline.pdf. For a discussion of the nature of complex, high-value goods, see Michael Hobday, Product Complexity Innovation and Industrial Organization, *Research Policy* 26, no. 6 (Feb. 1998), 689–710. See also Robert W. Rycroft and Don E. Kash, Innovation Policy for Complex Technologies, *Issues in Science and Technology*, Fall 1999, http://issues.org/16-1/rycroft/ (complex goods with multiple technologies embedded made up 43% of the most valuable goods in the top 30 world exports in 1970; by 1995 they made up 82%).

21. BLS, CES (employment in manufacturing industries).

22. Bureau of Economic Analysis (BEA), Fixed Assets Accounts (investments in private fixed assets – plant, equipment, IT - by industry), http://bea.gov.

23. Estimates from ITIF report, drawing on BEA data on manufacturing fixed investment quantity, measuring the actual quantity of fixed investment adjusting for cost changes. ITIF, Worse Than the Great Depression, 47–48.

24. BEA, Fixed Assets Accounts. See analysis in ITIF, Worse Than the Great Depression, 47–58.

25. *Wall Street Journal*, China Passes U.S. as Largest Manufacturer (citing IHS Global Insight report), March 14, 2011, http://247wallst.com/2011/03/14/china-passes-the-us-as-largest-manufacturer/.

26. ITIF, Worse Than the Great Depression, 30–42.

27. Susan Houseman, Christopher Kurz, Paul Lengermann, and Benjamin Mandel, Offshoring Bias in U.S. Manufacturing, *Journal of Economic Perspectives* 25, no. 2 (2011), 111–132, http://pubs.aeaweb.org/doi/pdfplus/10.1257/jep.25.2.111; Susan Helper, Timothy Krueger, and Howard Wial, Why Does Manufacturing Matter? Which Manufacturing Matters?, (Washington, DC: Brookings, Feb. 2012), 7, http://www.brookings.edu/~/media/Files/rc/papers/2012/0222_manufacturing_helper_krueger_wial/0222_manufacturing_helper_krueger_wial.pdf; Michael Mandel, How Much of the Productivity Surge of 2007–2009 Was Real, *Mandel on Innovation and Growth* (blog), March 28, 2011, http://innovationandgrowth.wordpress.com/2011/03/28/how-much-of-the-productivity-surge-of-2007-2009-was-real/.

28. BEA (value added by industry).

29. ITIF, Worse Than the Great Depression; see also Houseman et al., Offshoring Bias; Helper, Krueger, and Wial, Why Does Manufacturing Matter?

30. ITIF, Worse Than the Great Depression, 39.

31. Helper, Krueger, and Wial, Why Does Manufacturing Matter? 9–10. Compare Erik Brynjolfsson and Andrew McAfee, *Race against the Machine* (Lexington, MA: Digital Frontier Press, 2011).

32. ITIF, Worse Than the Great Depression, 39.

33. DG Trade Statistics, World Trade in Goods, Services, FDI, February 28, 2012, http://trade.ec.europa.eu/doclib/docs/2006/september/tradoc_122531.pdf.

34. US Census Bureau, Foreign Trade, U.S. International Trade in Goods and Services, Exhibits 1, 9, 15, https://www.census.gov/foreign-trade/Press-Release/current_press_release/exh1.pdf.

35. US Census Bureau, Trade in Goods with Advanced Technology Products, 2011, http://www.census.gov/foreign-trade/balance/c0007.html.

36. David Autor, Skills, Education, and the Rise of Earnings Inequality among the "Other 99 Percent," *Science* 344 (2014), 843–851.

37. BLS, Industries at a Glance, Manufacturing, NACIS 31-33, Workforce Statistics, http://www.bls.gov/iag/tgs/iag31-33.htm#iag31-33emp1.f.P.

38. Helper, Krueger, and Wial, Why Does Manufacturing Matter? 4–5.

39. Solow, Growth Theory.

40. Tassey, Rationales and Mechanisms, section 3, citing NSF data.

41. ITIF, Case for a National Manufacturing Strategy, April 2011, 13, http://www.itif.org/files/2011-national-manufacturing-strategy.pdf. See also Enrico Moretti, *The New Geography of Jobs* (New York: Houghton Mifflin Harcourt, 2012), 45–72 (regions that tie innovation talent and corresponding innovation capacity, along with advanced technology companies and production, have a multiplier effect of some 5 to 1, including nontradable service sectors that benefit from the regional economic gains).

42. ITIF, National Manufacturing Strategy.

43. For the concept of increasing returns, see Brian Arthur, *Increasing Returns and Path Dependence in the Economy* (Ann Arbor: University of Michigan Press, 1994).

Arthur defines increasing returns as "the tendency for that which is ahead to get further ahead, and for that which loses advantage to lose further advantage." For manufacturing job multiplier data, see, ITIF, Case for a National Manufacturing Strategy, 13.

44. The Industrial Revolution was the initial great scaler of wealth and corresponding enabler of population growth and the expansion of economic well-being. William Rosen, *The Most Powerful Idea in the World: A Story of Steam, Industry and Invention* (New York: Random House, 2010), 252–270.

45. As will be noted in chapter 7, software can scale rapidly, has features of both product and service, and can be incorporated into numerous products. It is perhaps best treated as a different category because of its unique features.

46. Barry C. Lynn, *End of the Line* (New York: Doubleday, 2005), 1–18.

47. Lynn, *End of the Line*, 1–18. See generally Joseph Fewsmith, The Political and Social Implications of China's Accession to the WTO, *China Quarterly* 167 (2001), 589–591. (WTO entry was a major step in bringing China into the world economy, and was sought by the United States to stabilize China's economic and political relations with major powers).

48. ITIF, Enough Is Enough: Confronting Chinese Innovation Mercantilism (report Feb. 2012), http://www2.itif.org/2012-enough-enough-chinese-mercantilism.pdf. Techniques include currency manipulation, tariffs, forced technology transfer, industrial subsidies, forced joint venture requirements, controls on foreign purchases, discriminatory standards, weak patenting, and IP theft. See also, re IP theft, Michael, Riley and Ashlee Vance, It's Not Paranoia If They're Stealing Your Secrets, *Bloomberg Business Week*, March 19, 2012, 76–84. Compare Edward S. Steinfeld, *Playing Our Game: Why China's Rise Doesn't Threaten the West* (New York: Oxford University Press, 2010), 230–234, with Carl J. Dahlman, *The World under Pressure: How China and India Are Influencing the Global Economy and Environment* (Stanford, CA: Stanford University Press, 2012), 182–205.

49. Dahlman, *The World under Pressure*.

50. Paul A. Samuelson, Where Ricardo and Mill Rebut and Confirm Arguments of Mainstream Economists Supporting Globalization, *Journal of Economic Perspectives* 18, no. 3 (Summer 2004), 135–137, 144–145, http://www.nd.edu/~druccio/Samuelson.pdf.

51. David Autor, David Dorn, and Gordon Hanson, The China Syndrome: Local Labor Market Effects of Import Competition in the United States, MIT economics paper, August 2011, http://economics.mit.edu/files/6613.

52. A. Michael Spence, The Impact of Globalization on Income and Employment: The Downside of Integrating Markets, *Foreign Affairs* 90, no. 4 (July–August 2011), 28–41, http://www.viet-studies.info/kinhte/MichaelSpence_Globalization_Unemployment.pdf. See also Autor, Skills, Education.

53. Ezra F. Vogel, *Japan as Number One: Lessons for America* (Cambridge, MA: Harvard University Press, 1979).

54. The tie between industrial strength and military strength is a widely accepted view among US defense analysts, where US technological superiority is considered its defense edge. See, for example, Michael E. O'Hanlon, The National Security Industrial Base: A Crucial Asset of the United States, Whose Future May be in Jeopardy, Washington, DC, Brookings, February 2011, http://www.brookings.edu/research/papers/2011/02/defense-ohanlon.

55. See, for example, Catherine L. Mann, Institute for International Economics, International Economics Policy Briefs, Globalization of IT Services and White Collar Jobs, N. PB03-11 (Dec. 2003), http://www.iie.com/publications/pb/pb03-11.pdf.

56. Gary Pisano and Willy Shih, Restoring American Competitiveness, *Harvard Business Review*, July–August 2009, 114–125, https://hbr.org/2009/07/restoring-american-competitiveness/ar/1.

57. Census Bureau, Foreign Trade Statistics, Trade in Goods with Advanced Technology Products.

58. ITIF, Worse Than the Great Depression. See also Houseman et al., Offshoring Bias, 111–32; Helper, Krueger, and Wial, Why Does Manufacturing Matter? 7; Mandel, How Much Was Real?

59. Clayton Christensen, *The Innovator's Dilemma* (Cambridge, MA: Harvard Business School Press, 1997).

60. Jonas Nahm and Edward Steinfeld, Scale-Up Nation: Chinese Specialization in Innovative Manufacturing, MIT working paper, March 12, 2012.

61. Gregory Tassey, Beyond the Business Cycle: The Need for a Technology-Based Growth Strategy, NIST working paper, February 2012, 3–8, http://www.nist.gov/director/planning/upload/beyond-business-cycle.pdf.

62. Susanto Basu, John Fernald, and Matthew Shapiro, Productivity Growth in the 1990s: Technology, Utilization, or Adjustment, NBER Working Paper 8359, 2001, http://www.nber.org/papers/w8359.pdf; Tassey, Beyond the Business Cycle.

63. Louis V. Gerstner, *Who Says Elephants Can't Dance? Leading a Great Enterprise through Dramatic Change* (New York: HarperCollins, 2003).

64. Suzanne Berger with the MIT Task Force on Production and Innovation Economy, *Making in America* (Cambridge, MA: MIT Press, 2013), 111–14.

65. OECD, Science, Technology and Industry Scoreboard 2013 (Paris: OECD, 2013), 47.

66. Arthur, *Increasing Returns*. Recall that much of what is counted as production in standard economic statistics would count as services if it were to be carried out by independent firms.

67. Rosen, *Most Powerful Idea*, 248–270, 317–319.

68. Bonvillian, Advanced Manufacturing Policies, 1173–1175, and sources listed therein.

69. Denis Fred Simon, ed., *The Emerging Technological Trajectory of the Pacific Rim* (Armonk NY: M.E. Sharpe, 1995).

CHAPTER 5

1. As detailed in chapter 3, the term "techno-economic paradigm" has been used extensively by growth economists Christopher Freeman and Carlota Perez to refer to a far-reaching cluster of technologies that creates "a new best practice frontier" with "pervasive effects throughout the economy," giving rise to a "great surge of development" that constitutes an innovation wave (or Kondratiev wave). We use the term, as noted in chapter 3, somewhat differently to refer to the technologies, and the related political-economic-social systems built around them, that form an entrenched legacy sector resistant to disruptive change. Freeman and Perez were studying the innovations that do happen, and we are studying innovations that don't, although the basic phenomena are comparable. There are additional features, as noted in chapter 3, in a legacy paradigm that Perez and Freeman didn't reach.

2. For disruptive innovations, as discussed in chapters 4 and 5, see Clayton M. Christensen, *The Innovator's Dilemma: When New Technologies Cause Great Firms to Fail* (Boston, MA: Harvard Business School Press, 1997). His definition of "disruptive innovation," as noted there, "describes a process by which a product or service takes root initially in simple applications at the bottom of a market and then relentlessly moves up-market, eventually displacing established competitors" (http://www.claytonchristensen.com/key-concepts/). As originally conceived, this process takes place entirely in the

private sector within particular industry segments. In his recent work, Christensen broadened this concept to include a product or organizational framework (as, for example, the rationalization of the hospital and indeed much of the healthcare system), whose introduction could lead to the rationalization of an entire industry. The latter process often exceeds the capacity of the private sector acting alone and requires substantial changes in public policy. See, for example, Clayton M. Christensen, Jerome H. Grossman, and Jason Huang, *The Innovator's Prescription: A Disruptive Solution to Health Care* (New York: McGraw-Hill, 2009).

3. For socio-technical systems, see, for example, *Research Policy* 39, no. 4 (May 2010), 435–510 (special section).

4. *Research Policy* 39, no. 4 (May 2010), 435–510 (special section).

5. The first four of these features are taken from Charles Weiss and William B. Bonvillian, Complex Established "Legacy" Systems: The Technology Revolutions That Do Not Happen, *Innovations* 6, no. 2 (2011), 162–163. Numbers 5 and 6 are added in order to bring our definition closer to the definition of the regime found in the literature on socio-technical systems, which emphasizes the link between technology and social systems, especially in firms and other organizations. See, for example, Stewart Russell and Robin Williams, Social Shaping of Technological Frameworks, and Knut H. Sorensen, Social Shaping on the Move: On the Policy Relevance of the Social Shaping of Technology Perspective, in *Shaping Technology, Guiding Policy: Concepts, Spaces and Tools*, ed. Knut H. Sorensen and Robin Williams (Cheltenham, UK: Edward Elgar, 2002), 128. Where our previous work emphasized the dimension of political economics, we now refer explicitly to the social dimension that underlies the politics that in turn often dictates the economics. In practice, all of these elements are intertwined. Numbers 7 and 8 are new to this work.

6. For analytic purposes, we distinguish between pricing structures (how prices differ between purchasers of the same product or input, or among types of input or product for the same purchaser), on the one hand, and the change in the prices themselves due to subsidy or other factors.

7. See, for example, Charles Weiss and William B. Bonvillian, *Structuring an Energy Technology Revolution* (Cambridge, MA: MIT Press 2009), 41 n. 10.

8. See summary in, Peter Singer, Federally Supported Innovations: 22 Examples of Major Technology Advances That Stem from Federal Research Support (Washington, DC: Information and Innovation Foundation (ITIF) February 2014), 17–19, http://www2.itif.org/2014-federally-supported-innovations.pdf. See also, 42 U.S. Code Sec. 16372, Ultra-deep water and unconventional onshore natural gas and other petroleum research and development program (collaborative industry-government R&D program), https://www.law.cornell.edu/uscode/text/42/16372.

9. See, for example, William B. Bonvillian, The Connected Science Model for Innovation: The DARPA Role, in National Research Council, *21st Century Innovation Systems for the U.S. and Japan* (Washington, DC: National Academies Press, May 2009), http://www.nap.edu/openbook.php?record_id=12194&page=206.

10. Udayan Gupta, ed., *Done Deals: Venture Capitalists Tell Their Stories* (Cambridge, MA: Harvard Business School Press, 2000), 1–11.

11. Elizabeth B. Reynolds, Hiram Semel, and Joyce Lawrence, Learning by Building: Complementary Assets and the Migration of Capabilities in U.S. Innovation Firms, in *Production in the Innovation Economy*, ed. Richard Locke and Rachel Wellhausen (Cambridge, MA: MIT Press, 2014), 81–108.

12. The broadcast examples cited are detailed in Tim Wu, *The Master Switch* (New York: Vintage Books, 2011). Wu calls the results cited here the Kronos effect, after the mythical king that ate his children because they were predicted to overthrow him.

For broadband, see Susan Crawford, *Captive Audience: The Telecom Industry and Monopoly Power in the New Gilded Age* (New Haven: Yale University Press, 2013).

13. Weiss and Bonvillian, *Structuring an Energy Technology Revolution*, 73–79.

14. Christensen, *The Innovator's Dilemma*, xviii–xxiv.

15. Geoffrey A. Moore, *Crossing the Chasm: Marketing and Selling Technology Products to Mainstream Customers*, rev. ed. (New York: Harper Business, 1999).

16. Everett M. Rogers, *Diffusion of Innovations* (Glencoe, NY: Free Press, 1962).

17. Weiss and Bonvillian, Complex Established "Legacy" Systems, 165ff.

18. McKinsey & Company, *Unlocking Energy Efficiency in the U.S. Economy*, July 2009, 4, 7–15, http://www.mckinsey.com/clientservice/electricpowernaturalgas/downloads/US_energy_efficiency_full_report.pdf.

19. Department of Energy CCS efforts are detailed in Peter Folger, Congressional Research Service, Carbon Capture and Sequestration: Research, Development and Demonstration at the US Department of Energy, February 10, 2014, http://fas.org/sgp/crs/misc/R42496.pdf. See also MIT CC&ST Program (MITEI website), Carbon Capture and Sequestration Technologies, US CCS Financing Overview, December 20, 2013, https://sequestration.mit.edu/tools/projects/us_ccs_background.html.

20. Folger, Carbon Capture and Sequestration, 10.

21. Ari Natter, DOE Suspends $1 Billion in FutureGen Funds, Bloomberg BNA Energy and Climate Report, February 5, 2015, http://www.bna.com/doe-suspends-billion-n17179922773/; Global CCS Institute, Large Scale CCS Projects, 2014, http://www.globalccsinstitute.com/projects/large-scale-ccs-projects.

22. This variant of the market imperfection of nonappropriability is also known technically as a "positive pecuniary externality." Typically these benefits operate through pricing mechanisms rather than through actual resource or technical advantages. See, for example, Christiano Antonelli, Pecuniary Externalities: The Convergence of Directed Technological Change and the Emergence of Innovation Systems, Bureau of Research on Innovation, Complexity and Knowledge (BRICK) Working Paper 3, February 2008, 1–4, http://www.carloalberto.org/files/brick_03_08.pdf.

23. This well-established paradigm favors input-intensive, industrial agriculture over organic agriculture, analyzed in chapter 10.

24. Larry Browning and Judy Shetler, *Sematech: Saving the U.S. Semiconductor Industry* (College Station: Texas A & M Press, 2000).

25. See, for example, Michael E. Levine, Revisionism Revised? Airline Deregulation and the Public Interest, *Law and Contemporary Problems*, 44, (January 1981), 179–195.

26. See, for example, Dorothy Robyn, *Braking the Special Interests: Trucking Deregulation and the Politics of Policy Reform* (Chicago: University of Chicago Press, 1987).

27. See, for example, Amy Johnston, How Deregulation Changed the Telecommunications Industry, *Management Quarterly* 36 no. 4 (1995) 24–28; Wu, *The Master Switch*.

28. Public Law 101–548 (Nov. 15, 1991); See, generally, A. Denny Ellerman, Paul L. Joskow, Richard Schmalensee, Juan-Pablo Montero, and Elizabeth M. Bailey, *Markets for Clean Air: The U.S. Acid Rain Program* (Cambridge: Cambridge University Press, 2000).

CHAPTER 6

1. This theme is explored in depth in Charles Weiss and William B, Bonvillian, *Structuring an Energy Technology Revolution* (Cambridge, MA: MIT Press, 2009).

2. Emily E. Adams, The Energy Game Is Rigged: Fossil Fuel Subsidies Topped $620 Billion in 2011, Earth Policy Institute, February 27, 2013, http://www.earthpolicy.org/data_highlights/2013/highlights36 (data from 25 nations on production and consumption subsidies); Congressional Budget Office, Federal Financial Support for the

Development and Production of Fuels and Energy Technologies, Issue Brief, March 2012), 4, http://www.cbo.gov/sites/default/files/cbofiles/attachments/03-06-Fuelsan-dEnergy_Brief.pdf (in shorter term stimulus legislation, renewables pass fossil fuels in tax subsidies); Congressional Research Service, Federal Renewable Energy R&D Funding History: A Comparison with Funding for Nuclear Energy, Fossil Energy and Efficiency R&D, March 7, 2012, http://www.fas.org/sgp/crs/misc/RS22858.pdf, http://www.hsdl.org/?view&did=10627 (FY2012, federal funding for renewable energy R & D amounted to about 17% of the energy R & D total, compared with 15% for energy efficiency, 25% for fossil, and 37% for nuclear).

3. Intergovernmental Panel on Climate Change (IPCC), Fifth Assessment Report, *Climate Change 2014: Mitigation of Climate Change* (Geneva: IPCC, 2014), http://mitigation2014.org.

4. American Clean Energy and Security Act of 2009, 111 Cong., 1st Sess., H.R. 2454 (Waxman-Markey Bill), passed the House of Representatives on June 26, 2009, on a 219-212 vote).

5. See the American Power Act of 2010 (the Kerry-Lieberman bill), which became S. 1733, 111th Cong., 2nd Sess., released May 12, 2010. Summarized at World Resources Institute, Summary of the American Power Act, June 2010, http://pdf.wri.org/wri_summary_american_power_act_2010-06-07.pdf. This legislation in turn descended from three earlier versions of the Climate Stewardship Act introduced in 2003 (S. 139), 2005 (S. 1151), and 2007 (S. 280) by Senators Lieberman and McCain.

6. Although neoclassical economist Robert Solow won the Nobel Prize in 1987 for developing economic growth theory that showed that technological and related innovation was the dominant factor in economic growth (Robert M. Solow, *Growth Theory: An Exposition*, 2nd ed. [New York: Oxford University Press, 2000], ix–xxvi [Nobel Prize Lecture, Dec. 8, 1987], http://nobelprize.org/nobel_prizes/economics/laureates/1987/solow-lecture.html), he treated it as exogenous to neoclassical theory because of the complexity of the innovation process and the corresponding difficulty in applying metrics and models to it. Economist Paul Romer developed endogenous growth theory (Paul Romer, Endogenous Technological Change, *Journal of Political Economy* 98 [1990], 72–102, http://artsci.wustl.edu/~econ502/Romer.pdf), but there has only been limited progress in neoclassical economics in fleshing out this approach since then. See Robert D. Atkinson and Darrene Hackler, Economic Doctrines and Approaches to Climate Change Policy, Washington, DC: ITIF, October 2010, http://www.itif.org/files/2010-econ-climate-change.pdf.

7. See, for example, Naomi Oreskes and Erik M. Conway, *Merchants of Doubt* (New York: Bloomsbury Press, 2009).

8. See, for example, Nicholas Stern, *Stern Review on the Economics of Climate Change* (London: H. M. Treasury, 2006), chap. 16, http://www.hm-treasury.gov.uk/media/4/3/Executive_Summary.pdf. (carbon pricing alone will not be sufficient to reduce emissions at the scale and pace required; government R & D and early-stage commercialization support will be needed); International Energy Agency (IEA), Energy Technology Perspectives 2008: Scenarios and Strategies to 2050, June 6, 2008, http://www.iea.org/Textbase/npsum/ETP2008SUM.pdf (major public and private investments will be required to implement new energy technologies); John Alic, David Mowery, and Edward Rubin, *U.S. Technology and Innovation Policies: Lessons for Climate Change* (Washington, DC: Pew Center on Global Climate Change, November 2003), ii (R & D support will not be enough; the federal government will need to back a balanced portfolio of technology support policies); Thomas L. Friedman, *Hot, Flat and Crowded: Why We Need a Green Revolution and How It Can Renew*

America (New York: Farrar, Straus and Giroux, 2008) (focus required on R & D and innovation spending); President's Council of Advisors on Science and Technology (PCAST), *The Energy Imperative: Technology and the Role of Emerging Companies* (Washington, DC: Executive Office of the President of the United States, November 2006), http://www.ostp.gov/pcast/PCAST-EnergyImperative_FINAL.pdf.

9. Gregory F. Nemet and Daniel M. Kammen, U.S. Energy R&D: Declining Investment, Increasing Need, and the Feasibility of Expansion, *Energy Policy* 35 (2007), 746–755, figures 1, 2, 4.

10. Congressional Research Service, Research and Development by Large Energy Production Companies, August 2011 (in 2010 the five largest US oil companies spent less than 2% of profits and less than 0.4% of total expenditures on R & D; calculations are based on total R & D spending of $3.6 billion in 2010); Nemet and Kammen, U.S. Energy R&D, figure 6.

11. National Venture Capital Association, *Yearbook 2013* (Thompson Reuters, March 2013), 47, figure 3.33, http://www.nvca.org/index.php?option=com_content&view=article&id=257&Itemid=103; Testimony of Will Coleman (representing the National Venture Capital Assoc.) Before the Senate Committee on Energy and Natural Resources, Hearing on Clean Energy Finance, July 18, 2013, 6–7, http://www.nvca.org/index.php?searchword=energy&ordering=&searchphrase=all&Itemid=101&option=com_search.

12. Breakthrough Institute, Brookings Institution, and World Resources Institute, Beyond Boom and Bust, April 12, 2012, 12–21, http://thebreakthrough.org/blog/Beyond_Boom_and_Bust.pdf; AAAS, Trends in Department of Energy R&D, 1997–2014, June 2013, http://www.aaas.org/spp/rd/Hist/DOE.jpg.

13. Breakthrough Institute et al., Beyond Boom and Bust.

14. Breakthrough Institute, Where the Shale Gas Revolution Came from: Government's Role in the Development of Hydraulic Fracturing in Shale, May 2012, http://thebreakthrough.org/images/main_image/Where_the_Shale_Gas_Revolution_Came_From2.pdf; Peter L. Singer, Federally Supported Innovation: 22 Examples of Major Technology Advances That Stem From Federal Research Support, ITIF, February 2014, 17–19.

15. Department of Energy, Energy Information Agency (EIA), Annual Energy Outlook 2013, The U.S. Becomes a Net Exporter of Natural Gas, Total U.S. Natural Gas Production, figure 2; Industrial and Electric Power Sectors Lead U.S. Gas Consumption, figure 85, http://www.eia.gov/forecasts/aeo/source_natural_gas_all.cfm#shale_gasa.

16. John Powell, EIA, Implications of Increasing U.S. Crude Oil Production, presentation to EIA 2013 Annual Energy Conference, June 18, 2013, 9, http://www.eia.gov/conference/2013/pdf/presentations/powell.pdf (citing EIA, Petroleum Supply Monthly and Annual Energy Review data).

17. IEA, *Energy Technology Perspectives 2008: Scenarios and Strategies to 2050*, June 6, 2008, http://www.iea.org/Textbase/npsum/ETP2008SUM.pdf (funding levels for energy R & D and implementation inadequate to meet climate challenge).

18. See, for example, Bloomberg New Energy Finance, Clean Energy Investment Falls for Second Year, January 15, 2014, http://about.bnef.com/press-releases/clean-energy-investment-falls-for-second-year/ (global venture capital and private equity clean technology funding fell to lowest level since 2005; global investment in renewable energy and new energy technologies fell 10% in 2010 and 11% in 2013).

19. Environmental Protection Administration (EPA), Transportation and Climate, Regulations and Standards: Light Duty, http://www.epa.gov/otaq/climate/regs-light-duty.htm.

20. Peter Folger, Carbon Capture and Sequestration: Research, Development and Demonstration at the U.S. Dept. of Energy, Congressional Research Service, February 10, 2014, 1–3, http://fas.org/sgp/crs/misc/R42496.pdf.

21. This summary relies on data and insights from Peter Fox-Penner, *Smart Power: Climate Change, the Smart Grid, and the Future of Electric Utilities* (Washington, DC: Island Press, 2010); MIT Energy Initiative, *The Future of the Electric Grid*, 2011, https://mitei.mit.edu/system/files/Electric_Grid_Full_Report.pdf; Yinuo Geng, Toward Implementation of the Smart Grid in the United States, unpublished paper, SAIS, Johns Hopkins University, October 13, 2010.

22. Mason Willrich, Electricity Transmission Policy for America: Enabling a Smart Grid, End-to-End, MIT-IPC-Energy Innovation Working Paper 09-003, MIT Industrial Performance Center, July 2009, 7, http://web.mit.edu/ipc/research/energy/pdf/EIP_09-003.pdf.

23. Willrich, Electricity Transmission.

24. See, for example, Alexandra B. Klass and Elizabeth J. Wilson, Interstate Transmission Challenges for Renewable Energy: A Federalism Mismatch, *Vanderbilt Law Review* 65, no. 6 (2012), 1801–1873 (which explores legal obstacles at the state level to investments in electricity transmission required for expanded use of wind or solar energy; notes (at 1872) it is illegal in some states to site transmission wires to make possible electricity exports to another state, even if required for integrated resource planning).

25. Department of Energy, Office of Electricity, *The Smart Grid, An Introduction* (Washington, DC: DOE, 2008), http://www.oe.energy.gov/DocumentsandMedia/DOE_SG_Book_Single_Pages(1).pdf.

26. Clark W. Gellings and Kurt E. Yeager, Transforming the Electric Infrastructure, *Physics Today* 57, no. 12 (December 2004), 45–51.

27. National Institute for Standards and Technology (NIST), smart grid homepage, http://www.nist.gov/smartgrid/.

28. American Recovery and Reinvestment Act (ARRA) of 2009, P.L. 111–115.

29. Department of Energy, Office of Energy Policy and Systems Analysis, Quadrennial Energy Review (QER), summary 2014, http://energy.gov/epsa/initiatives/quadrennial-energy-review-qer.

30. Department of Energy, Next Generation Power Electronics National Manufacturing Innovation Institute, http://energy.gov/eere/amo/next-generation-power-electronics-national-manufacturing-innovation-institute; Department of Energy, Wide Bandgap Semiconductors: Pursuing the Promise, April 2013, http://www.manufacturing.gov/docs/wide_bandgap_semiconductors.pdf.

31. Detailed recommendations along these lines are set out in MIT Energy Initiative, *Future of the Electric Grid*.

32. Energy Information Agency, *Emissions of Greenhouse Gasses in the United States 2001*, Report No. DOE/EIA-0573 (Washington, DC: EIA, December, 2002), http://www.eia.doe.gov/oiaf/1605/archive/gg02rpt/index.html.

33. McKinsey & Company, *Unlocking Energy Efficiency in the U.S. Economy*, July 2009, iii–xiv, http://www.mckinsey.com/client_service/electric_power_and_natural_gas/latest_thinking/unlocking_energy_efficiency_in_the_us_economy.

34. Stephen Pacala and Robert Socolow, Stabilization Wedges: Solving the Climate Problem for the Next 50 Years with Current Technologies, *Science* 305 (August 13, 2004), 968–972.

35. The energy efficiency potential cited in the report was divided across three building sectors of the US economy: industrial (40% of the end-use energy efficiency

potential), residential (35%), and commercial (25%). The savings in energy emissions could be achieved by technical changes that actually have a positive net present value in purely financial terms, making it an attractive investment. The discounted cash flow in actual dollars at a reasonable discount rate totaled approximately $1.2 trillion in present value against an estimated initial up-front total investment of approximately $520 billion. McKinsey & Company, *Unlocking Energy Efficiency*, vii.

36. See, for example, Consortium for Building Energy Innovation (CBEI, DOE's Building Hub), Research Digest, http://research.cbei.psu.edu; Department of Energy, EERE, Building Technologies Office (BTO), Appliance and Equipment Standards Program, http://energy.gov/eere/buildings/appliance-and-equipment-standards-program.

37. McKinsey & Company, *Unlocking Energy Efficiency*, viii.

38. Consortium for Building Energy Innovation (CBEI).

39. Consortium for Building Energy Innovation (CBEI), http://cms.engr.psu.edu/cbei/.

40. William F. Trimble, *Admiral William A. Moffett: Architect of Naval Aviation* (Annapolis, MD: Naval Institute Press, 2011), 111–199.

41. Peter Cohan, Boeing's Big Tanker Contract Has National—and State—Winners and Losers, *AOL Daily Finance*, February 25, 2011, http://www.dailyfinance.com/2011/02/25/boeing-airbus-tanker-contract-winners-losers/; Caroline Brother, Boeing and Airbus Prepare (Again) for Tanker Battle, *New York Times*, June 16, 2009, http://www.nytimes.com/2009/06/17/business/global/17boeing.html.

42. Norm Augustine, former CEO of Lockheed Martin, has estimated that if the current rate of cost increases for fighter aircraft continues, by 2054 the entire defense budget would be required to purchase one F-35 aircraft. *The Economist* cites "Augustine's Law" in Defense Spending in a Time of Austerity, August 26, 2010, http://www.economist.com/node/16886851?story_id=16886851.

43. Secretary Ray Mabus, Moving the Navy and Marine Corps off Fossil Fuels, posting, January 24, 2011, http://www.navy.mil/navydata/people/secnav/Mabus/Other/MovingtheNavyandMarineCorpsOffFossilFuels.pdf. See, generally, the navy website on energy, environment, and climate change at http://greenfleet.dodlive.mil/; Matt Hourihan and Matthew Stepp, *Lean, Mean and Clean: Energy Innovation and the Department of Defense* (Washington, DC: ITIF, March 2011), 13–22, http://www.itif.org/files/2011-lean-mean-clean.pdf

44. Biotechnow, June 6, 2014, http://www.biotech-now.org/environmental-industrial/2014/06/bio-fueling-the-navy#.

45. Sandra I. Erwin, Navy to Stay the Course with Biofuels, NDIA National Defense, January 20, 2014, http://www.nationaldefensemagazine.org/blog/Lists/Posts/Post.aspx?ID=1386.

46. Congressional Research Service, The Navy Biofuel Initiative under the Defense Production Act, June 22, 2012, http://www.fas.org/sgp/crs/natsec/R42568.pdf.

47. For an examination of the life cycle costs of transport biofuels, see Russell W. Stratton, Hsin Min Wong, and James I. Hileman, Quantifying Variability in Life Cycle Greenhouse Gas Inventories of Alternative Middle Distillate Transportation Fuels, *Environmental Science and Technology*, ACS online ed., April 22, 2011, http://pubs.acs.org/doi/full/10.1021/es102597f.

48. Hydrotreated renewable jet (HRJ) fuel is a term used to describe any feedstock or process that leads to fuel that is chemically identical to crude oil-based kerosene, the standard jet fuel. The US Air Force is testing such fuels derived from plant and seed oils, animal fat, and waste oils. The air force has been working to approve a 50% biofuel blend of such oils and petroleum that is expected to be approved for all air force jets.

49. James T. Bartis and Lawrence Van Bibber, *Alternative Fuels for Military Applications* (Santa Monica, CA: Rand, 2011), ix–xix, http://www.rand.org/pubs/monographs/MG969.html.

50. See breakdown from the US Department of Transportation of ITS technologies and research and strategic planning information, http://www.itsoverview.its.dot.gov/; http://www.its.gov/its_program/its_factsheets.htm.

51. The government of Singapore has been able to significantly reduce auto travel, building a highly efficient transit system and in parallel imposing systematic congestion pricing on its highways and heavy taxes for owning a car, treating cars as a luxury item. In other locations, congestion pricing to date has proved politically unpopular with drivers, despite congestion reduction, and made little headway elsewhere, despite attempts in highly congested cities like London and the New York.

52. US Census Bureau, Statistical Abstract of the United States: 2012, http://www.census.gov/compendia/statab/2012/tables/12s1105.xls.

53. DARPA Urban Challenge, November 3, 2007, darpa.mil/grand challenge/.

54. John J. Leonard, Jonathan How, Seth Teller, et al., A Perception Driven Autonomous Urban Vehicle, *Journal of Field Robotics* (2008), 727–774.

55. This technology discussion draws on Byron Stanley, Matthew Cornick, and Jeffrey Koechling, Ground Penetrating Radar Based Localization, paper presented at the National Defense Industry Association Ground Vehicle Systems Engineering and Technology Symposium, Autonomous Ground Systems Mini-Symposium, Troy, Michigan, August 21–22, 2013, and interview by author Bonvillian on July 24, 2013, with authors Stanley and Koechling.

56. A means of comparing an established reference point with a moving robot to locate the robot and obtain optimal path planning. See, for example, Edwin B. Olsen, Real-Time Correlative Scan Matching, paper, University of Michigan, 2009, http://april.eecs.umich.edu/pdfs/olson2009icra.pdf.

57. Byron Stanley, Jeffrey Koechling, and Matthew Cornick, Localization Using Ground Penetrating Radar, Presentation to MIT IdeaStream, April 5, 2013; interview with Byron Stanley and Jeffrey Koechling, July 24, 2013.

58. For a summary of regulatory developments, see Stanford Law Center for Internet and Society, Automated Driving, Legislative and Regulatory Action, http://www.Stanford.edu/wiki/index.php/Automated_Driving:_Legislative_and_Regulatory_Action. See also National Highway Traffic Safety Administration Preliminary Statement of Policy Concerning Automated Vehicles, May 30, 2013, http://www.nhtsa.gov/About+NHTSA/Press+Releases/U.S.+Department+of+Transportation+Releases+Policy+on+Automated+Vehicle+Development.

59. Bryant Walker Smith, Automated Vehicles are Probably Legal in the United States, *Texas A&M Law Review* 1 (2014), 411, http://ssrn.com/abstract=2303904.

60. Bryant Walker Smith, A Legal Perspective on Three Misconceptions in Vehicle Automation, in Gereon Meyer and Sven Beiker, eds., *Lecture Notes in Mobility, in Road Vehicle Automation* (Springer 2014), 85–91, http://ssrn.com/abstract=2459164.

61. William B. Bonvillian, Advanced Manufacturing Policies and Paradigms for Innovation, *Science* 342 (December 6, 2013), 1173. This problem is also discussed in detail in chapter 13 and in Dan Breznitz and Peter Cowhey, *America's Two Systems of Innovation: Recommendations for Policy Changes to Support Innovation, Production and Job Creation* (San Diego, CA: Connect Innovation Institute, February 2012).

62. Bureau of Economic Analysis, U.S. International Trade in Goods and Services (1992–2012), www.bea.gov/international/index.htm#trade; Organization for Economic Cooperation and Development (OECD), Goods Trade Balance, Trade: Key Tables

from OECD, table 3, January 8, 2013, www.oecd-ilibrary.org/trade/goods-trade-balance_20743920-table2.

63. William B. Bonvillian, The New Model Innovation Agencies: An Overview, *Science and Public Policy* 41, no. 4 (July 2014), 425–437.

64. Jonas Nahm and Edward S. Steinfeld, Scale-Up Nation: China's Specialization in Innovative Manufacturing, *World Development* 54 (2014), 288–300, http://dx.doi.org/10.1016/j.worlddev.2013.09.003; Dan Breznitz and Michael Murphree, *Run of the Red Queen* (New Haven, CT: Yale University Press, 2011).

65. Suzanne Berger with the MIT Task Force on Production and Innovation Economy, *Making in America* (Cambridge, MA: MIT Press, 2013). Author Bonvillian served as an advisor to this MIT study and is indebted to Prof. Berger and to his MIT colleagues for insights elaborated on here.

66. Berger, *Making in America*, 119–120; Suzanne Berger, How Finance Gutted Manufacturing, *Boston Review*, March–April 2014, 12–17; Clayton Christensen and Derek van Bever, The Capitalist's Dilemma, *Harvard Business Review*, June 2014, 60–69.

67. Berger, *Making in America*, 110–120.

68. Elizabeth B. Reynolds, Hiram Semel, and Joyce Lawrence, Learning by Building: Complementary Assets and the Migration of Capabilities in U.S. Innovation Firms, in *Production in the Innovation Economy*, ed. Richard Locke and Rachel Wellhausen (Cambridge, MA: MIT Press, 2014), 81–108.

69. Paul Osterman and Andrew Weaver, Skills and Skill Gaps in Manufacturing, in Locke and Wellhausen, *Production in the Innovation Economy*, 17–80.

70. Suzanne Berger, *Making in America*, 125–140. Compare Jonas Nahm and Edward S. Steinfeld, The Role of Innovative Manufacturing in High-Tech Product Development: Evidence from China's Renewable Energy Sector, in Locke and Wellhausen, *Production in the Innovation Economy*, 139–174.

71. William B. Bonvillian, Reinventing American Manufacturing, *Innovations* 7, no. 3 (2012), 106; Bonvillian, Advanced Manufacturing Policies, 1174.

72. William Rosen, *The Most Powerful Idea in the World: A Story of Steam, Industry and Invention* (New York: Random House, 2010).

73. Charles R. Morris, *The Dawn of Innovation: The First American Industrial Revolution* (New York: Public Affairs, 2012).

74. James Womack, Daniel Jones, and Daniel Roos, *The Machine That Changed the World* (New York: Free Press, 1990).

75. President's Council of Advisors on Science and Technology (PCAST), Advanced Manufacturing Partnership, *Capturing Domestic Competitive Advantage in Advanced Manufacturing*, July 2012, 14–25, http://www.whitehouse.gov/sites/default/files/microsites/ostp/pcast_amp_steering_committee_report_final_july_17_2012.pdf; Bonvillian, Reinventing American Manufacturing, 108–109.

76. ITIF, Enough Is Enough: Confronting Chinese Innovation Mercantilism, February 28, 2012, http://www.itif.org/publications/enough-enough-confronting-chinese-innovation-mercantilism.

77. Bonvillian, Reinventing American Manufacturing, 106–107.

78. ITIF, Restoring America's Lagging Investment in Capital Goods, October 2013, http://www2.itif.org/2013-restoring-americas-lagging-investment.pdf.

79. Berger, *Making in America*, 15–20, 44–58.

80. Gary P. Pisano and Willy C. Shih, *Producing Prosperity: Why America Needs a Manufacturing Renaissance* (Cambridge, MA: Harvard Business School Press, 2012).

81. Reynolds, Semel, and Lawrence, Learning by Building.

82. Berger, *Making in America*, 65–90.

83. Christina Romer, Do Manufacturers Need Special Treatment? *New York Times*, February 4, 2012, http://www.nytimes.com/2012/02/05/business/do-manufacturers-need-special-treatment-economic-view.html?_r=0; compare Stephen Ezell, Our Manufacturers Need a U.S. Competitiveness Strategy Not Special Treatment, ITIF blog, February 9, 2012, http://www.innovationfiles.org/our-manufacturers-need-a-u-s-competitiveness-strategy-not-special-treatment/.

84. Adam Smith, *The Wealth of Nations* (State College: Penn State Electronic Classics, 2005), see, for example, book 2, chap. 3, chap. 5; book 3, chap. 4; book 4, chap. 9.

85. Compare Rob Atkinson, Manufacturing Policy Is Not Industrial Policy, *The Innovation Files*, ITIF, February 6, 2012, http://www.innovationfiles.org/manufacturing-policy-is-not-"industrial-policy"/, with Jagdish Bhagwati, The Computer Chip vs. Potato Chip Debate, *Moscow Times*, September 2, 2010, http://www.themoscowtimes.com/opinion/article/the-computer-chip-vs-potato-chip-debate/414565.html.

86. Bonvillian, Advanced Manufacturing Policies, 1175.

87. PCAST, *Capturing Domestic Competitive Advantage*, 35–36.

88. PCAST, *Capturing Domestic Competitive Advantage*, 27–28, citing a Booz Allen survey.

89. Pisano and Shih, *Producing Prosperity*.

90. Berger, *Making in America*, 15–20.

91. Erica Fuchs and Randolph Kirchain, Design for Location? The Impact of Manufacturing Offshore on Technology Competitiveness in the Optoelectronics Industry, *Management Science* 56, no. 12 (2010), 2323–2349, http://papers.ssrn.com/sol3/papers.cfm?abstract_id=1545027.

CHAPTER 7

1. There has been a long debate as to whether software is a product or a service. Software has many of the attributes of a product: it is patentable and subject to copyright, interchangeable, and scalable—all key product characteristics. However, it is often tied to performance of a service, so that it has some of the attributes of a service as well. But it is also frequently reducible to a product: it is downloaded as a component into computers, laptops, and many auto and aircraft electronics products. So software—and lately the social networking technology it enables—is often considered a unique category, not a pure service or product.

2. We have chosen to review higher education rather than primary or secondary education because the entry of online technologies is moving more quickly in this sector, which makes it more relevant to an analysis of innovation entry.

3. Claudia Goldin and Lawrence Katz, *The Race between Education and Technology* (Cambridge, MA: Harvard University Press 2009). See also Claudia Goldin and Lawrence Katz, The Future of Inequality, *Milken Institute Review*, July 2009 (3rd Quarter), 26–33, http://assets1b.milkeninstitute.org/assets/Publication/MIReview/PDF/26-33mr43.pdf; David H. Autor, Skills, Education, and the Rise of Earnings Inequality among the 99%, *Science* 344, no. 6186 (May 23, 2014), 843–851, http://www.sciencemag.org/content/344/6186/843.abstract.

4. National Science Foundation, *Science and Engineering Indicators 2014*, chap. 2, International S&E Higher Education, 2-37-38, appendix table 2-34, http://www.nsf.gov/statistics/seind12/c2/c2s4.htm.

5. See, for example, Daron Acemoglu and David Autor, What Does Human Capital Do? A Review of Goldin and Katz's 'The Race between Education and Technology,' *Journal of Economic Literature* 50, no. 2 (2012), 426–463, http://economics.mit.edu/files/7490 (argues that Goldin and Katz's work accounts for broad labor market

trends but that there are richer interactions in skills and technologies than in their analysis).

6. Autor, Skills Education. Of course, there are other factors in this income disparity, including the decline in the size of the unionized workforce compared to the total workforce, the decline in the real value of the minimum wage, international competition, and automation affecting lower skill positions. Concerning intense international competition, particularly in industrial sectors, as discussed in chapter 4, see, for example, David Autor, David Dorn, and Gordon Hanson, The China Syndrome: Local Labor Market Effects of Import Competition in the United States, *American Economic Review* 103, no. 6 (2013), 2121–2168.

7. Robert B. Archibald and David H. Feldman, *Why Does College Cost So Much?* (New York: Oxford University Press 2011), 8–9.

8. The published average annual tuition and fees for an in-state student at a four-year public university was $8,655 in the 2011–2012 academic year; it averaged $15,172 at for-profit institutions and $29,056 at private nonprofit institutions. Association of Public and Land Grant Universities (APLU), Fact Sheet: College Costs, Answers to the Most Frequently Asked Questions about Public Higher Education, 2012, 1–2 (citing College Board data), https://www.aplu.org/document.doc?id=4287.

9. Most students don't pay the "sticker" price. Public universities provide over 70% of four-year undergraduate education in the United States. Seven million students were enrolled in more than 500 public universities and colleges in the United States in 2011–2012, and on average those that graduate obtain their bachelor's degree in 4.3 years. Sixty-eight percent of first-time students at public universities received financial aid, averaging $6,900. Full-time students at public universities received an average of $5,750 in financial aid, taking into account all aid sources, including federal Pell grants and education tax benefits. APLU, Fact Sheet, 1–2, 7, 9 (citing Department of Education data). This reduces the average annual cost of such education by 70% to $2,490—before including student loans. This is the "net price" of higher education—tuition and fees minus financial aid. At for-profit institutions, the average net tuition is $4,700 and at private nonprofit institutions, $12,970. College Board, Trends in College Pricing (2011).

10. Regardless of the type of higher education institution attended, tuition and fees appear to be a sound investment, given income and employment data. In a 2002 report the Census Bureau estimated that those with college degrees can be expected to earn on average $2.1 million over their working life, compared to $1.2 million for those with high school degrees. US Census Bureau, Special Study: The Big Payoff: Educational Attainment and Synthetic Estimates of Work-Life Earnings, July 2002, 3–4, http://usgovinfo.about.com/gi/o.htm?zi=1/XJ&zTi=1&sdn=usgovinfo&cdn=newsissues&tm=618&f=00&su=p284.13.342.ip_&tt=2&bt=0&bts=0&zu=http%3A//www.census.gov/prod/2002pubs/p23-210.pdf. See also Autor, Skills, Education; Anthony P. Carnevale, Stephen J. Rose, and Ban Cheah, Georgetown University Center on Education and the Workforce, The College Payoff, Education, Occupations, Lifetime Earnings, August 5, 2011, 2–4, https://cew.georgetown.edu/collegepayoff (college verses high school lifetime earnings differential increased to $2.3 million vs. $1.3 million in 2009 dollars). Higher education, then, has one of the highest average returns on investment. According to the Bureau of Labor Statistics, in July 2012 the unemployment rate for those with a bachelor's degree was 4.1%, compared to the 8.7% rate for high school graduates and the 12.7% rate for high school dropouts. Not all degrees are equal; in the recent recession, the unemployment rate for recent graduates in engineering, sciences, education, and health fields was relatively low, 5.4%;

unemployment was higher for nontechnical majors in the arts (11.1%) and social sciences (8.9%). Anthony Carnevale, Ban Cheah, and Jeff Strohl, Hard Times: College Majors, Unemployment and Earnings – Not All College Degrees are Created Equal, Georgetown University Center on Education and the Workforce, January 4, 2012.

11. Do student loans make the cost of education prohibitive? At public universities, 56% of bachelor degree recipients took on debt, while 44% graduated with no debt. For students who borrowed to attend college, the average debt was $22,000 in 2009–2010; for the average bachelor's degree recipient (both those who borrowed and those who did not), average total debt level was $12,300. College Board, Trends in Student Aid (2011). At current repayment rates of 3.4% for the federal direct unsubsidized loan program, a debt of $22,000 would result in a monthly payment of $217. These indebtedness numbers at public universities have not significantly changed in the past decade despite the recession; for those borrowing, average indebtedness was $19,800 in 1999–2000. At private four-year institutions, the average indebtedness for those borrowing was $28,100. Again, these numbers appear manageable when compared to the economic value of higher education. College Board, Trends in Student Aid (2011). Overall, the most thorough evaluation to date of the economics of higher education costs concludes that "rising college cost is not the cause of a national affordability crisis." Archibald and Feldman, *Why Does College Cost So Much?* 197–198.

12. APLU, Fact Sheet.

13. National Science Foundation, *Science and Engineering Indicators 2014*, chap. 2, appendix table 2-11.

14. For data on increases in higher education faculty salaries, see American Association of University Professors, Where Are the Priorities: Annual Report on the Economic Status of the Profession, 2007–08, March–April 2008, Percentage Increases in Average Nominal and Real Salaries 1971–72 through 2007–08 (for Continuing Faculty Members), 10, http://www.aaup.org/file/2007-08Economic-Status-Report.pdf (for 25 of the 29 years increases exceed inflation).

15. William Baumol and William Bowen, *Performing Arts: The Economic Dilemma* (New York: 20th Century Fund, 1966).

16. The subsequent sections of this subchapter draw on William B. Bonvillian and Susan R. Singer, The Online Challenge to Higher Education, *Issues in Science and Technology*, Summer 2013, http://www,issues.org/29.4/william.html. The authors appreciate Dr. Singer's and the editor's permission.

17. MIT News, MIT and Harvard Release Working Papers on Online Courses, January 21, 2014, http://newsoffice.mit.edu/2014/mit-and-harvard-release-working-papers-on-open-online-courses-0121 (data on MOOC registration and participation rates).

18. See, for example, Campaign for the Future of Higher Education, The 'Promises' of Online Higher Education: Profits, October 9, 2013, http://futureofhighered.org/wp-content/uploads/2013/10/Promises-of-Online-Higher-Ed-Profits1.pdf.

19. See generally, Alan Collins and Richard Halverson, *Rethinking Education in the Age of Technology: The Digital Revolution and Schooling in America* (New York: Teachers College Press, Columbia University, 2009).

20. A. J. Angulo, *William Barton Rogers* (Baltimore, MD: Johns Hopkins University Press, 2009).

21. US Department of Education, *Evaluation of Evidence-Based Practices in Online Learning: A Meta-analysis and Review of Online Learning Studies* (Washington, DC: US Department of Education, September 2010), viii, http://www2.ed.gov/rschstat/eval/tech/evidence-based-practices/finalreport.pdf ("The meta-analysis found on average, students in online learning conditions performed modestly better than

those receiving face-to-face instruction"; the difference was larger between blended learning and face-to-face). See also Kimberly Colvin, John Campaign, Alwins Liu, Quian Zhou, Colin Fredericks, and David Pritchard, Learning in Introductory Physics MOOC: All Cohorts Learn Equally Including an On-Campus Class, *International Review of Research in Open and Distance Learning* 15, no. 4 (September 2014), http://www.irrodl.org/index.php/irrodl/article/view/1902/3009 (learning occurs in a MOOC, with likely more conceptual learning than in a traditional lecture-based, on-campus course; concludes that not only college-trained professionals can learn in MOOCs, students with poorer educational backgrounds, and lower initial skill levels are able to learn in these environments).

22. Clayton Christensen, presentation, MIT-Harvard Summit, Online Learning and the Future of Residential Education, March 3–4, 2013, http://onlinelearningsummit.org/program.html.

23. See, for example, Carl Wieman, Applying New Research to Improve Science Education, *Issues in Science and Technology*, Fall 2012, http://issues.org/29-1/carl/. See also Carl Wieman, Expertise in Science and Engineering: How It Is Learned and Taught, xTalk, MIT, May 19, 2014, http://odl.mit.edu/events/carl-wieman-expertise-in-science-and-engineering-how-it-is-learned-and-taught/.

24. Sanjay Sarma and Isaac Chuang, The Magic behind the MOOCs, *MIT Faculty Newsletter* 25, no. 5 (June 2013), web.mit.edu.fnl/volume/255/sarmay_chuang.html.

25. Merrilea J. Mayo, Video Games: A Route to Large-Scale STEM Education? *Science* 323, no. 5910 (January 2, 2009), 79–82, http://www.sciencemag.org/content/323/5910/79.abstract.

26. Issuing students credentials or certificates for completing many online courses, as opposed to giving them a full-credit course grade in a college or university setting, may be an important adaptation to online education. The certificates need not be a second class of education, just a different kind of education. Employers, for example, may well be interested in systems where students obtain "stacks" of online credentials to demonstrate skills or content understanding. Online courses can be broken up into topical modules and resorted and restacked to fit different kinds of credentials. In 2010, US education institutions, led by community colleges, already granted over one million certificates annually in a range of specific semiprofessional programs—the fastest-growing form of higher education. Anthony P. Carnevale, Stephen J. Rose, and Andrew R. Hanson, Certificates: Gateway to Gainful Employment and College Degrees, Georgetown Center for Education and the Workforce, June 2012, http://www.insidehighered.com/sites/default/server_files/files/06_01_12%20Certificates%20Full%20Report%20FINAL.pdf. These certificates are increasingly recognized as valuable by employers. Employers are starting to offer pay differentials for them and to focus on hiring based on levels of core skills, such as applied math, critical listening, close observation, information compilation, and written expression that are matched to job requirements. J. Blevin and M. J. Mayo, The New World of Work, from Education to Employment, *Innovation Intake*, May 2013, http://www.theinnovationintake.com/latest-issue.html. Many of these skills may not be reflected in a traditional college education. The flexibility of online credentialing may better suit this trend toward lifelong skills assessment. In credentialing competition, online may be more flexible and adaptable and thus to have a competitive advantage over formal college education.

27. See, for example, Susan R. Singer, Natalie R. Nielsen, and Heidi A. Schweingruber, eds., *Discipline-Based Education Research: Understanding and Improving Learning in Undergraduate Science and Engineering* (Washington, DC: National Academies

Press, 2012), http://www.nap.edu/catalog.php?record_id=13362#toc; Carl Weiman, Applying New Research to Improve Science Education, *Issues in Science and Technology*, Fall 2012, http://www.issues.org/29.1/carl.html; Susan R. Singer and William B. Bonvillian, Two Revolutions in Learning, *Science* 339 (March 22, 2013), 1359.

28. These points are discussed in Singer and Bonvillian, Two Revolutions in Learning.

29. See, for example, Wieman, Expertise.

30. US Department of Education, *Evidence-Based Practices*; Rebecca Griffiths, Matthew Chingos, Christine Mulhern, and Richard Spies, *Interactive Online Learning on Campus: Testing MOOCs and Other Platforms in Hybrid Formats in the University System of Maryland*, report, Ithaka S&R, July 10, 2014, http://sr.ithaka.org/sites/default/files/reports/S-R_Interactive_Online_Learning_Campus_20140710.pdf (an 18-month study of 17 University of Maryland courses found that using online materials primarily from MOOCs in traditional classes can help colleges teach more efficiently; in side-by-side tests, which involved large, introductory courses, students in the hybrid sections "did as well or slightly better than students in the traditional sections in terms of pass rates and learning assessments." This finding "held across disciplines and subgroups of students"; faculty reported a number of benefits that came with using MOOCs, including "the ability to redesign classes without creating online content from scratch," and "replacing textbooks with more engaging content"); Steve Kolowich, San Jose State Adopts More edX Content for Outsources Trial, *Chronicle of Higher Education*, January 30, 2014, http://chronicle.com/blogs/wiredcampus/san-jose-state-u-adopts-more-edx-content-for-outsourcing-trial/49905 (in a traditional introductory electrical engineering course, pass rates were 57% and 74%; in an experimental section that "flipped" the classroom in a blended learning with MOOC content, the pass rate was 95%.)

31. Singer, Nielsen, and Schweingruber, *Discipline-Based Education Research*.

32. Steve Kolowich, "Outsourced Lectures Raise Concerns about Academic Freedom," *Chronicle of Higher Education*, May 28, 2013, http://chronicle.com/article/Outsourced-Lectures-Raise/139471/.

33. J. C. R. Licklider, Man Machine Symbiosis, *IRE Transactions on Human Factors in Electronics*, HFE-1, 4–11, March 1960.

34. The NRC's DBER report summarizes the still limited research work to date in STEM fields. Singer, Nielsen, and Schweingruber, *Discipline-Based Education Research*.

35. Rafael Reif, Better, More Affordable Colleges Start Online, *Time*, September 28, 2013, http://president.mit.edu/speeches-writing/better-more-affordable-colleges-start-online.

36. MIT, Institute-Wide Task Force on the Future of MIT Education, Preliminary Report, November 21, 2013, http://web.mit.edu/future-report/TaskForceOnFutureOfMITEducation_PrelimReport.pdf.

37. The problems facing innovations in the American system of healthcare delivery are discussed in detail in Clayton M. Christensen, Jerome H. Grossman, and Jason Hwang, *The Innovator's Prescription: A Disruptive Solution for Health Care* (New York: McGraw Hill, 2009).

38. US Centers for Medicare and Medicaid Services, Office of the Actuary, National Health Expenditures 2011–12, Forecast Summary, tables 1 and 2 (2011), http://www.cms.gov/Research-Statistics-Data-and-Systems/Statistics-Trends-and-Reports/NationalHealthExpendData/Downloads/Proj2011PDF.pdf.

39. In 2009, Congress attempted to reform the system through the Patient Protection and Affordable Care Act of 2010, P.L. 111–148, which was signed into law March 23, 2010. This legislation passed on party-line votes, an origin that threatens the

long-term political viability of the reforms. It expanded the scope of the entitlements in an attempt to resolve a fundamental structural problem in the system: the 40 million people outside the existing system, who face inadequate care because they lack affordable coverage. This expanded coverage was also included in order to build political support for the legislation. Overall, the legislation focused more on rearranging the system's financial "plumbing" than on confronting the contradictions between fee-for-service and performance and efficiency. Although it included provisions addressing the effectiveness of healthcare and on IT-based records, it did not focus strongly on ways to innovate, either in new medical technology or delivery systems.

40. President's Council of Advisors on Science and Technology (PCAST), *Big Data and Privacy: A Technological Perspective* (Washington, DC: White House Office of Science and Technology Policy, May 2014), 13–14, http://www.whitehouse.gov/sites/default/files/microsites/ostp/PCAST/pcast_big_data_and_privacy_-_may_2014.pdf.

41. Christensen and his colleagues proposed a major restructuring and rationalization of the US healthcare delivery system to bring stakeholder incentives in line with the needs of overall system efficiency. Christensen, Grossman, and Hwang, *Innovator's Prescription*; see especially chapters 6 and 7, and the epilogue.

42. Here we distinguish between IT systems for health records and those for "back office" functions like payroll, billing, and procurement. The latter provide direct benefit to the healthcare provider and do not face legacy obstacles of the kind we are discussing here.

43. PCAST, *Propelling Innovation in Drug Discovery, Development and Evaluation* (Washington, DC: White House Office of Science and Technology Policy, September 2012), http://www.whitehouse.gov/sites/default/files/microsites/ostp/pcast-fda-final.pdf; FDA, Innovation/Stagnation: Challenge and Opportunity on the Critical Path to New Medical Products, March 2004, http://www.fda.gov/ScienceResearch/SpecialTopics/CriticalPathInitiative/CriticalPathOpportunitiesReports/ucm077262.htm.

44. Infectious Disease Society of America, Bad Bugs, No Drugs: As Antibiotic Discovery Stagnates, A Public Health Crisis Brews (2004), updated in Helen W. Boucher et al., Bad Bugs, No Drugs: No Escape, *Clinical Infectious Diseases* 48, no. 1 (2009), 1–12; National Research Council, Board on Health Sciences Policy, *New Frontiers in Contraceptive Research* (Washington, DC: National Academies, Institute of Medicine, 2004).

45. MIT, The Third Revolution: The Convergence of the Life Sciences, Physical Sciences, and Engineering, MIT White Paper, January 4, 2011, http://web.mit.edu/dc/Policy/MIT%20White%20Paper%20on%20Convergence.pdf; National Research Council, Board on Life Sciences, *Convergence: Facilitating Transdisciplinary Integration of Life, Physical Science, Engineering and Beyond* (Washington, DC: National Academies Press, 2014), http://www.nap.edu/catalog.php?record_id=18722.

46. Phillip A. Sharp and Robert Langer, Promoting Convergence in Biomedical Science, *Science* 333 (July 29, 2011), 527, http://dc.mit.edu/sites/default/files/Sharp%20Langer%20Science.pdf; Philip A. Sharp, Meeting Global Challenges: Discovery and Innovation through Convergence, *Science* 345, no. 6215 (December 19, 2014), 1468–1471.

47. National Institute of Medicine, *Enhancing the Vitality of the National Institutes of Health: Organizational Changes to Meet New Challenges* (Washington, DC: National Academies Press, 2003), http://www.nap.edu/catalog/10779.html; FDA, Innovation/Stagnation.

48. See, for example, PCAST, *Better Health Care and Lower Costs: Accelerating Improvement through Systems Engineering* (Washington, DC: White House Office of Science and Technology Policy, May 2014), http://www.whitehouse.gov/sites/default/files/microsites/ostp/PCAST/pcast_systems_engineering_in_healthcare_-_may_2014.pdf (need to replace fee-for-service payment system with payments tied to outcomes); Daniel M. Fox, *Power and Illness: The Failure and Future of American Health Policy* (Berkeley: University of California Press, 1995) (problems with the focus of US health system on acute verses chronic care).

49. Robert Cook-Deegan, Does NIH Need a DARPA? *Issues in Science and Technology*, Winter 1996, http://www.issues.org/13.2/cookde.htm. DARPA formed a Bio-Tech Office.

50. For example, the BRAIN initiative, a cross-agency R & D effort on brain disease created by the Obama White House, is an inherently convergence-based approach. See White House, BRAIN Initiative, http://www.whitehouse.gov/blog/2013/04/02/brain-initiative-challenges-researchers-unlock-mysteries-human-mind; NIH, BRAIN Working Group Report to the Advisory Committee to the Director, June 5, 2014, http://www.nih.gov/science/brain/2025/index.htm.

51. Agency for Healthcare Research and Quality (AHRQ), Comparative Effectiveness Research, http://effectivehealthcare.ahrq.gov/index.cfm/what-is-comparative-effectiveness-research1/.

52. Department of Health and Human Services (HHS), Key Features of the Affordable Care Act, http://www.hhs.gov/healthcare/facts/timeline/timeline-text.html.

53. Walter Isaacson, *Steve Jobs* (New York: Simon and Shuster, 2011), 378–425.

54. Andrew Lo with David Fagnan, Jose Maria Fernandez, and Roger Stein, Can Financial Engineering Cure Cancer, presentation to the MIT LGO Webinar, March 1, 2013, http://lgosdm.mit.edu/VCSS/web_seminars/docs/AndrewLo_slides_20130301.pdf.

CHAPTER 8

1. William J. Perry, Perry on Precision Strike, *Air Force Magazine* 80, no. 4 (April 1997), 76, http://www.airforcemag.com/MagazineArchive/Pages/1997/April%201997/0497perry.aspx.

2. Richard H. Van Atta, Alethia Cook, Ivars Gutmanis, Michael J. Lippitz, Jasper Lupo, Rob Mahoney, and Jack H. Nunn, *Transformation and Transition: DARPA's Role in Fostering an Emerging Revolution in Military Affairs*, vol. 2, *Detailed Assessments*, IDA Paper P-3698 (Washington, DC: Institute for Defense Analysis, November 2003), I-1, www.darpa.mil/WorkArea/DownloadAsset.aspx?id=2687.

3. Perry, Perry on Precision Strike.

4. Barry D. Watts, The Evolution of Precision Strike, Center for Strategic and Budgetary Assessment, August 6, 2013, 6, http://www.csbaonline.org/publications/2013/08/the-evolution-of-precision-strike/.

5. Perry, Perry on Precision Strike.

6. Watts, Evolution of Precision Strike, 8.

7. Perry, Perry on Precision Strike.

8. Andrew W. Marshall, Some Thoughts on Military Revolutions, Second Version, DOD Office of Net Assessment, Memorandum for the Record, June 27, 1993, 3.

9. Andrew F. Krepineich Jr., The Military-Technical Revolution, Center for Strategic and Budgetary Assessment, 2002, 3 (reprint of DOD Office of Net Assessment paper July 1992), http://www.csbaonline.org/wp-content/uploads/2011/03/2002.10.02-Military-Technical-Revolution.pdf.

10. As noted in William B. Bonvillian, The Connected Science Model for Innovation: The DARPA Model, in *21st Century Innovation Systems for the U.S. and Japan*, ed.

Sadao Nagaoka, Masayuki Kondo, Kenneth Flamm, and Charles Wessner (Washington, DC: National Academies Press, 2009), 221–222, http://books.nap.edu/openbook.php?record_id=12194&page=206, the Revolution in Military Affairs defense transformation was built around many of the IT breakthroughs DARPA initially sponsored. Admirals William Owens and Arthur Cebrowski, and others, in turn, translated this IT revolution into a working concept of "network centric warfare," which further enabled the United States in the decade of the 1990s to achieve unparalleled dominance in conventional warfare. See William Owens with Edward Offley, *Lifting the Fog of War* (Baltimore, MD: Johns Hopkins University Press, 2001), chap. 3; David Alberts, John Garska, and Frederick Stein, *Network Centric Warfare* (Washington, DC: DOD Cooperative Research Program, August 1999), http://www.dodccrp.org/files/Alberts_NCW.pdf; Arthur Cebrowski and John Garska, Network Centric Warfare, Its Origin and Future, *U.S. Naval Institute Proceedings*, January 1998. See, generally, Richard O. Hundley, *Past Revolutions, Future Transformations: What Can the History of Revolutions in Military Affairs Tell Us about Transforming the US Military* (Washington, DC: Rand, National Research Institute, 1999), http://www.rand.org/content/dam/rand/pubs/monograph_reports/2007/MR1029.pdf. The foundation of this IT revolution that enabled this defense transformation was a great innovation wave that swept into the US economy in the 1990s, creating strong productivity gains and new business models that led to new societal wealth creation (see, for example, Dale Jorgenson, U.S. Economic Growth in the Information Age, *Issues in Science and Technology*, Fall 2001, http://www.issues.org/18.1/jorgenson.html (role of IT in driving 1990s growth), which, in turn, provided the funding base for the transformation in defense.

11. Andrew Krepinevich, *The Military-Technical Revolution*, 33, discussed in Watts, Evolution of Precision Strike, 8–9.

12. A vested technology is a technology deeply embedded in organization, value network, doctrine and mental habits of users, and hence resistant to change. It is often part of a larger paradigm or dominant product design.

13. Vernon W. Ruttan, *Is War Necessary for Economic Growth? Military Procurement and Technology Development* (New York: Oxford University Press, 2006).

14. This paragraph is drawn from William B. Bonvillian and Richard Van Atta, ARPA-E and DARPA: Applying the DARPA Model to Energy Innovation, *Journal of Technology Transfer*, October 2011, 499–500. The "connected" innovation system issue in US innovation organization is discussed in William B. Bonvillian, The New Model Innovation Agencies: An Overview, *Science and Public Policy* 41, July 2014; Bonvillian, Connected Science Model, 210–212.

15. See generally, John Alic, *Trillions for Military Technology* (New York: Palgrave Mc-Millan, 2007) (failures in defense technology foresight and planning were driven by a focus on nuclear strategy to the exclusion of other needs, failure by services to adequately define the technology requirements they need to fill, and a defense environment not well adapted to technological learning).

16. These market imperfections are over and above the need to simulate the operation of private markets within the defense procurement process, as for example by means of fly-offs between competing aircraft prototypes.

17. This section draws extensively on the chapter on stealth by Michael J. Lippitz and Richard Van Atta in Van Atta et al., *Transformation and Transition*, chap. 1, and on Ben Rich and Leo Janos, *Skunk Works* (Boston: Little, Brown, 1994), 16–41.

18. Pyotr Ya. Ufimtsev, *Methods of Edge Waves in the Physical Theory of Diffraction*, translated by the Foreign Technology Division, Air Force Systems Command,

National Technology Information Systems document FTD-HC-23-259-71, 1971, www.dtic.mil/cgi-bin/GetTRDoc?AD=AD0733203 (originally published, Moscow, Soviet Radio, 1962).

19. Van Atta et al., *Transformation and Transition*, I-4.

20. Rich and Janos, *Skunk Works*, 16–41.

21. Van Atta et al., *Transformation and Transition*, I-5–I-6.

22. Rich and Janos, *Skunk Works*, 271–280.

23. Van Atta et al., *Transformation and Transition*, IV-35.

24. DOD, *1997 Joint Warfighter S&T Plan*, chap. 4, Achieving Joint Warfighting Capability Objectives, Part B, Precision Force, 1. Definition, http://www.fas.org/spp/military/docops/defense/97_jwstp/jwstp.htm.

25. Van Atta et al., *Transformation and Transition*, chap. VI.

26. DOD, 1997 Joint Warfighter S&T Plan, chap. 4, part B.

27. Van Atta et al., *Transformation and Transition*, IV-38–IV-39.

28. The developments discussed in this paragraph are detailed in Van Atta et al., *Transformation and Transition*, VI-1–VI-11.

29. Norman Polmar, The Pioneering Pioneer, *Naval History* 27 no. 5 (October 2013), 14–15.

30. Developments discussed in paragraph detailed in Van Atta et al., *Transformation and Transition*, VI-11–VI-26.

31. L. Elaine Halchin, Other Transaction (OT) Authority, Congressional Research Service, July 15, 2011, http://fas.org/sgp/crs/misc/RL34760.pdf.

32. Developments discussed in this paragraph detailed in Van Atta et al., VI-26–VI-38.

33. Van Atta et al., *Transformation and Transition*, VI-39.

34. This discussion is drawn from Bonvillian, Connected Science Model.

35. Mitchell Waldrop, *The Dream Machine: J.C.R. Licklider and the Revolution That Made Computing Personal* (New York: Viking, 2001), chaps. 2, 5–7, and pp. 466–471.

36. Ruttan, *Is War Necessary*; Richard Van Atta, Fifty Years of Innovation and Discovery, DARPA, 2008, www.darpa.mil/WorkArea/DownloadAsset.aspx?id=2553.

37. Warren Bennis and Patricia Ward Biederman, *Organizing Genius* (New York: Basic Books, 1997) 1–30, 196–218.

38. Bennis and Biederman, *Organizing Genius*, 196–218.

39. Bonvillian, Connected Science Model, 214–225 ("great group" theory and DARPA's application of it).

40. This list is drawn from DARPA, *DARPA—Bridging the Gap, Powered by Ideas*, February 2005; DARPA, *DARPA over the Years*, October 27, 2003. For a more detailed evaluation of DARPA's ruleset, see Bonvillian and Van Atta, ARPA-E and DARPA.

41. Tammy L. Carleton, The Value of Vision in Radical Technological Innovation, dissertation, Department of Mechanical Engineering, Stanford University, September 2010, http://innovation.io/thesis/.

42. Francis Duncan, *Rickover: The Struggle for Excellence* (Annapolis, MD: Naval Institute Press, 2001); Thomas B. Allen and Norman Polmar, *Rickover* (Dulles, VA: Brassey's, 2007).

43. Neil Sheehan, *A Fiery Peace in a Cold War: Bernard Schriever and the Ultimate Weapon* (New York: Random House Vintage, 2009).

CHAPTER 9

1. The authors thank our Georgetown colleagues Joanna Lewis, Charles Wessner, Carl Dahlman, and Harley Balzer for very helpful discussions and comments on this chapter. We take full responsibility for any errors or misstatements.

2. See discussion in chapter 1; Bureau of Economic Analysis, GDP by Industry, Value Added to GDP by Industry—Annual (2012).

3. William B. Bonvillian, The New Model Innovation Agencies: An Overview, *Science and Public Policy*, September 2013 online edition, 3 ("innovation ecosystem"). The term "ecosystem" was applied to a university's innovation efforts in Edward B. Roberts and Charles Easley, *Entrepreneurship Impact*, Kauffman Foundation report 2010, 44–71. The term "ecosystem" was later applied to refer to the network of ancillary firms and institutions that provide various forms of technical support to local manufacturing firms in the MIT Production in the Innovation Economy study. Suzanne Berger with the MIT Task Force on Production and Innovation Economy, *Making in America* (Cambridge, MA: MIT Press, 2013). (See chapters 4 and 6 of the present book for further discussion.) We use it here differently for the larger innovation environment, as we define it here.

4. Bengt-Åke Lundvall, *Product Innovation and User-Producer Interaction* (Aalborg: Aalborg University Press, 1985); Chris Freeman, *Technology Policy and Economic Performance: Lessons from Japan* (London: Pinter, 1987); Chris Freeman, The National System of Innovation in Historical Perspective, *Cambridge Journal of Economics*, 19 (1995), 5–24; Bengt-Åke Lundvall, ed., *National Innovation Systems: Towards a Theory of Innovation and Interactive Learning* (London: Pinter, 1992); Richard R. Nelson and Nathan Rosenberg, Technical Innovation and National Systems, in *National Innovation Systems: A Comparative Analysis*, ed. Richard R. Nelson (New York: Oxford University Press, 1993), 3–21.

5. As a historical note, many of these factors were referred to as "implicit technology policy," as opposed to the "explicit technology policy" that deals directly with technological issues, in the science and technology policy literature of the 1970s. See, for example, Francisco Sagasti, National Science and Technology Policies for Development: A Comparative Analysis, in *Mobilizing Technology for Development*, ed. Jairam Ramesh and Charles Weiss (New York: Praeger, 1979). More recent literature has pointed out the importance of these factors in giving rise to the distinctiveness of the national innovation systems of different countries. See, for example, D. Archibugi and J. Michie, The Globalization of Technology: A New Taxonomy, *Cambridge Journal of Economics* 19 (1995), 121–140.

6. See, for example, Martina Fromhold-Eisebith, Bridging Scales in Innovation Policies: How to Link Regional, National and International Innovation Systems, *European Planning Studies* 15, no. 2 (2007), 217–233 and the many references therein.

7. Caroline S. Wagner, *The New Invisible College: Science for Development* (Washington, DC: Brookings Institution Press, 2008).

8. Hubert Schmitz and Simone Strambach, The Organisational Decomposition of Innovation and Global Distribution of Innovative Activities: Insights and Research Agenda, *International Journal of Technological Learning, Innovation and Development* 2, no. 4 (2009), 231–249.

9. The linear *value chain* of a commodity like coffee is distinct from the *supply chain* of a product like an automobile that must be assembled from a large number of component parts purchased from a large number of different suppliers.

10. Raphael Kaplinsky, *Globalization, Poverty and Inequality* (Cambridge, MA: Polity Press, 2005), 100–111.

11. The analogous value chain for physical infrastructure would encompass such elements as planning, techno-economic feasibility studies (including environmental impact assessment), engineering design, detailed engineering, construction, construction supervision, and postevaluation.

12. Carlo Pietrobelli and Roberta Rabellotti, Global Value Chains Meet Innovation Systems: Are There Learning Opportunities for Developing Countries? *World Development* 9, no. 7 (2011), 1261–1269

13. Torben M. Anderson et al., *The Nordic Model: Embracing Globalization and Sharing Risks* (Helsinki: Taloustieto Oy, 2007).

14. Marianne Ekman et al., *Learning Regional Innovation: Scandinavian Models* (Basingstoke, UK: Palgrave Macmillan, 2011), 61.

15. OECD, *OECD Science, Technology and Industry Scoreboard 2013: Innovation for Growth*, (Paris: OECD Publishing, 2013), 50.

16. OECD, *Scoreboard 2013*, 90, 91, 94.

17. National Research Council, *Rising to the Challenge: U.S. Innovation Policy for the Global Economy* (Washington, DC: National Academies Press, 2012), 299

18. For a thorough study of the extraordinarily pervasive top-to-bottom corruption in Putin's Russia, see Karen Dawisha, *Putin's Kleptocracy: Who Owns Russia* (New York: Simon & Schuster, 2014).

19. An example of such an innovative city, designed to overcome the disadvantages of a "disabling" innovation environment, is the $5.6 billion Skolkovo Innovation Center near Moscow, intended to promote technologically innovative industry through tax exemptions (and protection from organized crime), which has attracted investment from multinational companies including Microsoft, IBM, Intel, and Cisco, but lately has been hampered by loss of political support and affected by allegations of corruption in the construction phase. Loren Graham, *Lonely Ideas: Can Russia Compete?* (Cambridge, MA: MIT Press, 2013). See also note 26.

20. For a concise, hard-hitting summary of the top-to-bottom corruption in the Russian economy of 1999, see Richard L Palmer, Statement on the Infiltration of the Western Financial System by Elements of Russian Organized Crime, before the House Committee on Banking and Financial Services, Russian Law Institute, September 21, 1999, 324, http://www.russianlaw.org/palmer.htm, quoted in Karen Dawisha, *Putin's Kleptocracy*, 17.

21. Dawisha, *Putin's Kleptocracy*.

22. Loren Graham, *The Ghost of the Executed Engineer: Technology and the Fall of the Soviet Union* (Cambridge, MA: Harvard University Press, 1993).

23. John McNeill, *Something New under the Sun: An Environmental History of the Twentieth Century World* (New York: W.W. Norton, 2001).

24. Despite these obstacles, Soviet scientists and engineers did produce important innovations, especially within the military, notably *Sputnik* (the first artificial earth satellite), the hydrogen bomb, and a variety of deadly innovations in bacteriological warfare, such as antibiotic-resistant anthrax. Ken Alibek, *Biohazard: The Chilling True Story of the Largest Covert Biological Weapons Program in the World—Told from the Inside by the Man Who Ran It* (New York: Random House, 2008). Scientists in Maoist China, for their part, developed high-yielding varieties of rice more or less equivalent to the better known varieties produced by the International Rice Research Institute in the Philippines.

25. Graham, *Ghost of the Executed Engineer*.

26. The Skolkovo Institute outside Moscow is an attempt to build a modern research university, combining research and graduate education, through a collaboration with MIT and other Western universities, but it is not clear whether the current political leadership will be willing to sustain the effort over time. See note 19 and Skolkovo Institute for Science and Technology, http://www.skoltech.ru/en.

27. Charles Weiss, ed., Science and Technology Policy amid Change in Eastern Europe, special issue of *Technology in Society* 15, no. 1 (1993).

28. Christine Ebrahim-zadeh, Back to Basics—Dutch Disease: Too Much Wealth Managed Unwisely, *Finance and Development* 40, no. 1 (March 2003), http://www.imf.org/external/pubs/ft/fandd/2003/03/ebra.htm.

29. Graham, *Lonely Ideas.*

30. Massimiliano Granieri and Andrea Renda, *Innovation Law and Policy in the European Union: Towards Horizon 2020* (Milan: Springer, 2012); European Commission, *The ERA-NET Scheme,* http://cordis.europa.eu/fp7/coordination/about-era_en.html.

31. European Commission, *MEMO/10/473: Turning Europe into a True Innovation Union,* October 6, 2010, http://europa.eu/rapid/press-release_MEMO-10-473_en.htm?locale=en.

32. Granieri and Renda, *Innovation Law and Policy,* 143.

33. European Commission, *Improving Knowledge Transfer between Research Institutions and Industry across Europe: Embracing Open Innovation,* April 2007, http://ec.europa.eu/invest-in-research/pdf/com2007182_en.pdf.

34. David L Cleeton, Evaluating the Performance Record under the Lisbon Agenda, in *Europe and National Economic Transformation: The EU after the Lisbon Decade,* ed. Mitchell P. Smith (New York: Palgrave MacMillan, 2012); Paul Copeland and Dimitris Papadimitriou, eds., *The EU's Lisbon Strategy: Evaluating Success, Understanding Failure* (New York: Palgrave MacMillan, 2012).

35. National Research Council, *21st Century Manufacturing: The Role of the Manufacturing Extension Partnership Program* (Washington, DC: National Academies Press, 2012), 229.

36. Berger, *Making in America,* 125.

37. Berger, *Making in America,* 127.

38. National Research Council, *21st Century Manufacturing,* 225.

39. Alberto Alesina and Francesco Giavazzi, *The Future of Europe: Reform or Decline* (Cambridge, MA: MIT Press, 2006), 39.

40. Alesina and Giavazzi, *The Future of Europe,* 111–112.

41. Haibo Zhou, Ronald Dekker, and Alfred Kleinknech, Flexible Labor and Innovation Performance: Evidence from Longitudinal Firm-Level Data, *Industrial and Corporate Change* 20, no. 3 (2011), 944–945. Concerning German process innovation, see Berger, *Making in America,* 108–111, 134.

42. National Research Council, *21st Century Manufacturing,* 231.

43. The Fraunhofer Gesellschaft has been criticized for retaining the intellectual property resulting from this research and for carrying out functions that might otherwise have been performed by private industry, and in so doing perhaps blocking the emergence of a private consulting industry like that of the United States. Charles W. Wessner, ed., *21st Century Manufacturing: The Role of the Manufacturing Extension Partnership Program* (Washington, DC: National Research Council, 2013), appendix A-2.

44. Berger, *Making in America,* 131.

45. Charles Wessner, How Does Germany Do It? *Mechanical Engineering* 135 (2013), 42–47.

46. National Research Council, *Rising to the Challenge,* 273.

47. Reforms in 2002 introduced pay based on performance, although civil service rules have limited their application (*Bundesministerium des Innern*).

48. OECD, *OECD Economic Surveys: Germany* (Paris: OECD Publishing, 2013), 49.

49. Peter Gumbel, To Boost Entrepreneurship, France Tries to Change Its Attitude toward Failure, Reuters, January 23, 2014, http://blogs.reuters.com/great-debate/2014/01/23/to-boost-entrepreneurship-france-tries-to-change-its-attitude-toward-failure/.

50. Alesina and Giavazzi, *The Future of Europe,* 83. These investments include 3.9 billion euros to the Concorde program (electronic flight equipment) between 1970 and 1990,

8 billion to the Plan Calcul computing program, 3 billion at the start of Airbus, 2.1 billion for the first TGV line, and 1.2 billion for Minitel.

51. National Research Council, *21st Century Manufacturing*, 369.

52. Jacques Attali, *Rapport de la Commission pour la libération de la croissance française* (XO Éditions: La Documentation française, 2008), 48.

53. Alesina and Giavazzi, *The Future of Europe*, 58, 64.

54. National Research Council, *21st Century Manufacturing*, 370.

55. Blanka Vavakova, Reconceptualizing Innovation Policy: The Case of France, *Technovation* 46 (2006), 444–462.

56. Paul Slovic, Perceived Risk, Trust, and Democracy, in *Social Trust and the Management of Risk*, ed. George Cvetkovich and Ragnar E. Lofstedt (New York: Earthscan, 2013), 50–51.

57. Alesina and Giavazzi, *The Future of Europe*, 71.

58. National Research Council, *21st Century Manufacturing*, 370.

59. Vavakova, Reconceptualizing Innovation Policy.

60. National Research Council, *21st Century Manufacturing*, 372.

61. OECD, *Lisbon Strategy for Growth and Jobs: France National Reform Programme, 2008–2010* (Paris: OECD Publishing, 2008).

62. FSI France Investment 2020 Launched, http://www.caissedesdepots.fr/en/news/all-the-news/half-year-2009-2010-sales-up-10-on-a-reported-basis-03-like-for-like/fsi-france-investment-2020-launched.html.

63. Edward S. Steinfeld, *Playing Our Game: Why China's Rise Doesn't Threaten the West* (Oxford: Oxford University Press 2010), 142.

64. Dan Breznitz and Michael Murphree, *Run of the Red Queen: Government, Innovation, Globalization and Economic Growth in China* (New Haven: Yale University Press, 2011), 38–51.

65. Joanna Lewis, *Green Innovation in China* (New York: Columbia University Press, 2013).

66. Lewis, *Green Innovation in China*, 126–128.

67. Hardware Startups: Hacking Shenzhen: Why Southern China Is the Best Place in the World for a Hardware Innovator to Be, *Economist*, January 18, 2014.

68. Steinfeld, *Playing Our Game*, 152–153.

69. UNESCO Institute for Statistics, Global Flow of Tertiary-Level Students, 2014, http://www.uis.unesco.org/Education/Pages/international-student-flow-viz.aspx.

70. Carl J. Dahlman, *The World under Pressure* (Stanford, CA: Stanford University Press, 2012), 3.

71. The definition of a perverse subsidy is found in in chapter 5.

72. Nicholas R. Lardy, *Markets over Mao: The Rise of Private Business in China* (Washington, DC: Peterson Institute for International Economics, 2014).

73. Andrew Wedeman, *Double Paradox: Rapid Growth and Rising Corruption in China* (Ithaca, NY: Cornell University Press, 2012).

74. We thank our colleague Professor Harley Balzer for this insight.

75. Mancur Olson, *Power and Prosperity: Outgrowing Communist and Capitalist Dictatorships* (New York: Basic Books, 2000).

76. World Bank data, Gross Savings (% of GDP), 2013, http://data.worldbank.org/indicator/NY.GNS.ICTR.ZS.

77. Fion Li, China Mulls Trial Program for Individuals Investing Overseas, *Bloomberg*, January 12, 2013, http://www.bloomberg.com/news/2013-01-12/china-mulls-trial-program-for-individuals-investing-overseas.html.

78. Breznitz and Murphree, *Run of the Red Queen*, 46–47.

79. Breznitz and Murphree, *Run of the Red Queen*, 155–156. An analogous "dual economy" was typical of many developing countries before the mid-1980s, with larger, politically favored firms gaining privileged access to subsidized capital and other inputs while smaller firms were left to maximize their efficiency and productivity as best they could with limited access to capital and imported inputs.

80. Despite these issues, China was awarded favorable ratings in the 2014 Global Competitiveness Index. The Index does cite such problematic factors as access to financing, inefficient bureaucracy, corruption, and insufficient capacity to innovate. Nevertheless, China's extremely high scores for market size, macroeconomic environment, primary education, and other factors boost it to 29th out of the 144 countries rated. Klaus Schwab, ed., *The Global Competitiveness Report, 2013–2014* (Geneva: World Economic Forum 2013), http://reports.weforum.org/the-global-competitiveness-report-2013-2014/.

81. Lardy, *Markets over Mao.*

82. Jane Qiu, China Goes Back to Basics in Research Funding, *Nature* 507 (March 11, 2014), 148–149, http://www.nature.com/news/china-goes-back-to-basics-on-research-funding-1.14853.

83. Kristen Bound et al., *China's Absorptive State: Research, Innovation and the Prospects for China-U.K. Collaboration* (London: Nesta, 2013), http://www.nesta.org.uk/sites/default/files/chinas_absorptive_state_0.pdf.

84. We thank Professor Carl Dahlman of OECD, formerly of the Georgetown University School of Foreign Service, for these insights.

85. Breznitz and Murphree, *Run of the Red Queen*, 120.

86. In this case, the "broader social goal" is that of cutting-edge technological innovation, rather than environment or public health, as in most of the other cases we have considered. In another case of conflict between national policy and the incentives perceived by firms, efforts by the national government to protect local markets or even to dominate global markets by creating Chinese national standards and imposing them on global markets have had the paradoxical effect of discouraging local innovation by firms that fear that new technology resulting from their research may be incompatible with politically motivated standards about which they were not consulted (Breznitz and Murphree, *Run of the Red Queen*, 64, 72; Steinfeld, *Playing Our Game*, 173).

87. See Glenn R. Fong, Follower at the Frontier: International Competition and Japanese Industrial Policy, *International Studies Quarterly* 42 (1998), 339–366 (Japan's industrial policy had to become much more flexible and industry-led as it approached the innovation frontier).

88. Dieter Ernst, From Catching Up to Forging Ahead? China's Prospects in Semiconductors, East West Center Working Paper, Innovation and Economic Growth Series, Honolulu, HI, November 2014.

89. Kira Matus et al., Health Damages from Air Pollution in China, MIT Joint Program on the Science and Policy of Global Change, 2011, 8; World Bank, *Cost of Pollution in China: Economic Estimates of Physical Damages*, 2007, xiii, http://siteresources.worldbank.org/INTEAPREGTOPENVIRONMENT/Resources/China_Cost_of_Pollution.pdf.

90. World Health Organization, Global Burden of Disease Study, *Lancet*, December 13, 2014. http://www.thelancet.com/themed/global-burden-of-disease. See also Edward Wong, Air Pollution Linked to 1.2 Million Premature Deaths in China, *New York Times*, April 1, 2013, http://www.nytimes.com/2013/04/02/world/asia/air-pollution-linked-to-1-2-million-deaths-in-china.html?_r=0.

91. Edward Wong, Report Finds Widespread Water Pollution in China, *New York Times*, April 24, 2014, http://sinosphere.blogs.nytimes.com/2014/04/24/report-finds-widespread-water-pollution-in-china/?_php=true&_type=blogs&_r=0.

92. Alex L Wang, The Search for Sustainable Legitimacy: Environmental Law and Bureaucracy in China, *Harvard Environmental Law Review* 37 (2013), 376–440, http://www3.law.harvard.edu/journals/elr/files/2013/09/Wang-9-2.pdf. Wang argues that local officials were not receiving mixed signals from national authorities, but on the contrary understood their priorities correctly.

93. Wang, Search for Sustainable Legitimacy.

94. Wang, Search for Sustainable Legitimacy.

95. China Ministry of Science and Technology, *China Science and Technology Indicators 2010* (Beijing: Ministry of S&T, 2013), chap. 2. The average annual growth rate of China's R & D between 2001 and 2009 was 17% (table 2-1).

96. China Ministry of Science and Technology, *China Science and Technology Indicators 2010*, 54, 61. While some 20% of total US R & D is in basic research, less than 5% of China's R & D is in basic research; approximately 15% is in applied and 80% in development as of 2009 (figure 2-7). Sixty-one percent of total Chinese R & D is focused on manufacturing (table 2-6).

97. This refers to the many monopolistic segments of the economy that distort prices (Bloomberg). Increasing competition (mentioned below) seeks to address this problem.

98. Lardy, *Markets over Mao*.

99. Jawaharlal Nehru, speaking at the Indian Science Congress, 1938.

100. Pushpa M. Bhargava and Chandana Chakrabarti, *The Saga of Indian Science since Independence: In a Nutshell* (Hyderabad: Universities, 2003).

101. More precisely, India's First and Second Five-Year Plans provided for 0.18% and 0.45% of GNP to be spent on research and development for the periods 1951–1956 and 1956–1961, respectively. Mahesh Agnihotri, Risks to Economic Stability and Its Challenges: A Study of Chinese and Indian Economies, *Journal of Business Management & Social Sciences Research* 3, no. 6 (2014), 17–25, http://borjournals.com/a/index.php/jbmssr/article/view/1725/1074.

102. Daniel Yergin and Joseph Stanislaw, *The Commanding Heights: The Battle between Government and the Marketplace That Is Remaking the Modern World* (New York: Simon & Schuster, 1998), 68–73.

103. Dahlman, *The World under Pressure*, 55.

104. Ashok Parthasarathi, *Technology at the Core: Science and Technology with Indira Gandhi* (New Delhi: Dorling Kindersley, 2007), 11, 12–16, 183–184, 188, 311; R. M. Lala, *The Joy of Achievement: Conversations with J.R.D. Tata* (New Delhi: Viking 1995), 20; Anil K. Malhotra, *A Passion to Build: India's Search for Offshore Technology: A Memoir* (Raleigh, NC: Lulu Press, 2007).

105. Grappling with this development was what first alerted one of the authors (Weiss), working as the science and technology advisor at the World Bank, to the critical importance of the innovation context.

106. Dahlman, *The World under Pressure*, 56.

107. Dahlman, *The World under Pressure*, 58.

108. Mark Andrew Dutz, *Unleashing India's Innovation: Toward Sustainable and Inclusive Growth* (Washington, DC: World Bank, 2007), 7.

109. Navi Radjou et al., *Jugaad Innovation: A Frugal and Flexible Approach to Innovation for the 21st Century* (New York: Wiley, 2012). See also http://articles.economictimes.indiatimes.com/2012-07-and28/news/32906719_1_indian-innovations-frugality-incubator and http://www.nesta.org.uk/news/frugal-innovations.

110. Dahlman, *The World under Pressure*, 88–93.

111. Peter Foster, Revolution on India's Railway Runs out of Wheels, *Telegraph*, Telegraph Media Group, October 1, 2004, http://www.telegraph.co.uk/news/worldnews/asia/india/1473121/Revolution-on-Indias-railway-runs-out-of-wheels.htm.

112. Eugene M. Makar, *An American's Guide to Doing Business in India: A Practical Guide to Achieving Success in the Indian Market* (Avon: Adams Business, 2008), 35; Joint Economic Committee, US Congress, Challenges to Sustained Economic Growth in India, May 2007.

113. People and Society: India, *The World Factbook*, Central Intelligence Agency, https://www.cia.gov/library/publications/the-world-factbook/geos/in.html.

114. Dahlman, *The World under Pressure*, 61.

115. House of Commons, Science and Technology Committee, Bridging the Valley of Death: Improving the Commercialization of Research, June 20, 2012, Transcript of Oral Evidence, quoted in Charles W. Wessner, ed., *21st Century Manufacturing: The Role of the Manufacturing Extension Partnership Program* (Washington, DC: National Research Council, 2013), appendix A-2, 234. The member was referring here to the Fraunhofer institutes and the German industrial ecosystem rather than to disruptive innovation, but his words are broadly applicable.

CHAPTER 10

1. This chapter is drawn from Charles Weiss and William B. Bonvillian, Legacy Sectors: Barriers to Global Innovation in Agriculture and Energy, *Technology Analysis and Strategic Management* 25, no. 10 (November 2013), 1189–1208. The authors thank the managing editor for that journal for permission to use this material.

2. See, for example, Gates Foundation, Global Health Program Overview, 2011, http://www.gatesfoundation.org/global-health/Documents/global-health-program-overview.pdf.

3. See, for example, World Bank, Clean Technology Fund, https://www.climateinvestmentfunds.org/cif/node/2; US Department of Energy, US-China Clean Energy Cooperation: A Progress Report, 2013, http://www.uschinaecp.org/Downlond/ECP_Report_216x280_EN_713.pdf; and for more recent decisions, Department of State, China Climate Change Working Group Fact Sheets, http://asean.usmission.gov/factsheet11112014-11112008.html, http://www.state.gov/r/pa/prs/ps/2013/07/211768.htm, and http://www.state.gov/r/pa/prs/ps/2014/07/229308.htm. See also the Energy and Climate Partnership of the Americas (ECPA), http://ecpamericas.org/; the Global Bioenergy Partnership (GBEP), http://www.globalbioenergy.org/; the International Renewable Energy Agency (IRENA), http://www.irena.org; Clean Energy Ministerial (CEM), http://www.cleanenergyministerial.org/.

4. The term is from R. A. Mashelkar, Indian Science, Technology, and Society: The Changing Landscape, *Technology in Society* 30 (2008), 299–308.

5. This statement is a variant of the commonplace observation that technology embodies the economic factors and social values of the place where it was invented or commercialized, so that the importation of technology may either require an importation of these values or, alternatively, may be inappropriate to local conditions or factor proportions.

6. See, for example, Jenny C. Aker and Isaac M. Mbiti. Africa Calling: Can Mobile Phones Make a Miracle? *Boston Review*, 35, (March–April 2010), 17–19, 4, http://bostonreview.net/BR35.2/aker_mbiti.php.

7. C. K. Prahalad, *The Fortune at the Bottom of the Pyramid* (Philadelphia, PA: Wharton School Publishing, 2006). But see also Bernard Garrette and Aneel Karnani,

Challenges in Marketing Socially Useful Goods to the Poor, *California Management Review*, 52, (2010), 29–47.

8. Paul Roberts, *The End of Food* (Boston: Houghton Mifflin; New York: Bloomsbury, 2008). See also Michael Pollan, *Omnivore's Dilemma: The Natural History of Four Meals* (New York: Penguin, 2006).

9. Although overall agricultural production is decentralized, there are centralized, large-scale agribusiness elements in the system, including major equipment producers, agricultural chemical firms, and commodities trading firms.

10. US agricultural law states, "The term 'sustainable agriculture' means an integrated system of plant and animal production practices having a site-specific application that will, over the long-term (A) satisfy human food and fiber needs; (B) enhance environmental quality and the natural resource base upon which the agriculture economy depends; (C) make the most efficient use of nonrenewable resources and on-farm resources and integrate, where appropriate, natural biological cycles and controls; (D) sustain the economic viability of farm operations; and (E) enhance the quality of life for farmers and society as a whole." 7 U.S.C. 3103, Sec. 19. See also the definition used by the Department of Agriculture (USDA) Sustainable Agriculture Research and Education (SARE) Program of NIFA, https://www.cfda. gov/index?s=program&mode=form&tab=core&id=a3ae1d2fdc5e7d10cffef795b1 63e462. See, generally, National Research Council, Committee on 21st Century Agriculture Systems, Board on Agriculture and Natural Resources, *Toward Sustainable Agriculture Systems in the 21st Century* (Washington, DC: National Academies Press, 2010), chap. 1, http://books.nap.edu/catalog.php?record_id=12832. See also USDA, SARE, What Is Sustainable Agriculture? 2010, http://www.sare. org/Learning-Center/SARE-Program-Materials/National-Program-Materials/ What-is-Sustainable-Agriculture.

11. USDA, Agricultural Marketing Service, National Organic Program, http://www. ams.usda.gov/AMSv1.0/ams.fetchTemplateData.do?template=TemplateC&navID= NationalOrganicProgram&leftNav=NationalOrganicProgram&page=NOPConsum ers&description=Consumers&acct=nopgeninfo.

12. See, for example, Kathleen Merrigan and W. Lockeretz, Ensuring Comprehensive Organic Livestock Standards, presentation at the first IFOAM International Conference on Animals in Organic Production, 2009, http://www.ams.usda.gov/AMSv1.0/ getfile?dDocName=STELPRDC5066277. Merrigan became US deputy secretary of agriculture in the Obama administration.

13. The USDA supports farmers, ranchers, organizations, businesses, consumers, and others in improving agricultural sustainability through a number of activities and programs, including the Sustainable Agriculture Research and Education (SARE) program of the National Institute of Food and Agriculture (NFIA) (before 2008 in the Cooperative State Research, Education and Extension Service), http://www.sare. org/; Alternative Farming Systems Info Center, National Agricultural Library, http:// afsic.nal.usda.gov/nal_display/index.php?tax_level=1&info_center=2; Agricultural Research Service, ATTRA, National Sustainable Agriculture Information Service, https://attra.ncat.org/; National Agroforestry Center of the Forest Service and the Natural Resources Conservation Service, http://www.unl.edu/nac/; Cooperative State Research, Education and Extension Service, Sustainable Agriculture, http:// www.csrees.usda.gov/nea/ag_systems/ag_systems.cfm and http://www.csrees. usda.gov/sustainableagriculture.cfm; Agricultural Research Service National Program: Integrated Farming Systems, http://www.ars.usda.gov/research/programs/ programs.htm?NP_CODE=207; Economic Research Service publication: Green

Technologies for a More Sustainable Agriculture, http://www.ers.usda.gov/catalog/OneProductAtATime.asp?ARC=c&PDT=2&PID=46; Direct Marketing, Agricultural Marketing Service, National Organic Program, Agricultural Marketing Service, http://www.ams.usda.gov/AMSv1.0/nop.

14. For materials for small-scale farmers on sustainable agriculture, see the Rodale Institute website, http://rodaleinstitute.org/new_farm.

15. For a more optimistic assessment of this process in the United Kingdom, see Adrian Smith, Translating Sustainabilities between Green Niches and Socio-Technical Regimes, *Technology Analysis and Strategic Management* 19 (2007), 427–450.

16. See, for example, Elisabeth Rosenthal, Organic Agriculture May Be Outgrowing Its Ideals, *New York Times*, December 31, 2011 (labeled organic foods moving from emphasis on local growing and limited environmental strains), http://www.nytimes.com/2011/12/31/science/earth/questions-about-organic-produce-and-sustainability.html. Although large-scale farmers are beginning to mainstream organic, large food producers are also acquiring organic brands, which is part of the story discussed above of agriculture increasingly becoming embedded in a larger food system. For example, Colgate now owns "Tom's of Maine," Walmart has moved toward organic produce, Groupe Danone (Dannon) now owns Stonyfield yogurt, and MOM (formerly Malt-O Meal), is having success with organic food lines and certain sustainable practices. It economizes by substituting environmentally preferred bags for boxes, for example, http://www.malt-o-meal.com/category/sustainability/.

17. The 1913 Haber-Bosch process that allowed large-scale chemical fertilizer production was a significant enabler of world population growth. Vaclav Smil, *Enriching the Earth: Fritz Haber, Carl Bosch, and the Transformation of World Food Production.* (Cambridge, MA: MIT Press, 2001).

18. Pamela C. Ronald, From Lab to Farm: Applying Plant Research on Plant Genetics and Genomics to Crop Improvement, *PLoSBiology* 12, no. 6 (June 10, 2014), e1001878, http://www.plosbiology.org/article/fetchObject.action?uri=info%3Adoi%2F10.1371%2Fjournal.pbio.1001878&representation=PDF.

19. See Carl J. Dahlman, *The World under Pressure: How China and India Are Influencing the Global Economy and Environment* (Stanford, CA: Stanford University Press, 2012), chap. 6 (rapid industrialization of emerging nations is placing significant strain on world environmental resources).

20. The USDA is supporting adoption of renewable energy by US farmers in a number of programs. See, for example, USDA, Rural Development Energy Programs, http://www.rurdev.usda.gov/Energy.html.

21. Sustainable agriculture was emphasized at the June 2012 Rio+20 meeting on sustainable development. UN Conference on Sustainable Development, UNCSD Rio 2012 Issues Brief 9, Food Security and Sustainable Agriculture, December 2011, http://www.uncsd2012.org/index.php?page=view&type=400&nr=227&menu=45.

22. Susan McCouch et al., Agriculture: Feeding the Future, *Nature* 499 (July 4, 2013), 23–24, http://www.nature.com/nature/journal/v499/n7456/full/499023a.html.

23. Ronald, From Lab to Farm.

24. American Society of Plant Biologists, Unleashing a Decade of Innovation in Plant Science, 2013, http://plantsummit.files.wordpress.com/2013/07/plantsciencedecadalvision10-18-13.pdf.

25. National Research Council, Committee on a Review of USDA Agriculture and Food Research Initiative, *Spurring Innovation in Food and Agriculture: A Review of the USDA Agriculture and Food Research Initiative Program* (Washington, DC: National Academies Press, 2014); President's Council of Advisors on Science and Technology

(PCAST), Agricultural Preparedness and the Agricultural Research Portfolio, December 2012, http://www.whitehouse.gov/sites/default/files/microsites/ostp/pcast_agriculture_20121207.pdf ("Our most important conclusion is that our Nation's agricultural research enterprise is not prepared to meet the challenges that US agriculture faces in the 21st century for two major reasons. First, PCAST finds that the proportion of Federal funding for agricultural research allocated through competitive mechanisms is far below the proportion in other agencies, which fails to adequately encourage innovation. Second, PCAST finds that the current agricultural research portfolio is not optimally balanced; it overlaps with private-sector activities in several significant areas, while underfunding other important areas that are not addressed through private efforts").

26. US Department of Agriculture, Secretary Announces Creation of Foundation for Food and Agriculture Research, July 23, 2014, http://www.usda.gov/wps/portal/usda/usdahome?contentidonly=true&contentid=2014/07/0156.xml.

27. Ronald, From Lab to Farm.

28. Roberts, *The End of Food.*

29. Barry Commoner, *The Closing Circle: Nature, Man and Technology* (New York: Knopf. 1971); David Weir, *Circle of Poison: Food and Pesticides in a Hungry World* (San Francisco: Institute for Food and Development Policy, 1981). Certain controlled pesticides are barred from application but not production in the United States, and so are exported and applied on crops abroad, which are imported back into the United States.

30. For a comprehensive assessment of the state of agricultural technology in developing countries, see International Assessment of Agricultural Knowledge, Science and Technology for Development, Summary for Decision Makers, 2009, http://www.unep.org/dewa/agassessment/reports/IAASTD/EN/Agriculture%20at%20a%20Crossroads_Global%20Summary%20for%20Decision%20Makers%20(English).pdf. A review of this assessment by the Independent Evaluation Group of the World Bank is available at http://siteresources.worldbank.org/EXTGLOREGPARPROG/Resources/IAASTD_GPR.pdf. The full report can also be found in B. D. McIntyre, H. R. Herren, J. Wakhungu, and R. T. Watson, eds., *Agriculture at a Crossroads: Global Report* (Washington, DC: Island Press, 2008). The 2012 annual letter from Bill Gates of the Gates Foundation delineates the need for innovation in developing world farming as it faces the twin challenges of population growth (9.3 billion world population by 2050) and disruptive effects of climate change, http://www.gatesfoundation.org/annual-letter/2012/Pages/home-en.aspx.

31. World Bank, *Agriculture and Development* (Washington, DC: World Bank, 2008), chaps. 6–7, http://siteresources.worldbank.org/INTWDR2008/Resources/WDR_00_book.pdf.

32. World Bank, *Agriculture and Development*, chap. 4.

33. David Gale Johnson, *World Agriculture in Disarray*, 3rd ed. (New York: Macmillan, 1991). The first edition of Johnson's book was published in 1973. The picture he described then has not fundamentally changed.

34. The term was first used in a speech by W. S. Gaud, director of US Agency for International Development, to the Society for International Development, 1968, http://www.agbioworld.org/biotech-infotopics/borlaug-green.html.

35. Gordon Conway, *The Doubly Green Revolution* (Ithaca, NY: Cornell University Press, 1998); Noel Vietmeyer, *Borlaug*, vol. 2, *Wheat Whisperer, 1944–59* (Lorton, VA: Bracing Books, 2010); Noel Vietmeyer, *Borlaug*, vol. 3, *Bread Winner, 1960–69* (Lorton, VA: Bracing Books. 2011); Gregg Easterbrook, Forgotten Benefactor

of Humanity, *Atlantic*, January 1997, http://www.theatlantic.com/magazine/
archive/1997/01/forgotten-benefactor-of-humanity/306101/3/. Remarkably, Chinese
researchers succeeded in developing similar high-yielding varieties of rice during
the Maoist period, when communication with researchers in other countries was
largely cut off.

36. For a discussion of why African agriculture is so different from Asian agriculture
and why the Green Revolution has such differential success in the two settings,
see InterAcademy Council, *Realizing the Promise and Potential of African Agriculture* (Amsterdam: IAC, 2004), http://www.interacademycouncil.net/24026/
africanagriculture.aspx.

37. William Paddock and Paul Paddock, *Famine 1975! America's Decision: Who Will
Survive?* (Boston, MA: Little, Brown, 1967). See also Paul Ehrlich, *The Population
Bomb* (New York: Sierra Club / Ballantine 1969).

38. Noel Vietmeyer, *Wheat Whisperer* and *Bread Winner*.

39. National Research Council, Committee on 21st Century Agriculture Systems, Board
on Agriculture and Natural Resources, *Toward Sustainable Agriculture Systems in
the 21st Century* (Washington, DC: National Academies Press, 2010), chap. 8, http://
books.nap.edu/catalog.php?record_id=12832. See also Conway, *A Doubly Green Revolution* (calls for a second green revolution to offset some of the adverse environmental impacts of the first, stressing sustainable agriculture and conservation as well as
tripling production on small-scale farms in developing nations).

40. Concerning effects on prices from the use of corn for ethanol fuels, see, for example,
C. Ford Runge and Benjamin Senauer, How Biofuels Could Starve the Poor, *Foreign
Affairs* 86, no. 3 (May–June 2007), 41–53; Nicholas W. Minot, Transmission of World
Food Price Changes to Markets in Sub-Saharan Africa, International Food Policy
Research Institute, IFPRI Discussion Papers 1059, 2011; John Baffes and Tassos Ha-
niotis, Placing the 2006/08 Commodity Price Boom into Perspective, World Bank,
Development Prospects Group, Research Working Paper 5371, July 2010, http://
www-wds.worldbank.org/external/default/WDSContentServer/IW3P/IB/2010/07/
21/000158349_20100721110120/Rendered/PDF/WPS5371.pdf.

41. Robert Paarlberg with Norman Borlaug and Jimmy Carter, *Starved for Science: How
Biotechnology Is Being Kept out of Africa* (Cambridge, MA: Harvard University Press,
2009).

42. A similar lumpiness makes it uneconomic to develop commercial pesticides specific
to "minor" crops whose markets total "only" a few billion dollars, forcing growers to
use less effective and more environmentally harmful chemicals developed for other
crops.

43. See www.cgiar.org. See also Warren Baum and Michael Lejeune, *Partners against
Hunger* (Washington, DC: World Bank, 1986).

44. See, for example, the work of the International Service for the Acquisition of Agri-
biotech Applications, www.isaaa.org.

45. This approach reflects ongoing conceptual work by Prof. Sanjay E. Sarma, MIT.

46. Chris Reij and Ann Waters-Bayer, *Farmer Innovation in Africa: A Source of Inspiration for Agricultural Development* (London: Earthscan Publications, 2002).

47. See, generally Charles Weiss and William B. Bonvillian, *Structuring an Energy Technology Revolution* (Cambridge, MA: MIT Press, 2009); William B. Bonvillian and
Charles Weiss, Taking Covered Wagons East: A New Innovation Theory for Energy
and Other Established Sectors, *Innovations* 4, no. 4 (2009), 289–300.

48. See discussion of this balance in Weiss and Bonvillian, *Structuring an Energy Technology Revolution*, chap. 7.

49. See, for example, Clean Air Task Force, http://www.catf.us/coal/where/asia/; Asia Clean Energy Innovation Initiative, http://www.aceii.org/.

50. See, generally, US Department of Energy, U.S.-China Clean Energy Coopera-tion: A Progress Report, January 2011, http://www.pi.energy.gov/documents/USChinaCleanEnergy.PDF.

51. See, for example, Douglass M. Powell, M. T. Winkler, A. Goodrich, and Tonio Buonassisi, Modeling the Cost and Minimum Sustainable Price of Crystaline Sil-icon Photovoltaic Manufacturing in the U.S., *IEEE Journal of Photovoltaics* 3, no. 2 (April 2013), http://ieeexplore.ieee.org/xpl/articleDetails.jsp?reload=true&tp=&arnumber=6407638 (line of sight and other anticipated technology advances ex-pected to drive solar PV to competitive levels by 2020).

52. This pattern is already visible; see discussion of carbon capture and sequestration (CCS) in chapter 5. Although Department of Energy efforts to undertake carbon sequestration demonstrations began in 2003, the program was subsequently reor-ganized into seven regional partnerships, with limited progress on reaching the stage of injecting CO_2 for geological storage. Department of Energy, Office of Fossil Energy, Carbon Sequestration Regional Partnerships (2011), http://www.fe.doe.gov/programs/sequestration/partnerships/index.html. See, on carbon capture, Business Green, AEP: Lack of Climate Regulation Killed $668m CCS Project, July 18, 2011, http://www.businessgreen.com/bg/news/2094430/aep-lack-climate-regulation-killed-usd668m-ccs-project; Guardian Environment Network, U.S. Breaks Ground on First Industrial Scale Carbon Capture Project, August 26, 2011, http://www.guardian.co.uk/environment/2011/aug/26/us-carbon-capture-and-storage-biofuels. Importantly, as noted in chapter 5, DOE's FutureGen CCS project was scaled down in 2010 from a new plant to a retrofit of an existing power plant and was finally suspended in 2015 for lack of timely industry co-sponsorship support. Ari Natter, DOE Suspends $1 Billion in FutureGen Funds, Bloomberg BNA Energy and Climate Report, February 5, 2015, http://www.bna.com/doe-suspends-billion-n17179922773/; Global CCS Institute, Large Scale CCS Projects, 2014, http://www.globalccsinstitute.com/projects/large-scale-ccs-projects. The recent reclassification of carbon dioxide as a pollutant subject to EPA regulation may affect this possible trend if it survives the inevitable court and political challenges.

53. Breakthrough Institute and Information Technology and Innovation Foundation, *Rising Tigers, Sleeping Giant* (Washington, DC: ITIF, 2010), 23–24, 34–38, 48–52, and 67–74, http://www.itif.org/index.php?id=315; X. Tan and Z. Gang, World Resources Institute, An Emerging Revolution: Clean Technology Research, Development and Innovation in China, WRI Working Paper, December 2009. See, generally, Dahlman, *World under Pressure*, chap. 6; Daniel Breznitz and Michael Murphree, *Run of the Red Queen: Government, Innovation, Globalization and Economic Growth in China* (New Haven, CT: Yale University Press, 2011), 10–34; Edward Steinfeld, *Playing Our Game: Why China's Rise Doesn't Threaten the West* (New York: Oxford University Press, 2010).

54. See Pew Charitable Trusts, Who's Winning the Clean Energy Race, April 2014, 7–10, http://www.pewtrusts.org/en/research-and-analysis/reports/2014/04/03/whos-winning-the-clean-energy-race-2013. Concerning nuclear power advances, see, for example, Richard Martin, China Takes Lead in Race for Clean Nuclear Power, Wired.com, February 1, 2011, http://www.wired.com/wiredscience/2011/02/china-thorium-power/; see, generally, Mujid S. Kazimi, Thorium Fuel for Nuclear Energy, *American Scientist* 91, no. 5 (September–October 2003), 408–415; Robert Hargraves and Ralph W. Moir, Liquid Fluoride Thorium Reactors, *American Scientist* 98, no. 4 (July–August 2010), 304–313.

55. Joanna I. Lewis, The State of U.S.-China Relations on Climate Change: Examining the Bilateral and Multilateral Relationship, *China Environment Series* 11 (2010), 7–39.

56. Department of State, US Mission to ASEAN, U.S.-China Joint Announcement on Climate Change and Clean Energy Cooperation, November 11, 2014, http://asean.usmission.gov/factsheet11112014-11112008.html.

57. See, for example, Frances Stewart, *Technology and Underdevelopment*, 2nd ed. (London: Macmillan, 1977), and Frances Stewart, International Technology Transfer: Issues and Policy Options, in *Recent Issues in World Development: A Collection of Survey Articles*, ed. P. Streeten and R. Jolly (Oxford: Pergamon Press, 1981), 67–110.

58. Jose Goldemberg, Thomas B. Johannson, Amulya K. N. Reddy, and Robert H. Williams, *Energy for a Sustainable World* (New York: Wiley, 1981).

59. See, for example, Dahlman, *World under Pressure.*

60. Raphael Kaplinsky et al., Below the Radar: What Does Innovation in Emerging Economies have to Offer Other Low-Income Economies? *International Journal of Technology Management and Sustainable Development* 8 (2009), 177–197.

CHAPTER 11

1. Vannevar Bush, *Science: The Endless Frontier* (Washington, DC: Government Printing Office, 1945), 1–11, http://www.nsf.gov/od/lpa/nsf50/vbush1945.htm; discussed in Donald E. Stokes, *Pasteur's Quadrant: Basic Science and Technological Innovation* (Washington, DC: Brookings Institution Press, 1997).

2. The federal government funds 60% of all US basic research, and 31% of all US research and development, including basic research, applied research, and development. The other 69% of US R & D, primarily development, is funded by the private sector. NSF, *Science and Engineering Indicators 2014* (Washington, DC: NSF, 2014), figure 4.3, http://www.nsf.gov/statistics/seind14/index.cfm/etc/figures.htm.

3. William B. Bonvillian, The New Model Innovation Agencies: An Overview, *Science and Public Policy 41*, no. 4, July 2014, 425–437.

4. Peter L. Singer, Federally Supported Innovation: 22 Examples of Major Technology Advances That Stem from Federal Research, Information Technology and Innovation Foundation report, February 2014, http://www2.itif.org/2014-federally-supported-innovations.pdf.

5. Lewis Branscomb and Phillip Auerswald, *Between Invention and Innovation: An Analysis of Funding for Early-State Technology Development*, NIST GCR 02-841, November 2002, http://www.atp.nist.gov/eao/gcr02-841/contents.htm.

6. Vernon W. Ruttan, *Technology Growth and Development: An Induced Innovation Perspective* (New York: Oxford University Press 2001).

7. Ruttan, *Technology Growth and Development.*

8. Vernon W. Ruttan, *Is War Necessary for Economic Growth? Military Procurement and Technology Development* (New York: Oxford University Press, 2006). Ruttan, leading theorist of the induced model, turned in this his last book to what we term the extended pipeline model and the historic importance of the military in fostering radical and generative innovations. See also Bonvillian, New Model Innovation Agencies.

9. See, for example, Mariana Mazzucato, *The Entrepreneurial State: Debunking Public vs. Private Sector Myths* (New York: Anthem Press, 2013).

10. National Research Council, *Continuing Innovation in Information Technology* (Washington, DC: National Academies Press, 2012), figure 1, IT Sectors with Large Economic Impact; Glenn R. Fong, ARPA Does Windows: The Defense Underpinning

of the PC Revolution, *Business and Politics* 3, no. 3 (2001), 213–237, http://www.be-press.com/bap/vol3/iss3/art1/.

11. Mazzucato, *The Entrepreneurial State*, chap. 5. See generally, Gary Pisano and Willy Shih, Restoring American Competitiveness, *Harvard Business Review*, July–August 2009, 114–125, https://hbr.org/2009/07/restoring-american-competitiveness/ar/1.

12. Ruttan, *Is War Necessary*; William B. Bonvillian, The Connected Science Model for Innovation: The DARPA Model, in *21st Century Innovation Systems for the U.S. and Japan* (Washington, DC: National Academies Press, May 2009), 206–207, http://books.nap.edu/openbook.php?record_id=12194&page=206. See also John Alic, Lewis Branscomb, Harvey Brooks, Ashton Carter, and Gerald Epstein, *Beyond Spinoff: Military and Commercial Technologies in a Changing World* (Cambridge, MA: Harvard Business School Press, 1992).

13. David Roessner, Jennifer Bond, Sumiye Okubo, and Mark Planting, *The Economic Impact of Licensed Commercialized Inventions Originating in University Research, 1997–2007* (Washington, DC: Biotechnology Industry Organization, September 3, 2009), 32–33, 38.

14. Glenn R. Fong, Breaking New Ground or Breaking the Rules: Strategic Reorientation in US Industrial Policy, *International Security* 25, no. 2 (Fall 2000), 152–162, http://www.mitpressjournals.org/doi/pdf/10.1162/016228800560480; Bonvillian, New Model Innovation Agencies.

15. Discussion drawn from William B. Bonvillian, Advanced Manufacturing Policies and Paradigms for Innovation, *Science* 342, no. 6163 (December 6, 2013), 1173–1175, http://www.sciencemag.org/content/342/6163/1173.full.

16. John Womack, David Jones, and Daniel Roos, *The Machine That Changed the World* (New York: Free Press, 1990) (re: Japan); Suzanne Berger with the MIT Task Force on Production in the Innovation Economy, *Making in America* (Cambridge, MA: MIT Press, 2013), 121–154 (re: Germany).

17. Bureau of Economic Analysis, U.S. International Trade in Goods and Services (1992–2012), www.bea.gov/international/index.htm#trade; Organization for Economic Cooperation and Development, Goods Trade Balance, Trade: Key Tables from OECD, table 3, January 8, 2013, www.oecd-ilibrary.org/trade/goods-trade-balance_20743920-table2.

18. C. R. Morris, *The Dawn of Innovation: The First American Industrial Revolution* (New York: Public Affairs, 2012).

19. Berger, *Making in America*, 121–154; Jonas Nahm and Edward S. Steinfeld, Scale-up Nation: China's Specialization in Innovative Manufacturing, *World Development* 54, no. 288 (February 2014), 288–300; Daniel Breznitz and Michael Murphree, *Run of the Red Queen: Government, Innovation, Globalization and Economic Growth in China* (New Haven, CT: Yale University Press 2011).

20. Bonvillian, Connected Science Model, 206–237; Charles Weiss and William B. Bonvillian, *Structuring an Energy Technology Revolution* (Cambridge, MA: MIT Press, 2009), 13–36.

21. Branscomb and Auerswald, *Between Invention and Innovation*; Lewis M. Branscomb, and Philip E. Auerswald, *Taking Technical Risks: How Innovators, Executives, and Investors Manage High-Tech Risks* (Cambridge, MA: MIT Press, 2003).

22. James Wallace and Jim Erickson, *Hard Drive: Bill Gates and the Making of the Microsoft Empire* (New York: Harper Business, 1992), 73, 139–206.

23. Richard R. Nelson, *National Innovation Systems: A Comparative Analysis* (New York: Oxford University Press, 1993), 14.

24. Richard R. Nelson and Sidney R. Winter, *An Evolutionary Theory of Economic Change* (Cambridge, MA: Belknap Press of Harvard University Press, 1982).

25. Brian Arthur, *Increasing Returns and Path Dependence in the Economy* (Ann Arbor: University of Michigan Press, 1994).

26. Paul M. Romer, Economic Growth, in *The Concise Encyclopedia of Economics*, 2nd ed. (2007), http://www.econlib.org/library/Enc/EconomicGrowth.html. See also Paul M. Romer, Endogenous Technological Change, *Journal of Political Economy* 98, no. 5 (October 20000, S72.

27. Paul M. Romer, Should the Government Subsidize Supply or Demand in the Market for Scientists and Engineers? NBER Working Paper 7723, June 2000, 11.

28. Quoted in Bonvillian, Connected Science Model; William B. Bonvillian, Power Play: The DARPA Model and U.S. Energy Policy, *American Interest*, November 2006, 39–48.

29. William J. Abernathy and James M. Utterback, *Patterns of Industrial Innovation*, *Technology Review* 80 (July 1978), 40–47.

30. Avery Sen, Transformative Innovation: What 'Totally Radical' and 'Island-Bridge' Mean for NOAA Research, dissertation, George Washington University, March 2014, 18–56.

31. Council on Competitiveness, National Innovation Initiative, *Innovate America*, 2005, 8, http://www.compete.org/images/uploads/File/PDF%20Files/NII_Innovate_America.pdf.

32. Weiss and Bonvillian, *Structuring an Energy Technology Revolution*, 10, 38.

33. Romer, Endogenous Technological Change; Romer, Should the Government Subsidize.

34. Warren G. Bennis and Patricia W. Biederman, *Organizing Genius: The Secrets of Creative Collaboration* (New York: Basic Books, 1997).

35. Bonvillian, Connected Science Model; Bonvillian, Power Play.

36. Sen, Transformative Innovation, 44.

37. Robert D. Atkinson, *The Past and Future of America's Economy: Long Waves of Innovation That Power Cycle of Growth* (Cheltenham, UK: Edward Elgar. 2004); Carlota Perez, *Technological Revolutions and Finance Capital* (Cheltenham, UK: Edward Elgar, 2002).

38. Clayton Christensen, *The Innovator's Dilemma: When New Technologies Cause Great Firms to Fail* (Boston, MA: Harvard Business School, 1997).

39. Congressional Research Service, Federal Renewable Energy R&D Funding History: A Comparison with Funding for Nuclear Energy, Fossil Energy and Efficiency R&D, March 7, 2012, http://www.fas.org/sgp/crs/misc/RS22858.pdf.

40. Department of Energy, Office of Energy Efficiency and Renewable Energy, SunShot Initiative, http://energy.gov/eere/sunshot/sunshot-initiative.

41. While a series of low-cost start-up airlines, enabled by aviation deregulation legislation, failed in the 1980s, the advent of the Internet eventually displaced the oligopolistic control by three major carriers of computer reservation systems and the travel agents tied to these systems. This contributed to a return of new entrant air carriers.

42. Joby Warrick, Utilities wage campaign against rooftop solar, *Washington Post*, March 7, 2015, http://www.washingtonpost.com/national/health-science/utilities-sensing-threat-put-squeeze-on-booming-solar-roof-industry/2015/03/07/2d916f88-c1c9-11e4-ad5c-3b8ce89f1b89_story.html. Compare, MITEI, Future of Solar Energy (2015).

43. Marcus Wohlsen, New Jersey Bans Tesla to Ensure Buying a Car Will Always Suck, *Wired*, March 12, 2014, http://www.wired.com/2014/03/tesla-banned-ensure-process-buying-car-keeps-sucking/.

44. Suzanne Berger, How Finance Gutted Manufacturing, *Boston Review*, March–April 2014, 12–29; Elizabeth Reynolds, Hiram Semel, and Joyce Lawrence, Learning by

Building: Complementary Assets and the Migration of Capabilities in U.S. Innovation Firms, in *Production in the Innovation Economy*, ed. Richard Locke and Rachel Wellhausen (Cambridge, MA: MIT Press, 2014), 81–108.

45. Advanced Manufacturing Partnership, PCAST, *Report to the President on Accelerating U.S. Advanced Manufacturing*, October 2014, 41–43, http://www.whitehouse.gov/sites/default/files/microsites/ostp/PCAST/amp20_report_final.pdf (explores alternative financing mechanisms). This issue is detailed in chapter 13.

46. John Alic, Daniel Sarewitz, Charles Weiss, and William B. Bonvillian, A New Strategy for Energy Innovation, *Nature* 466 (July 15, 2010), 316–317.

47. HealthIT.gov, EHR Incentives and Certification, http://www.healthit.gov/providers-professionals/ehr-incentive-payment-timeline (EHR incentive system); HHS.gov/HealthCare, Secretary Kathleen Sebelius, *Innovation and Health Care*, May 28, 2013 (blog), http://www.hhs.gov/healthcare/facts/blog/2013/05/innovation.html (EHR use up 200%, expanding to half of physicians and four-fifths of hospitals).

48. Energy Power Research Institute, http://www.epri.com/About-Us/Pages/Our-Story.aspx.

49. Dan Fox, *The Convergence of Science and Governance: Research, Health Policy and American States* (Berkeley: University of California Press, 2010).

CHAPTER 12

1. The steps described in this section build on the discussion in Charles Weiss and William B. Bonvillian, *Structuring an Energy Technology Revolution* (Cambridge, MA: MIT Press, 2009).

2. William B. Bonvillian, The Connected Science Model for Innovation: The DARPA Role, in National Research Council, *21st Century Innovation Systems for Japan and the U.S.* (Washington, DC: National Academies Press, 2009), http://www.nap.edu/catalog.php?record_id=12194, 207.

3. Richard R. Van Atta, Fifty Years of Innovation and Discovery, in *DARPA: 50 Years of Bridging the Gap* (Arlington, VA: DARPA, 2008).

4. This discussion is drawn from William B. Bonvillian, The Connected Science Model for Innovation, in *21st Century Innovation Systems for the U.S. and Japan*, ed. Sadao Nagaoka, Masayuki Kondo, Kenneth Flamm, and Charles Wessner (Washington, DC: National Academies Press, 2009), 207, 209, 215.

5. William B. Bonvillian and Richard Van Atta, ARPA-E and DARPA: Applying the DARPA Model to Energy Innovation, *Journal of Technology Transfer*, October 2011.

6. Warren Bennis and Patricia Ward Beiderman, *Organizing Genius* (New York: Basic Books, 1997).

7. Bonvillian and Van Atta, ARPA-E and DARPA, 483–484. See also, on the origins of ARPA-E, Weiss and Bonvillian, *Structuring an Energy Technology Revolution*, 161–165, 185–186, 206, 260 n. 9, 262 nn. 17–19.

8. Bonvillian and Van Atta, ARPA-E and DARPA.

9. Tammy L. Carleton, The Value of Vision in Technological Innovation, dissertation, Stanford University, 2010, http://purl.stanford.edu/mk388mb2729; Bonvillian and Van Atta, ARPA-E and DARPA, 485.

10. See, for example, R. G. Cooper, S. J. Edgett, and E. J. Kleinschmidt, Optimizing the Stage Gate Process, *Research Technology Management* 45, no. 5 (2002), 21–27.

11. Warren G. Bennis and Patricia Ward Biederman, *Organizing Genius: The Secrets of Creative Collaboration* (New York: Basic Books, 1997), 206.

12. Ben Rich, *Skunkworks* (Boston: Little, Brown / Back Bay Books, 1996).

13. Michael A. Hiltzik, *Dealers of Lightning: Xerox PARC and the Dawn of the Computer Age* (New York: HarperCollins, 1999).

14. James Chposky and Ted Leonsis, *Blue Magic: The People, Power and Politics behind the IBM Personal Computer* (New York: Facts on File, 1986).

15. Douglas K. Smith, *Fumbling the Future: How Xerox Invented, Then Ignored the First Personal Computer* (New York: William Morrow, 1988).

16. Bonvillian and Van Atta, ARPA-E and DARPA, 486.

17. Although we group a number of his points within other categories, Avery Sen has taken the island/bridge model and applied to it to series of component elements, viewing it as a broad foundational model. These elements include, on the island side, limiting the size and duration of research projects ("Stay Small"), avoiding bureaucracy ("Feel Free"), focusing on the creative talent of scientists and engineers ("Herd Nerds"), and embracing talent diversity and attracting excellence ("Be Better"). On the bridge side, the elements he cites include: directing outcomes for societal, not simply scientific outcomes ("Make It Matter"), engaging a range of stakeholders ("Meet and Greet"), measuring concrete results ("Keep Clear"), and dialoging continuously with those with expertise and experience ("Listen and Learn"). Avery Sen, Transformative Innovation: What 'Totally Radical' and 'Island-Bridge' Mean for NOAA Research, dissertation, George Washington University, March, 78–101.

18. Henry W. Chesborough, The Era of Open Innovation, *MIT Sloan Review* 44, no. 3 (April 2003), http://sloanreview.mit.edu/article/the-era-of-open-innovation/.

19. Robert W. Rycroft and Don E. Kash, Innovation Policy for Complex Technologies, *Issues in Science and Technology* (Fall 1999), http://www.issues.org/16.1/rycroft.htm.

20. Brian Cathcart, *The Fly in the Cathedral* (New York: Farrar, Straus and Giroux, 2004).

21. Bonvillian and Van Atta, ARPA-E and DARPA, 476–477, 492.

22. Steven Miluvich and John M. A. Roy, The Next Small Thing: An Introduction to Nanotechnology, *Merrill Lynch Industry Comment*, September 4, 2001, 2.

23. Ronald W. Clark, *The Rise of the Boffins* (London: Phoenix House, 1962), 23–31.

24. Clark, *Rise of the Boffins*, 33–54.

25. Ronald W. Clark, *Tizard* (Cambridge, MA: MIT Press, 1965), 23–48, 105–192.

26. The term "operational research" was coined by A. V. Rowe in 1937 while working as assistant director at the RAF radar research and testing center at Bawdsey; "operations research" is the American term. Stephen Budiansky, *Blackett's War* (New York: Alfred A. Knopf, 2013), 87.

27. Clark, *Rise of the Boffins*, 8–9.

28. Budiansky, *Blackett's War*, 117–118.

29. Budiansky, *Blackett's War*, 113–166, 221–249.

30. Clark, *Tizard*, 248–272.

31. MIT's history of the Rad Lab states, "Running conferences [with Tizard Mission members] continued till October 13 [1940], and by that time practically everybody was agreed that what the program needed was a central laboratory built on the British lines: staffed by academic physicists, committed to fundamental research but committed even more than that to doing anything and everything needed to make microwaves [radar] work." MIT Radiation Laboratory, Five Years at the Radiation Laboratory, 1946, 12, https://archive.org/details/fiveyearsatradia00mass. See also Clark, *Tizard*, 265, 267 (Tizard meetings with V. Bush), 268–269 (mission meetings with Loomis).

32. Jennet Conant, *Tuxedo Park* (New York: Simon & Shuster 2002), 178–289.

33. Kai Bird and Martin J. Sherwin, *American Prometheus: J. Robert Oppenheimer* (New York: Alfred A. Knopf, 2005), 205–228, 255–259, 268–285, 293–297.

34. The discussion in this section is drawn from William B. Bonvillian and Charles Weiss, Taking Covered Wagons East: A New Innovation Theory for Energy and

Other Established Sectors, *Innovations* 4, no. 4 (Fall 2009), 289–300. The authors thank the journal's editors for permission to use this material. See also, Weiss and Bonvillian, *Structuring an Energy Technology Revolution*, 34–36, 44–50, 151–185.

35. Lewis M. Branscomb and Philip E. Auerswald, *Between Invention and Innovation: An Analysis of Funding for Early-State Technology Development, Part I—Early Stage Development*, NIST GCR 02-841, November 2002, http://www.atp.nist.gov/eao/gcr02-841/contents.htm, 2.

36. White House, Materials Genome Initiative website, http://www.whitehouse.gov/mgi.

37. This concept is discussed in Clayton Christensen, *The Innovator's Dilemma: When New Technologies Cause Great Firms to Fail* (Boston, MA: Harvard Business School Press, 1997).

38. Technology roadmapping is discussed in Weiss and Bonvillian, *Structuring an Energy Technology Revolution*, 171–177.

39. Larry Browning and Judy Shetler, *Sematech: Saving the U.S. Semiconductor Industry* (College Station: Texas A&M Press, 2000).

40. As an example of an R&D program designed to "drive down the production cost curve,", the Energy Department's SunShot initiative is organized to drive down the cost of solar power so it can compete with the cost of fossil fuel-based power by 2020. Department of Energy, SunShot Initiative, http://energy.gov/eere/sunshot-initiative.

41. This gap-filling approach in the energy sector is explored in detail in Weiss and Bonvillian, *Structuring an Energy Technology Revolution*, 151–185.

42. For example, ARPA-E was created to help fill this translational research gap in the energy sector. Bonvillian and Van Atta, ARPA-E and DARPA, 483–486. Other front-end innovation reforms in the Department of Energy are discussed in William B. Bonvillian, Time for Climate Plan B, *Issues in Science and Technology*, Winter 2011, http://issues.org/27-2/bonvillian-4/, 53–54.

CHAPTER 13

1. This chapter draws on William B. Bonvillian, Reinventing American Manufacturing: The Role of Innovation, *Innovations* 7, no. 3 (Fall 2012), 108–118. The authors thank the editors of that journal for permission to use this material.

2. Stephanie Shipp et al., *Emerging Global Trends in Advanced Manufacturing*, Report P-4603 (Alexandria, VA: Institute for Defense Analysis, March 2012), 9–17, http://www.wilsoncenter.org/sites/default/files/Emerging_Global_Trends_in_Advanced_Manufacturing.pdf.

3. Office of Science and Technology Policy and National Science and Technology Council, Materials Genome Initiative for Global Competitiveness, June 2011, http://www.whitehouse.gov/sites/default/files/microsites/ostp/materials_genome_initiative-final.pdf. See also OSTP, National Science and Technology Council Materials Genome Subcommittee, Materials Genome Initiative Strategic Plan, June 2014, http://www.nist.gov/mgi/upload/MGI-StrategicPlan-2014.pdf.

4. Advanced Manufacturing Partnership, President's Council of Advisors for Science and Technology, Capturing Domestic Competitive Advantage for Advanced Manufacturing, July 2012, 19, http://www.whitehouse.gov/sites/default/files/microsites/ostp/pcast_amp_steering_committee_report_final_july_17_2012.pdf. The AMP report, based on surveys of industry and university researchers, proposed 11 candidate technology paradigms: advanced sensing, measurement, and process control; advanced materials design, synthesis, and processing; sustainable manufacturing; nanomanufacturing; flexible electronics manufacturing; biomanufacturing and bioinformatics; additive manufacturing; advanced manufacturing equipment and testing

equipment; industrial robotics; and advanced forming and joining technologies. The second AMP report developed pilot technology strategies around three industry priority areas for advanced manufacturing. See Advanced Manufacturing Partnership, PCAST, Accelerating U.S. Advanced Manufacturing, AMP2.0 Report, October 2014, http://www.whitehouse.gov/sites/default/files/microsites/ostp/PCAST/amp20_report_final.pdf. See also The Third Industrial Revolution (special report), *Economist*, April 21, 2012, 15, 54ff.; Howard Harary, NIST, Findings from the Extreme Manufacturing Workshop, PowerPoint presentation, February 24, 2011, http://www.ndia.org/Divisions/Divisions/Manufacturing/Documents/119b%20presentations/10%20Harray.pdf.

5. Jeanne Mansfield, DARPA Administrators: Just Make It, *MIT News*, December 14, 2011 (with video of talk), http://web.mit.edu/newsoffice/2011/darpa-manufacturing-event-1214.html.

6. MIT Washington Office (Eliza Eddison), Survey of Federal Manufacturing Efforts, September 2010, http://web.mit.edu/dc/policy/MIT%20Survey%20of%20Federal%20Manufacturing%20Efforts.pdf. See also MIT Washington Office (Aneesh Anand), Survey of Selected Federal Manufacturing Programs at NIST, DOE, DOD and NSF, September 2014, http://dc.mit.edu/resources-links.

7. Advanced Manufacturing Partnership, Capturing Domestic Competitive Advantage.

8. David M. Hart, An Agent, Not a Mole: Assessing the White House Office of Science and Technology Policy, *Science and Public Policy*, August 25, 2013, 6–7, http://spp.oxfordjournals.org/content/early/2013/08/24/scipol.sct061.full.pdf.

9. National Nanotechnology Initiative, http://www.nano.gov.

10. Douglas Powell, Tonio Buonassisi, et al., Crystalline Silicon Photovoltaics: A Cost Analysis Framework for Determining Technology Pathways to Reach Baseload Electricity Costs, *Energy & Environmental Science* 5 (February 2012), 5874–5883; Alan Goodrich, Douglas Powell, Ted James, Michael Woodhouse, and Tonio Buonassisi, Assessing the Drivers of Regional Trends in Solar Photovoltaic Manufacturing, *Energy and Environmental Science* 6 (July 23, 2013), 2811–2821.

11. Tonio Buonassisi and Douglas Powell, Photovoltaic Research Lab, Photovoltaics (PV) Manufacturing, U.S. and China (slide presentation), October 14, 2011; Goodrich et al., "Assessing the Drivers," figures 2, 3, 4.

12. James P. Womack, Daniel T. Jones, and Daniel Roos, *The Machine That Changed the World* (New York: Free Press, 1990).

13. Industrie 4.0 Working Group, National Academy of Science and Engineering, *Securing the Future of German Manufacturing: Recommendations for Implementing the Strategic Initiative Industry 4.0*, sponsored by the Federal Ministry of Education and Research, April 2013, http://www.acatech.de/fileadmin/user_upload/Baumstruktur_nach_Website/Acatech/root/de/Material_fuer_Sonderseiten/Industrie_4.0/Final_report__Industrie_4.0_accessible.pdf; Technology Strategy Board (UK), High Value Manufacturing: Key Technology Area, 2008–11, http://webarchive.nationalarchives.gov.uk/20130221185318/www.innovateuk.org/_assets/pdf/corporate-publications/tsb_highvaluemanu.pdf; Shipp et al., *Emerging Global Trends*, 68–72.

14. As one of a number of examples, China, as noted in chapter 4, appears to be developing a new approach to systematic innovation in the scale-up of production, using multidirectional learning pathways shared between firms that lead to production speed, scaling and cost advantages. See also Chapter 9; Jonas Nahm and Edward Steinfeld, Scale-up Nation: China's Specialization in innovative Manufacturing, *World Development* 54 (February 2014), 288–300. Compare Suzanne Berger with the MIT Task Force

on Production and Innovation Economy, *Making in America* (Cambridge, MA: MIT Press, 2013), 125–140 (German manufacturing model).

15. Stephen J. Ezell and Robert D. Atkinson, The Case for a National Manufacturing Strategy, Information Technology and Innovation Foundation, April 2011, 12, http://www2.itif.org/2011-national-manufacturing-strategy.pdf (notes German manufacturing multiplier effect).

16. See technology roadmapping discussion in Weiss and Bonvillian, *Structuring an Energy Technology Revolution*, 171–177.

17. Department of Energy, Office of Energy Efficiency and Renewable Energy, SunShot Initiative, http://energy.gov/eere/sunshot/sunshot-initiative.

18. Department of Energy, Quadrennial Energy Review, http://energy.gov/epsa/initiatives/quadrennial-energy-review-qer.

19. Department of Energy, Quadrennial Technology Review, 2011, http://energy.gov/sites/prod/files/ReportOnTheFirstQTR.pdf.

20. Advanced Manufacturing Partnership, Accelerating U.S. Advanced Manufacturing.

21. Advanced Manufacturing Partnership, Accelerating U.S. Advanced Manufacturing, 58–70.

22. A number of these factors are evaluated in Advanced Manufacturing Partnership, Capturing Domestic Competitive Advantage, table 1, at 18. See also Advanced Manufacturing Partnership, Accelerating U.S. Advanced Manufacturing, 59–60.

23. Environmental Protection Agency (EPA), Global Greenhouse Gas Emissions Data (by Source), http://www.epa.gov/climatechange/ghgemissions/global.html.

24. Department of Energy, Energy Efficiency and Renewable Energy Office (EERE), Clean Energy Manufacturing Initiative, http://energy.gov/eere/cemi/clean-energy-manufacturing-initiative.

25. Erica Fuchs, The Impact of Manufacturing Offshore on Technology Competitiveness: Implications for U.S. Policy, Connect Innovation Institute report, San Diego, CA, 2012, 1, 6, http://www.connect.org/programs/innovation-institute/docs/fuchs-white-paper-0212.pdf.

26. Fuchs, Impact of Manufacturing Offshore, 11.

27. As first noted in chapter 6, the MIT Production in the Innovation Economy study of this start-up question, examining start-ups in the Boston area, found that for promising start-ups, the VC would stay in longer than the five to seven-year yardstick, through 10 years or more, but after the five to seven years it would effectively place the firm on what could be called "income maintenance." The study found that when the firm, after moving through the difficult product design phase, asked the VC for funds for production scale-up (which for complex, non-IT capital goods can require tens of millions), it was typically told that the VC doesn't finance that stage and directed to a contract manufacturer or sovereign wealth fund abroad. These entities are specialized in taking the production risk and/or organized to manage the costs. Elizabeth Reynolds, Hiram Semel, and Joyce Lawrence, Learning by Building: Complementary Assets and the Migration of Capabilities in U.S. Innovation Firms, in *Production in the Innovation Economy*, ed. Richard Locke and Rachel Wellhausen (Cambridge, MA: MIT Press, 2014), 81–108.

28. Reynolds, Semmel and Lawrence, Learning by Building, 84 93–97, 100–101.

29. See Advanced Manufacturing Partnership, Accelerating U.S. Advanced Manufacturing, 83–86. Programs noted in this subsection are discussed in Peter L. Singer, MIT Washington Office, Manufacturing Scale-Up: Summary of 14 Relevant Federal Financing Programs, May 27, 2014, http://dc.mit.edu/resources-links.

30. Andrew Lo, How Financial Engineering Can Cure Cancer, Stop Global Warming, and Solve the Energy Crisis, MIT Lecture, March 3, 2011, http://ttv.mit.edu/

videos/11921-mfin-faculty-speaker---andrew-lo; David E. Fagnan, Jose Maria Fernandez, Andrew Lo, and Roger M. Stein, Can Financial Engineering Cure Cancer? *American Economic Review* 103, no. 3 (May 2013), 406–411, http://dx.doi.org/10.1257/aer.103.3.406 (applies portfolio approach to cancer research).

31. See, generally, Robert M. Solow, *Growth Theory: An Exposition* (New York: Oxford University Press, 2000); Paul M. Romer, Endogenous Technological Change, *Journal of Political Economy* 98, no. 5 (1990), 72–102, http://artsci.wustl.edu/~econ502/Romer.pdf; William B. Bonvillian, The Connected Science Model for Innovation: The DARPA Model, in *21st Century Innovation Systems for the U.S. and Japan*, ed. Sadao Nagaoka, Masayuki Kondo, Kenneth Flamm, and Charles Wessner (Washington, DC: National Academies Press, 2009), 208–210. http://books.nap.edu/openbook.php?record_id=12194&page=206.

32. Weiss and Bonvillian, *Structuring an Energy Technology Revolution*, 13–34.

33. Daniel Breznitz and Peter Cowhey, *America's Two Systems of Innovation: Recommendations for Policy Changes to Support Innovation, Production and Job Creation* (San Diego, CA: Connect Innovation Institute, February 2012). See also William B. Bonvillian, Advanced Manufacturing Policies and Paradigms for Innovation, *Science* 392 (December 6, 2013), 1174.

34. Both systems are delineated in Weiss and Bonvillian, *Structuring an Energy Technology Revolution*, 13–26.

35. Daniel Breznitz, Why Germany Dominates the U.S. in Innovation, *Harvard Business Review*, blog, May 27, 2014, http://blogs.hbr.org/2014/05/why-germany-dominates-the-u-s-in-innovation/.

36. MIT Washington Office, Survey of Federal Manufacturing Efforts; MIT Washington Office, Selected Federal Manufacturing Programs.

37. Office of Science and Technology Policy, National Science and Technology Council, A National Strategic Plan for Advanced Manufacturing, February 2012, http://www.whitehouse.gov/sites/default/files/microsites/ostp/iam_advancedmanufacturing_strategicplan_2012.pdf.

38. A survey of partnership models is found in Institute for Defense Analysis, Science and Technology Policy Institute, *Advanced Manufacturing Partnerships: Identifying Areas of Investment: A Review of Methods Used by Federal, Private Sector and International Programs*, report draft, February 9, 2012.

39. Vernon W. Ruttan, *Is War Necessary for Economic Growth? Military Procurement and Technology Development* (New York: Oxford University Press, 2006).

40. Defense Science Board, *Technology and Innovation Enablers for Superiority in 2030*, October 2013), vii–ix, http://www.acq.osd.mil/dsb/reports/DSB2030.pdf.

41. Bonvillian, Connected Science Model, 206–207.

42. The DOD's Manufacturing Technology (ManTech) program (an approximately $250 million program across the services) understands and works within this strategic context. ManTech, The DOD Manufacturing Technology Program: Strategic Plan, March 2009, ES-1–ES-6, https://www.dodmantech.com/relatedresources/DoD_ManTech_Strat_Plan_Aug_18_Final_low_res.pdf.

43. The Advanced Manufacturing National Program Office, which includes NIST, DOD, NSF and DOE, could be a first step toward getting around these seams. http://manufacturing.gov/amp/ampnpo.html.

44. Gary P. Pisano and Willy Shih, *Producing Prosperity: Why America Needs a Manufacturing Renaissance* (Cambridge, MA: Harvard Business Press, 2012). See also Berger, *Making in America*.

45. Fraunhofer Institutes and Research Centers, http://www.fraunhofer.de/en/institutes-research-establishments.html.

46. Former DARPA director Regina Dugan, Statement to the House Subcommittee on Terrorism, Unconventional Threats and Capabilities of the House Armed Services Committee, 111th Cong., 1st Sess. (March 23, 2010), 11 ("What is the fundamental technical challenge in making new things? . . . It is in the seams. The seams between each 'stage' of development . . . design, prototyping, early production runs, limited and large-scale manufacturing").

47. Paul Osterman, and Andrew Weaver, Skills and Skill Gaps in Manufacturing, in *Production in the Innovation Economy,* ed. Richard Locke and Rachel Wellhausen (Cambridge, MA: MIT Press, 2014), 17–50.

48. Compare the MIT results with a 2011 survey by the Manufacturing Institute and Deloitte, which indicated that 82% of responding managers in manufacturing firms had had moderate to serious problems with the availability of skilled manufacturing candidates, with 74% of manufacturers reporting that this skills gap has affected their ability to expand operations. The respondents reported that 5% of manufacturing jobs were going unfilled, despite a high unemployment rate, because of skills problems. The survey did not study whether significant compensation increases could alter this problem, and unlike the IT survey, was more general and did not focus on actual time to fill vacant jobs data. National Association of Manufacturers, 2011 Skills Gap Report, 2011, http://www.themanufacturinginstitute.org/Research/Skills-Gap-in-Manufacturing/2011-Skills-Gap-Report/2011-Skills-Gap-Report.aspx; Tom Morrison, Bob Maciejewski, et al., Boiling Point? The Skills Gap in U.S. Manufacturing. A Report on Talent in the Manufacturing Industry, sponsored by Deloitte and the Manufacturing Institute, 2011, 6, http://www.themanufacturinginstitute.org/~/media/A07730B2A798437D98501E798C2E13AA.ashx.

49. Arvind Kaushal, Thomas Mayor, and Patricia Riedl, Manufacturing's Wake-Up Call, *Strategy & Business 64,* Booz & Company and Tauber Institute for Global Operations, University of Michigan, August 3, 2011, 38, http://www.tauber.umich.edu/docs/Manuf-WakeUp_w_Cover.pdf.

50. Joe Anderson, Council Chairman, and Mike Laszkiewicz, Workforce Development Subcommittee Chair to Department of Commerce Secretary Gary Locke, The Manufacturing Council, July 2011, http://www.trade.gov/manufacturingcouncil/documents/MC_Workforce_08222011.pdf.

51. New workforce training and apprenticeship models were a major focus of the companies, universities, community colleges, and unions undertaking the Advanced Manufacturing Partnership study. Advanced Manufacturing Partnership, Accelerating U.S. Advanced Manufacturing, 7–10, 30–37, 71–74.

52. Advanced Manufacturing Portal, National Network for Manufacturing Institutes, http://www.manufacturing.gov/nnmi.html.

53. Advanced Manufacturing Partnership, Capturing Domestic Competitive Advantage, recommendation 3, 22–23.

54. Susan Helper and Howard Wial, Accelerating Advanced Manufacturing Research Centers, report, Brookings Project on State and Metropolitan Innovation (Feb. 2011) (proposes that states shift from their role in attracting business to improving existing and new manufacturing capability).

55. Advanced Manufacturing Partnership, Accelerating U.S. Advanced Manufacturing, 73–87.

56. Advanced Manufacturing Partnership, Accelerating U.S. Advanced Manufacturing, 29.

57. White House Fact Sheet: President Announces New Actions to Further Strengthen U.S. Manufacturing, Office of the Press Secretary, October 27, 2014, http://www.whitehouse.gov/the-press-office/2014/10/27/fact-sheet-president-obama-announces-new-actions-further-strengthen-us-m.

58. HR 83, Consolidated and Further Continuing Appropriations Act of 2015, Rules Committee print 113-159, 113th Cong., 2nd Sess., passed by Congress on December 14, 2014, 226–251, http://docs.house.gov/billsthisweek/20141208/CPRT-113-HPRT-RU00-HR83sa.pdf.

59. The history and proposals of the two AMP projects are summarized at Advanced Manufacturing Portal, About the Advanced Manufacturing Partnership, http://www.manufacturing.gov/amp.html.

60. Maker Movement, Techopedia (definition), http://www.techopedia.com/definition/28408/maker-movement; White House, President Obama at the White House Maker Faire: Today's DIY Is Tomorrow's Made in America, June 18, 2014, http://www.whitehouse.gov/blog/2014/06/18/president-obama-white-house-maker-faire-today-s-diy-tomorrow-s-made-america.

61. Advanced Manufacturing Partnership, Capturing Domestic Competitive Advantage, recommendation 6, 35, appendix C. The Advanced Technological Education (ATE) centers program at NSF also sponsors workforce development at community colleges, with industry partnerships: http://atecenters.org/#t-slide-one. These NSF ATE grants have played an important role in establishing advanced manufacturing education programs at community colleges, http://www.nsf.gov/pubs/2011/nsf11692/nsf11692.htm. See also Maggie Lloyd, Review of the NSF's Advanced Technological Education (ATE) Program: ATE's Role in Advanced Manufacturing Education and Training, MIT Washington Office, February 2013, http://dc.mit.edu/sites/default/files/MIT%20Review%20of%20NSF%20ATE%20Program.pdf.

62. Lloyd, Review.

63. See for example, MIT, Masters of Engineering in Manufacturing, MIT Department of Mechanical Engineering, http://web.mit.edu/meng-manufacturing/,

64. In addition, degrees in science, technology, engineering and mathematics (STEM) have stagnated, and some 50% of those intending to major in STEM fields in US colleges drop out of those fields. PCAST, Engage to Excel, OSTP, Executive Office of the President, February 2012, 5, 47–66, http://www.whitehouse.gov/sites/default/files/microsites/ostp/pcast-engage-to-excel-final_feb.pdf; see, generally, Paul M. Romer, Should the Government Subsidize Supply or Demand in the Market for Scientists and Engineers? NBER Working Paper 7723, June 2000, http://time.dufe.edu.cn/article/romer/8.pdf; Richard B. Freeman, Does Globalization of the Scientific/Engineering Workforce Threaten U.S. Economic Leadership?, NBER Working Paper No. 11457 (July 2005), http://www.nber.org/papers/w11457.pdf?new_window=1.

65. A new approach developed by Prof. Suzanne de Treville and Prof. Norman Schurhoff of the University of Lausanne, using an in-depth operations research analysis, indicates that firms may have systematically overstated the gains of offshoring by failing to adequately account for a series of cost factors, such as inventory oversupply caused by additional shipping time. The Department of Commerce is now circulating to US manufacturers the online calculation tool these researchers have developed to assist firms in this analysis. See Susan Helper, Chief Economist, U.S. Department of Commerce, New Tool Shows Manufacturing in America Carries Huge Potential Savings, *The Commerce Blog*, October 1, 2014, http://www.commerce.gov/blog/2014/10/01/new-tool-shows-manufacturing-america-carries-huge-potential-savings-reshoring-success.

CHAPTER 14

1. Frederick Jackson Turner, *The Frontier in American History* (New York; Henry Holt, 1921), chap. 1. Available at http://xroads.virginia.edu/~HYPER/TURNER/home.html (note: first delivered as a paper in 1893 to the American Historical Association).

2. Robert M. Solow, *Growth Theory: An Exposition*, 2nd ed. (New York: Oxford University Press, 2000); Solow, Growth Theory and After (Nobel Prize Lecture, December 8, 1987, http://nobelprize.org/nobel_prizes/economics/laureates/1987/solow-lecture.html/.

3. Christopher Freeman, Innovation and Long Cycles of Economic Development, Department of Economics, University of Campinas, São Paulo, Brazil, August 25–27, 1982, http://www.globelicsacademy.net/pdf/JoseCassiolato_2.pdf; Carlota Perez, *Technological Revolutions and Financial Capital* (Cheltenham, UK: Edward Elgar, 2002), 3–46; Robert D. Atkinson, *The Past and Future of America's Economy: Long Waves of Innovation that Power Cycles of Growth* (Cheltenham, UK: Edward Elgar 2004), 3–40. As noted in chapter 13, the United States missed the quality manufacturing innovation wave launched by Japan in the 1970s–1980s.

4. The concept of a well-defended status quo setting in after a freewheeling period without rules is developed in Debora L. Spar, *Ruling the Waves: Cycles of Discovery, Chaos, and Wealth, from Compass to the Internet* (New York: Harcourt, 2001).

5. The concept of the complex established legacy sector is first discussed in chapter 1.

6. Information Technology and Innovation Foundation, Eroding Our Foundations: Sequestration, R&D and U.S. Economic Growth, September 2012, http://www2.itif.org/2012-eroding-foundation.pdf.

7. David Hart, *Forged Consensus* (Princeton, NJ: Princeton University Press, 1998), 17–29 (policy doctrine); Robert D. Atkinson, *Understanding and Maximizing America's Evolutionary Economy* (Washington, DC: Information Technology and Innovation Foundation, October 2014), 14–19, 34–44 (economic doctrine).

8. Mariana Mazzucato, *The Entrepreneurial State: Debunking Public vs. Private Sector Myths* (New York: Anthem Press 2013).

Glossary of Terms

applied research.   Research whose major motivation is the hope that the knowledge gained will lead to useful application. This research may or may not be **fundamental**.

asymmetric innovative capability.   The situation in which one country has more capacity to innovate than another, forcing the weaker country to import technology that may be suited more to the exporter's needs than to its own.

back end.   The phase of the innovation cycle in which a demonstrated technological idea becomes a commercialized product or process.

barrier to entry.   An obstacle to the entry of a firm or a technology into a business or market.

basic research.   Research intended to increase understanding of the natural world, whether motivated by curiosity or by the hope of practical application. See **curiosity-driven**, **fundamental**, and **applied research**.

Baumol's cost disease.   The characteristic of many services, such as live orchestras, by which labor requirements and productivity cannot change, so that costs inevitably go up when the price of labor increases.

"black boxing."   Assessing the impacts of a given technology without understanding its inner technical workings or scientific basis.

breakthrough.   A sudden, dramatic, and important discovery or development, especially one that occurs after a long period of relatively unsuccessful research or that leads to a technology that provides new functionality. See **radical innovation**.

buy, then make.   An approach to defense procurement through which the Defense Department contracts for a produced good before it is made. See **make, then buy**.

cap and trade.   An emission trading system in which a maximum amount of emission of a given pollutant is set (the *cap*) and in which potential polluters are allocated or sold (often by auction) allowances to emit that pollutant (also called *emission credits*) which they may trade among themselves. See **carbon charge**.

carbon charge.   Any system for increasing the cost to the emitter of emitting carbon dioxide into the atmosphere. The most prominent examples are **carbon taxes** and **cap-and-trade** regimes. Carbon here is shorthand for carbon dioxide.

carbon tax.   Direct taxes on carbon dioxide emissions.

carrots and sticks.   "Carrots" are incentives like tax credits, price guarantees, or government purchasing programs; "sticks" are regulatory mandates like renewable portfolio standards, emission taxes, and fuel economy standards.

challenge-based research.   A model of research management, typical of DARPA, that seeks research advances that will result in the solution to significant technological challenges. See **right-left model**.

change agent.   An institution or individual that pushes innovation advances through structural barriers protecting the paradigm of a legacy sector. See **meta-change agent**.

collective action. The phenomenon where many small units (for example, farmers or builders) join forces to protect their interests, for example by sharing the costs of research and development. The need for collective action is a **market imperfection** typical of **legacy sector paradigms**.

commercialization. Translation of an invention or other new development into a commercial product and introduction of that product into the marketplace.

complex, high-value goods. Engineering-intensive goods that often contain numerous components (which may be customized), require a wide breadth of knowledge and skills in their creation and production, embody technical novelty, and require groups of firms in their production.

component technology. A technology that is part of a larger **platform** or system containing other related technologies or systems. For example, carbon dioxide sequestration technology is a component of a larger system for carbon dioxide capture, transport, and sequestration.

connected science and technology. A model of research management whereby innovation actors from private, academic, and government sectors collaborate, working at all stages of the innovation process from research through to implementation and employing the **challenge** model.

contested launch. The launch of a technology that faces political or other nonmarket opposition from competitors or from the industrial sectors that must absorb it.

context. See **innovation context**.

convergence research. Integrated, cross-disciplinary research combining the life sciences, the physical sciences, and engineering.

cost disease. See **Baumol's cost disease**.

curiosity-driven research. **Basic research** whose major motivation is the desire of the researcher to learn more about the workings of the natural world.

demand pull. A model of the dynamic of **innovation** that portrays it as being driven by the pull of the market, rather than by advances in science and technology. Same as **market pull**.

demand-side policy. A policy intended to influence the demand for a technology or resource, especially energy, often through pricing but sometimes by a tax or **cap-and-trade** regime. This is also termed a *demand-oriented* policy.

demonstration. A full-scale operating model of a new technology, intended to show its practical utility to potential users and to gather data on its technical and economic characteristics under realistic conditions.

deployment. Installation and use of a technology or equipment on a substantial scale. Same as **implementation**.

detailed engineering. The full definition of the technical requirements for a product or project.

development. The process of turning a research result or an **invention** into a marketable product.

disabling environment. An **innovation environment** that discourages and is *un*favorable to innovation.

discontinuous innovation. An especially effective **secondary innovation**, that is, one that makes a major improvement in existing **functionality**.

disruptive technology. Originally, an **innovation** that begins in lower profit, low-end market segments ignored by well-established firms (which typically concentrate on adding extra functions to high-end, high-profit products) and improves, expands, and eventually displaces **incumbent technologies**. Examples include the personal computer that displaced mainframes, or the low-cost airlines that displaced legacy carriers.

The use of the term has been expanded to include any new technology that displaces a well-established **dominant** product **design** and its **value chain** or **value network**.

distributed manufacturing. Same as **unbundled manufacturing**.

dominant design. A product design that comes to dominate the market and to set the expectations customers and users regarding appearance, performance, and other characteristics.

dynamic comparative advantage. Comparative advantage achieved by strategic investment, as in education and research, rather than from natural resources or geographic characteristics.

dynamics of innovation. The forces that stimulate the process of innovation, and the patterns by which these forces operate.

economies of scale. A situation in which an increase in production volume or other scale gives rise to a decrease in unit cost.

"elephant" technology. A technology subject to the **market imperfection** of **lumpiness**.

embedded technology. Technology that was needed to design a machine or process, and that is in effect transferred to the purchaser or user through its purchase or use.

enabling environment. An **innovation environment** that facilitates and is favorable to innovation.

enabling innovation. An innovation that stimulates other innovations in different parts of the economy. Such an innovation typically creates a new **functionality** and corresponding gains in productivity. Examples include interchangeable machine parts, aircraft, nuclear energy, computing, the Internet, and spaceflight. Also known as a **generative innovation**.

extended pipeline. A model of innovation that describes the system that not only funds the early stages of research, as in the **pipeline model of innovation**, but also supports the follow-on stages, including **research, development,** product design, **prototype, demonstration,** and **test bed,** as well as often creating the initial market. This is the system established by the US Defense Department.

externality. A cost that is not borne or a benefit that is not gained by the makers, purchasers, or users of a product, or by the investors in or the beneficiaries of a project, and is therefore not counted in its accounting framework, such as an impact on environment, safety, or public health.

feasibility. See **techno-economic feasibility**.

first-mover advantage. The advantage accruing to the first firm or product to enter a new market. There are also first-mover *dis*advantages.

forcing mechanism. Any change in price, policy or other circumstances that induces a change in a technology.

front end. The phases of the innovation process that precede commercialization: **research, development,** and (in some cases) initial **prototyping** and **demonstration**.

frontier sector. A sector based on new, advanced, enabling technology, such as information technology and biotechnology. It is in contrast to a **legacy sector**.

Fulda Gap. A strategically important area of Western Europe through which invaders from the East could gain access to a favorable crossing of the Rhine River. During the Cold War, it was thought to be the most likely route of land invasion by the Soviet Union into Western Europe.

full-spectrum innovation. An innovation where an economy realizes the full gains from every stage of the innovation process, from research through production and implementation. This is in contrast to the situation in recent years, in which the United States has been realizing only partial gains from its innovation system because it has been offshoring much of its manufacturing capacity.

functionality. See **new functionality.**

fundamental research. Same as **basic research.**

generative innovation. Same as **enabling innovation.**

generic research. See **precompetitive research.**

GNP multiplier. The total added to the GNP by an innovation through both primary (direct employment and value added) and secondary effects (such as employment and value added in service and supplier industries), divided by the primary, direct effects.

governmental or regulatory impediment to innovation. Regulation, standard, or other governmental action that can protect incumbent technologies from more innovative new entrant technologies. Note that government and regulation can also stimulate or encourage innovation.

"great group(s)." Groups capable of breakthrough innovation by dint of their deep collaboration, remarkable talent in a range of complementary fields, strong leadership, focus on a competitive challenge, devotion to a mission, willingness to follow an organizational ruleset, and backing from an **innovation ecosystem.**

Habilitationsschrift. A sort of second Ph.D. required of most German academics that aspire to a teaching position in a German university.

implementation. Same as **deployment.**

increasing returns. The tendency, found in information and manufactured products, for a technology that moves ahead to get further ahead, often through the phenomenon of **technology lock in.**

incremental innovation. An innovation that provides relatively small improvements to the existing functionality of a technology, such as lowered costs or improved features. See also **innovation, radical innovation**, and **secondary innovation.**

incumbent technology. An established technology prominent among users.

induced innovation. An innovation provoked by a change in prices, and thus in costs, or more generally by a change in market conditions or policies, such as those for environment or safety. For example, rising energy prices may stimulate more rapid innovation in energy efficiency than would otherwise occur. See also **pipeline, extended pipeline, demand pull**, and **policy pull.**

"inducible" technologies. Technologies that are ready for implementation but that have lacked competitiveness because of perverse pricing or other external factors and that could be quickly implemented if these were to change. See also **"line of sight" innovations.**

industrial ecosystem. See **manufacturing ecosystem.**

innovation. The **implementation** of a new idea, invention, technology, or product on a substantial scale. See **technological innovation.**

innovation actor. Any person or institution that plays a role in the innovation process.

innovation context. Broad features of culture (especially attitudes toward novelty and risk), macroeconomic policy, business climate, legal structure, labor and trade policy, banking and finance that influence the speed and direction of innovation at the national or sectoral level. These factors contribute as much to the state of innovation in a country as do the institutions and policies that are established for the explicit purpose of encouraging, facilitating and supporting research, innovation, and the development of technological capacity. Like the **innovation environment**, this can be defined at either the national or sectoral level.

innovation ecosystem. Same as **innovation environment.**

innovation enabler. See **meta-change agent.**

innovation environment. The sum of the **innovation context** and the **innovation system**. This can be defined at either the national or the sectoral level. See **national innovation system** and **national innovation environment.**

innovation intensity. The ratio of national expenditure on R & D to GNP.

innovation organization. A model for the **dynamics of innovation** that is based on the orchestration of systems and organizations such as universities, government, and firms and the linkages and connections between them, and includes not only the **innovation system** but also the **innovation environment**, so as to address both technological issues and broader issues of the innovation environment. It requires a **change agent** to orchestrate these linkages.

innovation system. The institutions and policies that are established for the explicit purpose of encouraging, facilitating, and supporting research, innovation, and the development of technological capacity. At the national level, these institutions together are known in the literature as the **national innovation system**. Like the **innovation environment** and the **innovation context**, the **innovation system** can be defined at either the national or sectoral level.

innovation value chain. The value chain that links the actors involved in all the stages of innovation from conception of an idea (ideation) to research and through to final production.

invention. The first reduction to practice of a new technological idea. This typically includes **proof of concept** and the production of a **prototype**.

island-bridge model. A model of innovation management, typical of DARPA and its imitators, by which a relatively small, flexible, innovative organization lodged within a much larger bureaucracy is protected from normal bureaucratic influences and controls (the "island") but is permitted and is expected to cultivate special relationships (the "bridge") with top management and with the operators that would have to put the innovations it produces into practice.

jobless innovation. Innovation whose production is moved offshore, so that the benefits of the resulting manufacturing employment accrue to a country other than the one in which the innovation was conceived and in which the product was designed. In contrast to **full-spectrum innovation**.

jobs multiplier. The total additions to employment derived from an innovation through both primary effects and secondary effects (employment in service and supplier industries), divided by the direct employment effects.

knowledge spillover. See **spillover of knowledge**.

launch pathway. A series of steps by which a technology is (or can be) introduced into the marketplace or otherwise implemented at scale. See **point of market launch**.

learning by building. The process of improving efficiency or adapting and improving a technology during the course of its implementation.

legacy network. A group of economic, regulatory, legal, or political institutions not directly connected and pursuing their own interests, that, acting independently, can slow the introduction of innovation into a legacy sector.

legacy sector. An economic sector that is defended by a **technological/economic/ political/ social paradigm** characterized by barriers and **market imperfections** that favor existing technology and obstruct the **development** and **market launch** of disruptive innovations.

legacy sector paradigm. See **technological/economic/political/social paradigm**.

level playing field. An environment in which any technology has the same chances and is given the same support as other technologies, in particular as compared to an **incumbent technology** that is already established. Opposite of the **tilted playing field**.

linear model of innovation. See **pipeline model of innovation**.

"line of sight" innovation. Innovative technology that is now being explored and is within range of implementation. See **inducible innovation**.

lock-in. See **technology lock-in**.

lumpiness. A **market imperfection** in which certain innovations require a substantial minimum investment in order to be introduced at full scale against entrenched competition.

make, then buy. An approach to defense procurement in which a prospective vendor makes a product and then sells it to DOD. See **buy, then make**.

mandates. Government-imposed requirements. Examples include renewable portfolio and fuel economy standards. See **carrots and sticks**.

manufacturing. The process of making things, especially on a large scale. This has usually meant making tangible items—"things that hurt when you drop them on your foot." As software has increasingly been integrated into tangible products, the term has become increasingly synonymous with **production**, which see.

manufacturing ecosystem. The network of firms and institutions that support local manufacturing firms as trainers, vendors, providers of research and technical services, consultants, specialized journals, educators, university curricula, and locally owned providers of financial services. Also called the **industrial commons** or **industrial ecosystem**.

market imperfection. A difference between the actual situation and the assumptions of the free market model.

market launch. See **point of market launch**.

market pull. Same as **demand pull**.

meta-change agent. A high-level person who sets up a **change agent** within a bureaucracy, firm, or other system and mentors and protects agents so that they can do their job. Same as **innovation enabler**.

Moore's Law. The prediction, made by Intel cofounder Gordon Moore in 1965, that the number of transistors able to fit on an integrated circuit would increase exponentially, doubling approximately every two years. The time frame has since been reduced to eighteen months, and a sublaw added, that the price per transistor will drop by half in the same period.

mountain of death. The gap between the five- and seven-year time horizon of venture capitalists and angel investors, on the one hand, and the time horizon of 10 or more years in manufacturing and comparable sectors, on the other.

multiplier. See **GNP multiplier** and **jobs multiplier**.

national innovation context. See **innovation context**.

national innovation environment. The sum of the **national innovation system** and the **national innovation context**.

national innovation system. The network of public and private institutions within a country that support and encourage research and innovation. The network includes universities, research laboratories, entrepreneurs, bureaus of standards, consulting firms, technical services, and the policies and financing systems that support them.

network economies. A **market imperfection** in which the value of a network to any individual participant increases as the number of participants increases.

new functionality. A feature of a technology that makes it possible to do new kinds of things that were not possible with previous technologies.

niche market. A specialized segment of a larger market. It can be used as an accessible market in which to launch an innovation.

nonappropriability. A **market imperfection** in which the benefits of an investment accrue to someone other than the investor. Same as **split incentive**.

nonlevel playing field. See **tilted playing field**.

"normal" innovation. An innovation that does not need be introduced into a legacy sector and hence does not face the structural obstacles inherent in its paradigm.

offsets theory. The plan on the part of US defense officials in the 1970s and 1980s to undertake systematic technological advance so as to achieve parity and therefore deterrence in conventional battle and in this way to offset the Soviet advantage in force levels.

offshoring. Locating an operation or employment away from the country in which the headquarters of a company is located or in which a product was conceived and designed.

organic agriculture. Agriculture carried out without artificial fertilizer and pesticides, a definition sometimes extended to include free-range livestock, absence of genetic engineering, or other conditions.

organizational decomposition. See **unbundling**.

original equipment manufacturer. A firm that manufactures products for another firm, which sells the equipment under its own brand name and takes responsibility for it (OEM).

orphan technology. A technology for which there is a social need but no commercial market, and hence depends on the intervention of a governmental or other non-profit entity for its realization.

paradigm. See **technological/economic/political/social paradigm**.

paradigm-compatible innovation. An innovation that reinforces existing technological **paradigms** in a **legacy sector**, or is at least compatible with them. Same as **sustaining innovation**.

paradigm-incompatible innovation. An innovation that is incompatible with the economic, political, legal, and social aspects of a prevailing **paradigm** of a **legacy sector**.

Pasteur's quadrant. **Basic research** inspired not by pure curiosity but by the hope of practical application.

path dependence. Continuing use of a historical practice even when better alternatives are available. See **technology lock-in**.

pathway. See **launch pathway**.

perverse subsidy, price, or incentive. An incentive, subsidy, tax break, or other mechanism that encourages activities or products that are environmentally harmful or otherwise socially undesirable.

pilot project. a small-scale project undertaken to decide how and whether to launch a full-scale project. Compare with **demonstration**.

pipeline model of innovation. A model of the **dynamic of technological innovation** that portrays it as beginning with **basic scientific research**, then progressing through early- and late-stage **development**, including **proof of concept** or **prototyping**, leading to **invention**, design and **demonstration**, **manufacture**, and **commercialization**. Also called the **linear model of innovation**.

platform. A unit holding a variety of component technologies and systems (by extension of the military term for a multicomponent weapon system such as a ship or tank). For example, a plug-in car is a platform that contains an engine, advanced battery, electric power drive system, aerodynamic exterior design, and devices that connect to the electric grid and fuel infrastructure systems.

point of market launch. The time at which a technology is introduced into the market. This is the most difficult step in the development and deployment of technologies intended for legacy sectors, in contrast with the **valley of death**, which is the most difficult launch point for technologies that fit the **pipeline model of innovation**.

policy. The basic principles and declared objectives by which a government is guided, *or* a plan of action to achieve these objectives.

policy instrument. (or policy measure). A method by which to achieve a policy objective.

policy pull.   A model of the **dynamic** of **innovation** that describes innovations that are induced by changes in policy, such as for environment, safety, or energy conservation, rather than by changes in market prices or by advances in science and technology. (See **technology push, induced innovation**, and **market** or **demand pull**).

precompetitive research.   Research on generic problems affecting an entire industry that does not lead directly to the development of proprietary products. Same as **generic research**.

production.   The act of making something from its components or raw materials. Often used as a synonym for **manufacturing**, which see.

production ecosystem.   Same as **production value network**.

production value chain.   A **value chain** that connects all the steps involved in production from raw materials to final product.

production value network.   See **value network**.

proof of concept.   A demonstration in principle, sufficient to fulfill the purpose of verifying that a concept or theory has the potential of practical application but not as fully developed as a **prototype**.

prototype.   A preliminary working model of a new product, meant as a basis for later revisions to its design or function.

QWERTY keyboard.   The keyboard first introduced for typewriters and now standard for computers, often used as an example of **path dependence** and **technology lock-in**.

radical innovation.   An innovation that creates new products with new functional capabilities, as opposed to a **secondary** or **incremental innovation**. See **breakthrough** innovation.

regulatory impediment to innovation.   See **government or regulatory impediment to innovation**.

repurposing.   Applying a technology developed for one purpose for a different purpose, often in a different industry.

research.   Systematic investigation intended to achieve new knowledge and understanding of the natural world.

research-and-development intensity.   The ratio of the cost of research and development to a firm's overall revenues.

"right-left" model.   An approach to innovation, often associated with DARPA, whereby the **change agent** decides the technologies required from the "right" (requirement) side of the innovation pipeline, then looks for proposals for **breakthrough** research on the "left" side of the pipeline that will enable these technologies, and so nurtures the research into technologies that meet the requirements they have identified. See **challenge-based research**.

roadmapping.   A planning process, often coordinated across firms, to match short- and long-term goals for technological advance with specific technological development solutions to meet these goals. The analysis considers each element of technology relevant to the advance and its possible and preferred evolution pathways, and then ties each to the appropriate elements of **front-** and **back-end** support.

ruleset.   A set of organizational methodologies, approaches, and principles, such as those that govern DARPA. These include deep collaboration, remarkable talent in a range of complementary fields, strong leadership, facing a competitive challenge, and devotion to a mission.

scalable innovation.   An **innovation** that can rapidly expand its numbers and use.

secondary innovation.   An **innovation** that improves the existing **functionality** of a technology. See **discontinuous, incremental**, and **radical innovation**.

silver bullet.   A single solution, often technological in origin, that solves (or is purported to solve) a number of complicated problems at the same time.

spillover of knowledge.   The spread of know-how or other knowledge or capacity away from its point of origin, especially from an offshore firm to other firms in the country where it is located.

split incentive.   See **nonappropriability**.

stand up an innovation.   To see a technological or institutional innovation through to implementation or market launch, starting at as early a stage in the innovation process as necessary.

Sticks.   See **carrots and sticks**.

strategy.   A course of action chosen over other alternatives intended to make a desired future happen.

structural obstacle to innovation.   An obstacle to innovation imposed by a **legacy sector paradigm**. (This term is also used in the innovation literature to refer to an obstacle to innovation within firms or other organizations posed by their internal structure.)

structuring a technological revolution.   Providing a policy and institutional framework that considers the whole of the innovation process, removing structural and other obstacles and at the same time supporting its **front end**, thereby promoting **disruptive innovation** in a **legacy sector**.

sustainable agriculture.   Low-input agriculture that minimizes environmental disruption and resource use. More generally, agriculture that does not harm future generations.

sustaining innovation.   An innovation that is not only consistent with a paradigm but also strengthens it. See **paradigm-compatible innovation**.

technological capacity.   The ability to identify technically sound objectives, to choose, adapt, develop, implement and manage technology, and to carry out research.

techno-economic feasibility.   The ability of a **technology** to be successfully implemented, as judged by two criteria, its capacity to fulfill its function, and a satisfactory financial or economic rate of return.

technological/economic/political/social paradigm.   The combination of policies, regulations, incentives, institutions, public understanding, social systems, and political support that reinforces the stability of and helps to establish or entrench a legacy technology or sector and make it resistant to disruptive change.

technological fix.   A purely technological solution to a complicated policy or other problem. See **silver bullet**.

technological innovation.   Commercialization or widespread use of a **technology**. See also **innovation** and **deployment** (or **implementation**).

technological trajectory.   The course of evolution of the technology of a product or service, or of the technological capacity of a firm or organization.

technology.   A means of using technical knowledge to solve a practical problem. Contrary to frequent usage, this is not the same thing as the equipment that embodies that technology, and is not limited to computing and information technology.

technology challenge approach.   See **challenge-based research**.

technology lock-in.   The influence of a **dominant design** or otherwise dominant technology in limiting the possibility of alternative pathways for the evolution of technology for a particular purpose.

technology-push model.   A model of the **dynamic of technological innovation** that portrays innovation as being driven by the advance of a science or technology into the market through research and development (the **front end** of the innovation system), rather than by **demand** or **market pull**. Examples include the **pipeline, extended pipeline**, and **manufacturing-led models**.

technology-push policy. A policy to promote the entry or supply of new technology through **front-end** support to research and development. Also known as a technology supply-side policy.

technology taker. A country or firm that typically imports technology from world markets and uses it with at most relatively minor adaptation to local circumstances, usually because of a combination of aversion to risk and a lack of technological capacity.

technology visioning. The process of creating an image of how a technology is likely to develop in the future and what a successful technology would look like, as an aid to setting goals and motivating present action. This is an essential part of the **technology challenge approach** as practiced by DARPA.

test bed. A platform for experimentation for large, engineering-oriented development projects.

thinking community. A group of active researchers who are working on the same or related problems or toward the same or related goals, who are in regular touch with and support each other, and who build new concepts on the basis of one another's ideas.

tilted playing field. A nonlevel playing field on which some technologies are disadvantaged as compared to others, typically incumbent technologies that are already established but sometimes competing alternatives to established technologies. Same as **nonlevel playing field**. Opposite of **level playing field**.

trajectory. See **technological trajectory**.

transaction costs. Costs of a market transaction that do not figure directly in the price of the item being bought and sold, such as the cost of information gathering and technical advice.

transformative technology. An innovation whose introduction transforms a technological field or sector. See **disruptive innovation**.

translational research. An integrated approach to research management in which **applied research** is followed up, first by the translation of the results of this **research** into **technology**, and then by the launch of this technology through the **prototype** stage, keeping in mind the requirements of **deployment** and **commercialization**.

triple helix. The collaboration of government, university, and industry in innovation.

unbundling. Separation of tasks or steps in the production of goods (i.e., the links in the **value chain**) or in the innovation process so that they can be carried out by independent firms or firm subsidiaries, possibly located in different countries. Also known as **organizational decomposition**.

uncontested launch. Technology launch that will not be resisted by competitors or by the recipient industry if the new technology passes tests of **techno-economic feasibility**. Opposite of **contested launch**.

valley of death. The stage of technological innovation between early-stage **development** and **proof of concept** of an **invention** and its successful **commercialization**, a stage often shunned by private capital markets and traditionally deemed the most critical moment in technology launch in the innovation literature concerned with the **pipeline model**.

value chain. A series of linked actors that connect initial inputs and components to a final product. See **production value chain** and **innovation value chain**.

value network. A multidimensional network of supporting firm vendors, distributors, retail, and other services.

vertically integrated function. A function carried out entirely within a given firm, although not necessarily in the same country or in the country in which the firm's headquarters are located.

vested technology. A **technology**, deeply embedded in the organization, **value network**, doctrine, and mental habits of users, and hence resistant to change. It is often part of a larger **paradigm** or **dominant product design**.

References

Abbate, Janet. 1999. *Inventing the Internet*. Cambridge, MA: MIT Press.

Abernathy, William J., and James M. Utterback. 1978. "Patterns of Innovation in Technology." *Technology Review* 80, no. 7, 40–47.

Acemoglu, Daron, and David Autor. 2012. "What Does Human Capital Do? A Review of Goldin and Katz's 'The Race Between Education and Technology.'" *Journal of Economic Literature*. 50, no. 2, 426–463. http://economics.mit.edu/files/7490.

Adams, Emily E. 2013. "The Energy Game Is Rigged: Fossil Fuel Subsidies Topped $620 Billion in 2011." Earth Policy Institute. February 27. http://www.earth-policy.org/data_highlights/2013/highlights36.

Advanced Manufacturing Portal. 2014. "About the Advanced Manufacturing Partnership 2.0." http://www.manufacturing.gov/amp.html.

Advanced Manufacturing Portal. 2014. National Network for Manufacturing Institutes. http://www.manufacturing.gov/nnmi.html.

Agency for Healthcare Research and Quality. 2014. "What Is Comparative Effectiveness Research." http://effectivehealthcare.ahrq.gov/index.cfm/what-is-comparative-effectiveness-research1/.

Agnihotri, Mahesh. 2014. "Risks to Economic Stability and Its Challenges: A Study of Chinese and Indian Economies." *Journal of Business Management & Social Sciences Research* 3, no. 6, 17–25. http://borjournals.com/a/index.php/jbmssr/article/view/1725/1074.

Aker, Jenny C., and Isaac M. Mbiti. 2010. "Africa Calling: Can Mobile Phones Make a Miracle?" *Boston Review*, March–April. http://www.bostonreview.net/africa-calling-phones-economics-jenny-c-aker-isaac-m-mbiti.

Alberts, David, John Garska, and Frederick Stein. 1999. *Network Centric Warfare*. Washington, DC: Department of Defense Cooperative Research Program, August. http://www.dodccrp.org/files/Alberts_NCW.pdf.

Alesina, Alberto, and Francesco Giavazzi. 2006. *The Future of Europe: Reform or Decline*. Cambridge, MA: MIT Press.

Alibek, Ken. 2008. *Biohazard: The Chilling True Story of the Largest Covert Biological Weapons Program in the World—Told From the Inside by the Man Who Ran It*. New York: Random House.

Alic, John. 2007. *Trillions for Military Technology*. New York: Palgrave Macmillan.

Alic, John, Lewis Branscomb, Harvey Brooks, Ashton Carter, and Gerald Epstein. 1992. *Beyond Spinoff: Military and Commercial Technologies in a Changing World*. Cambridge, MA: Harvard Business School Press.

Alic, John, David Mowery, and Edward Rubin. 2003. *U.S. Technology and Innovation Policies: Lessons for Climate Change*. Washington, DC: Pew Center on Global Climate Change, November.

Alic, John, Daniel Sarewitz, Charles Weiss, and William Bonvillian. 2010. "A New Strategy for Energy Innovation." *Nature* 466 (July 15), 316–317.

Allen, Thomas B., and Norman Polmar. 2007. *Rickover*. Dulles, VA: Brassey's.

American Association for the Advancement of Science. 2013. "Trends in Department of Energy R&D, 1997–2014." June. http://www.aaas.org/sites/default/files/DOE_0.jpg.

American Association of University Professors. 2008. "Where Are the Priorities: Annual Report on the Economic Status of the Profession, 2007–2008." March–April. http://www.aaup.org/file/2007-2008Economic-Status-Report.pdf.

American Society of Plant Biologists. 2013. "Unleashing a Decade of Innovation in Plant Science." http://plantsummit.files.wordpress.com/2013/07/plantsciencedecadalvision10-18-13.pdf.

Anderson, Joe, and Mike Laszkiewicz. 2011. "The Manufacturing Council." July. http://www.trade.gov/manufacturingcouncil/documents/MC_Workforce_08222011.pdf.

Anderson, Torben M., et al. 2007. *The Nordic Model: Embracing Globalization and Sharing Risks*. Helsinki: Taloustieto Oy.

Angulo, A. J. 2009. *William Barton Rogers*. Baltimore, MD: Johns Hopkins University Press.

Antonelli, Christiano. 2008. "Pecuniary Externalities: The Convergence of Directed Technological Change and the Emergence of Innovation Systems." Bureau of Research on Innovation, Complexity and Knowledge Working Paper 3, February. http://www.carloalberto.org/files/brick_03_08.pdf.

Archibald, Robert B., and David H. Feldman. 2011. *Why Does College Cost So Much?* New York: Oxford University Press.

Archibugi, D., and J. Michie. 1995. "The Globalization of Technology: A New Taxonomy." *Cambridge Journal of Economics* 19, 121–140.

Arrow, Kenneth. 1962. "Economic Welfare and the Allocation of Resources for Invention." In *The Rate and Direction of Inventive Activity: Economic and Social Factors*, 609–626. Washington, DC: National Bureau of Economic Research. http://www.nber.org/chapters/c2144.pdf.

Arthur, W. Brian. 1989. "Competing Technologies, Increasing Returns, and Lock-in by Historical Events." *Economic Journal* 99, no. 394 (March), 116–131.

Arthur, W. Brian. 1994. *Increasing Returns and Path Dependence in the Economy*. Ann Arbor: University of Michigan Press.

Association of Public and Land Grant Universities. 2012. "Fact Sheet: College Costs. Answers to the Most Frequently Asked Questions about Public Higher Education." https://www.aplu.org/document.doc?id=4287.

Atkinson, Robert D. 2004. *The Past and Future of America's Economy: Long Waves of Innovation That Power Cycles of Growth*. Cheltenham, UK: Edward Elgar.

Atkinson, Robert D. 2006. "RFID: There's Nothing to Fear Except Fear Itself." Speech at the 16th Annual Computers, Freedom and Privacy Conference, May 4. http://www.itif.org/files/rfid.pdf.

Atkinson, Robert D. 2012. "Manufacturing Policy Is Not Industrial Policy." *The Innovation Files*. Information Technology and Innovation Foundation. February 6. http://www.innovationfiles.org/manufacturing-policy-is-not-"industrial-policy".

Atkinson, Robert D. 2014. "Understanding and Maximizing America's Evolutionary Economy." Information Technology and Innovation Foundation, October.

Atkinson, Robert D., and Stephen J. Ezell. 2012. *Innovation Economics*. New Haven, CT: Yale University Press.

Atkinson, Robert D., and Darrene Hackler. 2010. "Economic Doctrines and Approaches to Climate Change Policy." Information Technology and Innovation Foundation, October 1. http://www.itif.org/files/2010-econ-climate-change.pdf.

Attali, Jacques. 2008. "Rapport de la Commission pour la libération de la croissance française." XO Éditions, La Documentation française 16, 48. http://www.ladocumentationfrancaise.fr/var/storage/rapports-publics/084000041/0000.pdf

Autor, David H. 2014. "Skills, Education and the Rise of Earnings Inequality among the 'Other 99 Percent.'" *Science* 344, no. 6186 (May 23), 843–851. http://www.sciencemag.org/content/344/6186/843.full.

Autor, David H., David Dorn, and Gordon Hanson. 2011. "The China Syndrome: Local Labor Market Effects of Import Competition in the United States." *American Economic Review* 103, no. 6 (2013), 2121–2168. http://economics.mit.edu/files/6613.

Baffes, John, and Tassos Haniotis. 2010. "Placing the 2006/08 Commodity Price Boom into Perspective." World Bank, Development Prospects Group, Research Working Paper 5371, July. http://www-wds.worldbank.org/external/default/WDSContent-Server/IW3P/IB/2010/07/21/000158349_20100721110120/Rendered/PDF/WPS5371.pdf.

Bartis, James T., and Lawrence Van Bibber. 2011. *Alternative Fuels for Military Applications*. Santa Monica, CA: Rand. http://www.rand.org/pubs/monographs/MG969.html.

Baumol, William, and William Bowen. 1966. *Performing Arts: The Economic Dilemma*. New York: 20th Century Fund.

Basu, Susanto, John Fernald, and Matthew Shapiro. 2001. "Productivity Growth in the 1990s: Technology, Utilization, or Adjustment." NBER Working Paper 8359. http://www.nber.org/papers/w8359.pdf.

Baum, Warren, and Michael Lejeune. 1986. *Partners against Hunger* Washington, DC: World Bank.

Bennis, Warren, and Patricia Ward Biederman. 1997. *Organizing Genius: The Secrets of Creative Collaboration*. New York: Basic Books.

Berger, Suzanne. 2005. *How We Compete: What Companies around the World Are Doing to Make It in Today's Global Economy*. New York: Doubleday Currency.

Berger, Suzanne. 2014. "How Finance Gutted Manufacturing." *Boston Review*, March–April.

Berger, Suzanne, with the MIT Task Force on Production and Innovation Economy. 2013. *Making in America*. Cambridge, MA: MIT Press.

Berk, Joseph. 2009. *Systems Failure Analysis*. Material Park, OH: ASM International.

Betz, Frederick. 1993. *Strategic Technology Management*. New York: McGraw-Hill.

Bhagwati, Jagdish. 2010. "The Computer Chip vs. Potato Chip Debate." *Moscow Times*, September 2. http://www.themoscowtimes.com/opinion/article/the-computer-chip-vs-potato-chip-debate/414565.html.

Bhargava, Pushpa M., and Chandana Chakrabarti. 2003. *The Saga of Indian Science since Independence in a Nutshell*. Hyderabad, India: Hyderabad Universities Press.

Blevin, J., and M. J. Mayo. 2013. "The New World of Work, From Education to Employment." *Innovation Intake*, May. http://www.theinnovationintake.com/latest-issue.html.

Biomedical Advanced Research and Development Authority. 2014. Program description. http://www.phe.gov/about/barda/Pages/default.aspx.

Biotechnow. 2014. "Bio-Fueling the Navy." June 6. http://www.biotech-now.org/environmental-industrial/2014/06/bio-fueling-the-navy#.

Bird, Kai, and Martin J. Sherwin. 2005. *American Prometheus: J. Robert Oppenheimer*. New York: Alfred A. Knopf.

Bonvillian, William B. 2006. "Power Play: The DARPA Model and U.S. Energy Policy." *American Interest*, November–December, 40–47.

Bonvillian, William B. 2007. "Will the Search for New Energy Technologies Require a New R&D Mission Agency?" *Bridges* 14 (July). http://www.ostina.org/content/view/2297/721/.

Bonvillian, William B. 2009. "The Connected Science Model for Innovation: The DARPA Model." In *21st Century Innovation Systems for the U.S. and Japan*, ed. Sadao Nagaoka, Masayuki Kondo, Kenneth Flamm, and Charles Wessner, 206–237. Washington, DC: National Academies Press. http://books.nap.edu/openbook.php?record_id=12194&page=206.

Bonvillian, William B. 2011. "Time for Plan B for Climate." *Issues in Science and Technology*, Winter, 55–56. http://www.issues.org/27.2/bonvillian.html.

Bonvillian, William B. 2012. "Reinventing American Manufacturing: The Role of Innovation." *Innovations* 7, no. 3 (Fall), 108–118.

Bonvillian, William B. 2013. "Advanced Manufacturing Policies and Paradigms for Innovation." *Science* 392 (December 6), 1174.

Bonvillian, William B. 2013. "The New Model Innovation Agencies: An Overview." *Science and Public Policy*, September 26, 1–13.

Bonvillian, William B., and Susan R. Singer. 2013. "The Online Challenge to Higher Education." *Issues in Science and Technology*. http://issues.org/29-24/the-online-challenge-to-higher-education/.

Bonvillian, William B., and Richard Van Atta. 2011. "ARPA-E and DARPA: Applying the DARPA Model to Energy Innovation." *Journal of Technology Transfer*, 56, no. 5, October. 469–513.

Bonvillian, William B., and Charles Weiss. 2009. "Taking Covered Wagons East: A New Innovation Theory for Energy and Other Established Sectors." *Innovations* 4, no. 4, 289–300.

Bound, Kristen, et al. 2013. *China's Absorptive State: Research, Innovation and the Prospects for China-U.K. Collaboration*. London: Nesta. http://www.nesta.org.uk/sites/default/files/chinas_absorptive_state_0.pdf.

Branscomb, Lewis M., and Philip E. Auerswald. 2002. *Between Invention and Innovation: An Analysis of Funding for Early-State Technology Development, Part I: Early Stage Development*. NIST GCR 02-841, November. http://www.atp.nist.gov/eao/gcr02-841/contents.htm.

Branscomb, Lewis M., and Philip E. Auerswald. 2011. *Taking Technical Risks: How Innovators, Executives, and Investors Manage High-Tech Risks*. Cambridge, MA: MIT Press.

Breakthrough Institute. 2012. "Where the Shale Gas Revolution Came From: Government's Role in the Development of Hydraulic Fracturing in Shale." May. http://thebreakthrough.org/images/main_image/Where_the_Shale_Gas_Revolution_Came_From2.pdf.

Breakthrough Institute, Brookings Institution, and World Resources Institute. 2012. *Beyond Boom and Bust*, April 12. http://thebreakthrough.org/blog/Beyond_Boom_and_Bust.pdf.

Breakthrough Institute and Information Technology and Innovation Foundation. 2010. *Rising Tigers, Sleeping Giant*. Washington, DC: ITIF. http://www.itif.org/index.php?id=315.

Breznitz, Daniel. 2014. "Why Germany Dominates the U.S. in Innovation." *Harvard Business Review* blog, May 27. http://blogs.hbr.org/2014/05/why-germany-dominates-the-u-s-in-innovation/.

Breznitz, Daniel, and Peter Cowhey. 2012. *America's Two Systems of Innovation: Recommendations for Policy Changes to Support Innovation, Production and Job Creation*. San Diego, CA: Connect Innovation Institute, February.

Breznitz, Daniel, and Michael Murphree. 2011. *Run of the Red Queen: Government, Innovation, Globalization and Economic Growth in China*. New Haven, CT: Yale University Press.

Brother, Caroline. 2009. "Boeing and Airbus Prepare (Again) for Tanker Battle." *New York Times*, June 16. http://www.nytimes.com/2009/06/17/business/global/17boeing.html.

Browning, Larry, and Judy Shetler. 2000. *Sematech: Saving the U.S. Semiconductor Industry*. College Station: Texas A&M Press.

Brynjolfsson, Erik, and Andrew McAfee. 2011. *Race against the Machine*. Lexington, MA: Digital Frontier Press.

Brynjolfsson, Erik, and Andrew McAfee, 2014. *The Second Machine Age*. New York: W.W. Norton and Company.

Buderi, Robert. 1997. *The Invention That Changed the World*. New York: Simon & Schuster / Touchstone.

Budiansky, Stephen 2013. *Blackett's War*. New York: Alfred A. Knopf.

Buonassisi, Tonio, and Douglas Powell. 2011. "Photovoltaics (PV) Manufacturing, U.S. and China." Slide presentation, MIT Photovoltaic Research Lab, October 14.

Bureau of Economic Analysis. 2013. "U.S. International Trade in Goods and Services (1992–2012)." www.bea.gov/international/index.htm#trade.

Bureau of Labor Statistics. 2013. "Current Labor Statistics (CES) (manufacturing employment)." http://data.bls.ces.

Bureau of Labor Statistics. 2013. "Industries at a Glance, Manufacturing, NACIS 31-33, Workforce Statistics." http://www.bls.gov/iag/tgs/iag31-33.htm#iag31-33empl.f.P.

Bureau of Labor Statistics. 2012. "Current Labor Statistics." http://www.bls.gov/opub/mlr/department/current-labor-statistics.htm.

Bush, Vannevar. 1945. *Science: The Endless Frontier*. Washington, DC: Government Printing Office. http://www.nsf.gov/od/lpa/nsf50/vbush1945.htm.

Business Green. 2011. "AEP: Lack of Climate Regulation Killed $668m CCS Project." July 18. http://www.businessgreen.com/bg/news/2094430/aep-lack-climate-regulation-killed-usd668m-ccs-project.

Caisse des Dépôts. 2012. "FSI France Investment 2020 Launched." February 23. http://www.caissedesdepots.fr/en/news/all-the-news/half-year- 2009-2010-sales-up-10-on-a-reported-basis-03-like-for-like/fsi-france-investment-2020-launched.html.

Campaign for the Future of Higher Education. 2013. "The 'Promises' of Online Higher Education: Profits." October 9. http://futureofhighered.org/wp-content/uploads/2013/10/Promises-of-Online-Higher-Ed-Profits1.pdf.

Carleton, Tammy L. 2010. "The Value of Vision in Technological Innovation." Dissertation, Department of Mechanical Engineering, Stanford University. http://purl.stanford.edu/mk388mb2729.

Carnevale, Anthony P., Ban Cheah, and Jeff Strohl. 2012. "In Hard Times: College Majors, Unemployment and Earnings. Not All College Degrees Are Created Equal." Georgetown University Center on Education and the Workforce, January 4.

Carnevale, Anthony P., Stephen J. Rose, and Ban Cheah. 2011. "The College Payoff, Education, Occupations, Lifetime Earnings." Georgetown University Center on Education and the Workforce, August 5. https://cew.georgetown.edu/collegepayoff.

Carnevale, Anthony P., Stephen J. Rose, and Andrew R. Hanson. 2012. "Certificates: Gateway to Gainful Employment and College Degrees." Georgetown Center for Education and the Workforce, June. http://www.insidehighered.com/sites/default/server_files/files/06_01_12%20Certificates%20Full%20Report%20FINAL.pdf.

Cathcart, Brian. 2004. *The Fly in the Cathedral*. New York: Farrar, Straus and Giroux.

Cebrowski, Arthur, and John Garska. 1998. "Network Centric Warfare: Its Origin and Future." *U.S. Naval Institute Proceedings*, January.

Census Bureau. 2002. "Special Study: The Big Payoff: Educational Attainment and Synthetic Estimates of Work-Life Earnings." Washington, DC: Census Bureau, July.

http://usgovinfo.about.com/gi/o.htm?zi=1/XJ&zTi=1&sdn=usgovinfo&cdn=newsissues&tm=618&f=00&su=p284.13.342.ip_&tt=2&bt=0&bts=0&zu=http%3A//www.census.gov/prod/2002pubs/p23-210.pdf.

Census Bureau. 2012. "Trade in Goods with Advanced Technology Products, 2011." http://www.census.gov/foreign-trade/balance/c0007.html.

Census Bureau. 2012. Statistical Abstract of the United States: 2012. http://www.census.gov/compendia/statab/2012/tables/12s1105.xls.

Centers for Medicare and Medicaid Services, Office of the Actuary. 2011. "National Health Expenditures 2011–12, Forecast Summary." http://www.cms.gov/Research-Statistics-Data-and-Systems/Statistics-Trends-and-Reports/NationalHealthExpend-Data/Downloads/Proj2011PDF.pdf.

Central Intelligence Agency. 2014. "People and Society: India." *The World Factbook*. https://www.cia.gov/library/publications/the-world-factbook/geos/in.html.

Chesborough, Henry W. 2003. "The Era of Open Innovation." *MIT Sloan Review* 44, no. 3 (April). http://sloanreview.mit.edu/article/the-era-of-open-innovation/.

Chposky, James, and Ted Leonsis. 1986. *Blue Magic: The People, Power and Politics behind the IBM Personal Computer*. New York: Facts on File.

Christensen, Clayton. 1997. *The Innovator's Dilemma: When New Technologies Cause Great Firms to Fail*. Boston, MA: Harvard Business School Press.

Christensen, Clayton. 2013. "Online Learning and the Future of Residential Education." Slide presentation, MIT-Harvard Summit, March 3–4. http://onlinelearningsummit.org/program.html.

Christensen, Clayton M., Jerome H. Grossman, and Jason Hwang. 2009. *The Innovator's Prescription: A Disruptive Solution for Health Care*. New York: McGraw-Hill.

Christensen Institute. 2014. "Disruptive Innovation—Key Concepts." http://www.christenseninstitute.org/key-concepts/disruptive-innovation-2/.

Clark, Ronald W. 1962. *The Rise of the Boffins*. London: Phoenix House.

Clark, Ronald W. 1965. *Tizard*. Cambridge, MA: MIT Press.

Cleeton, David L. 2012. "Evaluating the Performance Record under the Lisbon Agenda." In *Europe and National Economic Transformation: The EU after the Lisbon Decade*, ed. Mitchell P. Smith. New York: Palgrave Macmillan.

Cohan, Peter. 2011. "Boeing's Big Tanker Contract Has National—and State—Winners and Losers." *AOL Daily Finance*, February 25. http://www.dailyfinance.com/2011/02/25/boeing-airbus-tanker-contract-winners-losers/.

Coleman, Will. 2013. Testimony (representing the National Venture Capital Association) before the Senate Committee on Energy and Natural Resources, Hearing on Clean Energy Finance, July 18, 6–7. http://www.nvca.org/index.php?searchword=energy&ordering=&searchphrase=all&Itemid=101&option=com_search.

Collins, Alan, and Richard Halverson. 2009. *Rethinking Education in the Age of Technology: The Digital Revolution and Schooling in America*. New York: Teachers College Press, Columbia University.

Colvin, Kimberly, John Campaign, Alwins Liu, Quian Zhou, Colin Fredericks, and David Pritchard. 2014. "Learning in Introductory Physics MOOC: All Cohorts Learn Equally Including an On-Campus Class." *International Review of Research in Open and Distance Learning* 15, no. 4 (September). http://www.irrodl.org/index.php/irrodl/article/view/1902/3009.

Congressional Budget Office. 2012. "Federal Financial Support for the Development and Production of Fuels and Energy Technologies." Issue brief, March. http://www.cbo.gov/sites/default/files/cbofiles/attachments/03-06-FuelsandEnergy_Brief.pdf.

Congressional Research Service. 2011. "Research and Development by Large Energy Production Companies." August.

Congressional Research Service. 2012. "Federal Renewable Energy R&D Funding History: A Comparison with Funding for Nuclear Energy, Fossil Energy and Efficiency R&D." March 7. http://www.fas.org/sgp/crs/misc/RS22858.pdf.

Congressional Research Service. 2012. "The Navy Biofuel Initiative under the Defense Production Act." June 22. http://www.fas.org/sgp/crs/natsec/R42568.pdf.

Conway, Gordon. 1998. *The Doubly Green Revolution*. Ithaca, NY: Cornell University Press.

Cook-Deegan, Robert. 1996. "Does NIH Need a DARPA?" *Issues in Science and Technology*, Winter. http://www.issues.org/13.2/cookde.htm.

Cooper, Robert G., Scott J. Edgett, and Elko J. Kleinschmidt. 2002. "Optimizing the Stage Gate Process." *Research Technology Management* 45, no. 5. 21–27. http://www.stage-gate.com/downloads/wp/wp_15.pdf.

Cooperative State Research, Education and Extension Service. 2014. "Sustainable Agriculture." http://www.csrees.usda.gov/nea/ag_systems/ag_systems.cfm and http://www.csrees.usda.gov/sustainableagriculture.cfm.

Copeland, Paul, and Dimitris Papadimitriou, eds. 2012. *The EU's Lisbon Strategy: Evaluating Success, Understanding Failure*. New York: Palgrave MacMillan.

Council on Competitiveness, National Innovation Initiative. 2005. *Innovate America*. http://www.compete.org/images/uploads/File/PDF%20Files/NII_Innovate_America.pdf.

Crawford, Susan. 2013. *Captive Audience: The Telecom Industry and Monopoly Power in the New Gilded Age*. New Haven, CT: Yale University Press.

Dahlman, Carl J. 2012. *The World under Pressure: How China and India Are Influencing the Global Economy and Environment*. Stanford, CA: Stanford University Press.

DARPA. 2003. *DARPA over the Years*. Report, October 27.

DARPA. 2005. *DARPA: Bridging the Gap, Powered by Ideas*. February.

DARPA. 2007. "Urban Challenge." November 3. darpa.mil/grand challenge/.

Dawisha, Karen. 2014. *Putin's Kleptocracy: Who Owns Russia?* New York: Simon & Schuster.

Defense Science Board. 2013. *Technology and Innovation Enablers for Superiority in 2030*. October. http://www.acq.osd.mil/dsb/reports/DSB2030.pdf.

Department of Agriculture. 2013. "Rural Development Energy Programs." http://www.rurdev.usda.gov/Energy.html.

Department of Agriculture. 2014. "Secretary Announces Creation of Foundation for Food and Agriculture Research." July 23. http://www.usda.gov/wps/portal/usda/usda home?contentidonly=true&contentid=2014/07/0156.xml.

Department of Agriculture. 2014. Agricultural Research Service National Program: Integrated Farming Systems. http://www.ars.usda.gov/research/programs/programs.htm?NP_CODE=207.

Department of Agriculture. "Green Technologies for a More Sustainable Agriculture." Economic Research Service publication. http://www.ers.usda.gov/publications/aib-agricultural-information-bulletin/aib752.aspx.

Department of Agriculture, Sustainable Agriculture Research and Education. 2010. "What Is Sustainable Agriculture?" http://www.sare.org/Learning-Center/SARE-Program-Materials/National-Program-Materials/What-is-Sustainable-Agriculture.

Department of Defense. 1997. *Joint Warfighter S&T Plan*. http://www.fas.org/spp/military/docops/defense/97_jwstp/jwstp.htm.

Department of Defense, ManTech. 2009. "The DOD Manufacturing Technology Program—Strategic Plan." March. https://www.dodmantech.com/relatedresources/DoD_ManTech_Strat_Plan_Aug_18_Final_low_res.pdf.

Department of Education. 2010. *Evaluation of Evidence-Based Practices in Online Learning: A Meta-Analysis and Review of Online Learning Studies*. Washington, DC: US

Department of Education, September. http://www2.ed.gov/rschstat/eval/tech/evidence-based-practices/finalreport.pdf.

Department of Energy. 2011. "U.S.-China Clean Energy Cooperation: A Progress Report." January. http://www.us-china-cerc.org/pdfs/US_China_Clean_Energy_Progress_Report.pdf.

Department of Energy. 2013. "Wide Bandgap Semiconductors: Pursuing the Promise." April. http://www.manufacturing.gov/docs/wide_bandgap_semiconductors.pdf.

Department of Energy, Office of Electricity. 2008. *The Smart Grid: An Introduction*. Washington, DC: DOE. http://www.oe.energy.gov/DocumentsandMedia/DOE_SG_Book_Single_Pages(1).pdf.

Department of Energy, Office of Energy Efficiency and Renewable Energy, Building Technologies Office. 2013. "Appliance and Equipment Standards Program." http://energy.gov/eere/buildings/appliance-and-equipment-standards-program.

Department of Energy, Office of Energy Efficiency and Renewable Energy. 2014. "Clean Energy Manufacturing Initiative." http://energy.gov/eere/cemi/clean-energy-manufacturing-initiative.

Department of Energy, Office of Energy Efficiency and Renewable Energy. 2014. "SunShot Initiative." http://energy.gov/eere/sunshot/sunshot-initiative.

Department of Energy, Office of Energy Policy and Systems Analysis. 2014. Quadrennial Energy Review" (summary). http://energy.gov/epsa/initiatives/quadrennial-energy-review-qer.

Department of Energy, Office of Fossil Energy. 2011. "Carbon Sequestration Regional Partnerships." http://www.fe.doe.gov/programs/sequestration/partnerships/index.html.

Department of Health and Human Services. 2013. Secretary Kathleen Sebelius, *Innovation and Health Care* (blog), May 28. http://www.hhs.gov/healthcare/facts/blog/2013/05/innovation.html.

Department of Health and Human Services. 2014. "Key Features of the Affordable Care Act." http://www.hhs.gov/healthcare/facts/timeline/timeline-text.html.

Department of State, U.S. Mission to ASEAN. 2014. "Fact Sheet: U.S.-China Joint Announcement on Climate Change." November 11. http://asean.usmission.gov/factsheet11112014-11112008.html.

Department of Transportation. 2012. "ITS Technologies and Research and Strategic Planning." http://www.itsoverview.its.dot.gov/; http://www.its.gov/its_program/its_factsheets.htm.

DG Trade Statistics. 2012. "World Trade in Goods, Services, FDI." February 28. http://trade.ec.europa.eu/doclib/docs/2006/september/tradoc_122531.pdf.

Drechsler, Wolfgang, et al., eds. 2009. *Techno-Economic Paradigms: Essays in Honour of Carlota Perez*. London: Anthem.

Dugan, Regina. 2010. Statement to the House Subcommittee on Terrorism, Unconventional Threats and Capabilities of the House Armed Services Committee, 111th Cong., 1st Sess., March 23.

Duncan, Francis. 2011. *Rickover: The Struggle for Excellence*. Annapolis, MD: Naval Institute Press.

Dutz, Mark Andrew. 2007. *Unleashing India's Innovation: Toward Sustainable and Inclusive Growth*. Washington, DC: World Bank.

Easterbrook, Gregg. 1997. "Forgotten Benefactor of Humanity." *Atlantic*, January. http://www.theatlantic.com/magazine/archive/1997/01/forgotten-benefactor-of-humanity/306101/3/.

Economic Times. 2012. "List of Indian Innovations That Exhibit Frugality and Inclusiveness." July 28. 28/news/32906719_1_indian- innovations-frugality-incubator.

Economist. 2010. "Defense Spending in a Time of Austerity." August 26. http://www.economist.com/node/16886851?story_id=16886851.

Economist. 2012. "The Third Industrial Revolution." Special report, April 21.

Economist. 2014. "Hardware Startups: Hacking Shenzhen. Why Southern China Is the Best Place in the World for a Hardware Innovator to Be." January 18.

Ehrlich, Paul. 1969. *The Population Bomb.* New York: Sierra Club / Ballantine.

Ekman, Marianne, et al. 2011. *Learning Regional Innovation: Scandinavian Models.* Basingstoke: Palgrave Macmillan.

Ellerman, A. Denny, Paul L. Joskow, Richard Schmalensee, Juan-Pablo Montero, and Elizabeth M. Bailey. 2000. *Markets for Clean Air: The U.S. Acid Rain Program.* Cambridge: Cambridge University Press.

Energy Information Agency. 2002. *Emissions of Greenhouse Gasses in the United States 2001.* Report No. DOE/EIA-0573. Washington, DC: EIA, December. http://www.eia.doe.gov/oiaf/1605/archive/gg02rpt/index.html.

Environmental Protection Agency. 2013. "Global Greenhouse Gas Emissions Data (by Source)." September 9. http://www.epa.gov/climatechange/ghgemissions/global.html.

Environmental Protection Agency. 2014. "Transportation and Climate, Regulations and Standards: Light Duty." November 7. http://www.epa.gov/otaq/climate/regs-light-duty.htm.

Ernst, Dieter. 2014. "From Catching Up to Forging Ahead? China's Prospects in Semiconductors." East West Center Working Paper, Innovation and Economic Growth Series, Honolulu, HI, November.

Erwin, Sandra I. 2014. "Navy to Stay the Course with Biofuels." *National Defense,* January. http://www.nationaldefensemagazine.org/blog/Lists/Posts/Post.aspx?ID=1386.

European Commission. 2007. "Improving Knowledge Transfer between Research Institutions and Industry across Europe: Embracing Open Innovation." April. http://ec.europa.eu/invest-in-research/pdf/com2007182_en.pdf.

European Commission. 2010. "MEMO/10/473: Turning Europe into a true Innovation Union." October 6. http://europa.eu/rapid/press-release_MEMO-10-473_en.htm?locale=en.

European Commission. "The ERA-NET Scheme." http://cordis.europa.eu/fp7/coordination/about-era_en.html.

Ezell, Stephen J. 2012. "Our Manufacturers Need a U.S. Competitiveness Strategy, Not Special Treatment." Information Technology and Innovation Foundation blog, February 9. http://www.innovationfiles.org/our-manufacturers-need-a-u-s-competitiveness-strategy-not-special-treatment/.

Ezell, Stephen J., and Robert D. Atkinson. 2011. *The Case for a National Manufacturing Strategy.* Information Technology and Innovation Foundation report, April. http://www.itif.org/files/2011-national-manufacturing-strategy.pdf.

Fagnan, David E., Jose Maria Fernandez, Andrew Lo, and Roger M. Stein. 2013. "Can Financial Engineering Cure Cancer?" *American Economic Review* 103, no. 3 (May), 406–411.

Fewsmith, Joseph. 2001. "The Political and Social Implications of China's Accession to the WTO." *China Quarterly* 167, 589–591.

Folger, Peter. 2014. "Carbon Capture and Sequestration: Research, Development and Demonstration at the US Department of Energy." Congressional Research Service, February 10. http://fas.org/sgp/crs/misc/R42496.pdf.

Fong, Glenn R. 2000. "Breaking New Ground or Breaking the Rules: Strategic Reorientation in US Industrial Policy." *International Security* 25, no. 2 (Fall), 152–162. http://www.mitpressjournals.org/doi/pdf/10.1162/016228800560480.

Fong, Glenn R. 2001. "ARPA Does Windows: The Defense Underpinning of the PC Revolution." *Business and Politics* 3, no. 3, 213–237. http://www.bepress.com/bap/vol3/iss3/art1/.

Fong, Glenn R. 2005. "The CIA in Silicon Valley: In-Q-Tel and the Search for a New Government-Industry Partnership." Paper presented at the annual meeting of the International Studies Association, Honolulu, HI, March 5. http://citation.allacademic.com/meta/p_mla_apa_research_citation/0/7/1/3/2/p71327_index.html.

Food and Drug Administration. 2004. "Innovation/Stagnation: Challenge and Opportunity on the Critical Path to New Medical Products." March. http://www.fda.gov/ScienceResearch/SpecialTopics/CriticalPathInitiative/CriticalPathOpportunitiesReports/ucm077262.htm.

Foster, Peter. 2004. "Revolution on India's Railway Runs out of Wheels." *Telegraph*, October 1. http://www.telegraph.co.uk/news/worldnews/asia/india/1473121/Revolution-on-Indias-railway-runs-out-of-wheels.html.

Fox, Daniel M. 1995. *Power and Illness: The Failure and Future of American Health Policy.* Berkeley: University of California Press.

Fox, Daniel M. 2010. *The Convergence of Science and Governance: Research, Health Policy and American States.* Berkeley: University of California Press.

Foxon, Timothy J. 2007. "Technological Lock-in and the Role of Innovation" In *A Handbook of Sustainable Development*, ed. Giles Atkinson, Simon Dietz, and Eric Neumayer, 140–152. Cheltenham, UK: Edward Elgar.

Fox-Penner, Peter. 2010. *Smart Power: Climate Change, the Smart Grid, and the Future of Electric Utilities.* Washington, DC: Island Press.

Freeman, Christopher. 1982. "Innovation and Long Cycles of Economic Development." Paper, Department of Economics, University of Campinas, São Paulo, Brazil, August 25–27. http://www.globelicsacademy.net/pdf/JoseCassiolato_2.pdf.

Freeman, Christopher. 1995. "The National System of Innovation in Historical Perspective." *Cambridge Journal of Economics* 19, 5–24.

Freeman, Christopher, John Clark, and Luc Soete. 1982. *Unemployment and Technical Innovation.* London: Pinter.

Freeman, Christopher, and Carlota Perez. 1988. "Structural Crises of Adjustment, Business Cycles and Investment Behavior." In *Technical Change and Economic Theory*, ed. Giovanni Dosi et al. London: Pinter.

Freeman, Richard B. 2005. "Does Globalization of the Scientific/Engineering Workforce Threaten U.S. Economic Leadership?" NBER Working Paper No. 11457, July. http://www.nber.org/papers/w11457.pdf?new_window=1.

Friedman, Thomas L. 2008. *Hot, Flat and Crowded: Why We Need a Green Revolution and How It Can Renew America.* New York: Farrar, Straus and Giroux.

Fromhold-Eisebith, Martina. 2007. "Bridging Scales in Innovation Policies: How to Link Regional, National and International Innovation Systems." *European Planning Studies* 15, no. 2, 217–233.

Fuchs, Erica. 2012. "The Impact of Manufacturing Offshore on Technology Competitiveness: Implications for U.S. Policy." Connect Innovation Institute report, San Diego, CA. http://connect.org/wp-content/uploads/2013/08/fuchs-white-paper-0212.pdf.

Fuchs, Erica, and Randolph Kirchain. 2010. "Design for Location? The Impact of Manufacturing Offshore on Technology Competitiveness in the Optoelectronics Industry." *Management Science* 56, no. 12. http://papers.ssrn.com/sol3/papers.cfm?abstract_id=1545027.

Garrette, Bernard and Aneel Karnani. 2010. "Challenges in Marketing Socially Useful Goods to the Poor." *California Management Review* 52, 29–47.

Gates, Bill. 2012. Gates Foundation Annual Letter, January. http://www.gatesfoundation. org/who-we-are/resources-and-media/annual-letters-list/annual-letter-2012.

Gates Foundation. 2011. "Global Health Program Overview." http://www.gatesfoundation. org/global-health/Documents/global-health-program-overview.pdf.

Gaud, W. S. 1998. Speech to the Society for International Development. http://www. agbioworld.org/biotech-info/topics/borlaug/borlaug-green.html.

Geels, Frank W. 2002. "Technological Transitions as Evolutionary Reconfiguration Processes." *Research Policy* 31, nos. 8–9 (December), 1257–1274.

Gellings, Clark W., and Kurt E. Yeager. 2004. "Transforming the Electric Infrastructure." *Physics Today* 57, no. 12 (December), 45–51.

Geng, Yinou. 2010. "Toward Implementation of the Smart Grid in the United States." (unpublished paper). School of Advanced International Studies, Johns Hopkins University, October 13.

Gerstner, Louis V. 2003. *Who Says Elephants Can't Dance? Leading a Great Enterprise through Dramatic Change.* New York: HarperCollins.

Goldemberg, Jose, Thomas B. Johannson, Amulya K. N. Reddy, and Robert H. Williams. 1981. *Energy for a Sustainable World.* New York: Wiley.

Goldin, Claudia, and Lawrence Katz. 2008. *The Race between Education and Technology.* Cambridge, MA: Harvard University Press.

Goldin, Claudia, and Lawrence Katz. 2009. "The Future of Inequality." *Milken Institute Review*, July, 3rd Quarter, 26–33. http://assets1b.milkeninstitute.org/assets/ Publication/MIReview/PDF/26-33mr43.pdf.

Goodrich, Alan, Douglas Powell, Ted James, Michael Woodhouse, and Tonio Buonassisi. 2013. "Assessing the Drivers of Regional Trends in Solar Photovoltaic Manufacturing." *Energy and Environmental Science* 6 (July 23), 2811–2821.

Graham, John. 2014. "No Time for Pessimism about Electric Cars." *Issues in Science and Technology* 31, 33–40. http://issues.org/31-31/no-time-for-pessimism-about-electric-cars.

Graham, Loren. 1993. *The Ghost of the Executed Engineer: Technology and the Fall of the Soviet Union.* Cambridge MA: Harvard University Press.

Graham, Loren. 2013. *Lonely Ideas: Can Russia Compete?* Cambridge, MA: MIT Press.

Granieri, Massimiliano, and Andrea Renda. 2012. *Innovation Law and Policy in the European Union: Towards Horizon 2020.* Milan: Springer.

Griffiths, Rebecca, Matthew Chingos, Christine Mulhern, and Richard Spies. 2014. *Interactive Online Learning on Campus: Testing MOOCs and Other Platforms in Hybrid Formats in the University System of Maryland.* Report, Ithaka S&R, July 10. http:// www.sr.ithaka.org/sites/default/files/reports/S-R_Interactive_Online_Learning_ Campus_20140710.pdf.

Guardian Environment Network. 2011. "U.S. Breaks Ground on First Industrial Scale Carbon Capture Project." August 26. http://www.guardian.co.uk/environment/2011/ aug/26/us-carbon-capture-and-storage-biofuels.

Gumbel, Peter. 2014. "To Boost Entrepreneurship, France Tries to Change Its Attitude toward Failure." Reuters, February 23. http://www.reuters.com/ article/2014/01/23/ gumbel-failure-idUSL2N0KX2IS20140123.

Gupta, Udayan, ed. 2000. *Done Deals: Venture Capitalists Tell Their Stories.* Cambridge, MA: Harvard Business School Press.

Halchin, L. Elaine. 2011. "Other Transaction (OT) Authority." Congressional Research Service, July 15. http://fas.org/sgp/crs/misc/RL34760.pdf.

Harary, Howard, NIST. 2011. "Findings from the Extreme Manufacturing Workshop." PowerPoint presentation, February 24. http://www.ndia.org/Divisions/Divisions/ Manufacturing/Documents/119b%20presentations/10%20Harray.pdf.

Hargraves, Robert, and Ralph W. Moir. 2010. "Liquid Fluoride Thorium Reactors." *American Scientist* 98, no. 4 (July–August), 304–313.

Hart, David M. 1998. *Forged Consensus*. Princeton, NJ: Princeton University Press.

Hart, David M. 2013. "An Agent, Not a Mole: Assessing the White House Office of Science and Technology Policy." *Science and Public Policy*, August 25, 6–7. http://spp.oxford-journals.org/content/early/2013/08/24/scipol.sct061.full.pdf.

HealthIT.gov. 2014. "EHR Incentives and Certification." http://www.healthit.gov/providers-professionals/ehr-incentive-payment-timeline.

Helper, Susan. 2014. "New Tool Shows Manufacturing in America Carries Huge Potential Savings." *Commerce Blog*, October 1. http://www.commerce.gov/blog/2014/10/01/new-tool-shows-manufacturing-america-carries-huge-potential-savings-reshoring-success.

Helper, Susan, Timothy Krueger, and Howard Wial. 2012. "Why Does Manufacturing Matter? Which Manufacturing Matters?" Brookings Institution, February. http://www.brookings.edu/~/media/Files/rc/papers/2012/0222_manufacturing_helper_krueger_wial/0222_manufacturing_helper_krueger_wial.pdf.

Helper, Susan, and Howard Wial. 2011. *Accelerating Advanced Manufacturing Research Centers*. Report, Brookings Project on State and Metropolitan Innovation, February.

Hiltzik, Michael A. 1999. *Dealers of Lightning: Xerox PARC and the Dawn of the Computer Age*. New York: HarperCollins.

Hobday, Michael. 1998. "Product Complexity, Innovation and Industrial Organization." *Research Policy*. 26, no. 6 (February), 689–710.

Hourihan, Matt, and Matthew Stepp. 2011. *Lean, Mean and Clean: Energy Innovation and the Department of Defense*. Washington, DC: Informational Technology and Innovation Foundation, March. http://www.itif.org/files/2011-lean-mean-clean.pdf.

House of Commons, Science and Technology Committee. 2012. "Bridging the Valley of Death: Improving the Commercialization of Research." June 20. Transcript of oral evidence, quoted in *21st Century Manufacturing: The Role of the Manufacturing Extension Partnership Program*, ed. Charles W. Wessner, (Washington, DC: National Research Council, 2013), appendix A-2, 234.

Houseman, Susan Christopher Kurz, Paul Lengermann, and Benjamin Mandel. 2011. "Offshoring Bias in U.S. Manufacturing." *Journal of Economic Perspectives* 25, no. 2, 111–132. http://pubs.aeaweb.org/doi/pdfplus/10.1257/jep.25.2.111.

Hughes, Thomas. 1993. *Networks of Power: Electrification in Western Society, 1880–1930*. Baltimore, MD: Johns Hopkins University Press.

Hundley, Richard O. 1999. *Past Revolutions, Future Transformations: What Can the History of Revolutions in Military Affairs Tell Us about Transforming the US Military*. Washington, DC: Rand / National Research Institute. http://www.rand.org/content/dam/rand/pubs/monograph_reports/2007/MR1029.pdf.

IARPA. Program description. 2014. http://www.iarpa.gov/.

Industrie 4.0 Working Group, National Academy of Science and Engineering. 2013. *Securing the Future of German Manufacturing: Recommendations for Implementing the Strategic Initiative Industry 4.0*. Sponsored by the Federal Ministry of Education and Research, April.

Infectious Disease Society of America. 2004. *Bad Bugs, No Drugs: As Antibiotic Discovery Stagnates, a Public Health Crisis Brews*. Updated in Helen W. Boucher et al. *Bad Bugs, No Drugs: No Escape*; *Clinical Infectious Diseases* 48, no. 1 (2009), 1–12.

Information Technology and Innovation Foundation. 2012. *Enough Is Enough: Confronting Chinese Innovation Mercantilism*. Washington, DC: ITIF, February 28. http://www.itif.org/publications/enough-enough-confronting-chinese-innovation-mercantilism.

Information Technology and Innovation Foundation. 2012. *Eroding Our Foundations: Sequestration, R&D and U.S. Economic Growth*. Washington, DC: ITIF, September. http://www2.itif.org/2012-eroding-foundation.pdf.

Information Technology and Innovation Foundation. 2012. *Worse Than the Great Depression: What the Experts Are Missing about American Manufacturing Decline*. Washington, DC: ITIF, March. http://www2.itif.org/2012-american-manufacturing-decline.pdf.

Information Technology and Innovation Foundation. 2013. *Restoring America's Lagging Investment in Capital Goods*. Washington, DC: ITIF, October. http://www2.itif.org/2013-restoring-americas-lagging-investment.pdf.

Institute for Defense Analysis, Science and Technology Policy Institute. 2012. *Advanced Manufacturing Partnerships: Identifying Areas of Investment—a Review of Methods Used by Federal, Private Sector and International Programs*. Report draft, February 9.

InterAcademy Council. 2004. *Realizing the Promise and Potential of African Agriculture* Amsterdam: IAC. http://www.interacademycouncil.net/24026/africanagriculture.aspx.

Intergovernmental Panel on Climate Change. 2014. Fifth Assessment Report, *Climate Change 2014: Mitigation of Climate Change*. Geneva: IPCC 2014. http://mitigation2014.org.

International Assessment of Agricultural Knowledge, Science and Technology for Development. 2008. "Agriculture at a Crossroads, Summary for Decision Makers." Full report also in B. D. McIntyre, H. R. Herren, J. Wakhungu, and R. T. Watson, eds., *Agriculture at a Crossroads: Global Report* (Washington, DC: Island Press, 2008). http://www.unep.org/dewa/agassessment/reports/IAASTD/EN/Agriculture%20at%20a%20Crossroads_Global%20Summary%20for%20Decision%20Makers%20%28English%29.pdf.

International Energy Agency. 2008. "Energy Technology Perspectives 2008: Scenarios and Strategies to 2050." June 6. http://www.iea.org/Textbase/npsum/ETP2008SUM.pdf.

Isaacson, Walter. 2011. *Steve Jobs*. New York: Simon & Shuster.

Jamshidi, Mo, ed. 2009. *System of Systems Engineering*. Hoboken, NJ: John Wiley & Sons.

Jaruzelski, Barry, and Kevin Dehoff. 2008. "Beyond Borders: The Global Innovation 1000." *Strategy & Business* 53 (Winter), 9. http://www.strategyand.pwc.com/media/file/Beyond-Borders-Global-Innovation-1000.pdf.

Johnson, Dale. 1991. *World Agriculture in Disarray*. 2nd ed. New York: Palgrave Macmillan.

Johnston, Amy. 1995. "How Deregulation Changed the Telecommunications Industry." *Management Quarterly* 36 no. 4, 24–28.

Jorgenson, Dale. 2001. "U.S. Economic Growth in the Information Age." *Issues in Science and Technology*, Fall. http://www.issues.org/18.1/jorgenson.html.

Kaplinsky, Raphael. 2005. *Globalization, Poverty and Inequality*. Cambridge MA: Polity Press.

Kaplinsky, Raphael, et al. 2009. "Below the Radar: What Does Innovation in Emerging Economies Have to Offer Other Low-Income Economies?" *International Journal of Technology Management and Sustainable Development* 8, 177–197.

Kaushal, Arvind, Thomas Mayor, and Patricia Riedl. 2011. "Manufacturing's Wake-Up Call." Strategy & Business 64, Booz & Company and Tauber Institute for Global Operations, University of Michigan, August 3, 38. http://www.strategyand.pwc.com/media/uploads/sb64-11306-Manufacturings-Wake-Up-Call.pdf.

Kazimi, Mujid S. 2003. "Thorium Fuel for Nuclear Energy." *American Scientist* 91, no. 5 (September–October). 1–16. http://www.ltbridge.com/assets/13.pdf.

Klass, Alexandra B., and Elizabeth J. Wilson. 2012. "Interstate Transmission Challenges for Renewable Energy: A Federalism Mismatch." *Vanderbilt Law Review* 65, no. 6, 1801–1873.

Kolowich, Steve. 2013. "Outsourced Lectures Raise Concerns about Academic Freedom." *Chronicle of Higher Education*, May 28. http://chronicle.com/article/Outsourced-Lectures-Raise/139471/.

Kolowich, Steve. 2014. "San Jose State Adopts More edX Content for Outsources Trial." *Chronicle of Higher Education*, February 30. http://chronicle.com/blogs/wiredcampus/san-jose-state-u-adopts-more-edx-content-for-outsourcing-trial/49905.

Krepinovich, Andrew F., Jr. 2003. *The Military-Technical Revolution*. Washington, DC: Center for Strategic and Budgetary Assessment. Reprint of DOD Office of Net Assessment paper, July 1992. http://www.csbaonline.org/wp-content/uploads/2011/03/2002.10.02-Military-Technical-Revolution.pdf.

Kuhn, Thomas. 1996. *Structure of Scientific Revolutions*. 3rd ed. Chicago: University of Chicago Press.

Lala, R. M. 1995. *The Joy of Achievement: Conversations with J.R.D. Tata*. New Delhi, India: Viking.

Lardy, Nicholas R. 2014. *Markets over Mao: The Rise of Private Business in China*. Washington, DC: Peterson Institute for International Economics.

Leonard, John J., Jonathan How, Seth Teller, et al. 2008. "A Perception Driven Autonomous Urban Vehicle." *Journal of Field Robotics*, 25, no. 10. 727–774. http://people.csail.mit.edu/lukesf/publications/leonardJFR08.pdf.

Levine, Michael E. 1981. "Revisionism Revised? Airline Deregulation and the Public Interest." *Law and Contemporary Problems*, January.

Lewis, Joanna I. 2010. "The State of U.S.-China Relations on Climate Change: Examining the Bilateral and Multilateral Relationship." *China Environment Series* 11, 7–39.

Lewis, Joanna I. 2013. *Green Innovation in China*. New York: Columbia University Press.

Li, Fion. 2013. "China Mulls Trial Program for Individuals Investing Overseas." *Bloomberg*, February 12. http://www.bloomberg.com/news/2013-2001-12/china-mulls-trial-program-for-individuals-investing-overseas.html.

Licklider, J. C. R. 1960. "Man Machine Symbiosis." *IRE Transactions on Human Factors in Electronics*, March.

Linden, Greg, Jason Dedrick, and Kenneth L Kraemer. 2011. "Innovation and Job Creation: The Case of Apple's iPod." *Journal of International Commerce and Economics*, May, 229–230. http://www.rrojasdatabank.info/innovation.pdf.

Lisbon Strategy for Growth and Jobs. 2008. "France National Reform Programme 2008–2010." October. http://ec.europa.eu/social/BlobServlet?docId=6111&langId=en.

Lloyd, Maggie. 2013. *Review of the NSF's Advanced Technological Education (ATE) Program: ATE's Role in Advanced Manufacturing Education and Training*. MIT Washington Office, February. http://dc.mit.edu/sites/default/files/MIT%20Review%20of%20NSF%20ATE%20Program.pdf.

Lo, Andrew. 2011. "How Financial Engineering Can Cure Cancer, Stop Global Warming, and Solve the Energy Crisis." MIT lecture, March 3. http://ttv.mit.edu/videos/11921-mfin-faculty-speaker---andrew-lo.

Lo, Andrew, with David Fagnan, Jose Maria Fernandez, and Roger Stein. 2013. "Can Financial Engineering Cure Cancer?" Presentation at MIT LGO Webinar. http://lgosdm.mit.edu/VCSS/web_seminars/docs/AndrewLo_slides_20130301.pdf.

Lundvall, Bengt-Åke. 1985. *Product Innovation and User-Producer Interaction*. Aalborg: Aalborg University Press.

Lundvall, Bengt-Åke, ed. 1992. *National Innovation Systems: Towards a Theory of Innovation and Interactive Learning.* London: Pinter.

Lynn, Barry C. 2005. *End of the Line.* New York: Doubleday.

Mabus, Ray. 2011. "Moving the Navy and Marine Corps Off Fossil Fuels." Blog post, February 24. http://www.navy.mil/navydata/people/secnav/Mabus/Other/MovingtheNavyandMarineCorpsOffFossilFuels.pdf.

Maker, Eugene M. 2008. *An American's Guide to Doing Business in India: A Practical Guide to Achieving Success in the Indian Market.* Avon: Adams Business.

Malhotra, Anil K. 2007. *A Passion to Build: India's Search for Offshore Technology: A Memoir.* Raleigh, NC: Lulu Press.

Mandel, Michael. 2011. "How Much of the Productivity Surge of 2007–2009 Was Real?" *Mandel on Innovation and Growth* blog, March 28. http://innovationandgrowth.wordpress.com/2011/03/28/how-much-of-the-productivity-surge-of-2007-2009-was-real/.

Mann, Catherine L. 2003. "Globalization of IT Services and White Collar Jobs." Institute for International Economics, International Economics Policy Briefs, N. PB03-11, December. http://www.iie.com/publications/pb/pb03-11.pdf.

Mansfield, Jeanne. 2011. "DARPA Administrators: Just Make It." *MIT News* (online), December 14 (with video of talk). http://web.mit.edu/newsoffice/2011/darpa-manufacturing-event-1214.html.

Marshall, Andrew W. 1993. "Some Thoughts on Military Revolutions." Second Version, DOD Office of Net Assessment, Memorandum for the Record, June 27.

Martin, Richard. 2011. "China Takes Lead in Race for Clean Nuclear Power." *Wired.com*, February 1. http://www.wired.com/wiredscience/2011/02/china-thorium-power/.

Mashelkar, R. A. 2008. "Indian Science, Technology, and Society: The Changing Landscape." *Technology in Society* 30, 299–308.

Matus, Kira, et al. 2011. "Health Damages from Air Pollution in China." MIT Joint Program on the Science and Policy of Global Change.

Mayo, Merrilea J. 2009. "Video Games: A Route to Large-Scale STEM Education?" *Science* 323, no. 5910 (February 2), 79–78. http://www.sciencemag.org/content/323/5910/79.abstract.

Mazzucato, Mariana. 2013. *The Entrepreneurial State: Debunking Public vs. Private Sector Myths.* New York: Anthem Press.

McCormack, Richard A. 2010. "China's Entry into the WTO 10 Years Ago Is Not What President Clinton Promised." *Manufacturing and Technology News* 17, no. 10 (June 15). http://www.manufacturingnews.com/news/10/0615/WTO.html.

McCouch, Susan, et al. 2013. "Agriculture: Feeding the Future." *Nature* 499 (July 4), 23–24. http://www.nature.com/nature/journal/v499/n7456/full/499023a.html.

McKinsey & Company. 2009. *Unlocking Energy Efficiency in the U.S. Economy.* July. http://www.mckinsey.com/clientservice/electricpowernaturalgas/downloads/US_energy_efficiency_full_report.pdf.

McNeill, John. 2001. *Something New under the Sun: An Environmental History of the Twentieth Century World.* New York: W.W. Norton.

Merrigan, Kathleen, and W. Lockeretz. 2009. "Ensuring Comprehensive Organic Livestock Standards." Presentation at 1st IFOAM International Conference on Animals in Organic Production. http://www.ams.usda.gov/AMSv1.0/getfile?dDocName=STELPRDC5066277.

Miluvich, Steven, and John M. A Roy. 2001. "The Next Small Thing: An Introduction to Nanotechnology." *Merrill Lynch Industry Comment.*

Minot, Nicholas W. 2011. "Transmission of World Food Price Changes to Markets in Sub-Saharan Africa." International Food Policy Research Institute, IFPRI Discussion Papers 1059.

MIT. 2011. "The Third Revolution: The Convergence of the Life Sciences, Physical Sciences, and Engineering." White paper, January 4. http://web.mit.edu/dc/Policy/MIT%20White%20Paper%20on%20Convergence.pdf.

MIT CC&ST Program. 2013. "Carbon Capture and Sequestration Technologies: U.S. CCS Financing Overview." Cambridge, MA: MITEI, December 20. https://sequestration.mit.edu/tools/projects/us_ccs_background.html.

MIT Energy Initiative. 2011. *The Future of the Electric Grid*. Cambridge, MA: MITEI. https://mitei.mit.edu/system/files/Electric_Grid_Full_Report.pdf.

MIT, Institute-Wide Task Force on the Future of MIT Education. 2013. Preliminary report, November 21. http://web.mit.edu/future-report/TaskForceOnFutureOfMITEducation_PrelimReport.pdf.

MIT, Masters of Engineering in Manufacturing, MIT Department of Mechanical Engineering, http://web.mit.edu/meng-manufacturing/.

MIT News. 2014. "MIT and Harvard Release Working Papers on Online Courses." February 21. http://newsoffice.mit.edu/2014/mit-and-harvard-release-working-papers-on-open-online-courses-0121.

MIT Radiation Laboratory. 1946. "Five Years at the Radiation Laboratory." https://archive.org/details/fiveyearsatradia00mass.

MIT Washington Office (Aneesh Anand). 2014. "Survey of Selected Federal Manufacturing Programs at NIST, DOE, DOD and NSF." September. http://dc.mit.edu/resources-links.

MIT Washington Office (Eliza Eddison). 2010. "Survey of Federal Manufacturing Efforts." September. http://web.mit.edu/dc/policy/MIT%20Survey%20of%20Federal%20Manufacturing%20Efforts.pdf.

Moore, Geoffrey A. 1999. *Crossing the Chasm: Marketing and Selling Technology Products to Mainstream Customers*. Rev. ed. New York: Harper Business.

Moretti, Enrico. 2012. *The New Geography of Jobs*. New York: Houghton Mifflin Harcourt.

Morris, Charles R. 2012. *The Dawn of Innovation: The First American Industrial Revolution*. New York: Public Affairs.

Morrison, Tom, Bob Maciejewski, et. al. 2011. "Boiling Point? The Skills Gap in U.S. Manufacturing: A Report on Talent in the Manufacturing Industry." Sponsored by Deloitte and the Manufacturing Institute. http://www.themanufacturinginstitute.org/~/media/A07730B2A798437D98501E798C2E13AA.ashx.

Myers, Norman, and Jennifer Kent. 2001. *Perverse Subsidies: How Tax Dollars Can Undercut the Environment and the Economy*. Washington, DC: Island Press.

Nahm, Jonas, and Edward S. Steinfeld. 2012. "Scale-up Nation: Chinese Specialization in Innovative Manufacturing." MIT Working Paper, March 12.

Nahm, Jonas, and Edward S. Steinfeld. 2014. "Scale-Up Nation: China's Specialization in Innovative Manufacturing." *World Development* 54 (February), 288–300. http://dx.doi.org/10.1016/j.worlddev.2013.09.003.

Nahm, Jonas, and Edward S. Steinfeld. 2014. "The Role of Innovative Manufacturing in High-Tech Product Development: Evidence from China's Renewable Energy Sector." In *Production in the Innovation Economy*, ed. Richard Locke and Rachel Wellhausen, 81–108. Cambridge, MA: MIT Press.

National Association of Manufacturers. 2011. "Skills Gap Report." Washington, DC: Manufacturing Institute. http://www.themanufacturinginstitute.org/Research/Skills-Gap-in-Manufacturing/2011-Skills-Gap-Report/2011-Skills-Gap-Report.aspx.

National Center for Appropriate Technology, ATTRA. 2014. National Sustainable Agriculture Information Service. https://attra.ncat.org/.

National Highway Traffic Safety Administration. 2013. "Preliminary Statement of Policy Concerning Automated Vehicles." May 30. http://www.nhtsa.gov/About+NHTSA/Press+Releases/U.S.+Department+of+Transportation+Releases+Policy+on+Automated+Vehicle+Development.

National Institute of Medicine. 2003. *Enhancing the Vitality of the National Institutes of Health: Organizational Changes to Meet New Challenges*. Washington, DC: National Academies Press. http://www.nap.edu/catalog/10779.html.

National Institutes of Health. 2014. "BRAIN Working Group Report to the Advisory Committee to the Director." June 5. http://www.nih.gov/science/brain/2025/index.htm.

National Research Council. 2012. *Continuing Innovation in Information Technology*. Washington, DC: National Academies Press.

National Research Council. 2013. *21st Century Manufacturing: The Role of the Manufacturing Extension Partnership Program*. Washington, DC: National Academies Press. http://www.nap.edu/openbook.php? record_id=18448&page=229.

National Research Council, Board on Health Sciences Policy. 2004. *New Frontiers in Contraceptive Research*. Washington, DC: National Academies, Institute of Medicine.

National Research Council, Board on Life Sciences. 2014. *Convergence: Facilitating Transdisciplinary Integration of Life, Physical Science, Engineering and Beyond*. Washington, DC: National Academies Press. http://www.nap.edu/catalog.php?record_id=18722.

National Research Council, Committee on a Review of USDA Agriculture and Food Research Initiative. 2014. *Spurring Innovation in Food and Agriculture: A Review of the USDA Agriculture and Food Research Initiative Program*. Washington, DC: National Academies Press.

National Research Council, Committee on 21st Century Agriculture Systems, Board on Agriculture and Natural Resources. 2010. *Toward Sustainable Agriculture Systems in the 21st Century*. Washington, DC: National Academies Press. http://books.nap.edu/catalog.php?record_id=12832.

National Research Council, Science and Telecommunications Board. 1999. *Funding a Revolution: Government Support for Computing Research*. Washington, DC: National Academy Press.

National Science Foundation. 2012. *Science and Technology Indicators 2012*. Washington, DC: National Science Foundation, January. http://www.nsf.gov/statistics/seind12/c4/c4s8.htm.

National Science Foundation. 2014. *Science and Engineering Indicators 2014*. Washington, DC: National Science Foundation. http://www.nsf.gov/statistics/seind12/c2/c2s4.htm.

National Venture Capital Association. 2013. *Yearbook 2013*. Thompson Reuters, March. http://www.nvca.org/index.php?option=com_content&view=article&id=257&Itemid=103.

Natter, Ari. 2015, "DOE Suspends $1 Billion in FutureGen Funds." Bloomberg BNA Energy and Climate Report, February 5, http://www.bna.com/doe-suspends-billion-n17179922773/.

Nelson, Richard R., ed. 1993. *National Innovation Systems: A Comparative Analysis*. New York: Oxford University Press.

Nelson, Richard R., and Nathan Rosenberg. 1993. "Technical Innovation and National Systems." In *National Innovation Systems: A Comparative Analysis*, ed. Richard R. Nelson, 3–21. New York: Oxford University Press.

Nelson, Richard R., and Sidney R. Winter. 1982. *An Evolutionary Theory of Economic Change*. Cambridge, MA: Belknap Press of Harvard University Press.

Nemet, Gregory F., and Daniel M. Kammen. 2007. "U.S. Energy R&D: Declining Investment, Increasing Need, and the Feasibility of Expansion." *Energy Policy* 35, 746–755.

Office of Science and Technology Policy and National Science and Technology Council. 2011. "Materials Genome Initiative for Global Competiveness", June. http://www.whitehouse. gov/sites/default/files/microsites/ostp/materials_genome_initiative-final.pdf.

Office of Science and Technology Policy and National Science and Technology Council. 2012. "A National Strategic Plan for Advanced Manufacturing." Washington, DC: OSTP, February. http://www.whitehouse.gov/sites/default/files/microsites/ostp/ iam_advancedmanufacturing_strategicplan_2012.pdf.

O'Hanlon, Michael E. 2011. "The National Security Industrial Base: A Crucial Asset of the United States, Whose Future May Be in Jeopardy." Brookings Institution, February. http://www.brookings.edu/research/papers/2011/02/defense-ohanlon.

Oldcomputers.net. 2014. "Apple II—1997." March 1. http://oldcomputers.net/appleii.html.

Olsen, Edwin B. 2009. "Real-Time Correlative Scan Matching." University of Michigan. http://april.eecs.umich.edu/pdfs/olson2009icra.pdf.

Olson, Mancur. 2000. *Power and Prosperity: Outgrowing Communist and Capitalist Dictatorships*. New York: Basic Books.

Oreskes, Naomi, and Erik M. Conway. 2009. *Merchants of Doubt*. New York: Bloomsbury Press.

Organization for Economic Cooperation and Development. 2012. "OECD Economic Surveys: Germany 2012." http://dx.doi.org/10.1787/eco_surveys-deu-2012-en.

Organization for Economic Cooperation and Development. 2013. "Goods Trade Balance, Trade: Key tables from OECD." January. http://www.oecd-ilibrary.org/trade/ goods-trade-balance_20743920-table2.

Organization for Economic Cooperation and Development. 2013. "OECD Economic Surveys: France." March. http://www.oecd.org/eco/surveys/Overview%20France%20 2013.pdf.

Organization for Economic Cooperation and Development. 2013. "OECD Science, Technology and Industry Scoreboard 2013: Innovation for Growth."

Osterman, Paul, and Andrew Weaver. 2014. "Skills and Skill Gaps in Manufacturing." In *Production in the Innovation Economy*, ed. Richard Locke and Rachel Wellhausen, 17–50. Cambridge, MA: MIT Press.

Owens William and Edward Offley. 2001. *Lifting the Fog of War*. Baltimore, MD: Johns Hopkins University Press.

Paarlberg, Robert, Norman Borlaug, and Jimmy Carter. 2009. *Starved for Science: How Biotechnology Is Being Kept out of Africa*. Cambridge, MA: Harvard University Press.

Pacala, Steven, and Robert Socolow. 2004. "Stabilization Wedges: Solving the Climate Problem for the Next 50 Years with Current Technologies." *Science* 305 (August 13), 968–972.

Paddock, William, and Paul Paddock. 1967. *Famine 1975! America's Decision: Who Will Survive?* Boston, MA: Little, Brown.

Parkinson, Robert. 1972. "The Dvorak Simplified Keyboard: Forty Years of Frustration." *Computers and Automation*, November 18–25. http://infohost.nmt.edu/~shipman/ ergo/parkinson.html.

Parthasarathi, Ashok. 2007. *Technology at the Core: Science and Technology with Indira Gandhi*. New Delhi: Dorling Kindersley.

Perez, Carlota. 2002. *Technological Revolutions and Financial Capital: The Dynamics of Bubbles and Golden Ages*. Cheltenham, UK: Edward Elgar.

Perry, William J. 1997. "Perry on Precision Strike." *Air Force Magazine* 80, no. 4 (April), 76. http://www.airforcemag.com/MagazineArchive/Pages/1997/April%201997/0497perry.aspx.

Pew Charitable Trusts. 2014. "Who's Winning the Clean Energy Race." April. http://www.pewtrusts.org/en/research-and-analysis/reports/2014/04/03/whos-winning-the-clean-energy-race-2013.

Pietrobelli, Carlo, and Roberta Rabellotti. 2011. "Global Value Chains Meet Innovation Systems: Are There Learning Opportunities for Developing Countries?" *World Development* 9, no. 7, 1261–1269.

Pisano, Gary P., and Willy Shih. 2009. "Restoring American Competitiveness." *Harvard Business Review*, July–August, 114–125. https://hbr.org/2009/07/restoring-american-competitiveness/ar/1.

Pisano, Gary P., and Willy Shih. 2012. *Producing Prosperity: Why America Needs a Manufacturing Renaissance.* Cambridge, MA: Harvard Business School Press.

Pollan, Michael. 2006. *Omnivore's Dilemma: The Natural History of Four Meals.* New York: Penguin.

Polmar, Norman. 2013. "The Pioneering Pioneer." *Naval History* 27, no. 5 (October). 14–15.

Powell, Douglas, Tonio Buonassisi, et al. 2012. "Crystalline Silicon Photovoltaics: As Cost Analysis Framework for Determining Technology Pathways to Reach Baseload Electricity Costs." *Energy & Environmental Science* 5 (February), 5874–5883.

Powell, John. 2013. "Implications of Increasing U.S. Crude Oil Production." Presentation to Energy Information Administration 2013 Annual Energy Conference, June 18. http://www.eia.gov/conference/2013/pdf/presentations/powell.pdf.

Prahalad, C. K. 2006. *The Fortune at the Bottom of the Pyramid.* Philadelphia, PA: Wharton School Publishing.

President's Council of Advisors on Science and Technology. 2006. *The Energy Imperative: Technology and the Role of Emerging Companies.* Washington, DC: White House Office of Science and Technology Policy, November. http://www.ostp.gov/pcast/PCAST-EnergyImperative_FINAL.pdf.

President's Council of Advisors on Science and Technology. 2011. *Ensuring American Leadership in Advanced Manufacturing.* Washington, DC: White House Office of Science and Technology Policy, June. http://www.whitehouse.gov/sites/default/files/microsites/ostp/pcast-advanced-manufacturing-june2011.pdf.

President's Council of Advisors on Science and Technology. 2012. Advanced Manufacturing Partnership, *Capturing Domestic Competitive Advantage in Advanced Manufacturing.* Washington, DC: White House Office of Science and Technology Policy, July. http://www.whitehouse.gov/sites/default/files/microsites/ostp/pcast_amp_steering_committee_report_final_july_17_2012.pdf.

President's Council of Advisors on Science and Technology. 2012. "Agricultural Preparedness and the Agricultural Research Portfolio." December. http://www.whitehouse.gov/sites/default/files/microsites/ostp/pcast_agriculture_20121207.pdf.

President's Council of Advisors on Science and Technology. 2012. *Engage to Excel.* Washington, DC: White House Office of Science and Technology Policy, February 5. http://www.whitehouse.gov/sites/default/files/microsites/ostp/pcast-engage-to-excel-final_feb.pdf.

President's Council of Advisors on Science and Technology. 2012. *Propelling Innovation in Drug Discovery, Development and Evaluation.* Washington, DC: White House Office of Science and Technology Policy, September. http://www.whitehouse.gov/sites/default/files/microsites/ostp/pcast-fda-final.pdf.

President's Council of Advisors on Science and Technology. 2014. *Better Health Care and Lower Costs: Accelerating Improvement through Systems Engineering.* Washington, DC: White House Office of Science and Technology Policy, May. http://www.white-house.gov/sites/default/files/microsites/ostp/PCAST/pcast_systems_engineering_in_healthcare_-_may_2014.pdf.

President's Council of Advisors on Science and Technology. 2014. *Big Data and Privacy: A Technological Perspective.* Washington, DC: White House Office of Science and Technology Policy, May. http://www.whitehouse.gov/sites/default/files/microsites/ostp/PCAST/pcast_big_data_and_privacy_-_may_2014.pdf.

President's Council of Advisors on Science and Technology. 2014. *Report to the President on Accelerating U.S. Advanced Manufacturing.* October. http://www.whitehouse.gov/sites/default/files/microsites/ostp/PCAST/amp20_report_final.pdf.

Qiu, J. 2014. "China Goes Back to Basics in Research Funding." *Nature* 507 (March 11), 148–149. http://www.nature.com/news/china-goes-back-to-basics-on-research-funding-1.14853.

Radjou, Navi, et al. 2012. *Jugaad Innovation: A Frugal and Flexible Approach to Innovation for the 21st Century.* San Francisco: Jossey-Bass.

Reif, Rafael. 2013. "Better, More Affordable Colleges Start Online." *Time*, September 2. http://president.mit.edu/speeches-writing/better-more-affordable-colleges-start-online.

Reij, Chris, and Ann Waters-Bayer. 2002. *Farmer Innovation in Africa: A Source of Inspiration for Agricultural Development.* London: Earthscan.

Renda, Andrea. 2012. *Innovation Law and Policy in the European Union: Towards Horizon 2020.* Milan: Springer.

Reynolds, Elizabeth B., Hiram Semel, and Joyce Lawrence. 2014. "Learning by Building: Complementary Assets and the Migration of Capabilities in U.S. Innovation Firms." In *Production in the Innovation Economy*, ed. Richard Locke and Rachel Wellhausen, 81–108. Cambridge, MA: MIT Press.

Rich, Ben, and Leo Janos. 1994. *Skunk Works.* Boston: Little, Brown.

Riley, Michael, and Ashlee Vance. 2012. "It's Not Paranoia if They're Stealing Your Secrets." *Bloomberg Business Week*, March 19, 76–84.

Roberts, Edward B., and Charles Easley. 2010. *Entrepreneurship Impact.* Kansas City, MO: Kauffman Foundation. Report. 44–71.

Roberts, Paul 2008. *The End of Food.* Boston and New York: Houghton Mifflin/Bloomsbury.

Robyn, Dorothy. 1987. *Braking the Special Interests: Trucking Deregulation and the Politics of Policy Reform.* Chicago: University of Chicago Press.

Roessner, David, Jennifer Bond, Sumiye Okubo, and Mark Planting. 2009. *The Economic Impact of Licensed Commercialized Inventions Originating in University Research, 1997-2007.* Washington, DC: Biotechnology Industry Organization, September 3.

Rogers, Everett M. 1962. *Diffusion of Innovations.* Glencoe, New York: Free Press.

Romer, Christina. 2012. "Do Manufacturers Need Special Treatment?" *New York Times*, February 4. http://www.nytimes.com/2012/02/05/business/do-manufacturers-need-special-treatment-economic-view.html?_r=0 ITIF.

Romer, Paul M. 1990. "Endogenous Technological Change." *Journal of Political Economy* 98, no. 5, 72–102. http://www.nber.org/papers/w3210.pdf.

Romer, Paul M. 2000. "Should the Government Subsidize Supply or Demand in the Market for Scientists and Engineers." NBER Working Paper 7723, June. 11. http://www.nber.org/papers/w7723.

Romer, Paul M. 2007. "Economic Growth." In *The Concise Encyclopedia of Economics.* 2nd ed. http://www.econlib.org/library/Enc/EconomicGrowth.html.

Ronald, Pamela C. 2014. "From Lab to Farm: Applying Plant Research on Plant Genetics and Genomics to Crop Improvement." *PLoSBiology* 12, no. 6 (June 10), e1001878. http://www.plosbiology.org/article/fetchObject.action?uri=info%3Adoi%2F10.1371%2Fjournal.pbio.1001878&representation=PDF.

Rosen, William. 2010. *The Most Powerful Idea in the World: A Story of Steam, Industry and Invention*. New York: Random House.

Rosenthal, Elisabeth. 2011. "Organic Agriculture May Be Outgrowing Its Ideals." *New York Times*, December 31. http://www.nytimes.com/2011/12/31/science/earth/questions-about-organic-produce-and-sustainability.html.

Runge, C. Ford, and Benjamin Senauer. 2007. "How Biofuels Could Starve the Poor." *Foreign Affairs* 86, no. 3 (May–June), 41–53.

Ruttan, Vernon. 2001. *Technology Growth and Development: An Induced Innovation Perspective*. New York: Oxford University Press.

Ruttan, Vernon. 2006. *Is War Necessary for Economic Growth? Military Procurement and Technology Development*. New York: Oxford University Press.

Rycroft, Robert W., and Don E. Kash. 1999. "Innovation Policy for Complex Technologies." *Issues in Science and Technology*, Fall. http://www.issues.org/16.1/rycroft.htm.

Sagasti, Francisco. 1979. "National Science and Technology Policies for Development: A Comparative Analysis." In *Mobilizing Technology for Development*, ed. Jairam Ramesh and Charles Weiss. New York: Praeger.

Samuelson, Paul A. 2004. "Where Ricardo and Mill Rebut and Confirm Arguments of Mainstream Economists Supporting Globalization." *Journal of Economic Perspectives* 18, no. 3 (Summer), 135–137, 144–145. http://www.nd.edu/~druccio/Samuelson.pdf.

Sarma, Sanjay, and Isaac Chuang. 2013. "The Magic behind the MOOCs." *MIT Faculty Newsletter*, 25, no. 5, June. http://web.mit.edu/fnl/volume/255/sarmay_chuang.html.

Schilling, Melissa. 2005. *Strategic Management of Technological Innovation*. 2nd. ed. New York: McGraw-Hill.

Schmitz, Hubert, and Simone Strambach. 2009. "The Organisational Decomposition of Innovation and Global Distribution of Innovative Activities: Insights and Research Agenda." *International Journal of Technological Learning, Innovation and Development* 2, no. 4, 231–249.

Schumpeter, Joseph A. 1975. *Capitalism, Socialism and Democracy*. New York: Harper.

Schwab, Klaus, ed. 2013. *The Global Competitiveness Report, 2013–2014*. Geneva: World Economic Forum. http://reports.weforum.org/the-global-competitiveness-report-2013-2014/.

SciDevnet. 2012. "Science and Technology in the Islamic World." January–February. http://www.scidev.net/en/science-and-innovation-policy/science-in-the-islamic-world/.

Sen, Avery. 2014. "Transformative Innovation: What 'Totally Radical' and 'Island-Bridge' Mean for NOAA Research." Dissertation, George Washington University, March.

Sharp, Phillip A. 2014. "Meeting Global Challenges: Discovery and Innovation through Convergence." *Science* 345, no. 6215 (December 19), 1468–1471.

Sharp, Phillip A., and Robert Langer. 2011. "Promoting Convergence in Biomedical Science." *Science* 333 (July 29), 527. http://dc.mit.edu/sites/default/files/Sharp%20Langer%20Science.pdf.

Sheehan, Neil. 2009. *A Fiery Peace in a Cold War: Bernard Schriever and the Ultimate Weapon*. New York: Random House Vintage.

Shipp, Stephanie, et al. 2012. *Emerging Global Trends in Advanced Manufacturing*. Report P-4603. Arlington, VA: Institute for Defense Analysis, March. http://www.wilsoncenter.org/sites/default/files/Emerging_Global_Trends_in_Advanced_Manufacturing.pdf.

Simon, Denis Fred, ed. 1995. *The Emerging Technological Trajectory of the Pacific Rim*. Armonk, NY: M.E. Sharpe.

Singer, Peter L. 2014. "Federally Supported Innovation: 22 Examples of Major Technology Advances That Stem from Federal Research Support." Information Technology and Innovation Foundation report, February. http://www2.itif.org/2014-federally-supported-innovations.pdf.

Singer, Susan R., and William B. Bonvillian. 2013. "Two Revolutions in Learning." *Science* 339 (March 22), 1359.

Singer, Susan R., Natalie R. Nielsen, and Heidi A. Schweingruber, eds. 2012. *Discipline-Based Education Research: Understanding and Improving Learning in Undergraduate Science and Engineering*. Washington, DC: National Academies Press. http://www.nap.edu/catalog.php?record_id=13362#toc.

Slovic, Paul. 2013. "Perceived Risk, Trust, and Democracy." In *Social Trust and the Management of Risk*, ed. George Cvetkovich and Ragnar E. Lofstedt . New York: Earthscan.

Smihula, Daniel. 2009. "The Waves of the Technological Innovation of the Modern Age and the Present Crisis." *Studia Politica Slovaca* 1, 32–47. http://papers.ssrn.com/sol3/papers.cfm?abstract_id=2353600.

Smil, Vaclav. 2001. *Enriching the Earth: Fritz Haber, Carl Bosch, and the Transformation of World Food Production*. Cambridge, MA: MIT Press.

Smith, Adam. 2005. *The Wealth of Nations*. State College: Penn State Electronic Classics.

Smith, Adrian. 2007. "Translating Sustainabilities between Green Niches and Socio-technical Regimes." *Technology Analysis and Strategic Management* 19 (July), 427–450.

Smith, Bryant Walker. 2014. "Automated Vehicles are Probably Legal in the United States" *Texas A&M Law Review* 1, 411. http://ssrn.com/abstract=2303904.

Smith, Bryant Walker. 2014. "A Legal Perspective on Three Misconceptions in Vehicle Automation," Lecture Notes in Mobility, in Gereon Meyer and Sven Beiker, eds. *Road Vehicle Automation* (Springer). http://ssrn.com/abstract=2459164.

Smith, Douglas K., and Robert C. Alexander. 1999. *Fumbling the Future*. Lincoln, NE: iUniverse.

Solow, Robert M. 1987. "Growth Theory and After." Nobel Prize Lecture, December 8. http://nobelprize.org/nobel_prizes/economics/laureates/1987/solow-lecture.html.

Solow, Robert M. 2000. *Growth Theory: An Exposition*. 2nd ed. New York: Oxford University Press.

Sorensen, Knut H., and Robin Williams, eds. 2002. *Shaping Technology, Guiding Policy: Concepts, Spaces and Tools*. Cheltenham, UK: Edward Elgar.

Spar, Deborah L. 2001. *Ruling the Waves: Cycles of Discovery, Chaos, and Wealth, from Compass to the Internet*. New York: Harcourt.

Spence, Michael A. 2001. "The Impact of Globalization on Income and Employment: The Downside of Integrating Markets." *Foreign Affairs* 90, no. 4 (July–August), 28–41. http://www.viet-studies.info/kinhte/MichaelSpence_Globalization_Unemployment.pdf.

Stanford Law Center for Internet and Society. 2012. "Automated Driving, Legislative and Regulatory Action." http://cyberlaw.stanford.edu/wiki/index.php/Automated_Driving:_Legislative_and_Regulatory_Action.

Stanley, Byron, Matthew Cornick, and Jeffrey Koechling. 2013. "Ground Penetrating Radar Based Localization." Paper presented at the National Defense Industry Association Ground Vehicle Systems Engineering and Technology Symposium, Autonomous Ground Systems Mini-Symposium, Troy, Michigan, August 21–22.

Stanley, Byron, Jeffrey Koechling, and Matthew Cornick. 2013. "Localization Using Ground Penetrating Radar." Presentation to MIT IdeaStream conference, April 5.

Steinfeld, Edward S. 2010. *Playing Our Game: Why China's Rise Doesn't Threaten the West*. New York: Oxford University Press.

Stern, Nicholas. 2006. *Stern Review on the Economics of Climate Change*. London: H. M. Treasury. Report. http://www.hm-treasury.gov.uk/media/4/3/Executive_Summary.pdf.

Stewart, Frances. 1977. *Technology and Underdevelopment*. 2nd ed. London: Macmillan.

Stewart, Frances 1981. "International Technology Transfer: Issues and Policy Options." In *Recent Issues in World Development: A Collection of Survey Articles*, ed. P. Streeten and R. Jolly, 67–110. Oxford: Pergamon Press.

Stokes, Donald E. 1997. *Pasteur's Quadrant: Basic Science and Technological Innovation*. Washington, DC: Brookings Institution Press.

Stratton, Russell W., Hsin Min Wong, and James I. Hileman. 2011. "Quantifying Variability in Life Cycle Greenhouse Gas Inventories of Alternative Middle Distillate Transportation Fuels." *Environmental Science and Technology*, ACS online ed., April 22. http://pubs.acs.org/doi/full/10.1021/es102597f.

Tan, X., and Z. Gang. 2009. "An Emerging Revolution: Clean Technology Research, Development and Innovation in China." World Resources Institute Working Paper, December.

Tassey, Gregory. 2010. "Rationales and Mechanisms for Revitalizing US Manufacturing R&D Strategies." *Journal of Technology Transfer* 35, no. 3 (June). http://www.nist.gov/director/planning/upload/manufacturing_strategy_paper.pdf.

Tassey, Gregory. 2012. "Beyond the Business Cycle: The Need for a Technology-Based Growth Strategy." National Institute of Standards and Technology working paper, February. http://www.nist.gov/director/planning/upload/beyond-business-cycle.pdf.

Technology Strategy Board (UK). 2008. "High Value Manufacturing: Key Technology Area, 2008–2011." http://webarchive.nationalarchives.gov.uk/20130221185318/www.innovateuk.org/_assets/pdf/corporate-publications/tsb_highvaluemanu.pdf.

Techopedia. N.d. "Maker Movement." http://www.techopedia.com/definition/28408/maker-movement.

Trimble, William F. 2011. *Admiral William A. Moffett: Architect of Naval Aviation*. Annapolis, MD: Naval Institute Press.

Turner, Frederick Jackson. 1921. *The Frontier in American History*. New York; Henry Holt. First delivered as a paper in 1893 to the American Historical Association. http://xroads.virginia.edu/~HYPER/TURNER/home.html.

Ufimtsev, P. Ya. "Methods of Edge Waves in the Physical Theory of Diffraction." 1971. Trans. Foreign Technology Division, Air Force Systems Command. National Technology Information Systems document FTD-HC-23-259-71. Sept. 7. www.dtic.mil/cgi-bin/GetTRDoc?AD=AD0733203.

UNESCO Institute for Statistics. 2014. "Global Flow of Tertiary-Level Students." http://www.uis.unesco.org/Education/Pages/international-student-flow-viz.aspx.

United Nations Conference on Sustainable Development. 2011. "Food Security and Sustainable Agriculture." UNCSD Rio 2012. Issues Brief 9, December. http://www.uncsd2012.org/content/documents/227Issues%20Brief%209%20-%20FS%20and%20Sustainable%20Agriculture%20CLCnew.pdf

United States Navy. 2014. "Energy, Environment and Climate Change." http://greenfleet.dodlive.mil/.

US Census Bureau 2012. "Foreign Trade, U.S. Int'l Trade in Goods and Services." https://www.census.gov/foreign-trade/Press-Release/current_press_release/exh1.pdf.

US Census Bureau. 2012."Trade in Goods with Advanced Technology Products, 2011." http://www.census.gov/foreign-trade/balance/c0007.html.

US Centers for Medicare and Medicaid Services. 2011. Office of the Actuary. "National Health Expenditures 2011–2021, Forecast Summary."http://www.cms.gov/Research-Statistics-Data-and-Systems/Statistics-Trends-and-Reports/NationalHealthExpend Data/Downloads/Proj2011PDF.pdf.

US Code, 42 U.S.C. Sec. 16372, Ultra-deepwater and unconventional onshore natural gas and other petroleum research and development program (collaborative industry-government R&D program), https://www.law.cornell.edu/uscode/text/42/16372.

Utterback, James. 1979. *Technological Innovation for a Dynamic Economy*. New York: Pergamon Press.

Van Atta, Richard H. 2008. "Fifty Years of Innovation and Discovery." In *DARPA: 50 Years of Bridging the Gap*. Washington, DC: DARPA. www.darpa.mil/WorkArea/DownloadAsset.aspx?id=2553.

Van Atta, Richard H., Alethia Cook, Ivars Gutmanis, Michael J. Lippitz, Jasper Lupo, Rob Mahoney, and Jack H. Nunn. 2003. *Transformation and Transition: DARPA's Role in Fostering an Emerging Revolution in Military Affairs*. Vol. 2, *Detailed Assessments*. IDA Paper P-3698. Washington, DC: Institute for Defense Analysis, November. www.darpa.mil/WorkArea/DownloadAsset.aspx?id=2687.

Vavakova, Blanka. 2006. "Reconceptualizing Innovation Policy: The Case of France." *Technovation* 46, 444–462.

Vernon, Raymond. 1966. "International Investment and International Trade in the Product Cycle." *Quarterly Journal of Economics* 81–89.

Vietmeyer, Noel. 2010. *Borlaug*. Vol. 2, *Wheat Whisperer, 1944–59*. Lorton, VA: Bracing Books.

Vietmeyer, Noel. 2011. *Borlaug*. Vol. 3, *Bread Winner, 1960–69*. Lorton, VA: Bracing Books.

Wagner, Caroline S. 2008. *The New Invisible College: Science for Development*. Washington, DC: Brookings Institution Press.

Waldrop, Mitchell. 1992. *Complexity*. New York: Simon & Shuster.

Waldrop, Mitchell. 2001. *The Dream Machine: J.C.R. Licklider and the Revolution that Made Computing Personal*. New York: Viking.

Wall Street Journal. 2011. "China Passes U.S. as Largest Manufacturer." March 14. http://247wallst.com/2011/03/14/china-passes-the-us-as-largest-manufacturer/.

Wallace, James, and Jim Erickson. 1992. *Hard Drive: Bill Gates and the Making of the Microsoft Empire*. New York: Harper Business.

Wang, Alex L. 2013. "The Search for Sustainable Legitimacy: Environmental Law and Bureaucracy in China." *Harvard Environmental Law Review* 37. http://www3.law.harvard.edu/journals/elr/files/2013/09/Wang-9-2.pdf.

Warrick, Joby. 2015. "Utilities wage campaign against rooftop solar," *Washington Post*, March 7. http://www.washingtonpost.com/national/health-science/utilities-sensing-threat-put-squeeze-on-booming-solar-roof-industry/2015/03/07/2d916f88-c1c9-11e4-ad5c-3b8ce89f1b89_story.html.

Watts, Barry D. 2013. "The Evolution of Precision Strike." Center for Strategic and Budgetary Assessments, August 6. http://www.csbaonline.org/publications/2013/08/the-evolution-of-precision-strike/.

Wedeman, Andrew. 2012. *Double Paradox: Rapid Growth and Rising Corruption in China*. Ithaca, NY: Cornell University Press.

Weiss, Charles, and William B. Bonvillian. 2009. *Structuring an Energy Technology Revolution*. Cambridge, MA: MIT Press.

Weiss, Charles, and William B. Bonvillian. 2011. "Complex Established 'Legacy' Systems: The Technology Revolutions that Do Not Happen." *Innovations* 6, no. 2, 157–187.

Weiss, Charles, and William B. Bonvillian. 2013. "Legacy Sectors: Barriers to Global Innovation in Agriculture and Energy." *Technology Analysis and Strategic Management* 25, no. 10 (November), 1189–1208.

Wessner, Charles. 2013. "How Does Germany Do It?" *Mechanical Engineering* 135, 42–47.

Wessner, Charles, ed. 2013. *21st Century Manufacturing: The Role of the Manufacturing Extension Partnership Program.* Washington, DC: National Research Council.

Wessner, Charles W., Alan W. Wolff, Committee on Comparative National Innovation Policies: Best Practice for the 21st Century, Board on Science, Technology, and Economic Policy, Policy and Global Affairs, and National Research Council. 2012. *Rising to the Challenge: U.S. Innovation Policy for the Global Economy.* Washington, DC: National Academies Press.

White House. 2014. "President Obama at the White House Maker Faire: Today's DIY Is Tomorrow's Made in America." June 18. http://www.whitehouse.gov/blog/2014/06/18/president-obama-white-house-maker-faire-today-s-diy-tomorrow-s-made-america.

White House Blog. 2013. "BRAIN Initiative Challenges Researchers to Unlock Mysteries of Human Mind." April 4. http://www.whitehouse.gov/blog/2013/04/02/brain-initiative-challenges-researchers-unlock-mysteries-human-mind.

White House, Office of Press Secretary. 2014. "White House Fact Sheet: President Announces New Actions to Further Strengthen U.S. Manufacturing." October 27. http://www.whitehouse.gov/the-press-office/2014/10/27/fact-sheet-president-obama-announces-new-actions-further-strengthen-us-m.

Wieman, Carl. 2012. "Applying New Research to Improve Science Education." *Issues in Science and Technology*, Fall. http://issues.org/29-21/carl/.

Wieman, Carl. 2014. "Expertise in Science and Engineering: How It Is Learned and Taught." xTalk, MIT, May 19. http://odl.mit.edu/events/carl-wieman-expertise-in-science-and-engineering-how-it-is-learned-and-taught/.

Willrich, Mason. 2009. "Electricity Transmission Policy for America: Enabling a Smart Grid, End-to-End." MIT-IPC-Energy Innovation Working Paper 09-003. Cambridge MA: MIT Industrial Performance Center, July. http://web.mit.edu/ipc/research/energy/pdf/EIP_09-003.pdf.

Wohlsen, Marcus 2014. "New Jersey Bans Tesla to Ensure Buying a Car Will Always Suck." *Wired*, March 12. http://www.wired.com/2014/03/tesla-banned-ensure-process-buying-car-keeps-sucking/.

Womack, James, Daniel Jones, and Daniel Roos. 1990. *The Machine That Changed the World.* New York: Free Press.

Wong, Edward. 2013. "Air Pollution Linked to 1.2 Million Premature Deaths in China." *New York Times*, April 1. http://www.nytimes.com/2013/04/02/world/asia/air-pollution-linked-to-1-2-million-deaths-in-china.html?_r=0.

Wong, Edward. 2014. "Report Finds Widespread Water Pollution in China." *New York Times*, April 24. http://sinosphere.blogs.nytimes.com/2014/04/24/report-finds-widespread-water-pollution-in-china/?_php=true&_type=blogs&_r=0. (Accessed 2014-2007-15).

World Bank. 2007. *Cost of Pollution in China: Economic Estimates of Physical Damages.* http://siteresources.worldbank.org/INTEAPREGTOPENVIRONMENT/Resources/China_Cost_of_Pollution.pdf.

World Bank. 2008. *Agriculture and Development.* World Development Report. Washington, DC: World Bank. http://siteresources.worldbank.org/INTWDR2008/Resources/WDR_00_book.pdf.

World Bank. 2008. "Proposal for a Clean Technology Fund, Report on Design Meeting on Climate Investment Funds." April 3. http://siteresources.worldbank.org/INTCC/Resources/Proposal_For_A_Clean_Technology_Fund_April_3_2008.pdf.

World Bank. 2013. "Data: Gross Savings (% of GDP)." http://data.worldbank.org/indicator/NY.GNS.ICTR.ZS.

World Health Organization. 2013. "Global Burden of Disease, Injuries, and Risk Factors Study 2013." *Lancet.* http://www.thelancet.com/themed/global-burden-of-disease.

Wu, Tim. 2011. *The Master Switch.* New York: Vintage Books.

Yannuzzi, Rick E. 2000. "In-Q-Tel: A New Partnership between the CIA and the Private Sector." *Defense Intelligence Journal* 9, no. 1, 25–38.

Yergin, Daniel, and Joseph Stanislaw. 1998. *The Commanding Heights: The Battle between Government and the Marketplace That Is Remaking the Modern World.* New York: Simon & Schuster.

Zhou, Haibo, Ronald Dekker, and Alfred Kleinknecht. 2011. "Flexible Labor and Innovation Performance: Evidence from Longitudinal Firm-Level Data." *Industrial and Corporate Change* 20, no. 3, 944–945.

Zittrain, Jonathan. 2008. *The Future of the Internet and How to Stop It.* New Haven, CT: Yale University Press.

Index

Note: Locators followed by the letter 'n' refer to notes